THE GW-BASIC® REFERENCE

THE GW-BASIC® REFERENCE

Don Inman and Bob Albrecht

Osborne **McGraw-Hill**

Berkeley   New York   St. Louis   San Francisco
Auckland   Bogotá   Hamburg   London   Madrid
Mexico City   Milan   Montreal   New Delhi   Panama City
Paris   São Paulo   Singapore   Sydney
Tokyo   Toronto

Osborne **McGraw-Hill**
2600 Tenth Street
Berkeley, California 94710
U.S.A.

Osborne **McGraw-Hill** offers software for sale. For information on software, translations, or book distributors outside of the U.S.A., please write to Osborne **McGraw-Hill** at the above address.

This book is printed on recycled paper.

The GW-BASIC® Reference

 234567890 DOC 99876543210

ISBN 0-07-881644-0

Contents at a Glance

Part **III**

Applications

Part **IV**

Appendixes

Contents

Part II
The GW-BASIC Language

Part III
Applications

Part IV
Appendixes

BASIC

Introduction

This book is divided into four functional parts: Part I, "Honing GW-BASIC Tools;" Part II, "The GW-BASIC Language;" Part III, "Applications;" and Part IV, "Appendixes."

The first part provides a slow-paced general background and review of GW-BASIC. Its tutorial style allows beginners to learn fundamental concepts and more advanced users to brush up their skills. The reference section is task-oriented, grouping GW-BASIC functions, statements, and commands according to the jobs they perform. Examples and demonstration programs offer practical illustrations of the use of GW-BASIC keywords. The third section contains utility programs that demonstrate a wide variety of GW-BASIC capabilities. These programs use GW-BASIC keywords in meaningful applications. The fourth section contains a series of appendixes that provide helpful reference material that can be easily located.

Part I: Honing GW-BASIC Tools

If you have an IBM personal computer or an IBM PC "clone," you probably have used BASICA or GW-BASIC. The two versions are virtually the same. Part I presents an overview of GW-BASIC, a bit of its history, how it works, and descriptions of programming conventions and style used in this book. Also included in Part I are some terms and concepts to help you write and understand GW-BASIC programs.

A chapter is devoted to using GW-BASIC in the direct mode. In this mode, the statements that you enter are executed immediately. Methods of controlling the display screen are discussed, along with both setting and reading the date and time. Performing arithmetic operations and using variables are also demonstrated. You also learn to use, list, and change function key assignments.

You are then introduced to the program mode and learn to write, list, save, load, and run programs. You will find a full chapter on editing and merging programs. You learn to insert, alter, and delete characters, words, and lines of your programs. Merging includes saving a program in ASCII format, then merging the ASCII-saved program with a program in memory. You also learn how to renumber lines of your completed programs.

The concluding chapter of Part I discusses the use of numbers, strings, and variables. You learn to classify variables, numbers, and strings by their type, and how GW-BASIC converts the value of variables from one type to another when necessary. Arrays are introduced. Dimensioning an array and the use of subscripts for array elements are also explained. Exponential notation is described and illustrated, and you learn to perform arithmetic, relational, and logical operations.

Part II: The GW-BASIC Language

Part II contains the formal syntax for each GW-BASIC statement, command, and function. These essential parts of the language are grouped by function: assignment and program flow; remarks, constants, variables, and expressions; terminal I/O; program control; editing; arrays; string manipulation; file and device I/O; graphics; sound; memory access and control; error handling; and joystick, light pen, and COM and I/O ports.

This section of the book provides a quick reference for any keyword in the GW-BASIC language. If you need to find the chapter in which a discussion of a particular keyword is given, you can look in Appendix A, "GW-BASIC Keywords." If you want the exact page of the keyword, look in the index.

In addition to the formal syntax, the syntax box of each keyword includes the purpose of the keyword, the meaning of the parameters used in its syntax, and notes that give expanded information and warnings. If you need more information, read the text following the syntax box. Examples are given for most individual keywords, and a demonstration program is provided for related keywords to show their use in the context of a meaningful program.

Part III: Applications

Part III contains three types of application programs: a program to dynamically create a tile pattern, two programs for creating menus in windows, and a program to create graphic figures with instant DRAW commands executed with simple keystrokes. The programs show the use of GW-BASIC keywords in the context of a utility program. Each program is discussed in detail so you can understand why and how the keywords are used.

xxviii   GW-BASIC: The Reference

The first program not only allows you to create a tile pattern one pixel at a time, but on completion of the pattern displays the hexadecimal codes and the paint statement necessary to use the pattern to fill a closed geometric figure.

From the window programs, you will learn to overlay a window on the information displayed on the screen. When the information in the window has been used, you will learn how to remove the window from the screen and restore the screen to the condition existing before the window was displayed.

The final application uses the DRAW command. Rather than writing a number of DRAW statements to draw a figure, this program allows you to select individual commands from the keyboard. You can make your drawings one step at a time without the need for extensive preplanning.

Appendixes

Appendix A lists each GW-BASIC keyword and the chapter in which it appears. You can use this appendix to quickly find the chapter in which a keyword is discussed. Exact page locations can be found in the index.

Appendix B is a list of ASCII codes 0-255 and the action or printable character assigned to each code.

Appendix C contains a list of scan codes and the HEX key codes used by the computer for determining keystrokes from the keyboard.

Appendix D contains a list of error codes and messages displayed when errors occur.

Appendix E contains equivalents in the decimal, hexadecimal, and octal systems.

Appendix F contains additional information on the use of assembly (machine) language.

Appendix G is a glossary of terms used in this book and the meaning of each.

Appendix H contains descriptions of the display screens that can be used and the colors available in each screen mode.

Conventions Used in This Book

Several conventions are used throughout this book to assist you in distinguishing between narrative text and items that have special meanings. Special items might be cautions, reminders, introductory technical terms, or items that you should type.

For example, when you are asked to enter data you will see the word "Type" followed by a colon and the data to be typed (in boldface characters). On subsequent lines there may be instructions to press one or more keys. These lines are printed as a block, separate from narrative text, and appear as in the following example.

Type: **RUN**
and press ENTER

In some instances, you will be asked to press two keys in combination. Key combinations like this are indicated by a plus sign (+) between the two keys, as:

Press ALT + F

When new terms are introduced, they are printed in *italics*. For example,

The *indirect mode* is used for entering programs.

The text following such an italicized word will explain its meaning and its use.

Program messages or parts of the program screen that appear in text are printed in a monospace font (similar to their appearance on the screen) to distinguish them from the narrative text, as follows:

```
PRINT 2 * 14 + 10
 38
Ok
_
```

This book also uses three special notations to emphasize specific material or concepts. The word NOTE, CAUTION, or REMEMBER (capitalized and in bold face characters) follows the special notation.

 NOTE

 **CAUTION**

REMEMBER

In Part II of this book, each GW-BASIC statement, command, and function is described within a text box with separate sections: Syntax, Purpose, Notes, and Parameters. The headings are printed in boldface.

Figures, programs, and tables are also set off from narrative text with box enclosures.

Save your fingers . . . and your patience . . .

The Convenience Disk
for "The GW-BASIC Reference"

. . . You'll be able to take any program in The Reference and modify it to suit your own particular needs. It should make "The GW-BASIC Reference" even more pleasant and instructive.

The programs in just the last three chapters would justify the purchase of this convenience disk. These programs are fairly long and would be particularly tough on your fingers and patience.

We refer to this disk as the "convenience disk" for still another reason: it has a "Read Me" file that will give you brief descriptions of all the programs in the book and their specific locations.

We want to make this clear: as the authors, we *encourage* you to use these programs. Use them in any way you want; we just want you to enjoy and learn. That's why we set so low a price on the disk: just $9.95, and why we don't worry about our copyright.

As the authors, we thank you for buying and using our book.

— Don Inman and Bob Albrecht

To order:

The disk is $9.95 (plus 70¢ sales tax if you're a California resident). Please include on your order your name and address (printed, please); the number of disks you'll want, and the size (5 1/4" or 3 1/2"). And enclose a check or money order for the proper amount.

Mail this information to:

THE MAIL ORDER EMPORIUM
530 HILMAR ST.
SANTA CLARA, CA 95050

Why This Book Is for You

This book has been written so that it can be used by both beginning and experienced programmers. It is assumed that you have a working knowledge of your computer's disk operating system (DOS), and a little knowledge of some version of BASIC would be helpful.

The material is organized so that you can read the book from the beginning or use it as a reference. The first five chapters provide a background for using the rest of the book: a bit of BASIC history and a description of GW-BASIC symbols, punctuation, and syntax conventions; programming conventions and style; keywords; editing and merging programs; uses of numbers, strings, and variables; and the types of operations that can be performed.

Chapters 6 through 20 provide a formal presentation of individual keywords and detailed discussions of their use. You will find yourself returning to this section for information applicable to specific programming conditions.

Chapters 21 through 23 provide practical applications using a wide variety of GW-BASIC keywords. You can use these applications as a base for writing more extensive programs.

The fourth section of the book contains a series of appendixes containing material for handy reference.

This book should find a permanent place on the bookshelves of your home or office. Keep it in an easily located place so that it can provide instant help when you need it.

Learn More About GW-BASIC

Here is an excellent selection of other Osborne/McGraw-Hill books on GW-BASIC and QuickBASIC that will help you build your skills.

For an easy and fun introduction to GW-BASIC, see *GW-BASIC Made Easy,* by Bob Albrecht and Don Inman. Step by step, this book helps you establish excellent programming fundamentals.

For those who enjoy learning through hands-on exercises and skill checks, *Teach Yourself GW-BASIC,* by Bob Albrecht will soon have you writing your own programs.

For users who wish to increase the speed and ease of their programming by installing Microsoft's QuickBASIC program, the following books should be of interest: *QuickBASIC Made Easy,* by Albrecht, Wenden Wiegand, and Dean Brown, is a great introduction to QuickBASIC version 4.5. *Using QuickBASIC 4.5, Second Edition,* by Don Inman and Bob Albrecht, and *QuickBASIC: The Complete Reference,* by Steven Nameroff, are excellent guides written for users at all levels of programming ability.

I

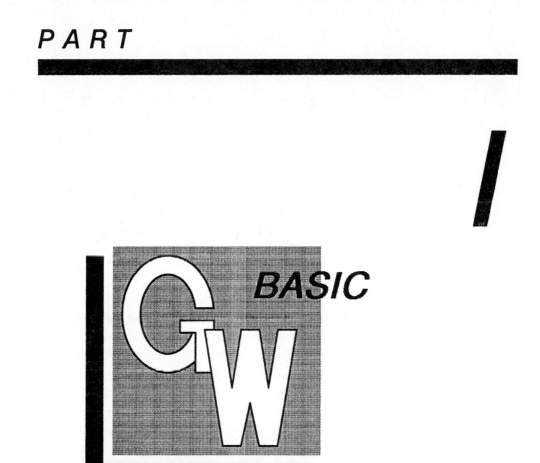

Honing GW-BASIC Tools

Part I contains an informal background of how BASIC began and a review of how GW-BASIC performs its tasks. Although this part assumes the reader has had some background in some version of BASIC, the pace is slow, and much information that is not usually available in BASIC reference manuals is offered.

After discussing background information in Chapter 1, "Overview," the direct operating mode is discussed. This includes examples of what you can do in GW-BASIC without writing a program. You will also learn how to use the indirect operating mode to write your programs. Discussions of automatic line numbering, listing programs, saving programs, and running programs are included. A full chapter is devoted to editing and merging programs. Part I concludes with a discussion of numbers, strings, and variables.

CHAPTER

1

Overview

If you have a computer, you probably have some version of BASIC. Since BASIC is often bundled with (or built into) personal computer packages, it is readily available to millions of computer users. Most versions of BASIC in use today are some form of Microsoft BASIC, or conform to Microsoft BASIC's standards. Here are some of the Microsoft BASIC versions most commonly in use today.

- GW-BASIC is the generic form of Microsoft BASIC. If you have an IBM PC "clone," you probably have this version (or a compatible one), perhaps on your MS-DOS disk or on a separate disk.

- BASICA, licensed and distributed by IBM, is virtually the same as GW-BASIC.

5

- Tandy BASIC is also virtually the same as GW-BASIC, and it is bundled with the Tandy 1000 series of computers. This is the version used by the authors in writing this book.

In this book, the term GW-BASIC is used to mean any of the above versions of Microsoft BASIC. Since there are 20 or 30 million copies of GW-BASIC in the hands of computer users, this version of BASIC has become the worldwide standard. Even compiled BASICs, such as Microsoft's QuickBASIC and Spectra Software's PowerBasic, have their roots in GW-BASIC.

If you are a beginning programmer, GW-BASIC is a great way to start. It provides a quick way to explore or solve a problem. The programming concepts and methods that you learn with GW-BASIC can be easily transferred to other versions of BASIC, and even to other computer languages.

In this chapter, you will find a little history about BASIC, and you will begin to use GW-BASIC. In particular, you will learn

1. How GW-BASIC began

2. The relationship between GW-BASIC and the Microsoft Disk Operating System (MS-DOS)

3. A little about GW-BASIC's two modes of operation (direct and indirect)

4. How a GW-BASIC program works

5. The programming conventions and style used in this book

6. Some terms and concepts to help you write and understand GW-BASIC programs

7. The syntax used to describe GW-BASIC statements, commands, and functions

It is assumed that you have a working knowledge of your computer's disk operating system (referred to in this book as DOS), as well as some knowledge of a version of BASIC. The following keywords used in this first chapter are common to all versions of BASIC, and you should be familiar with them.

REM
PRINT
END
INPUT
RUN
SAVE
LOAD

A Bit of History

Created in 1964 by Dartmouth College professors John G. Kemeny and Thomas E. Kurtz, BASIC has grown and improved over the years. The original BASIC language was created as an instructional tool for training novice programmers. It was designed to be easy to learn, but still useful for any programming task. The success of the original goals is demonstrated by BASIC's widespread use because of its simplicity, ease of use, and general-purpose computing power.

In 1965 BASIC became available outside Dartmouth, initially through terminals connected to large, time-sharing computer systems. When microcomputers were introduced to the public in the 1970s as personal computers, the computer arena was enlarged to include not only the professional programmer but also the creative amateur. Enthusiastic amateurs began to experiment with everything—from building their own computers from kits, to writing their own programs.

For some time, BASIC was the only high-level computer language available to personal computer users. Perhaps some of you remember the early computers, like the ALTAIR 8800, introduced in 1975 by Ed Roberts. Then Bill Gates gave us ALTAIR BASIC, later called Microsoft BASIC. The early BASIC was primitive, and personal computers had a limited amount of memory. Therefore, BASIC programs were crunched into the smallest possible space — unreadable to any but the most dedicated user. Fortunately, computers improved, memory capacities grew larger, and BASIC got better and better, in answer to the needs of the people. In its most recent manifestations, Microsoft BASIC has become the worldwide de facto standard.

BASIC has been criticized for its lack of structure. However, you can create BASIC programs in a style that is easy to read and understand. You can learn to express yourself in BASIC, and you can use BASIC to make your computer do what you want it to do, in the way you want it done.

Who knows what direction BASIC will take in the future? Will we see an object-oriented version? Will a version of BASIC become a macro language used in other software applications? Time will tell (and we will tell as soon as we know). In the meantime, let's enjoy what we have.

The Relationship Between GW-BASIC and MS-DOS

Microsoft GW-BASIC is a programming language with English-like vocabulary, and mathematical notation similar to that used in math, science, and other technical literature. It runs under MS-DOS (Microsoft Disk Operating System) and has close relationships with that system. This book assumes you have a working knowledge of your computer's DOS.

How to Install GW-BASIC
with No Hard Disk

If you have a hard disk system, skip this section and go to the next section. If you do not have a hard disk system, make a backup copy of your DOS disk (or disks, if you have a two-disk set) now, before doing anything else. Then put the original disks away, and use your backup copies to load DOS.

Users who do not have a hard disk drive should consider making a GW-BASIC Work Disk that contains the MS-DOS COMMAND.COM file and the GWBASIC.EXE file. (Your own BASIC's EXE file may be named differently, such as BASICA.EXE for an IBM PC or BASIC.EXE for a Tandy 1000. Check the directory of your DOS to find the correct name for your GW-BASIC version.)

To create the Work Disk, format a blank disk with the DOS command

```
FORMAT A: /S
```

The /S is a switch (or parameter) that tells DOS to make a system-formatted disk containing the COMMAND.COM file plus two hidden files necessary for starting (booting) your system from the Work Disk.

In this book, DOS commands appear in all uppercase.

The next step is to copy your BASIC's EXE file from your DOS disk to the Work Disk. In the copy command, use the unique filename assigned to your EXE file.

When these files have been copied to your Work Disk, look at the directory of the Work Disk to make sure COMMAND.COM and the GWBASIC.EXE file have been copied. The directory should look something like this for a 5 1/4-inch 360K floppy disk.

```
Volume in drive A has no label
Directory of  A:

COMMAND  COM    23612  10-16-87   3:00p
GWBASIC  EXE    79168  10-16-87   3:01p

        2 File(s)     214016 bytes free
```

If you use a 3 1/2-inch 720K disk, the directory will look the same, except that more bytes will be free.

Regardless of the size of your disks, there will be plenty of room for several GW-BASIC programs on the Work Disk. When you are ready to go to work, you need only the Work Disk; there is no need to switch disks to load or save your GW-BASIC programs. Use the Work Disk to do it all: boot the computer, load BASIC, and save and load your program files. After you make the first Work Disk, make several copies, so you will have some ready when the first one fills up with programs.

How to Install GW-BASIC on a Hard Disk

If you have a hard disk in your computer, you can copy the GWBASIC.EXE file to your hard disk along with other DOS files. Copy all of the DOS files into the root directory of your hard disk or into an appropriately named subdirectory. You may have more than one version of BASIC and want to include these versions in their own specific subdirectory, too. You would then copy the GWBASIC.EXE file into that subdirectory. Assuming you have already created a subdirectory named BASIC, you could copy GW-BASIC to that subdirectory with the command

```
A>COPY GWBASIC.EXE C:\BASIC
```

Getting from DOS to GW-BASIC

When you turn on your computer, you first see messages giving copyright dates, version numbers, and other information about DOS. A typical opening message on a Tandy 1000TX computer is shown in Figure 1-1. This example is from a computer with no clock or calendar; notice the prompts that require the date and time to be entered. If your system has a built-in clock and calendar, these prompts will not appear.

The default drive (the one currently active) is followed by the DOS prompt. Your default drive depends upon the configuration of your system. Two examples are shown here.

```
A>_            (No hard disk)
```

```
C:\>_          (Hard disk)
```

This opening line, the DOS *command line,* is where you enter your DOS commands, with their various parameters and switches.

Figure 1-1.

```
BIOS ROM version 01.03.00
Compatibility Software
Copyright (C) 1984,1985,1986,1987
Phoenix Software Associates Ltd.
and Tandy Corporation.
All rights reserved.

Microsoft MS-DOS version 3.20
Tandy version 03.20.22
Licensed to Tandy Corp.
All rights reserved


Current date is Tue  1-01-1980
Enter new date (mm-dd-yy): 1-01-91
Current time is 0:01:33:31
Enter new time: 14:35


Microsoft(R) MS-DOS(R)  version 3.20
(C)Copyright Microsoft Corp 1981 - 1986

A>_
```

A typical opening MS-DOS screen

Parameters and switches are extra bits of information that determine how the command executes. See your DOS reference for more details.

Your GW-BASIC file is loaded from the DOS command line. In your GW-BASIC user's guide, find the name of your GW-BASIC file. It may be BASICA, BASIC, GW-BASIC, GWBASIC, or something similar. Typical commands to load GW-BASIC from the active drive are shown here. You may need to change directories to access the GW-BASIC file.

```
A>GWBASIC              (Non-hard disk system, with GW-BASIC in drive A)

C:\>GWBASIC            (Hard disk system, with GW-BASIC in root
                          directory of drive C)

C:\>BASIC\GWBASIC      (Hard disk system, with GW-BASIC in BASIC
                          subdirectory of drive C)
```

GW-BASIC, when loaded, displays version and copyright messages similar to those of DOS. Also displayed are the number of memory bytes free for use by GW-BASIC. A typical opening screen is shown in Figure 1-2.

The GW-BASIC prompt, "Ok," is shown here with the cursor on the next line, ready for an entry.

```
Ok
_
```

At the bottom of the opening GW-BASIC screen is a list of the function keys F1 through F10. This list indicates actions that have been preassigned to the function keys. When you press one of the function keys, the assigned action takes place. Function keys can be used to avoid typing long or frequently used GW-BASIC statements or commands. The function keys are usually located across the top or on the left side of the keyboard.

Figure 1-2.

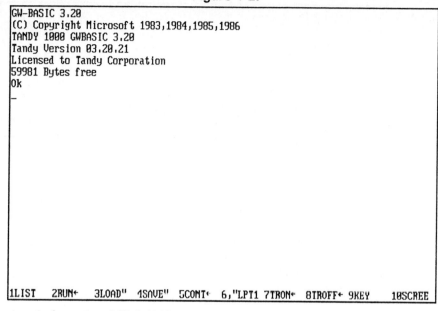

```
GW-BASIC 3.20
(C) Copyright Microsoft 1983,1984,1985,1986
TANDY 1000 GWBASIC 3.20
Tandy Version 03.20.21
Licensed to Tandy Corporation
59981 Bytes free
Ok
_
```

1LIST   2RUN←   3LOAD" 4SAVE" 5CONT← 6,"LPT1 7TRON← 8TROFF← 9KEY   10SCREE

A typical opening GW-BASIC screen

The function key assignments are shown in Figure 1-3. An arrow following the assignment means the action performed by the function will be carried out immediately, for example,

     2RUN←   (Immediately executes the program in memory)

If no arrow follows the assignment description, BASIC expects additional information to be supplied before it will carry out the action for this function key.

     3LOAD"   (Waits for name of the program to load)

Figure 1-3.

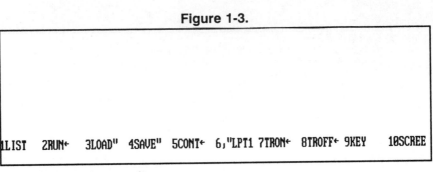

```
1LIST   2RUN←   3LOAD"  4SAVE"  5CONT←  6,"LPT1 7TRON←  8TROFF← 9KEY    10SCREE
```

Function key assignment line

Function key use is also discussed in Chapter 2, "Direct Mode Operations," and in Chapter 8, "Terminal I/O."

Exiting from GW-BASIC to DOS

When you wish to return to DOS from GW-BASIC, enter the SYSTEM command at the GW-BASIC cursor.

SYSTEM

When you type **SYSTEM** and press ENTER, the computer immediately leaves GW-BASIC, returns you to DOS, and displays the DOS prompt followed by the cursor.

A>_   *(Active disk drive depends on*
                  your system)

Entry Modes

When the GW-BASIC prompt appears, you can use either one of two entry modes: the direct mode or the indirect mode.

The Direct Entry Mode

In the *direct mode,* GW-BASIC statements and commands are executed immediately when you press the ENTER key. This mode is useful for testing short parts of programs, or when using the computer as a calculator. For example, type **BEEP** at the GW-BASIC prompt, to hear a beep and see the following:

```
Ok              (GW-BASIC prompt)
BEEP            (Your entry)
Ok              (Short beep is heard; then prompt reappears)
_               (Cursor blinks)
```

After the beep, type **PRINT 2 * 14 + 10** at the new prompt, and press ENTER to calculate the result of your entry, as shown here.

```
PRINT 2 * 14 + 10    (Your entry)
 38                  (Result is displayed)
Ok                   (Another prompt)
_                    (Cursor)
```

The direct entry mode is discussed in more detail in Chapter 2, "Direct Mode Operations."

The Indirect Entry Mode

The *indirect mode* is used for entering programs. Each line in the program is preceded by a line number and is stored in memory when you press the ENTER key. When a program has been stored, it can be executed by pressing the F2 function key. Pressing F2 is equivalent to typing RUN and pressing ENTER.

The statements in a program are executed in the order of the ascending line numbers, unless a control statement redirects the program flow to a specified line number.

Programs in this Book

GW-BASIC's LIST command displays programs in all uppercase letters, except characters in REM (remark) statements and text enclosed in double quotation marks. In addition, GW-BASIC's LIST command eliminates blank lines you may have left between program lines. (To make programs easy to read, some conventions are used in this book that deviate from the listings produced by GW-BASIC LIST.)

Program listings in this book use the following conventions —except when the listings are from GW-BASIC's LIST, AUTO, and other commands that produce all-uppercase output.

- All BASIC keywords are in uppercase (REM, PRINT, INPUT).

- Program variables are in lowercase, or mixed upper- and lowercase (number, akey$, Rate, SalesTax).

- Functional blocks of programs are separated by one blank line.

- Each functional block (except the first) begins with a remark whose line number is a multiple of 100.

- The first block of a program consists of several remarks that include the program's title, the chapter in which it is used, the filename, and other possible identifying remarks.

Other conventions will be discussed later in this chapter, and when they are used in specific programs.

You should save your GW-BASIC programs in ASCII format. If you use the ASCII format when saving a program to a disk file, you can then merge the program file with other programs, using GW-BASIC's MERGE command. MERGE is discussed in

Chapter 4, "Editing and Merging Programs," and Chapter 9, "Program Control."

With your word processor, you can create, modify, print, and otherwise manipulate ASCII-saved program files. With TYPE and PRINT commands, you can look at ASCII files from DOS. GW-BASIC programs saved in ASCII format can also be loaded into some of the newer BASIC language packages (such as QuickBASIC and PowerBasic). When you move up to a compiled version of BASIC, you can compile most ASCII-saved GW-BASIC programs under the new language with little or no modification.

How a GW-BASIC Program Works

GW-BASIC programs are made up of statements that you enter at the command level, after GW-BASIC's "Ok" prompt has been displayed. You number each line of the program to execute it in a specific order.

The computer does not execute all statements. Statements that are not executed are called *remarks*. Remarks begin with the key word, REM, or an apostrophe that is used in place of REM. The remarks explain what the program is doing. For example, all the programs in this book begin with a series of remarks that identify the program.

GW-BASIC looks at each numbered line in the program one at a time, in the ascending order of the line numbers. If a line begins with a remark (REM or '), GW-BASIC moves to the next line without doing anything. If the line does not begin with a remark, GW-BASIC interprets the statements on the line, and then performs the actions specified.

The computer continues reading and executing one line at a time, until all lines have been scanned. It then returns to the command level, ready for a new command.

Program 1-1.

```
1 REM ** Print Date and Time -- Then BEEP **
2 ' GW-BASIC Reference, Chapter 1. File: GWRF0101.BAS

100 REM ** Initialize **
110 CLS

200 REM ** Print Date and Time, then BEEP and End **
210 PRINT DATE$
220 PRINT TIME$
230 BEEP
240 END
```

Print Date and Time - Then Beep (GWRF0101.BAS)

A Sample GW-BASIC Program

Program 1-1, Print Date and Time - Then BEEP, is structured in three functional blocks.

The first block, containing only remarks, identifies the program. Our first program opens with the following lines.

```
1 REM ** Print Date and Time - Then BEEP **
2 ' GW-BASIC Reference, Chapter 1.  File: GWRF0101.BAS
```

The first line gives the title of the program. Line 2 shows the book title, the chapter in which this program first appears, and the filename under which the program is saved (GWRF0101.BAS).

In this book, the elements of a program filename describe the program in the following way:

Filename Element	Indication
GWRF	Abbreviation for *GW-BASIC: The Reference*
01	Program appears in Chapter 1
01	Number of the program within the chapter
.BAS	A BASIC program

The second block clears the screen (CLS). In more complex programs, this block will contain more than one statement. The final block prints the current date and the current time, sounds a beep, and ends the program with an END statement. (Although the END statement is optional in GW-BASIC programs, it is included in this book to clearly mark the end of a program.)

Enter this program and save it in ASCII format (by typing a comma, a space, and the letter *A* following the filename). If you are saving it to a disk in the default drive, use this SAVE command:

```
SAVE "GWRF0101.BAS", A
```

To save Program 1-1 to a specific disk drive (for example, drive B, or the BASIC subdirectory of drive C), type

```
SAVE "B:GWRF0101.BAS", A
```

or

```
SAVE "C:\BASIC\GWRF0101.BAS", A
```

You might want to indicate that this is an ASCII-saved program by using ASC as the filename extension.

```
SAVE "B:GWRF0101.ASC", A
```

SAVE is also discussed in Chapter 9, "Program Control." After saving the program, run it. You will hear a beep after the date and time are printed. Here is how the program output might look:

```
05-08-1991
10:15:33
Ok
_
```

When Program 1-1 is run, GW-BASIC performs its actions in the order shown in Table 1-1. Table 1-2 shows a list of GW-BASIC keywords introduced in Program 1-1, and their use in the program.

Program 1-2, Sample Program, calculates the sales tax on the amount you enter from the keyboard. In Program 1-2, lines 1, 2, and 100 are remarks and are not executed. Line 110 is executed first, then 120, then 130, then 140, and finally 150.

Table 1-1.

Line	Action Performed
1	A remark, not executed
2	A remark, not executed
100	A remark, not executed
110	Clears the screen
200	A remark, not executed
210	Prints the current date
220	Prints the current time
230	Sounds a beep
240	Ends the program

Actions Performed in Program 1-1

Table 1-2.

Keyword	Use
REM	Explanatory remark
CLS	Clears the screen
PRINT	Displays information on the screen
DATE$	Retrieves the current date
TIME$	Retrieves the current time
BEEP	Sounds the speaker for 1/4 of a second
END	Terminates the program, closes all open files, and returns to the command level

GW-BASIC Keywords Used in Program 1-1

The program contains keywords in all uppercase, but other elements are in mixed upper- and lowercase. A blank line separates the opening description block from the operational part of the program. Function key F1 is another typing shortcut. If you press F1 to list the program, the blank line will be removed. Also,

Program 1-2.

```
1 REM ** Sample Program **
2 ' GW-BASIC Reference, Chapter 1. File: GWRF0102.BAS

100 REM ** BEEP, Input, Calculate **
110 CLS
120 TaxRate = 6 / 100
130 BEEP: INPUT SalesAmount
140 PRINT SalesAmount * TaxRate
150 END
```

Sample Program (GWRF0102.BAS)

Figure 1-4.

```
1 REM ** Sample Program **
2 ' GW-BASIC Reference, Chapter 1. File: GWRF0102.BAS

100 REM ** BEEP, Input, Calculate **
110 CLS
120 TAXRATE = 6 / 100
130 BEEP: INPUT SALESAMOUNT
140 PRINT SALESAMOUNT * TAXRATE
150 END
```

LIST of Program 1-2

lowercase letters are changed to uppercase in all lines, except for remarks and strings contained within quotation marks. These changes are shown in Figure 1-4. Figure 1-5 shows a series of inputs and outputs from Program 1-2.

Save Program 1-2 as GWRF0102.BAS in ASCII format. You will then have two GW-BASIC programs saved to your Work Disk.

Figure 1-5.

```
? 1234
 74.04
OK
-

? 350
 21
OK
-

? 22
 1.32
OK
-
```

Output of Program 1-2

To look at a directory of your Work Disk without returning to DOS, use the FILES command. If your files were saved to the currently active disk drive,

Type: **FILES**
and press ENTER.

If your files were saved to a specific disk drive (B in the following example),

Type: **FILES "B:"**
and press ENTER.

Figure 1-6 shows a typical directory when a specific drive has been entered with the FILES command.

The FILES command is discussed in more detail in Chapter 9, "Program Control."

Programming Conventions and Style

A computer accepts information, processes the information according to specific instructions, and provides the results of the process as new information. In programming, you quickly learn how to define a problem and break it down into small, manageable parts. You can then write a series of instructions, each block of which solves a particular part of your original problem. You complete the solution by linking the blocks together into a complete program.

It is important that your instructions to the computer (your program) are written so that your computer can understand them. It is equally important that you write the instructions so that they are easy for you or anyone else to read, understand, and use.

Figure 1-6.

```
Ok
FILES "B:"
B:\
COMMAND .COM       BASIC   .EXE      GWRF0101.BAS      GWRF0102.BAS
 211968 Bytes free

Ok
_
```

FILES command output

Throughout this book you will find carefully designed examples that use a consistent set of programming conventions and structured style. This section discusses the conventions used in this book to promote good programming style and structure.

REM Statements

Each program begins with a series of remark statements. GW-BASIC accepts either an apostrophe (') or REM to indicate remark statements. You have learned that these statements are not executed, but are included for explanation and information. In the programs of this book, the first REM states the name of the program. Additional explanatory information is displayed in a second (and possibly a third) remark statement. You will remember that the opening remarks of Program 1-1 were

```
1 REM ** Print Date and Time - Then BEEP **
2 ' GW-BASIC Reference, Chapter 1.  File: GWRF0101.BAS
```

Each functional block of the program also includes a REM statement to indicate clearly the function of that part of the program. In Program 1-1, these REMs were:

```
100 REM ** Initialize **
200 REM ** Print Date and Time, then BEEP and End **
```

Double asterisks are used to emphasize main remarks. REM statements are discussed in Chapter 7, "Remarks, Constants, Variables, and Expressions."

GW-BASIC Keywords

Although you may type keywords in either uppercase or lowercase, the keywords appear in uppercase when listed. This book consistently uses uppercase for keywords. Here are some keywords used in Programs 1-1 and 1-2.

REM
CLS
PRINT
INPUT
BEEP
DATE$
TIME$
END

Variables

GW-BASIC recognizes long, unique variables (up to 40 characters). It is important that you choose meaningful names for variables. Names should have a close relationship to the function they represent. This book uses lowercase and mixed uppercase and lowercase for variable names to distinguish them from keywords. This makes the programs easier for you to read. Remember, however, that the GW-BASIC LIST command lists variables in all uppercase letters.

Two variables, TaxRate and SalesAmount, were used in Program 1-2. Variables are discussed in Chapter 7, "Remarks, Constants, Variables, and Expressions."

Line Numbers

Line numbers are required for each logical GW-BASIC line. The opening remark of programs in this book begins with line one. In the first block, the line numbers are incremented by one for each additional line.

```
1 REM ** Sample Program **
2 ' GW-BASIC Reference, Chapter 1.  File: GWRF0102.BAS
```

All other blocks in the main part of programs in this book begin with a multiple of 100. The line increment for these blocks is 10.

```
100 REM ** BEEP, Input, Calculate **
110 CLS
120 TaxRate = 6 / 100
130 BEEP: INPUT SalesAmount
140 PRINT SalesAmount * TaxRate
150 END
```

Any subroutine begins with a multiple of 1000. The opening line of a functional block or a subroutine is a remark. When a GOSUB or GOTO statement is used, the line referenced therein is never a remark. Instead, the reference is made to the first line following a remark, such as 110, 210, or 1010. Program 1-3, Date and Time Stamp, demonstrates a GOSUB to a subroutine at line 1010. This subroutine can be added to any program, to date- and time-stamp the use of the program. You can also use LPRINT statements to stamp the date and time on the output of the program. Save Program 1-3 in ASCII format as: GWRF0103.BAS.

PRINT and LPRINT are discussed in Chapter 8, "Terminal I/O." GOSUB and RETURN are discussed in Chapter 6, "Assignment and Program Flow."

Punctuation

A comma, semicolon, or colon is normally followed by a space. Exceptions to this convention are when punctuation is used within

Program 1-3.

```
1 REM ** Date and Time Stamp **
2 ' GW-BASIC Reference, Chapter 1. File: GWRF0103.BAS

100 REM ** Initialize **
110 CLS                             '1st executed

200 REM ** Call subroutine, then end **
210 GOSUB 1010                      '2nd executed
220 END                             '6th and last executed

1000 REM ** SUBROUTINE: Print date and time **
1010 PRINT DATE$                    '3rd executed
1020 PRINT TIME$                    '4th executed
1030 RETURN                         '5th executed
```

Date and Time Stamp (GWRF0103.BAS)

a string, and when a colon immediately follows a semicolon. These conventions are illustrated here.

```
210 CLS: worth# = 0: shares = 1
430 PRINT: PRINT "Total Electric = "; TotElec
540 format$ = "$$###,###,###.##"
620 PRINT "Total Value = ";: PRINT USING format$; worth#
```

Operational and Relational Symbols

Liberal spacing between elements of a program line makes it much easier to read. This book places one space before and after the operational symbols + − * / ^ and the relational symbols = < > <= >= <>. There is one exception: when a minus sign (−) is used to indicate a negative number. Here are some examples.

```
130 WHILE shares <> 0
160 worth# = worth# + shares * price#
210 worth# = INT(worth# * 100) + .5) / 100
240 FOR here = bottom TO top STEP -1
```

Indent Loops

The lines of FOR/NEXT and WHILE/WEND loops are indented two spaces, to indicate clearly where a loop starts and ends. Variable names are always included with the appropriate NEXT statement in FOR/NEXT loops. A FOR/NEXT loop:

```
240 FOR item = 1 TO NumInSet
250   PRINT "Score #"; item;: INPUT score!
260   SumOfAll! = SumOfAll! + score!
270   SumOfSet! = SumOfSet! + score!
280 NEXT item
```

A WHILE/WEND loop:

```
130 WHILE shares <> 0
140   INPUT "Number of shares "; shares
150   INPUT "Price per share  "; price#
160   worth# = worth# + shares * price#
170   PRINT
180 WEND
```

WHILE/WEND and FOR/NEXT loops are discussed in Chapter 6, "Assignment and Program Flow."

Multiple Statements

Multiple statements are used only when they form a compound function—that is, the statements together perform some related action. One example is when the screen is cleared and the key line turned off. Another example is when a comment is added to a program line. Here are lines using these multiple statements.

```
110 CLS: KEY OFF
240 BigMoney = 1325          'Opening balance
```

Another example is when printed information is placed at a specific location on the screen (row 3, column 5).

```
210 LOCATE 3,5: PRINT Title$
```

Helpful Terms and Concepts

This section presents some terms and concepts that will help you understand computer languages in general, and GW-BASIC in particular.

Statement Syntax

The description of each program statement in this book includes the syntax used for the statement. Usually some of the items listed in the syntax description are optional. Let's look at the unique symbols that are used to standardize syntax descriptions, to make them more quickly and easily understood.

Symbols used in syntax descriptions include commas, semicolons, square brackets, braces, and vertical lines.

```
, ; [ ] { } ¦
```

The *simplest statement* contains only the statement, with no options. An example is

```
BEEP
```

BEEP produces a short sound from the computer's speaker, and is discussed in Chapter 16, "Sound."

A *single word* may be the syntax description for more than one item, as in

```
DATA constants
```

In this DATA statement, the single word constants represent one or more numeric constants assigned to variables by a READ statement. Here is an example of such a data list.

```
DATA 10, 20, 30, 40
```

The READ statement also uses a single word (variablelist) in its syntax to represent one or more variables to be assigned values from a DATA statement.

```
READ variablelist
```

Here is an example of a variablelist.

```
READ NumberOfShares, CostPerShare!
```

DATA and READ statements are discussed in Chapter 6, "Assignment and Program Flow."

Square brackets, [and], are used to surround a part of a statement that is optional. For example, a subroutine's RETURN statement may include a line number to which control returns following the end of the subroutine.

```
RETURN [linenumber]          (Control returns to specified line number)
```

See Chapter 6, "Assignment and Program Flow," for more information on GOSUB and RETURN.

Two or more pairs of brackets are used in the syntax of some statements. Some of these brackets may be nested within others. This makes the interpretation more difficult. Here is the syntax for the COLOR statement used for the text screen mode (SCREEN 0).

```
COLOR [foreground][,[background][,border]]
```

In this syntax, foreground is an integer 0-31, background is an integer 0-7, and border is an integer 0-15. The COLOR statement allows many formats, as indicated by the multiple brackets. Some are listed here.

```
COLOR 5            (Foreground only)
COLOR , 7          (Background only)
COLOR 4, 7         (Foreground and background)
COLOR 5, 0, 2      (Foreground, background, and border)
```

More information on the COLOR statement is in Chapter 8, "Terminal I/O," and in Chapter 15, "Graphics."

Three periods (called an ellipsis) following an item enclosed in brackets indicates that you can include zero, one, or more than one occurrence of the item. The syntax for a CLOSE statement is

```
CLOSE [[#] filenumber[,[#] filenumber]...]
```

Here are some examples.

```
CLOSE                (Closes all open files)
CLOSE 5              (Closes file 5)
CLOSE #5             (Also closes file 5)
CLOSE #5, 6, 7       (Closes files 5, 6, and 7)
```

The CLOSE statement is discussed in more detail in Chapter 14, "File and Device I/O."

Braces, { and }, enclose a set of options, one of which must be chosen. The items are separated by a vertical line ¦.

```
INPUT [;][promptstring {;¦,}] variablelist
```

In this example, the first option (semicolon) is separated by a vertical line (¦) from the second option (comma). One of the two options must be used, but not both.

Here are a few possible INPUT statements:

```
INPUT "An integer, please "; Number
INPUT; "An integer, please "; Number
INPUT "An integer, please ", Number
INPUT "Two integers, please "; Number1, Number2
```

For more detailed information on the INPUT statement, see Chapter 8, "Terminal I/O."

Hardware Considerations

Early computers used one of three kinds of displays: TV set, composite monitor, or RGB monitor. Today, displays are usually classified by the type of graphics adapter used in the computer. Both monochrome (two colors) and color (many colors) adapters are used. Common color adapters are: Color Graphics Adapter (CGA), Enhanced Graphics Adapter (EGA), and Video Graphics Array (VGA).

CGA adapters provide basic graphics capability, which is enough for most typical uses. It has three modes: text mode, a low-resolution mode using three drawing colors, and a medium-resolution mode using one drawing color. In the text mode, the screen size can be set to 80 (columns) by 25 (rows), or to 40 by 25. Graphics statements do not work in the text mode.

EGA adapters provide better resolution and more drawing colors than CGA. Capabilities vary according to the type of EGA monitor used: color display monitor (CDM), extended color display monitor (ECDM), or monochrome display monitor (MDM). In the text mode, the EGA adapters can set the screen size to 80 by 25 and 40 by 25. The ECDM and MDM also support modes with 43 lines of text.

VGA adapters are the most versatile (and most expensive) that can be used by GW-BASIC. VGA provides many more drawing colors than any of the other color adapters. In the text mode, the screen size can be set to 80 by 25, 80 by 43, 80 by 50, 40 by 25, 40 by 43, or 40 by 50.

Special consideration for adapter hardware must be made with some GW-BASIC statements and functions discussed in this book. Some graphics statements and functions will not work if your computer does not contain the appropriate graphics adapter. Similarly, some communications statements and functions cannot be used without an RS-232 communications card.

Summary

This chapter has given you some background information about BASIC, and some specific facts about GW-BASIC. You began by learning a bit of BASIC history. You found out how to move back and forth between DOS and GW-BASIC. You then read about some of the programming conventions used in this book.

After loading GW-BASIC from DOS, you learned to use the direct entry mode to execute GW-BASIC commands and statements immediately. You then learned how to write a program in the indirect, or program, entry mode. You saw how a program works by examining the action performed by each line of a short program that printed the date and time.

In the sections about programming conventions and style, you learned these things about the programs in this book:

- Programs are separated into functional blocks.

- REM statements begin each functional block.

- GW-BASIC keywords are shown in all uppercase characters.

- Variables are shown in lowercase or mixed upper- and lower-case characters.

- Line numbers increase by 10 for each line within a functional block. Functional blocks begin with a multiple of 100, and subroutines begin with a multiple of 1000. The exception is the opening description block, which begins with line 1, and where line numbers increase by one.

- Punctuation conventions are used to produce easy-to-read programs.

- Control loops are indented for clarity.

- Multiple statements on a single line are related.

You learned to read and interpret syntax symbolism used to describe GW-BASIC commands, statements, and functions. The chapter closed with a brief discussion of hardware considerations when using certain GW-BASIC statements.

You now have some BASIC background and an inkling of what to expect in future chapters. The conventions and style have been set. You are ready to use the GW-BASIC tools that have been presented in this chapter, and there are other tools to sharpen up in the next chapter.

Direct Mode
Operations

Most GW-BASIC commands and statements can be executed without including them in a program. They can be executed from the GW-BASIC prompt, one at a time, without line numbers. When used in this way, they are called *direct statements* or *direct commands*. You are thus operating in the *direct mode* (also called the *immediate mode*). Certain other keywords, such as DATA, DEF FN, RETURN, and ON TIMER, only have meaning within a program and cannot be used in the direct mode.

You will learn to use many direct statements and commands in this chapter. In particular, you will learn to

- Clear the display screen
- Change screen modes
- Change screen and printer widths
- Read and set the date and time
- Use some typing shortcuts
- Perform instant arithmetic
- Use variables in the direct mode
- Turn the function key line off and on
- Change the function key assignments, and disable function keys

Controlling the Display

GW-BASIC has many commands that control the appearance of the display screen. For example, the opening screen shown in Chapter 1, Figure 1-2, contains information about the version of GW-BASIC that you are using. You can erase that information by using a CLS statement in the direct mode.

Type: **CLS**
and press ENTER

When the screen is cleared with a CLS statement, only the prompt (Ok) and the cursor (＿) at the top of the screen, and the key assignment line at the bottom of the screen, remain displayed.

You can also clear the screen by using the CTRL+L key combination as a shortcut. This key combination is performed by holding down the CTRL key and pressing the L key. (In this book, combining two keys in this manner to perform an action will always be indicated by connecting the two key names with a plus (+) sign.)

Press CTRL+L

by holding down the CTRL key and pressing the L key. Notice that the screen clears, except for the cursor at the top of the screen and the function key assignments at the bottom of the screen. The prompt (Ok) does not appear.

Changing Colors

If you have color graphics capability (a color monitor and appropriate adapter), you can control the colors used on your screen. You can change the foreground, background, and border colors in the text mode with a COLOR statement. For example, change the colors in the text mode to bright white foreground, blue background, and gray border with this command:

```
COLOR 15, 1, 8
```

When you enter this command, notice that only the text you type *after* entering the COLOR statement is printed with the new background color. As you type characters at the cursor position, each new character appears in bright white on a blue background. The rest of the screen's background area is still the original color. To completely fill the screen's background in the new color, you must also clear the screen. When the previous COLOR statement is followed by a CLS statement, the entire background changes to the specified color. You can put both statements on the same line, separated by a colon, like this:

```
COLOR 15, 1, 8: CLS
```

When you have been using nonstandard colors, it is always a good idea to return to the default screen colors after completing a task. To return to the default colors in the text mode, use the following direct statements:

```
COLOR 7, 0, 0: CLS
```

The default colors are white foreground, black background, and black border. Using a border color that is different from the background can produce a distracting display. However, you may have special situations in which you do want these two colors to be different.

Experiment with the COLOR statement using other numbers.

CAUTION Do not use the same number for foreground and background colors. If you do, you will not be able to see any text characters. This makes it difficult to recover to a screen with the default colors. You can press the F10 key to return to SCREEN 0 with the default colors, but the screen may not have the default WIDTH 80 (if you return from SCREEN 1, for example). SCREEN and WIDTH 80 statements are explained in the next section.

The COLOR statement is described in more detail in Chapter 8, "Terminal I/O," and in Chapter 15, "Graphics."

Changing Screen Modes

You can change from the text mode (SCREEN 0) to one of the graphics modes by using the SCREEN statement. To change to the low-resolution graphics screen, type:

```
SCREEN 1
```

This graphics screen provides low-level color graphics capability—providing you have the appropriate hardware to support it. See the discussion of the SCREEN statement in Chapter 8, "Terminal I/O," and Chapter 15, "Graphics."

When you change from text mode to this graphics mode, notice that the Ok prompt and cursor become twice as wide as in the text mode. SCREEN 1 permits only 40 text characters per line, whereas there can be as many as 80 characters per line in SCREEN 0.

After accessing SCREEN 1, you can use graphics statements to draw shapes. The following statement draws a cyan rectangle near the center of the screen and fills it with color:

```
LINE (80, 90)-(240, 110), 1, BF
```

This statement draws a rectangle whose upper-left coordinates are (80, 90) and whose lower-right coordinates are (240, 110). Cyan is color 1. The letters BF specify a Box Filled with color. Figure 2-1 shows the display screen after this LINE statement is entered.

Figure 2-1.

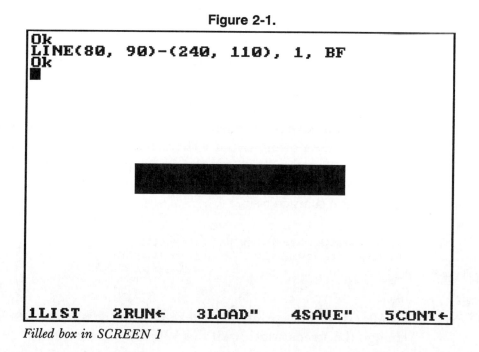

Filled box in SCREEN 1

The LINE statement is discussed in more detail in Chapter 15, "Graphics."

Here are two ways to return to the text mode from a graphics mode. The simplest way is to press the F10 function key.

Press the F10 key

A second way is to enter the following SCREEN command:

```
SCREEN 0, 0, 0
```

You may notice that when you return to the text mode with the SCREEN 0 command, the screen is cleared. The size of the text characters, however, does not change from the 40-character-per-line size of SCREEN 1. The prompt and cursor are in double-width characters.

Changing Screen Width in the Text Mode

Suppose you have just returned from SCREEN 1 to SCREEN 0. The text size is now double-size characters (40 per line), and only five of the function key assignments fit on the key line at the bottom of the screen. Enter the following PRINT command to confirm the character size:

```
PRINT "Character size is now 40."    (Enter this)
Character size is now 40.            (This is printed in
Ok                                   double-size characters)
_
```

After you have printed the text with 40 characters per line, change the screen width with this WIDTH statement:

Type: **WIDTH 80**
and press ENTER

Not only does this command return the screen to 80 characters
per line, but it also clears the screen. Only the prompt, cursor, and
key line remain, and the characters printed on the 40-character-
per-line screen are gone.

 REMEMBER   You can change the number of characters printed
on a line in the text mode (SCREEN 0) by using the WIDTH
statement in the direct mode or from within a program. Using the
WIDTH statement will also clear the screen.

Changing Printer Widths

There may be times when you want to set your printer width to
the same character-per-line length as the screen, so that printouts
will correspond to the printing on the screen. The maximum
number of characters per line for a printer can also be set with a
direct WIDTH statement, such as

```
WIDTH "LPT1:", n   (n is the number of characters per line)
```

Set the screen width to 40 characters per line, and clear the
screen. Then set the printer width to 40, and print a string of 60
asterisks with the following statements:

Type: **WIDTH "LPT1:", 40**
and press ENTER

Type: **PRINT STRING$(60,"*")**
and press ENTER

Type: **LPRINT STRING$(60,"*")**
and press ENTER

STRING$ is a GW-BASIC function that returns a string of specified length (60 in this example), using the character specified (here, an asterisk). STRING$ is discussed in Chapter 13, "String Manipulation."

Figure 2-2 shows the printer's WIDTH command, the PRINT statement that displays the string, and an LPRINT statement that sends the string to the printer.

Because you set the printer width to 40, it prints the string of asterisks as follows:

Notice that the number of asterisks printed per line corresponds to the number of asterisks per line on the screen—40 asterisks on the first line, and 20 on the second line. The printer's asterisks are printed at their normal width; the printer WIDTH statement changes only the number of characters, not their size.

The WIDTH statement can also be used when you want the printer's character-per-line width to be different from that of the screen. WIDTH is also discussed in Chapter 8, "Terminal I/O."

Date and Time

The computer stores a date and time in memory. You can read the computer's date and time, and you can set a new date and

Figure 2-2.

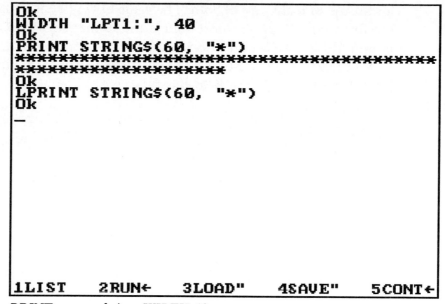

```
Ok
WIDTH "LPT1:", 40
Ok
PRINT STRING$(60, "*")
************************************************************
********************
Ok
LPRINT STRING$(60, "*")
Ok
_




1LIST    2RUN←    3LOAD"    4SAVE"    5CONT←
```

PRINT commands in a WIDTH 40 screen

time. Both of these direct operations are performed using the DATE$ and TIME$ keywords, but the keywords are used in different ways. You use the keyword as a variable to *read* the date or time. When you *set* the date or time, you use the keyword as a statement.

Reading the Date

You can read the date by using a direct PRINT statement with DATE$ as a variable. For example,

```
PRINT DATE$        (Direct statement with DATE$ as a variable)
12-04-1990         (The printed date)
Ok
_
```

You can type the keywords PRINT and DATE$ in uppercase, lowercase, or a mixture of both. The value of DATE$ is printed in the form mm-dd-yyyy, where mm is the numerical value of the month, dd is the day, and yyyy is the year.

You can use the question mark (?) as a shortcut for typing the PRINT statement, in the following way:

Type: **? DATE$**
and press ENTER.
The computer prints:

```
12-04-1990
```

Another shortcut for typing the PRINT keyword is to hold down the ALT key and press the P key. (This action will hereafter be designated: ALT+P.)

Hold down the ALT key
and press the P key.
Then release both.
The computer prints:

```
PRINT _
```

Then type: **DATE$**
and press ENTER

Naturally, the same date is printed as in the previous examples—unless much time has passed since you tried the other methods.

REMEMBER   You can use ALT+P as a shortcut to print the keyword PRINT followed by a space. The ALT key can be used with other keys to produce shortcuts for entering many GW-BASIC keywords. A complete list is shown in Table 2-1.

When the computer is first turned on, the value of DATE$ is automatically set to 01-01-1980. However, this value is changed to the current date by your response to a DOS prompt for the date, or by an installed hardware clock and calendar.

You can also assign the date to a string variable and print the variable's value, as shown here.

```
Today$ = DATE$       (Assign DATE$ to Today$)
Ok
PRINT Today$         (Direct PRINT statement)
12-04-1990           (Printed date)
Ok
—
```

Table 2-1.

Keyword	Press	Keyword	Press
AUTO	ALT+A	MOTOR*	ALT+M
BSAVE	ALT+B	NEXT	ALT+N
COLOR	ALT+C	OPEN	ALT+O
DELETE	ALT+D	PRINT	ALT+P
ELSE	ALT+E	RUN	ALT+R
FOR	ALT+F	SCREEN	ALT+S
GOTO	ALT+G	THEN	ALT+T
HEX$	ALT+H	USING	ALT+U
INPUT	ALT+I	VAL	ALT+V
KEY	ALT+K	WIDTH	ALT+W
LOCATE	ALT+L	XOR	ALT+X

*The MOTOR keyword is a holdover from earlier versions of BASIC, used when computers stored files on cassette tapes instead of disks.

ALT Key Shortcuts

Reading the Time

To read the time, you use a procedure similar to that for reading the date. The TIME$ keyword can be used in a direct PRINT statement, as in

```
PRINT TIME$          (Direct statement)
10:33:47             (Printed time)
Ok
_
```

When you enter PRINT TIME$, the computer immediately prints the current time in the form hh:mm:ss, where hh is hours (using a 24-hour clock), mm is minutes, and ss is seconds. Remember, you can always use the typing shortcuts discussed previously for the PRINT statement.

The hours from noon to midnight on a 24-hour clock are printed with values in the range 12-23. Table 2-2 shows some examples of 12-hour clock times converted to a 24-hour clock.

Table 2-2.

12-hour Clock	*24-hour Clock*
01:00:00 A.M.	01:00:00
08:20:30 A.M.	08:20:30
11:05:45 A.M.	11:05:45
12:00:00 Noon	12:00:00
01:00:00 P.M.	13:00:00
08:20:30 P.M.	20:20:30
11:05:45 P.M.	23:05:45
12:00:00 Midnight	00:00:00

12-Hour and 24-Hour Clock Equivalents

The time may also be assigned to a variable by a direct statement, and then printed as follows:

```
StartTime$ = TIME$          (Direct assignment to StartTime$)
Ok
PRINT StartTime$            (Direct PRINT statement)
10:35:03                    (Printed time)
Ok
_
```

After waiting a few seconds, try printing the value of the variable StartTime$ again. Then print TIME$.

```
PRINT StartTime$            (Print it again)
10:35:03                    (The same time is printed)
Ok
PRINT TIME$  \              (Print the new time)
10:35:35                    (The latest time is printed)
Ok
_
```

Notice that the value of StartTime$ did not change, even though the time did. StartTime$ was originally assigned the time of 10:35:03, and will keep that value until some new value (such as a new TIME$) is assigned to it. Time passes on, but variables stay the same until a new value is assigned to them.

Setting the Date

To set the computer's date, you can use DATE$ as a direct statement, as shown here.

```
DATE$ = "12/5/90"
Ok
_
```

Notice that double quotes are used around the value assigned to
DATE$. Since DATE$ is in string format, the value assigned to it
must also be in string format. Slashes separate the month, day,
and the last two digits of the year.

You can verify that the date has been set correctly by printing
the value of DATE$ with a direct PRINT statement, as you did
previously.

```
DATE$ = "12/5/90"          (You set the date)
Ok
PRINT DATE$                (Direct statement)
12-05-1990                 (Printed date)
Ok
_
```

You can set the date in several ways. Some are shown here.

```
DATE$ = "12/5/90"

DATE$ = "12-5-1990"

DATE$ = "12/05/1990"
```

For each of these settings, the date is printed as:

```
12-05-1990
```

You could also assign the date to a variable and use a DATE$
statement, as follows:

```
Today$ = "12/6/90"         (Assign value to Today$)
Ok
DATE$ = Today$             (DATE$ assignment)
Ok
PRINT DATE$                (Direct PRINT statement)
12-06-1990
Ok
_
```

Setting the Time

Remember, the computer uses a 24-hour clock. When setting the time, you must use 24-hour clock values. For example, you can set 9:05 A.M. (ante meridiem) as follows:

Type: **TIME\$ = "9:05"**
and press ENTER

You can set 9:05 P.M. (post meridiem) as follows:

Type: **TIME\$ = "21:05"**   *(9:05 plus 12 hours)*
and press ENTER

Once again, TIME\$ is in string format, so double quotes must be used around the value assigned.

You can verify the time you set by using TIME\$ as a variable, like this:

```
PRINT TIME$
21:05:20
Ok
_
```

DATE\$ and TIME\$ can also be used in programs, to stamp the output of your programs with the current date and time. You can also stamp a direct mode session with the date, time, and your name, as in the following sequence of direct statements:

```
MyName$ = "Albert Outlander"
Ok
PRINT DATE$, TIME$, MyName$
12-06-1991    21:13:08      Albert Outlander
Ok
_
```

Another useful technique is to create and use a file to record the usage of your programs by writing the date, time, and program name to the file each time a program is used. You can no doubt find many other uses for DATE$ and TIME$, which are discussed in more detail in Chapter 18, "System Routines."

Instant Arithmetic

You can use your computer as a calculator in the direct mode. It can perform the operations of addition (+), subtraction (−), multiplication (*), division (/), integer division (\), modulo arithmetic (MOD), and even exponentiation (^). Of course, the PRINT statement must be used if you want to see the results.

BASIC's various types of numbers are discussed in Chapter 5, "Numbers, Strings, and Variables," and in Chapter 7, "Remarks, Constants, Variables, and Expressions." Here are some examples.

Addition:

```
PRINT 3 + 4      (Integers)
 7
Ok
 _
```

Notice that positive numbers are preceded by a blank space. Negative numbers have a minus sign in that place.

Subtraction:

```
PRINT 57.2958 - 3.14159      (Single precision numbers)
 54.15421
Ok
 _
```

Multiplication:

```
PRINT 3.14159 * 57.2958      (Single precision numbers)
 179.9999
Ok
_
```

Notice that only seven digits are printed in the result. The default number type is single precision, accurate to seven places at most.

Division:

```
PRINT 57.2958  /  3.14159        (Single precision numbers)
 18.23784
Ok
_
```

Notice again that only seven places arc printed in the result.

Integer division:

```
PRINT 3 \ 4          (Integers)
 0
Ok
PRINT 33.3 \ 5.1     (Single precision numbers)
 6
Ok
_
```

Notice that the results of division using the integer division sign (\ ) are integers. Remainders are ignored. Single and double precision numbers are converted to integers before the division is made. The second division operation is therefore performed as $33 \setminus 5 = 6$. Also, see the MOD operation that follows.

Modulo arithmetic:

```
PRINT 3 MOD 4
 3
Ok
```

```
PRINT 57.2958 MOD 3.14159     (Floating point numbers)
 0
Ok
_
```

The MOD operator computes the remainder for an integer division. In the case of single or double precision numbers, the numbers are first rounded to integers, and then the MOD operation is performed. Thus the previous calculation has no remainder, since 57 MOD 3 = 0.

Exponentiation:

```
PRINT 3 ^ 4
 81
PRINT 345 ^ 6
 1.686221E+15
Ok
_
```

Notice the format in which the result of the second exponentiation example is displayed. In BASIC, very large numbers are printed as *floating point numbers*. The number in the example (1.686221E+15) is 1.686221 times 10 to the 15th power, or

$$1.686221 \times 10 \char`\^ 15$$

Floating point notation is a short way to express very large numbers. To write the number in the example in normal Arabic figures, you would have to move the decimal point 15 places to the right.

1,686,221,000,000,000

Floating point numbers have two parts: the *mantissa* and an *exponent*. These two parts are separated by the letter E when the numbers are single precision, or by the letter D when the numbers are double precision.

1.686221E+15   (Single precision number)
$$\diagup \quad | \quad \diagdown$$
mantissa   E   exponent

7.714286485714363D−07   (Double precision number)
$$\diagup \quad | \quad \diagdown$$
mantissa   D   exponent

The exponent normally includes a plus (+) sign for positive exponents and a minus (−) sign for negative exponents. The plus sign can be omitted for positive exponents.

The Function Keys

The function keys are usually located across the top or at the left side of the keyboard. Enhanced keyboards have 12 function keys, numbered F1 through F12. Some keyboards have only ten function keys, numbered F1 through F10. GW-BASIC has preassigned some of the most frequently used commands and statements to function keys F1 through F10.

After clearing the screen, press the F9 key. At the top of the screen you see

```
KEY _
```

Pressing F9 is equivalent to typing three letters (K, E, and Y) and a space.

Now, press the F1 key. You see

```
KEY LIST _
```

Pressing F1 is equivalent to typing four letters (L, I, S, and T) and a space.

After pressing F9 and F1, press ENTER. In this book, a sequence of keypresses such as this will hereafter be referred to in this format:

Press: F9, F1, ENTER

A complete list of function key assignments is printed vertically on the screen, as shown in Figure 2-3. The advantage of this vertical listing is that it shows each entire key assignment. The assignment listing at the bottom of the screen only shows the first five characters.

Notice that some of the function key assignments have an arrow following the assignment, as shown in Figure 2-4. These

Figure 2-3.

```
Ok
KEY LIST
F1 LIST
F2 RUN←
F3 LOAD"
F4 SAVE"
F5 CONT←
F6 ,"LPT1:"←
F7 TRON←
F8 TROFF←
F9 KEY
F10 SCREEN 0,0,0←
F11
F12
Ok
─


1LIST    2RUN←    3LOAD"  4SAVE"  5CONT←  6,"LPT1 7TRON←  8TROFF← 9KEY    10SCREE
```

Default function key assignments

Figure 2-4.

```
RUN←
CONT←
,"LPT1:"←
TRON←
TROFF←
SCREEN 0,0,0←
```

Functions giving immediate action

commands or statements (with the trailing arrow) are executed without the need for pressing the ENTER key. Other functions require the ENTER key to be pressed before they are executed.

After the list is printed, press the F10 key. This is the equivalent of the direct screen statement SCREEN 0, 0, 0, which calls for the text mode and clears the screen. A complete list of the predefined function key assignments, with their descriptions, is shown in Table 2-3.

Turning Key Line Descriptions Off and On

The key line descriptions at the bottom of the screen can be distracting when you are running a program. You can turn off the

Table 2-3.

Key	Default Function	Description
F1	LIST	Lists a program. You must press the ENTER key.
F2	RUN ←	Runs a program. The program runs immediately.
F3	LOAD″	Loads a program. You enter the name of the desired program; then press ENTER to load the program.
F4	SAVE″	Saves a program. You enter the name of the program after the quote; then press ENTER to save the program.
F5	CONT ←	Restarts (continues) a program after it has been interrupted by STOP. Program execution resumes immediately.
F6	,″LPT1:″ ←	Selects printer as I/O device. I/O command precedes the comma. The command is executed immediately.
F7	TRON ←	Turns on the tracing function. The command is executed immediately.
F8	TROFF ←	Turns off the tracing function. The command is executed immediately.
F9	KEY	Use for the KEY functions. Complete the command, then press ENTER.
F10	SCREEN 0,0,0 ←	Invokes the text mode. The command is executed immediately.

Function Key Assignments

key descriptions *before* running a program, or by using a statement *within* the program.

To turn the key line off,

Type: **KEY OFF**
and press ENTER

To turn the key line back on,

Type: **KEY ON**
and press ENTER

Changing Function Key Assignments

Although GW-BASIC has predefined function keys F1 through F10, you may change the assignment for any of these keys. To do so, you use KEY followed by the function key number to be changed, a comma, and a string of 15 characters or less (additional entered characters are ignored). Let's look at an example of assigning function keys in order to streamline a common task.

After using one of the graphics modes, you will usually want to return to the text mode, with the black and white default screen colors and 80 characters per line. If you don't use the TRON and TROFF function keys very much, you can change either of those two keys to functions that will help you quickly restore the text mode display.

First, make the following new assignment to F7:

Press: F10   (*Clear the screen*)
Then type: **KEY 7, "WIDTH 80"**   (*Make new assignment*)
and press: ENTER   (*Complete the entry*)

Notice that the assignment is a string, enclosed in double quotes.

When you have completed the new assignment, look at the key line at the bottom of the screen. The assignment for F7 has been changed. Notice that the line does not show the full assignment for some keys due to space limitations. To see the full key assignments, list them with this sequence:

Press: F9, F1, ENTER

You will see a new list of the active key functions, as shown in Figure 2-5. Notice that the assignment for F7 has changed.

Try out your new key assignment by drawing a rectangle in SCREEN 1, as follows:

Type: **SCREEN 1**
and press ENTER

Type: **COLOR 1, 1: CLS**
and press ENTER

Type: **LINE (80, 90)-(240, 110), 1, BF**
and press ENTER

A rectangle appears near the center of the display of SCREEN 1. The screen is blue with white letters, and the colored rectangle is filled with cyan.

Now, to return to SCREEN 0 with the default colors, use the following sequence:

Press: F10, F7, ENTER

The screen is cleared to the text mode by F10, and the width is set to 80 by F7. The GW-BASIC prompt and cursor appear at the top of the screen. The key line is displayed at the bottom of the screen (unless you have turned if off with a KEY OFF statement).

When you use F7 as defined in the previous example, you have to press the ENTER key to execute the WIDTH 80 command that

Figure 2-5.

```
Ok
KEY LIST
F1 LIST
F2 RUN←
F3 LOAD"
F4 SAVE"
F5 CONT←
F6 ,"LPT1:"←
F7 WIDTH 80
F8 TROFF←
F9 KEY
F10 SCREEN 0,0,0←
F11
F12
Ok
_




1LIST    2RUN←   3LOAD"  4SAVE"  5CONT←  6,"LPT1 7WIDTH  8TROFF← 9KEY     18SCREE
```

Altered function key assignments

was assigned. The ENTER keypress can also be included in the F7 assignment, by adding the ASCII character code 13 (for ENTER), like this:

Type: **KEY 7, "WIDTH 80" + CHR$(13)**
and press ENTER

The + CHR$(13) part of this assignment is counted as a single character. Therefore, "WIDTH 80" + CHR$(13) is considered nine characters. GW-BASIC catenates (joins) the equivalent of an ENTER keypress (CHR$ 13) to the assignment string within the quotes. Thus, after making this new assignment, the ENTER keystroke is part of the WIDTH command; you do not have to press the ENTER key after the F7. The sequence that restores the screen to its default conditions is now

Press: F10, F7

The function keys will revert to their default assignments when you leave GW-BASIC, and the next time you load it, F7 will again be TRON. If you want to, you can write a short GW-BASIC program to make the key changes you need most often. See Program 2-1, F-Key (Function Key) Changes. Save your program, then load and run it after you load GW-BASIC. You can also load and run the program when you load GW-BASIC directly from the DOS command line, by appending the program's filename as shown here.

```
A>GW-BASIC GWRF0201
```

Disabling the Function Keys

Not only can you change the actions performed by the function keys, you can also disable a key altogether, by assigning the null string (a string with nothing in it) to it. For example, to disable F1,

Type: **KEY 1, ""**   *(A pair of double quotes; no space)*

and press ENTER

The same key statement, with a different key number, will disable other function keys.

Use of KEY is discussed in Chapter 8, "Terminal I/O."

Program 2-1.

```
1 REM ** F Key Changes **
2 ' GW-BASIC Reference, Chapter 2. File: GWRF0201.BAS
3 ' Changes key assignments

100 REM ** Make new assignments **
110 KEY 7, "WIDTH 80" + CHR$(13)
120 ' Add any other key changes in this section

200 REM ** Clear screen and end **
210 CLS: END
```

F-Key (Function Key) Changes (GWRF0201.BAS)

Summary

This chapter has shown you many uses of GW-BASIC in the direct mode. Most GW-BASIC keywords can be used within programs, too. The indirect mode (programming mode) is discussed in the next chapter.

You began by learning how to clear the display.

You then learned how to change the screen's foreground, background, and border colors, with a COLOR statement followed by a CLS statement.

COLOR 15, 1, 8: CLS

You also saw how to change screen modes with a SCREEN statement.

SCREEN 1   For low-resolution color
                                graphics
SCREEN 0   For the text mode

You found out how to change the number of characters displayed on a screen line in the text mode—and on your printer—using the WIDTH statement containing the number of desired characters per line.

WIDTH 80	Screen display to normal text
WIDTH 40	Screen display to double-width characters
WIDTH "LPT1:", 40	Printer to 40 characters per line

You learned to read and set the computer's date and time by using DATE$ and TIME$ in a PRINT statement, and as a variable.

PRINT DATE$	Read the date
PRINT TIME$	Read the time
DATE$ = "12/5/90"	Set the date
TIME$ = "9:05"	Set the time

You performed each of GW-BASIC's arithmetic operations (addition, subtraction, multiplication, division, integer division, exponentiation, and modulo arithmetic), and used the PRINT statement to display the results.

Finally, you learned how to list the function key assignments, and to turn the key line off and on with KEY OFF and KEY ON. You also learned to change the keys' assignments by specifying a key number and entering its new function assignment in a string. You learned to disable a function key by specifying its number and entering a null string.

3

The Program Mode

This chapter gets you started with programming in GW-BASIC. It introduces some of the commands and statements used to instruct the computer—that is, to tell it what you want to accomplish. You will learn to enter simple GW-BASIC programs in the *Indirect,* or *Programming, mode.* You will also learn to list, run, and save programs that have been created in the Indirect mode.

As you learned in Chapter 2, a Direct mode instruction tells the computer to do something immediately. In contrast, instructions entered in the Indirect, or Programming, mode seem to do nothing immediately. Combined, however, they make up a series of things for the computer to do at a later time (called a program).

As you enter instructions in the Indirect mode, they are stored in the computer's memory. The instructions in a program are not carried out by the computer until the program is executed with a RUN statement.

In this chapter, you will learn to

- Use the AUTO command to provide automatic line numbers at equally spaced intervals for an entire program
- Enter and exit from the Automatic Line Number mode, using the AUTO command, to provide equally spaced line numbers within program blocks
- List your programs to the screen, to a printer, to a file, or to a communications adapter
- Save your programs in normal (compressed binary) format, ASCII format, and protected (encoded binary) format
- Load programs that have been previously saved
- Run programs
- Load and run programs with one command

The following GW-BASIC keywords are used in this chapter: REM, PRINT, AUTO, CLS, DATE$, TIME$, BEEP, LIST, LLIST, SAVE, LOAD, RUN, INPUT, MERGE, and END.

Comparing the Indirect and Direct Modes

Each line of a program must have a unique line number. Lines in a program are executed in ascending order of their numbers, unless the flow of execution is altered by statements like GOTO or GOSUB. GW-BASIC knows an Indirect mode operation from a

Direct mode operation by whether or not it is preceded by a line number.

In a Direct mode operation, the action specified is carried out immediately. Then the "Ok" prompt and cursor appear. Here is how the screen looks after a Direct mode operation using a PRINT statement.

```
PRINT 5 + 6
 11
Ok
_
```

In an Indirect mode operation, there is no apparent action. The cursor appears ready for another instruction (which can be either direct or indirect). Here is how the screen looks when the PRINT statement is used in the Indirect mode.

```
110 PRINT 5 + 6
_
```

Even though it looks like nothing happens when you enter an indirect operation in this way, the computer performs an unseen task. When you press ENTER after an Indirect mode statement, that line is stored in memory as part of a program. After a complete program has been entered, you can execute it with a RUN command. You can also save it to a file for use at a later time.

Programs in memory are lost when you leave GW-BASIC. If you want to keep a program for future use, you must store it on a disk with a SAVE command. Later, you will use the LOAD command to load programs that have been previously saved.

Automatic Line Numbering

The AUTO command provides automatic line numbering, so that you do not have to enter each line number as you enter programs.

The AUTO command has a basic form, and also has many variations. Its basic form is

```
AUTO 100, 10
```

The number immediately following the AUTO keyword tells the computer to use 100 for the first program line. The second number (10) tells the computer how much to increment each line number. Both numbers in the AUTO command must be positive integers.

Other forms for AUTO are:

Command Form	Result
AUTO	AUTO by itself defaults to line 10 for the first line number and an increment of 10.
AUTO 200	Start numbering with 200, and use the default increment value of 10.
AUTO 300,	Start numbering with 300, and use the current increment value.
AUTO, 2	Start numbering with 0, and increment by 2.
AUTO.	Start at the current line, and use the current increment value.
AUTO., 10	Start at the current line, and increment by 10.

Using AUTO in Its Basic Form

Program 1-1, Print Date and Time - Then BEEP (from Chapter 1), is used again here to demonstrate the basic form of automatic line numbering. This simple program prints the current date and time, and sounds a beep to announce the end of the program.

The program was originally written in three functional blocks, with a blank line space between each block. GW-BASIC eliminates blank lines when listing or saving a program. The closest way that you can approximate a blank line is to use a line number followed by an apostrophe (shortcut for REM). This is a good way to indicate the block separations.

Even though you probably have Program 1-1 saved in a file, let's enter it again following the steps in this section, to practice entering a program with the aid of the AUTO command.

Correcting Your Typing Errors   Most people make a few mistakes when typing. You can correct simple typing errors that you notice before the line is entered by using the BACKSPACE key to step backwards (erasing letters as you go) until the error is deleted. Then retype the line from that point.

If the line has already been entered, you can exit the Automatic Line Numbering mode when you discover the error, correct the error by retyping the line, and then return to the Automatic Line Numbering mode to continue. Exiting and reentering automatic line numbering is discussed in the next section.

If a program is short, you can leave the errors until all lines of the program have been entered. Then you can exit from automatic line numbering and retype the incorrect lines, pressing ENTER after each line is typed.

A more complete discussion of editing programs is in Chapter 4, "Editing and Merging Programs."

Using AUTO to Enter Program 1-1   Any number can be specified for the starting line number. In this example, 100 is used for the starting line number, and 10 is the increment value for the ascending line numbers. The number 10 is not a magic number, but it does leave some line numbers unused between each program line, so that you can add more lines later, if needed.

Enter the first AUTO command.

```
AUTO 100, 10
```

When you press ENTER, line number 100 is displayed, followed by a blank space and the cursor, like this:

```
AUTO 100, 10
100 _
```

Next enter the REM of the first program line. When you press ENTER, the line is entered. GW-BASIC now moves the cursor to the next line and displays the number 110, a space, and the cursor; it is ready to accept line 110. Enter line 110.

```
AUTO 100, 10
100 REM ** Print Date and Time - Then BEEP **
110 ' GW-BASIC Reference, Chapter 1.  File: GWRF0101.BAS
120 _
```

Pause for a moment when the cursor appears at line 120. This line will be used for a block separator. Type an apostrophe and press ENTER. Then continue with the next two lines.

```
120 '
130 REM ** Initialize **
140 CLS
150 _
```

Make line 150 another block separator; enter an apostrophe. Then continue with the rest of Program 1-1 as shown here.

```
150 '
160 REM ** Print Date, Time: BEEP and End **
170 PRINT DATE$
180 PRINT TIME$
190 BEEP
200 END
210 _
```

The program has now been completely entered. Even though line 210 was displayed while AUTO was in effect, it is not part of the program. Press CTRL+BREAK or CTRL+C to terminate the AUTO command now in effect.

Using AUTO in Other Forms

You may not want to number the lines of your programs with regular increments such as those used in the last section. You can use other forms of the AUTO command to get line numbers like the ones in Program 1-1's original form.

Number the first two lines by using the following AUTO command:

```
AUTO 1, 1
```

After this AUTO command is entered, the number 1 is provided for the first line. After typing the first two lines, you see the following display:

```
AUTO 1,1
1 REM ** Print Date and Time - Then BEEP **
2 ' GW-BASIC Reference, Chapter 1.  File: GWRF0101.BAS
3 _
```

Instead of line 3, you may want to insert a different line number, followed by a space and an apostrophe, to separate the blocks of the program. To do so, you must first leave the Automatic Line Numbering mode by pressing CTRL+BREAK or CTRL+C.

```
3                    (Press CTRL+BREAK here)
Ok
_
```

At the cursor,

> Type: **99** '
> and press ENTER.

You now want to change the next line number and the increment, so that the next block of the program begins at line 100 and increments by 10. Enter a new AUTO command as follows:

```
99 '
AUTO 100, 10          (Enter new command)
100 _                 (New line number and cursor appear,
                       ready for a program line)
```

Now enter the 100 block of program lines. Each time you press ENTER this time, the line number will be incremented by 10. When the line number for line 120 appears, pause again.

```
100 REM ** Initialize **
110 CLS
120 _
```

Since there is no line 120, again press CTRL+BREAK or CTRL+C to terminate the AUTO command now in effect. The computer returns to the direct mode.

```
100 REM ** Initialize **
110 CLS
120                   (Press CTRL+BREAK here)
Ok
_
```

Now that you are out of the automatic line numbering mode, enter line number 199 followed by a space and an apostrophe. This provides a separator line between the second and third blocks of the program. (The line numbers at which you pressed CTRL+BREAK or CTRL+C are not entered as part of the program.) Here is the program so far:

```
1 REM ** Print Date and Time - Then BEEP **
2 ' GW-BASIC Reference, Chapter 1.  File: GWRF0101.BAS
99 '
100 REM ** Initialize **
110 CLS
199 '
```

To enter the 200 block, you can use another form of the AUTO command. Type only the AUTO command, followed by the number 200. When no comma and increment value are entered, the AUTO command is executed with the default increment value of 10. When the line number 200 appears, you are back in the Indirect mode. As you enter the lines of block 200, a new number appears after each press of the ENTER key.

```
AUTO 200
200 REM ** Print Date and Time, then BEEP and End **
210 PRINT DATE$
220 PRINT TIME$
230 BEEP
240 BEND          (Oops!  A misspelled word)
250 _
```

The GW-BASIC keyword, END, was misspelled in line 240. Press CTRL+BREAK at line 250 to terminate the current AUTO command. Then enter the following form of AUTO:

```
250                (Press CTRL+BREAK here)
AUTO., 10          (New AUTO command)
```

This form of the AUTO command causes the next line to be numbered the same as the most recently entered line (240). An asterisk appears after the line number to warn you that the current line will be overwritten by the new one.

```
AUTO., 10
240*_
```

This is just what you want! Whatever you enter here will replace the previous line 240 that contained the error.

Type: **END**
and press ENTER.

After line 240 has been corrected, the AUTO command is still in effect, and the line number 250 is displayed followed by a blank space and the cursor.


```
240*END              (Your corrected line)
250 _
```


You can use this method to correct errors whenever you spot them *before* you enter the next line.

Look over your program again, carefully. If you see an error in any line, type the line number and retype the line. When you press the ENTER key, the new line replaces the one that contained the error.

More advanced methods of editing are discussed in Chapter 4, "Editing and Merging Programs," and in Chapter 10, "Editing." AUTO is also discussed further in Chapter 10.

Listing the Program

Programs may be listed to the display screen, the printer, a communications adapter, or a file. For this task, the LIST command is most often used when writing and debugging programs, because it puts program lines in numerical order and allows you to look at any part of a program.

Listing to the Screen

You can list the program currently in memory to the display screen by typing the keyword **LIST** at the GW-BASIC prompt. Then press ENTER. You can also list the program by pressing the F1 function key. A third way to list a program is to enclose the screen device driver (SCRN:) in quotes following the LIST command and a comma. Try all three of these list operations.

Type: **LIST**
and press ENTER.

Press: F1
and then press ENTER.

Type: **LIST ,"SCRN:"**
and press ENTER.

A listing of Program 1-1, as entered in this chapter with the AUTO command, is shown in Figure 3-1.

Figure 3-1.

```
LIST
1 REM ** Print Date and Time - Then BEEP **
2 ' GW-BASIC Reference, Chapter 1.  File: GWRF0101.BAS
99 '
100 REM ** Initialize **
110 CLS
199 '
200 REM ** Print Date and Time, then BEEP and End **
210 PRINT DATE$
220 PRINT TIME$
230 BEEP
240 END
```

Listing of Program 1-1

REMEMBER   Any blank lines originally entered in a program are removed when the program is listed. All letters that were originally entered in lowercase are capitalized when a program is listed (except those contained in REM statements or within quotes). If you want to save the line spaces between blocks of the program, you can enter a line number with a lone REM, or with an apostrophe (')—for example, 9 ', or 199 ' as shown in Figure 3-1.

Following are some other options you may find useful:

- To list only part of a program, you can use the keyword LIST followed by the range of lines desired. The beginning and ending line numbers you enter do not have to exist in the program. The computer will list any existing lines between the two lines specified.

- To list lines 100 through 199, type **LIST 100—199** and press ENTER. You will see

```
LIST 100-199
100 REM ** Initialize **
110 CLS
199 '
Ok
_
```

- To list all lines from the beginning through line 200, type **LIST—200** and press ENTER. The result is shown in Figure 3-2.

- To list all lines from 200 to the end of the program, type **LIST 200 —** and press ENTER. Figure 3-3 shows the resulting display.

Figure 3-2.

```
LIST -200
1 REM ** Print Date and Time - Then BEEP **
2 ' GW-BASIC Reference, Chapter 1.  File: GWRF0101.BAS
99 '
100 REM ** Initialize **
110 CLS
199 '
200 REM ** Print Date and Time, then BEEP and End **
```

LIST −200 of Program 1-1

LIST can also be used with a period (.) as shown here.

Command Form	Instruction
LIST .	List the most recently displayed line
LIST . −100	List all lines, from the most recently displayed line to line 100
LIST 100 −.	List all lines, from line 100 to the most recently displayed line
LIST −.	List all lines, from the first line to the most recently displayed line
LIST . −	List all lines, from the most recently displayed line to the last line of the program

You can also list any single line, by entering LIST followed by the desired line number.

LIST 200   *(Lists line 200 if it exists)*

Figure 3-3.

```
LIST 200-
200 REM ** Print Date and Time, then BEEP and End **
210 PRINT DATE$
220 PRINT TIME$
230 BEEP
240 END
```

LIST 200— of Program 1-1

Copying and Moving Lines with LIST

By changing the line numbers, you can copy lines of code from one place in a program to another, thus duplicating them. First, list the lines to be copied. After they are listed, move the cursor to each line number and renumber it, pressing ENTER after each change. The old lines are still in their original place in the program. In addition, they are also in the new line numbers. Thus the lines are duplicated.

Lines can also be moved to new locations. To move lines, follow the same procedure described for copying the lines. When the lines have been copied, remove the old lines by typing the old line numbers all by themselves, and pressing ENTER after each line number.

For example, Program 1-2 from Chapter 1 could be rearranged to conform with the style used for other programs in this book, if you move a few lines to a new block and insert one line.

Program 1-2 as originally written is shown in Figure 3-4. To make the changes, first list lines 100-150 with the LIST command.

```
LIST 100-150
100 REM ** BEEP, Input, Calculate **
110 CLS
120 TAXRATE = 6 / 100
130 BEEP: INPUT SALESAMOUNT
140 PRINT SALESAMOUNT * TAXRATE
150 END
```

After listing these lines, move the cursor to line 100, and change the line number to 200.

```
200 REM ** BEEP, Input, Calculate **
```

In the same way, change line numbers 120 to 210, 130 to 220, 140 to 230, and 150 to 240. The lines should now look like this:

```
200 REM ** BEEP, Input, Calculate **
110 CLS
210 TAXRATE = 6 / 100
220 BEEP: INPUT SALESAMOUNT
230 PRINT SALESAMOUNT * TAXRATE
240 END
```

Leave line 110 as it is, but delete old lines 100, 120, 130, 140, and 150 by typing in each of those line numbers and pressing ENTER after each one.

Figure 3-4.

```
1 REM ** Sample Program **
2 ' GW-BASIC Reference, Chapter 1.  File: GWRF0102.BAS

100 REM ** BEEP, Input, Calculate **
110 CLS
120 TaxRate = 6 / 100
130 BEEP: INPUT SalesAmount
140 PRINT SalesAmount * TaxRate
150 END
```

Listing of Program 1-2

```
100                  (Press ENTER here,
120                    and after each line number)
130
140
150
```

Finally, enter the following lines:

```
99 '
100 REM ** Initialize **
199 '
```

A listing of the revised program is shown in Figure 3-5.

Listing to the Printer

You can also list all or part of the program currently in memory to the line printer. The usual way to list to your printer is to use the LLIST command, just as you used LIST to list to the screen.

Figure 3-5.

```
1 REM ** Sample Program **
2 ' GW-BASIC Reference, Chapter 1.  File: GWRF0102.BAS
99 '
100 REM ** Initialize **
110 CLS
199 '
200 REM ** BEEP, Input, Calculate **
210 TAXRATE = 6 / 100
220 BEEP: INPUT SALESAMOUNT
230 PRINT SALESAMOUNT * TAXRATE
240 END
```

Listing of revised Program 1-2

Here are forms of the LLIST command:

```
LLIST           (Print a complete program)
LLIST 150       (Print only line 150)
LLIST 100-199   (Print lines 100 through 199)
LLIST -200      (Print from start through line 200)
LLIST 200-      (Print from line 200 to the end)
```

You can also list the program to your printer by using the LIST statement in the following ways:

```
LIST ,"LPT1:"          (Print a complete program)
LIST 150,"LPT1:"       (Print only line 250)
LIST 100-199,"LPT1:"   (Print lines 100 through 199)
LIST -200,"LPT1:"      (Print from start through line 200)
LIST 200-,"LPT1:"      (Print from line 200 to the end)
```

A shortcut for typing LIST ,"LPT1:" is to press F1, and then press F6. The complete program, or the lines you have specified, is then immediatcly printed, providing your printer is on line.

Listing to a File

You can list a program to a file by using the LIST command followed by a space, a comma, and the file path and filename (enclosed in double quotes). Here is the command to list the previous demonstration program to drive B:

```
LIST ,"B:GWRF0102"      (List the current program
                        to a file named GWRF0102
                        on a disk in drive B)
```

Listing a program to a file produces the same result as saving a program in ASCII format to a file, as described in the next section. This list technique can be used to save all or part of a program for use in another program via the MERGE command. For example:

```
LIST 1000-1999,"B:GWRFPART"    (List lines 1000-1999 to
                                the file GWRFPART.BAS on a
                                disk in drive B)
```

If there is a program in memory, "GWRFPART" can be merged into this program by

```
MERGE "B:GWRFPART"
```

   MERGE is discussed in Chapter 4, "Editing and Merging Programs," and in Chapter 10, "Editing."

Listing to a Communications Adapter

If you want to send a program or part of a program to someone, by way of a modem or other device connected to a communications adapter in your computer, you can send it with a LIST command. The line numbers are listed, and the specifications of the adapter must also be included, like this:

```
LIST 100-300, "COM1:2400, N, 8"
```

In this example, COM1 is the adapter, 2400 is the baud rate, N means No Parity, and 8 specifies the number of data bits. Of course, the device connected to COM1 in this example must be an output device, such as a modem or serial printer.
   Communications adapters are discussed in Chapter 20, "Commands for Ports, Joystick, Light Pen, and Function/Cursor Keys."

Saving the Program

A program is a file, similar to a data file. In order to use the program at a later time, you must save the program to a file.

Include the disk drive specification in the filename unless you want to save the file to the default drive. If the file is saved to a subdirectory, include the subdirectory's name, also.

Here are forms of the SAVE command:

```
SAVE "GWRF0102"              (Saves the program
                              to the default drive)
SAVE "B:GWRF0102"           (Saves the program to drive B)
SAVE "B:\PROGRAMS\GWRF0102"  (Saves the program to the
                              subdirectory PROGRAMS on
                              the disk in drive B)
```

The F4 function key invokes the SAVE command. Press F4, and the keyword SAVE with opening double quotes is displayed.

```
SAVE"
```

You can then enter the name of your program file.

Filename Extensions for Programs

If you do not append an extension to the filename when you save a program, GW-BASIC adds the extension BAS, as in

```
GWRF0102.BAS
```

To differentiate between various types of GW-BASIC files, you can add a three-character extension denoting the type, such as

GWRF0309.DAT   For a data file
GWRF0310.BAS   For a GW-BASIC program file
GWRF0311.LST   For a listed file

Appending the filename extension is unnecessary when you are loading or running a program that has been saved with a BAS extension, or merging a program that has been listed to a file with a BAS extension. You must, however, use the extension to rename a program file with NAME or to erase a program file with KILL. (These commands are explained in Chapter 14, "File and Device I/O.")

Formats for Program Files

Programs can be saved in three different formats. Let's use Program 1-1 for demonstration.

The normal (and default) method for saving a program is in *compressed binary format.* Save Program 1-1 this way now, using no extension.

```
SAVE "B:GWRF0101"
```

You can also save a program in *ASCII format,* by appending a comma and the letter *A* to the file specification. Save Program 1-1 now, using the *A* option, as shown here. (The extension used in this demonstration is ASC, to indicate that the file has been saved in ASCII format. However, you may use any valid extension.)

```
SAVE "B:GWRF0101.ASC", A
```

ASCII format should be used when you will be

- Merging the program at a later time with another program, with the MERGE command

- Using a word processor to edit the program or to insert the program in a document

- Sending the program over the phone lines to another source

- Loading the program into a compiled BASIC language such as PowerBasic or QuickBASIC

The third file format is *encoded binary* (also called *protected*) *format*. To use this, append the letter *P* after the filename, instead of the *A* used for ASCII format. Save Program 1-1 once more, using this format.

```
SAVE "B:GWRF0101.BIN", P
```

When a program is saved in encoded binary format, it is "protected." After it is loaded from the disk via the LOAD command, it cannot be listed or edited by LIST or EDIT commands. Therefore, no one can look at the program code. If you try to list the protected program, you will see the following messages:

```
LIST
Illegal function call
Ok
EDIT 210
210
Illegal function call
Ok
_
```

To examine a protected program, you can load it and then save it under a different name, without the *P* option. Then load the unprotected file, and examine it with LIST or EDIT.

Comparing File Formats

After you have saved Program 1-1 in all three formats, look at the directory of the disk to which they were saved. Compare the number of memory bytes used for each format. The version of

Program 1-1 used in this demonstration shows the following amounts of memory used:

```
GWRF0101.BAS   228
GWRF0101.ASC   250
GWRF0101.BIN   228
```

Notice that programs saved in compressed binary or encoded binary format require less disk space than programs saved in ASCII format; they also load faster. However, if you expect that your program will be merged with another program, used by a word processor, or sent over phone lines for use by a different computer system, an ASCII format is the only one that will work. Because future plans are often unknown when a file is saved, you may want to consider saving all your files in ASCII format.

Figure 3-6 illustrates how a compressed binary (BAS) file is stored. You can produce a similar display on the screen by exiting GW-BASIC and using a DOS TYPE command, as follows:

```
TYPE B:GWRF0101.BAS
```

For comparison, Figure 3-7 shows the way an ASCII (ASC) file is stored (when the *A* option is appended to the SAVE command). As you can see, ASCII files are stored character by character, just like text in a word processor. You can also produce this display on the screen with a DOS TYPE command.

```
TYPE B:GWRF0101.ASC
```

If you want to preserve lowercase characters and other formatting features that GW-BASIC changes when it compresses your files, create your programs with a word processor and save them in ASCII format. This way, your source file will contain all those nice formatting features. Program 1-1 was first created using a

Figure 3-6.

```
C:\>TYPE B:GWRF0101.BAS
 ⌐‼◙ Â ** Print Date and Time - Then BEEP ** §¶◙ :Â┘ GW-BASIC REFFERENCE, Chapte
r 1.  File: GWRF0101.BAS •¶c :Â┘ 4¶d Â ** Initialize ** :¶n └ B¶‖ :Â┘ m¶▙ Â ** P
rint Date, Time: BEEP and End ** ∪¶╥ ▫ ▪╏ ∆¶▄ ▫ ▪Â à¶ψ ┼ Y¶▆ ∪
C:\>
```

Compressed binary (BAS) file of Program 1-1

word processor, and was saved in ASCII format as file
GWRF0101.ASC. Notice that ASC was used as the extension to
indicate the program was saved in ASCII format.

If you save a GW-BASIC program in ASCII format, you can
load it into a compiled BASIC language such as PowerBasic or
QuickBASIC. Many GW-BASIC programs saved in ASCII can be
compiled and run in such languages with little or no change.

Figure 3-7.

```
C:\>TYPE B:GWRF0101.ASC
1 REM ** Print Date and Time - Then BEEP **
2 ' GW-BASIC Reference, Chapter 1.  File: GWRF0101.BAS
99 '
100 REM ** Initialize **
110 CLS
199 '
200 REM ** Print Date, Time: BEEP and End **
210 PRINT DATE$
220 PRINT TIME$
230 BEEP
240 END

C:\>
```

ASCII file of Program 1-1

You can also send the ASCII source program to your printer from DOS with the PRINT command, and to the screen with the TYPE command.

```
PRINT B:GWRF0101.ASC          (To your printer)
TYPE B:GWRF0301.ASC           (To the screen)
```

Loading the Program

The LOAD command is used to access a file that has been created in the indirect mode and saved to disk.

When the LOAD command is executed, the file is loaded into memory. The name of the file, included in the LOAD command, must be enclosed in double quotes. If you press the F3 key, the keyword and opening quotes are displayed, and you can add the filename.

Press: F3
The computer prints:

```
LOAD"_
```

If the filename extension is BAS, it may be omitted—otherwise, include the extension.

```
LOAD"B:GWRF0101"              (If extension is BAS)
LOAD"B:GWRF0101.ASC"          (If extension is ASC or another
                              extension, include it)
```

When used with just the filename, the LOAD command closes all open files and deletes all variables and program lines currently in memory before it loads the specified program. After the program is loaded, it may be listed, edited, or run.

You can load and also immediately run a program, by appending a comma and the letter *R* following the filename, like this:

```
LOAD"B:GWRF0101.ASC", R
```

When you use the *R* option, all open data files remain open. This allows you to load one program from within another, and to use the same data files. Be aware, however, that the values of the variables in the first program are *not* preserved by the LOAD command with the *R* option. The CHAIN command (discussed in Chapter 9, "Program Control") is more appropriate for preserving variables when control is passed from one program to another.

Filenames are always specified in string form when using the SAVE, LOAD, and RUN commands. You can therefore use string variables to load one program from another. Program 3-1, Menu Selector, allows you to select a program from a menu, that is, to run one program from within another program.

Program 3-1.

```
1 REM ** Menu Selector **
2 ' GW-BASIC Reference, Chapter 3.  File: GWRF0301.DOC
3 ' Used to demonstrate the R LOAD option
99 '
100 REM ** Initialize **
110 CLS
199 '
200 REM ** Print program selections **
210 PRINT "Program Selections"
220 PRINT : PRINT "  B:GWRF0101.ASC"
230 PRINT "  B:GWRF0102.ASC"
240 PRINT "  B:GWRF0103.ASC"
299 '
300 REM ** Make selections & run program **
310 PRINT
320 INPUT "Enter the name of the program desired:", Program$
330 LOAD Program$, R
340 END
```

Menu Selector

Suppose you have a disk on which Programs 1-1, 1-2, and 1-3 from Chapter 1 are saved with an ASC extension, in ASCII format. (If you do not have such a disk, prepare one now.) On this disk, enter Program 3-1 and save it in ASCII format with an ASC extension. Use an appropriate disk drive designation. (Be sure to save Program 3-1 in ASCII format, as it will be used in that form in Chapter 4.)

Here are two examples of the SAVE command to save Program 3-1:

```
SAVE "B:GWRF0301.ASC", A
```

```
SAVE "C:\BASIC\GWRF0301.ASC", A
```

This disk will be used in the next section to demonstrate how a program can be loaded and run from within another program.

Running the Program

Programs that have been created in the indirect operating mode are executed by the RUN command. If the program to be executed is in memory, you can start it by entering the keyword RUN only, or by pressing the F2 function key. Either method runs the program currently in memory starting with the lowest-numbered program line.

Load Program 3-1 (file GWRF0301.ASC) now if it is not already in memory. If you didn't save it previously, type in the program now. After it is loaded or typed in,

Type: **RUN**
and press ENTER.
or
Press F2.

You will see the menu as shown in Figure 3-8. To make a selection, you type in the complete filename of the program desired. There are more sophisticated ways to select from a menu, but for now let's keep things simple. As it is now written, the program will load and try to run any program you name that is on the disk in the specified drive — even if it is not on the menu.

If the filename you enter matches one of the three listed on the menu, that file is immediately loaded and run by the LOAD

Figure 3-8.

```
Program Selections

 B:GWRF0101.ASC
 B:GWRF0102.ASC
 B:GWRF0103.ASC

Enter the name of the program desired:_


















1LIST   2RUN←   3LOAD"  4SAVE"  5CONT←  6,"LPT1 7TRON← 8TROFF← 9KEY    10SCREE
```

Menu produced by Program 3-1

statement at line 330. If the name is entered incorrectly or is not on the disk in the specified drive, you will see the message "File not found in 330."

Figure 3-9 shows the result of a RUN of this program. In this example, the first selection (B:GWRF0101.ASC) was made from the menu in Figure 3-8. The selected program clears the screen and displays the current date and time—gives a beep, and then ends. The computer returns to GW-BASIC's direct operation mode, displaying the "Ok" prompt and cursor.

Since Program 3-1 loaded the program selected from the menu, Program 3-1 is no longer in memory. The file named B:GWRF0101.ASC was loaded by your selection; therefore, the selected program replaced Program 3-1 and remains in memory at the end of the run.

In this situation, you can run Program 3-1 again by adding its

Figure 3-9.

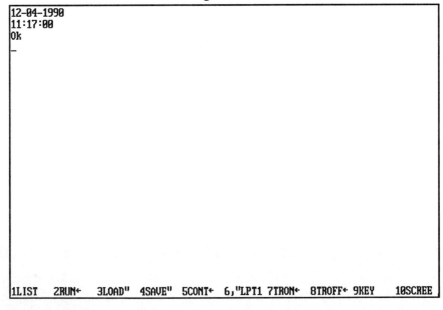

Output of Program B:GWRF0101.ASC selected from menu

filename to the RUN command.

```
RUN "B:GWRF0301.ASC"
```

When used in this form, the RUN command first closes all open files and deletes what is currently in memory. Then the command loads the specified file from the disk in drive B into memory and executes it.

If you want to keep files open when using the RUN command, add a comma and the letter *R* to the end of the command.

```
RUN , R
RUN 110, R
RUN "B:GWRF0301.ASC", R
```

If you want to start the program in memory from a line other than the lowest-numbered line, add the desired starting line number to the RUN command, for example,

```
RUN 100
```

Summary

In this chapter, you used the AUTO command in many forms to automatically number the lines of Program 1-1. You learned that AUTO's basic form is

```
AUTO 100, 10
```

where the first number (100) is the first line to be supplied for automatic numbering. The second number (10) is the amount each line number is increased.

You learned to interrupt the automatic line numbering by pressing CTRL+C or CTRL+BREAK. You used several different AUTO commands to number the blocks of the program.

You listed a complete program, or parts of a program, to the screen, to a printer, to a disk file, and to a communications adapter, with various LIST commands.

Command Form	Where Program Is Listed
LIST	The screen
LIST ,"SCRN:"	The screen
LLIST	A printer
LIST ,"LPT1:"	A printer
LIST ,"B:GWRF0301"	A file named GWRF0301 on disk B
LIST ,"COM1:2400, N, B"	A communications adapter

You saw how to use SAVE to save a program in normal format (compressed binary), ASCII format and protected (encoded binary) format. When a program is saved in ASCII format, it can be merged with other programs. It can also be displayed from DOS by the TYPE command or printed by the DOS PRINT command. When a program is saved in protected format, it cannot be listed by a LIST command or edited by an EDIT command.

Command Form	Type of Format
SAVE "B:GWRF0301"	Compressed binary format
SAVE "B:GWRF0301.ASC", A	ASCII format
A SAVE "B:GWRF0301.ASC", P	Protected format

You also loaded a program that had been previously saved, and learned how to use the *R* option to both load and immediately run a program.

Command Form	Instruction
LOAD "B:GWRF0301"	Load a program
LOAD "B:GWRF0301", R	Load and run a program

Finally, you got to execute a program with the RUN command. You learned to start a program from a specified line. You also read about running a program from within another program, and about using the *R* option to keep the current data files open.

Command Form	Instruction
RUN	Run the program in memory
RUN 100	Run the program in memory starting with line 100
450 RUN "B:GWRF0301"	From a line within another program, run the program named
450 RUN "B:GWRF0301", R	From a line in another program, run the program named and keep current files open

CHAPTER

4

Editing and Merging Programs

Once you have created a program, you will usually want to improve it or revise it to fit different situations. Editing a program, and merging bits and pieces of other programs, are tasks that play an important part in a programmer's life.

In this chapter you will learn to edit and merge programs that have previously been created and saved. In particular, you will learn how to do the following:

97

- Edit lines while they are being typed
- Delete and insert characters in lines that have been previously entered, using both the Overtype entry mode and the Insert entry mode
- Use the EDIT command to display the current program line or a specified line that you want to change
- Edit a previous program to improve its output format
- Insert new lines between existing lines
- Create programs and subroutines separately, save them in ASCII format, and merge them into a single program
- Renumber parts of merged program files
- Keep a library file of useful subroutines
- Create and maintain a REM file of your programs

Editing a Program

You can edit GW-BASIC program lines as you type, or after the lines have been entered and the program is still in memory. You can also edit lines in a program that has been previously saved in a file, by reloading that file into memory.

Although the NEW command is normally used to clear memory prior to entering a new program, it can also be used as an editing feature to delete the entire program currently in memory. Then you can start over, entering lines from the beginning.

Editing Lines As You Type Them

When you are entering programs, type carefully to avoid simple errors. This will eliminate the need for extensive editing of your programs. However, no one is perfect. If you notice an incorrect character as you are typing a line, you can delete it by using the BACKSPACE key, the DELETE key, or the CTRL+H key combination. After the character has been deleted, continue typing on that line. Don't forget the typing shortcuts discussed in Chapter 2, such as ALT+P. Using these shortcuts can reduce the amount of typing that is necessary, as well as the chance for errors.

Suppose you are entering the first line of a new program and spot an error while you are on the first line. Two ways to correct the error are demonstrated here.

Using the BACKSPACE or CTRL+H key:

```
1 REM ** Menuu_      (Oops!  An extra u was typed;  press
                      the BACKSPACE key)

1 REM ** Menu_       (BACKSPACE or CTRL+H moves the cursor
                      left one position and deletes the
                      character to the left of the cursor)
```

Using the DELETE key:

```
1 REM ** Menuu Selector_           (Error discovered here)
```

Move the cursor to the
   second *u* of "Menuu."
Press: DELETE   (*Deletes the u*)
Press: END   (*Moves cursor to end of line*)
Continue typing the line.

When you pressed the DELETE key in the second technique, the letter *u* was deleted. All the text to its right moved left one place to fill the deleted space.

After the misspelling is corrected, enter the balance of line 1. Now suppose you make another typing error in line 2 and want to retype the whole line. There is a third way to correct an error in a line if the ENTER key has not yet been pressed.

The ESC key will delete a line that is in the process of being typed, before the ENTER key has been pressed.

```
1 REM ** Menu Selector **
2 ' FQ-VAIX_                    (Press ESC while cursor is still
                                 on the line)
```

All of line 2 is erased (including the line number) when you press ESC while the cursor is still on that line. The cursor then appears at the beginning position on that line.

```
1 REM ** Menu Selector **

_
```

You then retype the line number and enter the line correctly.

Editing Previously Entered Lines

Either of two modes can be used while editing: *Overtype* or *Insert*. In the Overtype mode, the character under the cursor is replaced when you type another character. In the Insert mode, the character at the cursor position (and all characters to the right of the cursor) are moved one place to the right when you type another character.

You can toggle between the Insert mode and the Overtype mode by pressing the INS key. The cursor appears as a solid block (■) in the Insert mode and an underline (_) in the Overtype mode. When you toggle to the Insert mode, you remain in this mode only as long as you are inserting consecutive characters. If you use an arrow key to move the cursor, GW-BASIC automatically reverts to Overtype mode. You also revert to Overtype mode when you press the ENTER key.

After a line has been entered, you can still edit the line by moving the cursor with the arrow keys to the place where the change is to be made. Then use one or more of the following editing methods:

- *Type over the characters* to be changed, in the Overtype mode.
- *Delete characters to the left of the cursor* by using the BACKSPACE key or CTRL+H, in either Overtype or Insert mode.
- *Delete characters at the cursor position* by using the DELETE key, in either Overtype or Insert mode.
- *Insert characters at the cursor position* in the Insert editing mode.
- *Add characters at the end of a program line* in either Overtype or Insert mode.
- *Truncate characters at the end of a program line* by moving the cursor to the desired position and pressing CTRL+END, or by pressing CTRL+E and then ENTER in either Overtype or Insert mode.

NOTE Program lines that you see on the screen can be different from the program lines stored in memory. Remember, when you are writing a program, each line is not entered into memory until you press the ENTER key. In the same way, when you edit a program line, be sure to press the ENTER key to store the edited line in memory.

When you edit more than one line, be sure to press the ENTER key on *each* modified line. When you alter characters in the middle of a line, you can press the ENTER key immediately after the change. You don't have to move the cursor to the end of the line before pressing ENTER to complete the modification.

If you have edited a previously saved program, be sure to save the program again after making the editing changes. Otherwise, your changes will only be in effect while the program is in memory. They will not be permanent until the program is saved.

The EDIT Command

You can edit any of the lines of a program that are visible on the screen. GW-BASIC has an EDIT command that will display any specified line and place the cursor at the beginning of the line, ready for editing. The EDIT command only displays one line. If you want to edit several consecutive lines, use LIST. The advantage of the EDIT command is that it places the cursor automatically on the line to be edited. With LIST, you have to move the cursor to the line to be edited.

Table 4-1.

Key Combination	Cursor Movement
DOWN ARROW or CTRL + −	Down one line.
LEFT ARROW or CTRL +]	Left one position.
RIGHT ARROW or CTRL + /	Right one position.
UP ARROW or CTRL + 6	Up one line.
CTRL + LEFT ARROW or CTRL + B	To beginning of the previous "word."
CTRL + RIGHT ARROW or CTRL + F	To beginning of the next "word."
END or CTRL + N	To end of the logical line.
CTRL + ENTER or CTRL + J	To beginning of the next line; lets you create logical lines that are longer than the screen width.
HOME or CTRL + K	To upper-left corner of the screen.
TAB or CTRL + I	To next tab stop; tab stops occur every eight columns.

Key Combination Shortcuts for Cursor Movement

When editing a program, you can use the shortcut key combinations shown in Table 4-1 and Table 4-2. The tables show shortcuts for cursor movement, editing, and other computer actions. Table 4-1 shows special key combinations for moving the cursor while editing. Table 4-2 shows key combinations that provide other editing and control commands.

For each combination, the two keypresses are separated by a plus (+) sign to indicate that the keys are used together. However, don't press the + key. Simply hold down the first key while you press the second key; then release both.

For example, CTRL+B means

Hold down: CTRL
Press: the *B* key
and then release both.

In this section we will use the Menu Selector Program 3-1, which you saved in Chapter 3, for editing purposes. Load Program 3-1 now; it was saved in ASCII format in Chapter 3 as GWRF0301.ASC. The program is shown again in Figure 4-1. In this program, the menu title and items appeared in the upper-left part of the screen. In the discussions that follow, the files in menu items 1, 2, and 3 are assumed to be on a disk in drive B. If your files are on drive A or some other drive, make the appropriate changes to the program.

Suppose you wish to move the menu title so that it is near the center of screen line 5. You can edit the PRINT statement in line 210 of Program 3-1, by entering the EDIT command followed by a space and the number 210.

```
EDIT 210                    (Enter this EDIT command)
210 PRINT "Program Selections"
```

Table 4-2.

Key Combination	Resulting Action
BACKSPACE or CTRL + H	Deletes character to left of cursor; character at cursor and characters to right of cursor move left one place.
DELETE	Deletes character at cursor; all characters to right of cursor move one place left.
CTRL + END or CTRL + E	Erases from cursor position to end of line.
ESC or CTRL + [	Erases entire logical line on which cursor is located.
INSERT or CTRL + R	Toggles the editing modes (Insert or Over-type).
CTRL + BREAK or CTRL + C	Returns to direct mode without saving changes on current line. Also exits AUTO line numbering mode (if in effect).
CTRL + PRTSC	Toggles on/off the echoing of characters on screen to the printer.
SHIFT + PRTSC	Sends current screen contents to the printer. If contents are from graphics mode, GRAPHICS.COM file must have been loaded from DOS.
CTRL + HOME or CTRL + L	Clears screen and puts cursor in upper-left corner.
CTRL + S or CTRL + NUMLOCK	Pauses computer; press again to continue execution.
CTRL + G	Beeps the computer's speaker.
CTRl + HOLD	For computers having a HOLD key—causes same action as CTRL + NUM LOCK or CTRL + S.

Key Combination Shortcuts for Editing and Other Tasks

Figure 4-1.

```
1 REM ** Menu Selector **
2 ' GW-BASIC Reference, Chapter 3.  File: GWRF0301.ASC
3 ' Used to demonstrate the R LOAD option
99 '
100 REM ** Initialize **
110 CLS
199 '
200 REM ** Print program selections **
210 PRINT "Program Selections"
220 PRINT: PRINT "  B:GWRF0101.ASC"
230 PRINT "  B:GWRF0102.ASC"
240 PRINT "  B:GWRF0103.ASC"
299 '
300 REM ** Make selections & run program **
310 PRINT
320 INPUT "Enter the name of the program desired:", PROGRAM$
330 LOAD PROGRAM$, R
340 END
```

Listing of Program 3-1

When the EDIT command is entered, line 210 is displayed with the cursor at the first character (the 2 of 210), as shown in the previous listing. You may now edit the line.

Press: CTRL+RIGHT ARROW   *(Moves the cursor to the letter P*
                                    of the keyword PRINT)

Press: INSERT   *(Enters the Insert mode)*
Type: **LOCATE 5, 31:**
followed by a space
and then press ENTER.

The CTRL+RIGHT ARROW keypress moves the cursor from its current position to the beginning of the next "word" to the right.

To assure that line 210 has been edited correctly, enter the keyword EDIT, followed by one space and a period. This form of the EDIT command presents the most recently displayed program line (line 210 in this example), ready for editing.

```
EDIT .
210 LOCATE 5, 31: PRINT "Program Selections"
```

The line is correct. Press ENTER to continue.

Now the title will be placed as desired, but the menu items will still be printed at the leftmost position of the lines they occupy. To place them directly below the title, you need to precede their PRINT statements in lines 220, 230 and 240 with a LOCATE statement. Use the LIST command with the starting and ending lines, since there are three lines to be edited.

```
LIST 220-240
220 PRINT: PRINT "  B:GWRF0101.ASC"
230 PRINT "  B:GWRF0102.ASC"
240 PRINT "  B:GWRF0103.ASC"
Ok
```

Move the cursor to the first 2 in the line number 220. Then press CTRL+RIGHT ARROW to move the cursor one "word" to the right. It will move to the *P* of the leftmost PRINT statement in line 220. Delete this keyword and make sure you are in the Insert mode. Then enter a LOCATE statement. Follow this sequence:

Press: DELETE five times
Press: INSERT   *(Enters the Insert mode)*
Type: **LOCATE 7, 31**
and press ENTER.

Line 220 is modified, and the cursor moves to the first number in line 230.

```
220 LOCATE 7, 31: PRINT "  B:GWRF0101.ASC"
230 PRINT "  B:GWRF0102.ASC"
240 PRINT "  B:GWRF0103.ASC"
```

In the same way that **LOCATE** 7, 31 was inserted in line 220, type **LOCATE 8, 31:** in line 230 and **LOCATE 9, 31:** in line 240. Remember to enter the Insert mode before making the insertion on each line. When you have finished editing the three lines, they should read as follows:

```
220 LOCATE 7, 31: PRINT "  B:GWRF0101.ASC"
230 LOCATE 8, 31: PRINT "  B:GWRF0102.ASC"
240 LOCATE 9, 31: PRINT "  B:GWRF0103.ASC"
```

Using the LIST command, list lines 200-240, the complete block, to verify that the edited lines are correct in memory, as well as on the screen.

```
LIST 200-240
200 REM ** Print program selections **
210 LOCATE 5, 3: PRINT "Program Selections"
220 LOCATE 7, 31: PRINT "  B:GWRF0101.ASC"
230 LOCATE 8, 31: PRINT "  B:GWRF0102.ASC"
240 LOCATE 9, 31: PRINT "  B:GWRF0103.ASC"
Ok
_
```

One last revision is needed to modify the program's title, the chapter in which it appears, and the filename. Since there are two lines to correct, list lines 1-2 to make the corrections, instead of using the EDIT command twice.

```
LIST 1-2
1 REM ** Menu Selector **
2 ' GW-BASIC Reference, Chapter 3.  File: GWRF0301.ASC
Ok
_
```

Use UP ARROW to move the cursor to line 1. Then press END to move the cursor to the end of the line. Use LEFT ARROW to back up to the left asterisk of the last pair of asterisks.

Type: **- Version 2** and a space
and press ENTER.

Then move the cursor to the chapter number (3). Instead of deleting the 3 and replacing it with a 4, you can type over the character while you are in the Overtype entry mode. Remember, use the Insert mode to insert characters; use the Overtype entry mode to replace characters. With the cursor on the number 3 of "Chapter 3",

Type: **4**

Last of all, move the cursor to the number 3 of the filename (B:GWRF0301). While still in the Overtype mode, type the number 4. Then press the ENTER key.

The revised program is now named Program 4-1, Menu Selector - Version 2. Save the program as GWRF0401.ASC in ASCII format. When the program is run, the menu appears as shown in Figure 4-2.

Menu selections should be as simple as possible. For example, it isn't necessary to type in the complete name of the desired program. A section of code added between blocks 200 and 300 will

Program 4-1.

```
1 REM ** Menu Selector - Version 2 **
2 ' GW-BASIC Reference, Chapter 4.  File: GWRF0401.ASC
3 ' Used to demonstrate the R LOAD option
99 '
100 REM ** Initialize **
110 CLS
199 '
200 REM ** Print program selections **
210 LOCATE 5, 31: PRINT "Program Selections"
220 LOCATE 7, 31: PRINT "  B:GWRF0101.ASC"
230 LOCATE 8, 31: PRINT "  B:GWRF0102.ASC"
240 LOCATE 9, 31: PRINT "  B:GWRF0103.ASC"
299 '
300 REM ** Make selections & run program **
310 PRINT
320 INPUT "Enter the name of the program desired:", Program$
330 LOAD Program$, R
340 END
```

Menu Selector - Version 2 (GWRF0401.ASC)

make menu item selection simpler in this program. To make room for the new section, you need to change the line numbers of what is now block 300.

Renumbering Lines

The GW-BASIC keyword RENUM is used to renumber program lines. Change the numbers of the lines in block 300 by entering the following command:

```
RENUM 400, 300, 10
```

This command will change all line numbers from the second line number in the command (300) to the end of the program. The

Figure 4-2.

```
                    Program Selections

                     B:GWRF0101.ASC
                     B:GWRF0102.ASC
                     B:GWRF0103.ASC

Enter the name of the program desired:? _

1LIST  2RUN←  3LOAD"  4SAVE"  5CONT←  6,"LPT1 7TRON←  8TROFF← 9KEY    10SCREE
```

Menu from Program 4-1

first line number used for the new number sequence will be the
first number in the RENUM command (400). The third number
(10) provides the increment used in the new number sequence. A
list of the renumbered program is shown in Figure 4-3.

The RENUM command can also be used in the following
forms:

```
RENUM               (Renumbers the complete program,
                       starting at line 10 with an increment of 10)
RENUM 1000, , 20    (Renumbers the complete program, with
                       1000 as the first line and an increment of 20)
```

The RENUM command also changes the line numbers referred to in other statements, such as GOTO, GOSUB, THEN,
and ELSE.

Figure 4-3.

```
LIST
1 REM ** Menu Selector - Version 2 **
2 ' GW-BASIC Reference, Chapter 4.  File: GWRF0401.ASC
3 ' Used to demonstrate the R LOAD option
99 '
100 REM ** Initialize **
110 CLS
199 '
200 REM ** Print program selections **
210 LOCATE 5, 31: PRINT "Program Selections"
220 LOCATE 7, 31: PRINT "  B:GWRF0101.ASC"
230 LOCATE 8, 31: PRINT "  B:GWRF0102.ASC"
240 LOCATE 9, 31: PRINT "  B:GWRF0103.ASC"
299 '
400 REM ** Make selections & run program **
410 PRINT
420 INPUT "Enter the name of the program desired:", PROGRAM$
430 LOAD PROGRAM$, R
440 END
Ok

—
```

Listing of renumbered Program 4-1

Inserting New Lines

One of the easiest ways to select from a menu is to number each item on the menu. Then you can select an item by entering its number, rather than its complete name. You can then have the computer supply the appropriate names that match the numbers on the menu.

Since you have renumbered the old 300 block to be a 400 block, you can now use the 300 numbers for the new block of code to be inserted.

```
300 REM ** Select from the menu **
310 LOCATE 11, 5
320 INPUT "Press the number of desired program: ", number
```

```
330 IF number = 1 THEN Program$ = "B:GWRF0101.ASC"
340 IF number = 2 THEN Program$ = "B:GWRF0102.ASC"
350 IF number = 3 THEN Program$ = "B:GWRF0103.ASC"
399 '
```

Use the LIST command to see the program as it now exists (shown in Figure 4-4).

There is one important additional revision to make in Program 4-1. In lines 220, 230, and 240, you need to insert the appropriate numbers before the menu choices. First, list these three lines. Then, using your new editing knowledge, make the appropriate changes to make the lines read as follows:

```
220 LOCATE 7, 31 : PRINT "1  B:GWRF0101.ASC"
230 LOCATE 8, 31 : PRINT "2  B:GWRF0102.ASC"
240 LOCATE 9, 31 : PRINT "3  B:GWRF0103.ASC"
```

List the program again to see the program as it now exists (Figure 4-5).

Lines 410 and 420 of the revised program are no longer needed, because the menu item choice is now made at line 320. To eliminate lines 410 and 420,

Type: **410**
and press ENTER.   (*Deletes line 410*)
Type: **420**
and press ENTER.   (*Deletes line 420*)

Then renumber block 400 again with

```
RENUM 400, 400, 10
```

This time the RENUM command says: Start at line 400 and renumber all lines from line 400 to the end of the program, using an increment of 10.

Figure 4-4.

```
LIST
1 REM ** Menu Selector - Version 2 **
2 ' GW-BASIC Reference, Chapter 4.  File: GWRF0401.ASC
3 ' Used to demonstrate the R LOAD option
99 '
100 REM ** Initialize **
110 CLS
199 '
200 REM ** Print program selections **
210 LOCATE 5, 31: PRINT "Program Selections"
220 LOCATE 7, 31: PRINT "  B:GWRF0101.ASC"
230 LOCATE 8, 31: PRINT "  B:GWRF0102.ASC"
240 LOCATE 9, 31: PRINT "  B:GWRF0103.ASC"
299 '
300 REM ** Select from the menu **
310 LOCATE 11, 5
320 INPUT "Press the number of the desired program: ", NUMBER
330 IF NUMBER = 1 THEN PROGRAM$ = "B:GWRF0101.ASC"
340 IF NUMBER = 2 THEN PROGRAM$ = "B:GWRF0102.ASC"
350 IF NUMBER = 3 THEN PROGRAM$ = "B:GWRF0103.ASC"
399 '
400 REM ** Make selections & run program **
410 PRINT
420 INPUT "Enter the name of the program desired:", PROGRAM$
430 LOAD PROGRAM$, R
440 END
Ok
_
```

Menu Selector Program with block 300

The title of the last block is no longer accurate, because the INPUT statement (where the selection was previously made) has been removed. EDIT line 400 to make the correction.

```
EDIT 400
400 REM ** Make selections and run program"
```

Figure 4-5.

```
LIST
1 REM ** Menu Selector - Version 2 **
2 ' GW-BASIC Reference, Chapter 4.  File: GWRF0401.ASC
3 ' Used to demonstrate the R LOAD option
99 '
100 REM ** Initialize **
110 CLS
199 '
200 REM ** Print program selections **
210 LOCATE 5, 31: PRINT "Program Selections"
220 LOCATE 7, 31: PRINT "1  B:GWRF0101.ASC"
230 LOCATE 8, 31: PRINT "2  B:GWRF0102.ASC"
240 LOCATE 9, 31: PRINT "3  B:GWRF0103.ASC"
299 '
300 REM ** Select from the menu **
310 LOCATE 11, 5
320 INPUT "Press the number of the desired program: ", NUMBER
330 IF NUMBER = 1 THEN PROGRAM$ = "B:GWRF0101.ASC"
340 IF NUMBER = 2 THEN PROGRAM$ = "B:GWRF0102.ASC"
350 IF NUMBER = 3 THEN PROGRAM$ = "B:GWRF0103.ASC"
399 '
400 REM ** Make selections & run program **
410 PRINT
420 INPUT "Enter the name of the program desired:", PROGRAM$
430 LOAD PROGRAM$, R
440 END
Ok
_
```

Menu Selector Program with menu choice numbers

Use CTRL+RIGHT ARROW to move the cursor to the letter *M* of "Make" in line 400. Then

   Press: CTRL+END

This erases line 400 from the cursor position to the end of the line. At the cursor,

Type: **Run program ***
and press ENTER

The last change you need to make is to modify the first two lines of the program. List lines 1 and 2, and use the editing techniques you have learned to make the lines read

```
1 REM ** Menu Selector - Version 3 **
2 ' GW-BASIC Reference, Chapter 4.  File: GWRF0402.ASC
Ok
_
```

Program 4-2.

```
1 REM ** Menu Selector - Version 3 **
2 ' GW-BASIC Reference, Chapter 4.  File: GWRF0402.ASC
3 ' Used to demonstrate the R LOAD option
99 '
100 REM ** Initialize **
110 CLS
199 '
200 REM ** Print program selections **
210 LOCATE 5, 31: PRINT "Program Selections"
220 LOCATE 7, 31: PRINT "1  B:GWRF0101.ASC"
230 LOCATE 8, 31: PRINT "2  B:GWRF0102.ASC"
240 LOCATE 9, 31: PRINT "3  B:GWRF0103.ASC"
299 '
300 REM ** Select from the menu **
310 LOCATE 11, 19
320 INPUT "Press the number of desired program: ", number
330 IF number = 1 THEN Program$ = "B:GWRF0101.ASC"
340 IF number = 2 THEN Program$ = "B:GWRF0102.ASC"
350 IF number = 3 THEN Program$ = "B:GWRF0103.ASC"
399 '
400 REM ** Run program **
410 LOAD Program$, R
420 END
```

Menu Selector - Version 3 (GWRF0402.ASC)

Program 4-2, Menu Selector - Version 3, has now been completed. Figure 4-6 shows the new menu and prompts used by this version of the program.

Merging a Program

As discussed in the "Saving the Program" section of Chapter 3, a file saved to a disk in ASCII format can be merged with a program, by a MERGE command. The MERGE command specifies the name of the file to be merged. If the file to be merged is not on the disk in the default drive, the disk on which the file is located must be included with the filename. If the filename has an extension other than BAS, the extension must be appended to the filename. For example,

```
MERGE "B:GWRF0404.ASC"
```

Figure 4-6.

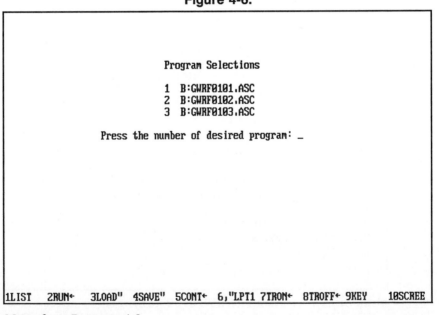

```
                    Program Selections

                    1   B:GWRF0101.ASC
                    2   B:GWRF0102.ASC
                    3   B:GWRF0103.ASC

          Press the number of desired program: _
```

```
1LIST    2RUN←   3LOAD"  4SAVE"  5CONT←  6,"LPT1 7TRON←  8TROFF← 9KEY    10SCREE
```

Menu from Program 4-2

CAUTION   Use some care when merging files. If any line numbers in the file to be merged are the same as the program in memory, the lines in the file to be merged will replace (overwrite) these identically numbered lines of the program in memory.

If you try to merge a file that was not saved in ASCII format, a "Bad file mode" message will be displayed. The file will not be merged.

A Demonstration of MERGE

In this section, you will enter a subroutine and save it in ASCII format. You will then enter a new program in memory, and merge the subroutine with the program in memory.

REMEMBER   When you are entering files that you expect to merge with other programs, avoid low-numbered lines. Start with a very large number. Lines from 60000 upward are used in the demonstrations in this book.

Program 4-3, SUBROUTINE: Date and Time Stamp, is the subroutine to be saved in ASCII format. Lines 60000 to 60005 are

Program 4-3.

```
60000 REM ** SUBROUTINE: Date and Time Stamp **
60001 ' GW-BASIC Reference, Chapter 4.  File: GWRF0403.SUB
60002 ' Saved in ASCII format.
60003 ' Use to send the date and time to the screen.
60004 ' Renumber the subroutine to fit the program
60005 ' being used.

60100 REM ** Send date and time to screen **
60110 PRINT DATE$
60120 PRINT TIME$
60130 RETURN
```

SUBROUTINE: Date and Time Stamp (GWRF0403.SUB)

used for descriptive remarks to remind you what is in the subroutine and how it will be used. The executable lines of the program follow line 60100 (with an increment of 10), in the same manner as for regular programs in this book.

This subroutine can be used in many situations to stamp the date and time on your work. If you want to stamp the date and time on information sent to the printer, change the PRINT keywords to LPRINT. In fact, you may want to create a separate, ASCII-saved subroutine to use when sending the date and time to your printer.

REMEMBER Save subroutines in ASCII format. You may want to save all your mergeable subroutines with a special filename extension (such as SUB).

When you have entered Program 4-3, if you are saving it to drive B, use

```
SAVE "B:GWRF0403.SUB", A          (Don't forget the A)
```

After you have entered and saved the subroutine in ASCII format, enter Program 4-4, Purchase Record. Do not run the program yet, because line 210 has a GOSUB statement to a line number that does not yet exist.

After the subroutine has been merged, this Purchase Record program will let you keep a record of purchases that you make on a given date. You enter the number of purchases to be recorded at line 320. The FOR/NEXT loop in block 400 allows you to enter the amount of each purchase. In the same block, a running total of your purchase amounts is assigned to the variable total#. Since the variables amount# and total# are double precision numbers, you can afford to be a high-spender. Line 510 prints the grand total, and then the program pauses at line 610. When you press a key, the default screen is restored and the program ends.

Program 4-4.

```
1 REM ** Purchase Record **
2 ' GW-BASIC Reference, Chapter 4.  File: GWRF0404.ASC
3 ' Saved in ASCII format.  Used to demonstrate MERGE

100 REM ** Initialize **
110 CLS: KEY OFF: DEFINT A-Z
120 Form$ = "$$###,###,###,###.##": total# = 0

200 REM ** Display date and time **
210 GOSUB 1010

300 REM ** Get number of purchases **
310 LOCATE 5, 1
320 INPUT "How many purchases "; purchases

400 REM ** Get purchase amounts and total **
410 FOR number = 1 TO purchases
420    INPUT "Amount "; amount#
430    total# = total# + amount#
440 NEXT number

500 REM ** Print total **
510 PRINT: PRINT "Total: ";
520 PRINT USING Form$; total#

600 REM ** Wait for keypress, then end **
610 akey$ = INPUT$(1)
620 CLS: KEY ON: END
```

Purchase Record (GWRF0404.ASC)

A PRINT USING statement is used in line 520 so that the dollar amount is printed with normal appearance, as defined by Form$ in line 120.

```
120 Form$ = "$$###,###,###,###.##": total# = 0
520 PRINT USING Form$; total#
```

The double dollar sign ($$) places a dollar sign just to the left of the first digit of total# when it is printed. Each number sign (#) reserves a place for one digit of the total. The commas tell the computer to separate with a comma each three places to the left of the decimal point. The two number signs to the right of the decimal point reserve spaces for cents.

Now is the time to merge the subroutine which was saved as B:GWRF0403.SUB. Enter the MERGE command and filename. The filename must be enclosed in double quotation marks. Also include the disk drive, unless the default drive holds the subroutine file.

```
MERGE "B:GWRF0403.SUB"
```

The numbering of the subroutine starts at 60000. Renumber it after it is merged, using a starting number of 1000 with an increment of 1.

```
RENUM 1000, 60000, 1
```

The previous command renumbers the subroutine, as shown in Figure 4-7. You can now delete some remarks (lines 1001-1006)

Figure 4-7.

```
1000 REM ** SUBROUTINE: Date and Time Stamp **
1001 ' GW-BASIC Reference, Chapter 4.  File: GWRF0403.SUB
1002 ' Saved in ASCII format.
1003 ' Use to send the date and time to the screen.
1004 ' Renumber the subroutine to fit the program
1005 ' being used.
1006 REM ** Send date and time to screen **
1007 PRINT DATE$
1008 PRINT TIME$
1009 RETURN
```

Renumbered subroutine

and renumber the remaining lines in increments of 10, like this:

```
DELETE 1001-1006
Ok
RENUM 1000, 1000, 10
Ok
_
```

This completes the program. Retitle it "Purchase Record with Subroutine." Change lines 1 and 2 to reflect the new title, and also change the filename. Save it in ASCII format with the filename GWRF0405.ASC. A run of Program 4-5, Purchase Record with Subroutine, is shown in Figure 4-8.

Merging Another Subroutine

Program 4-5 does not include sales tax on the purchases. You can add a section to the main program to calculate the sales tax on the total of the purchases. However, you may prefer to write the sales tax calculation as a separate program (a subroutine), and merge it with Program 4-5 as it now exists. If you save the sales tax subroutine as an ASCII file, you can merge it with any program you want.

Enter Program 4-6, SUBROUTINE: Calculate Sales Tax, and save it in ASCII format as GWRF0406.SUB.

Since you saved both Programs 4-5 and 4-6 in ASCII format, it doesn't matter which one is merged with the other. The subroutine is now in memory, so you can merge Program 4-5 with it using the following MERGE command:

```
MERGE "B:GWRF0405.ASC"
```

List the merged programs; the merged result is shown in Figure 4-9.

Program 4-5.

```
1 REM ** Purchase Record with Subroutine **
2 ' GW-BASIC Reference, Chapter 4.  File: GWRF0405.ASC
3 ' Saved in ASCII format.  Used to demonstrate MERGE

100 REM ** Initialize **
110 CLS: KEY OFF: DEFINT A-Z
120 Form$ = "$$###,###,###,###.##": total# = 0

200 REM ** Display date and time **
210 GOSUB 1010

300 REM ** Get number of purchases **
310 LOCATE 5, 1
320 INPUT "How many purchases "; purchases

400 REM ** Get purchase amounts and total **
410 FOR number = 1 TO purchases
420    INPUT "Amount "; amount#
430    total# = total# + amount#
440 NEXT number

500 REM ** Print total **
510 PRINT: PRINT "Total: ";
520 PRINT USING Form$; total#

600 REM ** Wait for keypress, then end **
610 akey$ = INPUT$(1)
620 CLS: KEY ON: END

1000 REM ** SUBROUTINE: Date and Time Stamp **
1010 PRINT DATE$
1020 PRINT TIME$
1030 RETURN
```

Purchase Record with Subroutine (GWRF0405.ASC)

Figure 4-8.

```
12-10-1990
16:43:19


How many purchases ? 3
Amount ? 9456.88
Amount ? 123.99
Amount ? 22.45

Total:          $9,603.32
_
```

Output of Program 4-5

Program 4-6.

```
60000 REM ** SUBROUTINE: Calculate Tax **
60001 ' GW-BASIC Reference, Chapter 4.  File: GWRF0406.SUB
60002 ' Saved in ASCII format.
60003 ' Use to calculate sales tax on purchases
60004 ' Renumber the subroutine to fit the program
60005 ' being used.

60100 REM ** Calculate Sales Tax **
60110 TaxRate# = .06#
60120 Tax# = int(total# * TaxRate# + .005) * 100) / 100
60130 RETURN
```

SUBROUTINE: Calculate Tax (GWRF0406.SUB)

Figure 4-9.

```
LIST
1 REM ** Purchase Record with Subroutine **
2 ' GW-BASIC Reference, Chapter 4.  File: GWRF0405.ASC
3 ' Saved in ASCII format.  Used to demonstrate MERGE
100 REM ** Initialize **
110 KEY OFF: CLS: DEFINT A-Z
120 FORM$ = "$$###,###,###,###.##": TOTAL# = 0
200 REM ** Display date and time **
210 GOSUB 1010
300 REM ** Get number of purchases **
310 LOCATE 5, 1
320 INPUT "How many purchases "; PURCHASES
400 REM ** Get purchase amounts and total **
410 FOR NUMBER = 1 TO PURCHASES
420    INPUT "Amount "; AMOUNT#
430    TOTAL# = TOTAL# + AMOUNT#
440 NEXT NUMBER
500 REM ** Print total **
510 PRINT: PRINT "Total: ";
520 PRINT USING FORM$; TOTAL#
600 REM ** Wait for keypress, then end **
610 AKEY$ = INPUT$(1)
620 CLS: KEY ON: END
1000 REM ** SUBROUTINE: Date and Time Stamp **
1010 PRINT DATE$
1020 PRINT TIME$
1030 RETURN
60000 REM ** SUBROUTINE: Calculate Tax **
60001 ' GW-BASIC Reference, Chapter 4.  File: GWRF0406.SUB
60002 ' Saved in ASCII format.
60003 ' Use to calculate sales tax on purchases
60004 ' Renumber the subroutine to fit the program
60005 ' being used.
60100 REM ** Calculate Sales Tax **
60110 TAXRATE# = .06#
60120 TAX# = INT(TOTAL# * TAXRATE# + .005) * 100) / 100
60130 RETURN
```

Listing of merged Programs 4-5 and 4-6

Delete lines 60001 through 60100. Then renumber the remaining part of the subroutine, using an increment of 10, starting with line 2000.

```
DELETE 60001-60100
Ok
RENUM 2000, 60000, 10
Ok
_
```

The new subroutine is now

```
2000 REM ** SUBROUTINE: Calculate Tax **
2010 TaxRate# = .06#
2020 tax# = (INT(total# * TaxRate# + .005) * 100) / 100
2030 RETURN
```

Of course, you must add lines to call the new subroutine, print the amount of tax, and add the tax to the total purchase price. You can insert these lines at the end of the 400 block:

```
450 GOSUB 2010
460 PRINT "Tax =   "; tax#
470 total# = total# + tax#
```

Finally, change lines 1 and 2 to reflect a new title and filename.

```
1 REM ** Purchase Record with Two Subroutines **
2 ' GW-BASIC Reference, Chapter 4.  File: GWRF0407.ASC
```

This completes Program 4-7, Purchase Record with Two Subroutines. The output of a run of this program (using the same purchases displayed previously in Figure 4-8) is shown in Figure 4-10.

Other Useful Subroutines

You can build a complete file of useful subroutines like the two used in the previous merge demonstrations. Save in ASCII format

Program 4-7.

```
1 REM ** Purchase Record with Two Subroutines **
2 ' GW-BASIC Reference, Chapter 4.  File: GWRF0407.ASC
3 ' Saved in ASCII format.  Used to demonstrate MERGE

100 REM ** Initialize **
110 CLS: KEY OFF: DEFINT A-Z
120 Form$ = "$$###,###,###,###.##": total# = 0

200 REM ** Display date and time **
210 GOSUB 1010

300 REM ** Get number of purchases **
310 LOCATE 5, 1
320 INPUT "How many purchases "; purchases

400 REM ** Get purchase amounts and total **
410 FOR number = 1 TO purchases
420   INPUT "Amount "; amount#
430   total# = total# + amount#
440 NEXT number
450 GOSUB 2010
460 PRINT "Tax =  "; : PRINT USING Form$; tax#
470 total# = total# + tax#

500 REM ** Print total **
510 PRINT: PRINT "Total: ";
520 PRINT USING Form$; total#

600 REM ** Wait for keypress, then end **
610 akey$ = INPUT$(1)
620 CLS: KEY ON: END

1000 REM ** SUBROUTINE: Date and Time Stamp **
1010 PRINT DATE$
1020 PRINT TIME$
1030 RETURN

2000 REM ** SUBROUTINE: Calculate Tax **
2010 TaxRate# = .06#
2020 tax# = (INT(total# * TaxRate# + .005) * 100) / 100
2030 RETURN
```

Purchase Record with Two Subroutines (GWRF0407.ASC)

Figure 4-10.

```
12-12-1990
21:26:17


How many purchases ? 3
Amount ? 9456.88
Amount ? 123.99
Amount ? 22.45
Tax =              $576.20

Total:        $10,179.52
—
```

Output of Program 4-7

all the subroutines that you expect to reuse, so that you can merge them with any program you like.

For example, here is a subroutine that might prove useful in many programs. It prints a prompt at the bottom of the screen, requesting whether you want to end a program or continue. If you press the ESC key, the program ends. Press a different key, and the program continues.

```
60000 REM ** SUBROUTINE: More INPUT or END? **
60010 LOCATE 25, 1: PRINT "Press ESC to end - ";
60020 PRINT "any other key for more.";
60030 akey$ = INPUT$(1): LOCATE 25, 1: PRINT SPACE$(42);
60040 RETURN
```

When any key is pressed at this point in the subroutine, the prompt message is erased. Control returns to the main program.

At that point in the main program, there must be a statement that tells the computer what to do, depending on the keypress made in the subroutine, such as

```
750 IF akey$ = CHR$(27) THEN END
```

Here, if ESC is pressed, the program ends. If a different key is pressed, the computer goes to the statement following line 750, and the program continues. You could save this subroutine in ASCII format with a filename such as ENDER.SUB.

You will no doubt think of program code segments that you will frequently use. Instead of entering them in each program you write, save them separately in ASCII format as subroutines. Group them together on a disk, which you can label as your Subroutine Library.

Creating and Maintaining a REM File

You have collected quite a number of programs in these first four chapters. The filenames for these programs were chosen to indicate the book, chapter, and program number in the chapter. On a directory of a disk, these names won't mean much to you. You can remedy this by creating a program consisting only of REM statements that contain information about the programs on the disk. The REM program will not be executed, but can be viewed by using LIST. Your REM file might look like the one shown in Figure 4-11.

The REM file in this example lists the programs in blocks, with the filename on the first line and the program title on the second line. Subsequent lines contain information about the program. You can use this file, or make your own, to add other programs as you create them through the rest of this book. Just add the new

Figure 4-11.

```
1 REM ** GW-BASIC Reference REM File **
2 ' GW-BASIC Reference file information
3 ' Description of program files
4 ' This file saved in ASCII format

1101 REM ** GWRF0101.BAS **
1102 ' Print Date and Time - Then BEEP
1103 ' Prints the current date and time
1104 ' Saved in compressed binary format

1111 REM ** GWRF0101.ASC **
1112 ' Same as GWRF0101.BAS but in ASCII format

1121 REM ** GWRF0101.BIN **
1122 ' Same as GWRF0101.BAS but in protected
1123 ' binary format

1201 REM ** GWRF0102.BAS **
1202 ' Sample Program
1203 ' Calculates the tax on entered amount
1204 ' Saved in ASCII format

1301 REM ** GWRF0103.BAS **
1302 ' Date and Time Stamp
1303 ' Calls a subroutine to print date and time
1304 ' Saved in ASCII format

2101 REM ** GWRF0201.BAS **
2102 ' F Key Changes
2103 ' Changes function key 7 to "WIDTH 80"
2104 ' Other changes can be added
2105 ' Saved in ASCII format

3101 REM ** GWRF0301.ASC **
3102 ' Menu Selector
3103 ' Prints a menu for selecting a program
3104 ' The selected program is loaded and run
3105 ' Saved in ASCII format
```

REM file (continued on next page)

Figure 4-11.

```
4101 REM ** GWRF0401.ASC
4102 ' Menu Selector - Version 2
4103 ' Same as GWRF0301.ASC but centers title
4104 ' and items
4105 ' Saved in ASCII format

4201 REM ** GWRF0402.ASC **
4202 ' Menu Selector - Version 3
4203 ' Same as GWRF0401, but numbers menu items
4204 ' and provides item selection by number
4205 ' Saved in ASCII format

4301 REM ** GWRF0403.SUB **
4302 ' SUBROUTINE: Date and Time Stamp
4303 ' A subroutine for printing date and time
4304 ' Saved in ASCII format
4305 ' Can be merged with other programs

4401 REM ** GWRF0404.ASC **
4402 ' Purchase Record
4403 ' Main program for demonstrating MERGE
4404 ' Calculates total for entered number of amounts
4405 ' Saved in ASCII format

4501 REM ** GWRF0405.ASC **
4502 ' Purchase Record with subroutine
4503 ' A merge of GWRF0403.SUB and GWRF0404.ASC
4504 ' Date and time stamps purchase record
4505 ' Saved in ASCII format

4601 REM ** GWRF0406.SUB **
4602 ' SUBROUTINE: Calculate Sales Tax
4603 ' A subroutine to calculate sales tax
4604 ' Saved in ASCII format
4605 ' Can be merged with other programs

4701 REM ** GWRF0407.ASC **
4702 ' Purchase Record with Two Subroutines
4703 ' A merge of GWRF0406.SUB and GWRF0405.ASC
4704 ' Date and time stamps purchase record
4705 ' and includes sales tax on purchases
4706 ' Saved in ASCII format
```

REM file

programs to the end of the REM file, along with as many comments about each program as you want. You can look at your REM file directly from DOS with the DOS TYPE command.

```
TYPE A:\PROGRAMS\REMFILE      (Hard disk with subdirectory)
```

or

```
TYPE B:REMFILE                (Two floppy disk drives)
```

Summary

This chapter has discussed numerous editing and merging techniques. It began with editing the current line on which the cursor resided. You deleted characters with the DELETE and BACKSPACE keys. The ESC key was used to delete a whole line.

Then various ways were shown to use the Insert mode and the Overtype mode to delete, insert, and add characters to lines that had been previously entered. You truncated characters at the end of a program line by using the CTRL+END or CTRL+E key combinations. You also learned that

- The ENTER key must be pressed to make editing changes permanent.
- Programs must be saved after they are edited to make the changes permanent.

You used the EDIT command to display lines that you wished to edit. It has two forms:

```
EDIT 240       (To edit line 240)
EDIT .         (To edit the currently displayed line)
```

The RENUM command was used to renumber parts of a program so that you could insert new lines between existing lines.

The MERGE command was used to join two separate programs into a single program. The programs that you want to merge must be saved in ASCII format. You joined two subroutines to a main program to demonstrate the merging procedure.

You were urged to create a library of useful subroutines, saved in ASCII format, on a separate Subroutine Library disk.

Finally, you learned how to create and maintain a program of only REM statements that describes a group of programs in a directory or on a disk, such as those used in this book.

5

Numbers, Strings, and Variables

GW-BASIC programs use keywords, such as INPUT, PRINT, READ, and DATA. You supply the program with the information on which the computer performs these actions. The information you supply is in the form of either strings or numbers. As you have discovered in earlier chapters, GW-BASIC also has specific symbols that tell the computer what operation to carry out on the information.

You will learn in this chapter how GW-BASIC distinguishes between the different types of information that you supply, and how it stores and uses each type. You will also examine how string and numeric constants are assigned to variables, and how they are used with operational and relational symbols to form expressions. *Constants* are static values that GW-BASIC uses during execution of your program. These components, along with GW-BASIC's keywords and control structures, allow you to write programs that tell the computer exactly what you want it to do.

In particular, you will

- Differentiate between string and numeric constants
- Enter and use string constants
- Enter and use many types of numeric constants
- Understand and use exponential notation
- Classify variables by type, and use the appropriate type
- Specify a variable type by a range of beginning letters
- Specify the dimension of arrays and use subscripts to define elements of arrays
- See how memory space is used to store different variable types
- See how GW-BASIC converts variables from one type to another when necessary
- Use arithmetic, relational, and logical operators

String Constants

A *string constant* is any sequence of up to 255 alphanumeric characters. A string can be any of the following:

a word: educational
a name: Albert Outlander
an address: 1218 Exchange St.
a phone number: 707-555-3131
meaningless characters: GWRF22*&#99

Usually strings are enclosed in double quotation marks.

String	Description
""	Null string; no characters
"Enter a number"	Instruction
"$1,500.00"	Money string
"12-11-90"	Date

The double quotation marks are not considered a part of the string and are not displayed when a string is printed.

You can use strings in direct statements, as in the following PRINT statement:

```
PRINT "12-21-90"      (String used in a direct statement)
12-21-90              (Printed without quotes)
```

Since double quotation marks are used to mark the beginning and end of a string, you cannot use double quotes within the string. Suppose you want to print the following:

Don't say, "It will not work."

To print this sentence as a string, the complete sentence must be enclosed in double quotations in the PRINT statement.

Consider this statement:

```
PRINT "Don't say, "It will not work.""
```

Look at what happens when you try it:

```
PRINT "Don't say, "It will not work.""
Don't say,  0  0 -1
Ok
_
```

The computer interprets the first part of the PRINT statement as the string "Don't say,". Then it interprets the next four words as numeric variables and prints their values.

It = 0   (*No numeric value assigned to* It)
will = 0   (*No numeric value assigned to* will)
not work = −1 (work = *0 or false, so* not work = *−1 or true*)

If you need to use double quotation marks inside a string, you can use the ASCII character code for the double quotation mark. Break up the string into two parts, like this:

```
PRINT "Do say, " CHR$(34) "It will work." CHR$(34)
Do say, "It will work."
Ok
_
```

This time, the PRINT statement is interpreted as two separate strings ("Do say, " and "It will work."). Using the CHR$ function in the appropriate place provides the desired quotation marks (ASCII code 34). The CHR$ function is discussed in more detail in Chapter 13, "String Manipulation."

A string can be assigned to a *string variable* if the appropriate type declaration character ($) is appended to the variable. The variable name can be any combination of letters and numbers, but the first character must be a letter. Here are some examples of valid names.

Name1$ Naym$ City$
Address$ Agent007$ Word$

 NOTE   Most keywords cannot be used as variables. For example, you cannot use Name$ as a string variable, because NAME is a GW-BASIC reserved word. A reserved word may be embedded in a variable, such as Name1$.

Here are two examples of strings assigned to variables.

```
Name1$ = "Albert Outlander"
Ok
Name2$ = "Outlander, Albert"
Ok
_
```

Assign the strings to Name1$ and Name2$ in the Direct mode, and use the variables in direct PRINT statements.

```
PRINT Name1$, Name2$
Albert Outlander          Outlander, Albert
Ok
_
```

Notice that commas can be used within strings, provided the strings are contained within double quotation marks.

There are times when strings may be used without the double quotation marks. For instance, the double quotes can sometimes be omitted when entering a string for an INPUT statement that assigns the string to a variable. Enter and run the following short program:

```
110 CLS
210 INPUT "Enter your name, please "; Naym$
220 PRINT Naym$
230 END
```

If no commas are contained in the name that is entered in this short program, the entry and name will be printed as shown here.

```
Enter your name, please ? Albert Outlander
Albert Outlander
Ok
_
```

However, suppose you wish to enter the last name first, then a comma, then a space, and then the first name. Here is what happens.

```
Enter your name, please ? Outlander, Albert
?Redo from start
Enter your name, please ? _
```

GW-BASIC interprets the comma in the entry as a *delimiter* (a symbol that separates entries). It thinks you are trying to enter two names where only one is called for by the program. Therefore, it asks you to redo the entry from the start.

This time try enclosing the entry in double quotes.

```
Enter your name, please ? "Outlander, Albert"
Outlander, Albert
Ok
_
```

It now works. If a string contains punctuation marks, enclose that string within double quotation marks.

Two strings may be joined together by using a plus sign (+) to catenate the strings. When used with strings, the plus sign works differently from the way it works with numbers. With numbers, the + means addition. When used between strings, the + says to join the strings together. Thus,

"Albert" + " Outlander"
is equivalent to
"Albert Outlander"

To demonstrate this, run the following short program:

```
110 CLS
210 Name1$ = "Albert": Name2$ = "Alexander"
230 Name3$ = "Outlander"
240 PRINT Name1$ + CHR$(32) + Name2$ + CHR$(32) + Name3$
250 END
```

Here is the result of a run. The spaces are created by CHR$(32).

```
RUN
Albert Alexander Outlander
Ok
_
```

The assignment of a string to a variable can also occur in a READ statement. In some cases, double quotation marks around strings in DATA statements are unnecessary. The following FOR/NEXT loop assigns names from a DATA statement to the string variable Name$. Double quotation marks are not used in the first two names.

```
FOR number = 1 to 3
   READ Naym$: PRINT Naym$
NEXT number
DATA John Brown, Bill Smith, "Jones, Tom"
```

The commas in the DATA statement are used to separate the strings; therefore, the computer does not need the double quotation marks to interpret where a string starts and ends. However, if you have commas included in your strings, you need the double quotation marks around the strings, as shown for the string "Jones, Tom" in the DATA statement above.

If you are not sure whether double quotation marks are needed, play it safe and use them to enclose your strings.

Numeric Constants

Numeric constants can be either positive or negative. GW-BASIC uses three types of numeric constants: *integers, single precision,* and *double precision.* Hereafter in this chapter the words "numeric constant" and "number" are used interchangeably.

Integers are stored as whole numbers in the range of −32768 to +32767, inclusive. These values are the largest and smallest values (expressed in powers of 2) that can be stored in the two bytes of memory reserved for integers. Numbers are specified as integers by a trailing percent sign (%). Here are three integers with their type designation appended to the number.

742%   7000%   −215%

Single precision numbers are stored with 7 digits. Use the exclamation mark (!) to specify a single precision number. Here are three single precision numbers with the type designation appended.

29.3!   -3.141593!   6.28!

Double precision numbers are stored with 17 digits, but the maximum number of digits printed is 16. Use a trailing number (or pound) sign (#) to declare a double precision number. Here are three double precision numbers.

3.14159265#   123.456789012345#   123.05#

You may perform arithmetic operations on all three types of numbers. You may even mix different types of numbers in any of the arithmetic operations. In such operations, GW-BASIC results assume the precision of the number that has the greatest precision. This may produce misleading results, as shown here.

```
PRINT .1! * 2.204622341#
 .2204622373851433
Ok
_
```

Multiplying the double precision number by .1 should merely move the decimal point one place to the left. However, the printed result shows that a round-off error has occurred in the ninth digit.

In GW-BASIC, numbers are stored and operations are performed in binary form. Integers in the proper range can be expressed in binary form with no loss of precision. However, single and double precision numbers cannot always be converted to an exact equivalent value in binary form. Unless the single or double precision number can be expressed as the sum of powers of a finite number of powers of 2, there will be some round-off error.

Table 5-1 shows several examples of different number types used in performing arithmetic, and the results obtained. The results shown with an asterisk have round-off errors due to the lack of precision of a number involved in the operation.

Table 5-1.

First Number	Operation	Second Number	Result
2% (I)	+	3! (S)	5
.1! (S)	+	3# (D)	3.100000001490116*
2% (I)	*	3# (D)	6
.1! (S)	*	3# (D)	.3000000044703484*
3! (S)	/	2% (I)	1.5
3# (D)	/	.1! (S)	29.99999955296517*

Note: (I) = integer
(S) = single precision
(D) = double precision

Operations Using Mixed Number Types

Integers

GW-BASIC can use integers in three different number systems: *decimal, hexadecimal,* and *octal.* The decimal system is the primary one used. Hexadecimal and octal numbers, because they can be converted directly to binary form with no loss of precision, are used in special situations where an exact conversion is necessary.

The range of integers used by GW-BASIC is specified as −32768 through +32767. If you like to experiment, you may discover some interesting results while testing this integer range. Study the results of Direct mode statements, shown in Table 5-2. You can see that GW-BASIC accepts integers and results beyond the specified range when a PRINT statement is used. However, the assignment of an out-of-range integer is not accepted. The value of the variable remains at zero.

Table 5-3 shows a one-line program, and three versions of a FOR/NEXT loop that prints the increasing integer values as-

Table 5-2.

Statement Entered	Printed Result	Comment
PRINT 32768%	32768	*Accepted*
PRINT 32768% + 32768%	65536	*Accepted*
number% = 32768% PRINT number%	Overflow 0	*Number too big* Zero was assigned
number% = 32769% PRINT number%	Overflow 0	*Number too big* Zero was assigned
number% = -32769% PRINT number%	Overflow 0	*Absolute value too big* Zero was assigned

Direct Mode Integer Experiments

Table 5-3.

Program	Result of Run
210 PRINT 32768%	32768
210 FOR number% = 32764 TO 32766 220 PRINT number% 230 NEXT number%	32764 32765 32766
210 FOR number% = 32764 TO 32767 220 PRINT number% 230 NEXT number%	32764 32765 32766 32767 Overflow in 230
210 FOR number% = 32764 TO 32768 220 PRINT number% 230 NEXT number%	Overflow in 210

Program Mode Integer Experiments

signed to a variable. The first program, the one-liner, prints an out-of-range number successfully. The second program successfully accepts and prints three successive integers within the integer range. The third program accepts and prints four successive integers within the specified range, but prints an "Overflow in 230" message. This happens when number% is increased to 32768 by the NEXT statement, at the last pass through the FOR/NEXT loop. The last program immediately prints an "Overflow in 210" message when the out-of-range integer is detected in the FOR statement.

A more precise way to state the limits of integer use would be this: The range of integers that can be *assigned to a variable* is −32768 through 32767.

Hexadecimal numbers consist of these 16 symbols: 0, 1, 2, 3, 4, 5, 6, 7, 8, 9, A, B, C, D, E, and F. Hexadecimal numbers, as integers, can be converted to binary numbers with no round-off error. Table 5-4 shows the decimal and binary equivalents of each hexadecimal symbol. As you can see in the table, a group of four binary bits is equivalent to one hexadecimal symbol. Hexadecimal numbers are useful in situations where binary relationships must be expressed.

When you enter hexadecimal numbers, prefix them with the symbols &H. This tells the computer the value is to be interpreted

Table 5-4.

Hexadecimal Symbol	Decimal	Binary
0	0	0000
1	1	0001
2	2	0010
3	3	0011
4	4	0100
5	5	0101
6	6	0110
7	7	0111
8	8	1000
9	9	1001
A	10	1010
B	11	1011
C	12	1100
D	13	1101
E	14	1110
F	15	1111

Hexadecimal Symbols and Equivalents

as a hexadecimal number rather than a decimal number. Here are three hexadecimal numbers.

&H4F   &H41F   &HA5A5

Each position in a hexadecimal number represents a power of 16, not 10, as in the decimal system. For example,

$$\&H41F \quad = (4 * 16\char`^2) + (1 * 16\char`^1) + (15 * 15\char`^0)$$
$$= (4 * 256) + (1 * 16) + (15) = 1055$$

Quite often the value of a hexadecimal number is unimportant, but the pattern produced by its binary equivalent is important. For example,

&HFF00 = 1111111100000000 binary

This number can define the pattern used to print a broken line segment. The patterns defined by &HFF00, &HE0E0, and &HFF10 are shown in Figure 5-1. The shaded circles of the pattern are printed. The unshaded circles are skipped over (a space is provided but no character is printed).

Program 5-1, Print Line Patterns, draws three boxes. The sides of each box use one of the patterns shown in Figure 5-1. The completed boxes of the program are shown in Figure 5-2.

You can convert a decimal integer to its hexadecimal equivalent by using GW-BASIC's HEX$ function. Enclose the decimal integer in parentheses following the keyword HEX$.

```
PRINT HEX$(40)
28
Ok
PRINT HEX$(200)
C8
Ok
_
```

Figure 5-1.

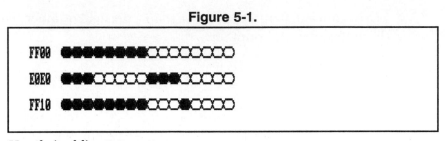

Hexadecimal line patterns

The octal number system uses the symbols 0, 1, 2, 3, 4, 5, 6, and 7. Octal numbers are entered with the prefix &O. (If you ever use octal numbers, be sure that you type the capital letter *O* in the prefix, not the number *0* (zero).) Octal numbers are used similarly to hexadecimal numbers. Although popular in the past, octal numbers are not used as much now.

Program 5-1.

```
1 REM ** Print Line Patterns **
2 ' GW-BASIC Reference, Chapter 5.  File: GWRF0501.BAS

100 REM ** Initialize **
110 SCREEN 1: CLS: KEY OFF: DEFINT A-Z

200 REM ** Label and draw lines **
210 LOCATE 4, 2: PRINT "FF00"
220 LINE (30, 35)-(300, 160), , B, &HFF00
230 LOCATE 8, 8: PRINT "E0E0"
240 LINE (60, 67)-(270, 140), , B, &HE0E0
250 LOCATE 11, 14: PRINT "FF10"
260 LINE (110, 92)-(240, 120), , B, &HFF10

300 REM ** Wait for keypress, then restore screens **
310 akey$ = INPUT$(1)
320 CLS: SCREEN 0: KEY ON
330 END
```

Print Line Patterns (GWRF0501.BAS)

Here are three octal numbers and their decimal equivalents.

&O35 = 29 decimal
&O213 = 139 decimal
&O502 = 322 decimal

You can use the OCT$ function to convert a decimal integer to an octal number.

```
PRINT OCT$(29)
35
Ok
PRINT OCT$(322)
502
Ok
_
```

Figure 5-2.

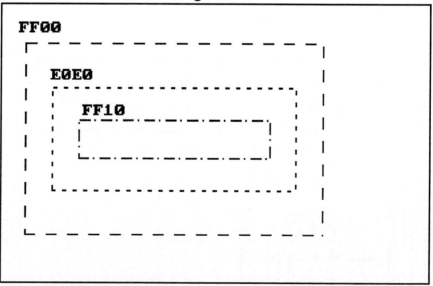

Boxes with different line styles

Single Precision Numbers

A single precision number has seven or fewer digits and can be an integer or a noninteger. Four bytes of memory are used to store a single precision number — twice as much memory as that used for an integer. Here are a few single precision numbers.

6   2.2   2.718282   0.01745329

The exclamation mark (!) is appended to a number to designate it as single precision.

3.14159!   2.204!

Single precision numbers can also be expressed in *floating point* form. Floating point numbers are either positive or negative numbers represented in *exponential* form. A floating point number consists of these two parts:

- A mantissa greater than or equal to 1, but less than 10
- A signed integer portion called the exponent

The two parts of a floating point, single precision number are separated by the letter *E*.

2.23E+08

mantissa E exponent

The allowable range for the absolute value of floating point numbers is from 3.0 times 10^{-39}, to 1.7 times 10^{38}. If the sign of the exponent is positive, it may be omitted. Exponents may be expressed with one or two digits.

Floating point notation is similar to the scientific notation format used in math and science books. The only difference is in the way the exponent is denoted. Compare the two notations in these expressions of the approximate speed of light through water, measured in meters per second (223 million):

Scientific notation	2.23×10^{8}
Floating point notation	$2.23E+08$

Floating point notation is a shorthand way of expressing very large or very small numbers. A very small number has a negative exponent, as in the number of feet in one centimeter (0.03280833).

Number of feet in 1 centimeter: $3.280833E-02$

You can change a number from exponential form to the usual decimal notation. If the exponent is *negative,* move the decimal point in the mantissa to the *left* as many places as the value of the exponent, as shown here:

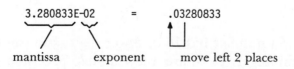

mantissa   exponent   move left 2 places

If the exponent is *positive,* move the decimal point in the mantissa to the *right* as many places as the value of the exponent, like this:

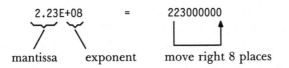

Figure 5-3 shows several examples of direct operations involving numbers printed in exponential form. Notice that the decimal point is always printed one place to the right of the first nonzero digit in exponential notation. The exponent part consists of a sign (+ or −) followed by two digits. Very small numbers are interpreted as zero. Numbers of very large magnitude (positive or negative) cause an overflow and may produce erroneous results.

Figure 5-4 shows how floating point numbers are treated when their values are beyond GW-BASIC's range. Negative numbers of very large magnitude (on the left), positive numbers of very large magnitude (on the right), and zero for very small positive or negative numbers (at the center) all cause overflow. Overflow values are treated as follows:

−1.701412E+38 for negative overflow
1.701412E+38 for positive overflow

All floating point number results that are between approximately −3.0E−39 and +3.0E−39 are treated as zero.

Double Precision Numbers

A double precision number has 16 or fewer digits and can be an integer or a noninteger. Here are a few double precision numbers.

12345678   0.0174532925   2.718281828459045

Figure 5-3.

```
PRINT 33333333333333333      (17 threes in a row)
 3.333333333333333D+16       (16 digits printed)

PRINT 33.33E-07
 3.333E-06                   (Decimal moved behind first digit)

PRINT 3.45E7                 (Accepts this form)
 3.45E+07                    (But prints it like this)

PRINT 3.12E-40               (Very small number)
 0                           (Because less than smallest
                              representable number)

PRINT 1.701411E+38           (Largest single precision number
 1.701411E+38                 that can be represented)

PRINT 1.701412E+38           (Outside allowable limit)
Overflow                     (Warning is printed)
 1.701412E+38

PRINT -1.701412E+38          (Outside allowable limit)
Overflow                     (Warning is printed)
-1.701412E+38

PRINT -1.701411E+38          (Negative limit for single
-1.701411E+38                 precision number)
```

Floating point number printouts

The number or pound sign (#) can be appended to a number to designate it as double precision.

3.1415926536#   2.204622341#   .1#

Double precision numbers can also be expressed in floating point form. They consist of the same two parts described for single precision, floating point numbers: a mantissa greater than or

Figure 5-4.

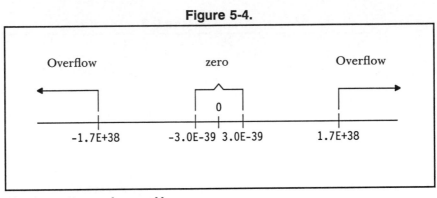

Floating point number trouble areas

equal to 1, but less than 10, and a signed integer portion called the exponent. The two parts of a floating point, double precision number are separated by the letter *D*.

The allowable range for the absolute value of floating point, double precision numbers is the same as floating point, single precision numbers: from 3.0 times 10^{-39} to 1.7 times 10^{38}. Double precision numbers are more precise than single precision numbers or integers.

The overflow limits for double precision numbers are the same as for single precision numbers. Very small numbers are interpreted as zero. Numbers of very large magnitude (positive or negative) cause an overflow and may produce erroneous results. Overflow values are treated as follows:

$-1.701411733192644D + 38$ for negative overflow

$1.701411733192644D + 38$ for positive overflow

All floating point results between approximately $-3.0D - 39$ and $+3.0D - 39$ are treated as zero.

See Figure 5-4 for the treatment of double precision values beyond GW-BASIC's range.

Variables

Variables are names to which you assign values in programs. You may assign a specific value, or you may assign the value of an expression that is calculated. When a program runs, all numeric variables are initialized to zero, and all string variables are assigned the null string (""). Even though RUN initializes variables to zero, it is good programming practice to explicitly initialize variables used in a program.

Variable names may be any length, but only the first 40 characters will be used; the rest are discarded. Characters allowed in variable names are letters, numbers, and the decimal point. One of the special *type declaration characters* (%, !, #, or $) may be appended to the variable name. The first character of the name must be a letter. Here are some examples.

a   a$ Alpha   Al.pha   Zebra!

Reserved words (AUTO, REM, WIDTH, and so on) cannot be used as variable names, but may be embedded within a name. For example,

AUTO is a reserved word and is not permitted.
Automat is permitted (AUTO is embedded in Automat).

Table 5-5.

Variable Type	Character	Example
String	$	FirstName$
Numeric		
Integer	%	begin%
Single precision	!	frequency!
Double precision	#	BigMoney#

Variable Type Declaration Characters

Do not use the combination "FN" as the first two letters of a variable name. GW-BASIC considers names that begin with "FN" to be user-defined functions.

Variable Types and Names

The *type declaration characters* (%, !, and #) indicate numeric variables. The dollar sign ($) indicates string variables. The variable's name type must match the value type—string variables with strings, and numeric variables with numbers. Table 5-5 shows the type declaration characters and the variable types they represent.

The GW-BASIC DEFtype statements (DEFSTR, DEFINT, DEF-SNG, and DEFDBL) are used in a program to declare all or a range of variables as a specific type. A variable falling within the specified range then assumes the specified type without the need of a type declaration character in its name.

```
DEFINT A-Z     (Declares all variables integer type)
DEFSNG L-P     (Declares variables beginning with letters
                L, M, N, O, or P to be single precision)
```

```
DEFDBL Q-S       (Declares variables beginning with letters
                  Q, R, or S to be double precision)
DEFSTR T-U       (Declares variables beginning with letters
                  T or U to be strings)
```

A type declaration character appended to a variable name will override any of the above DEFtype declarations. If no type declaration is appended to a variable name and no DEFtype statement has been executed, the default type is single precision.

When a number assigned to a numeric variable is of a type different from that of the variable, the number will be converted to the precision of the variable. For example, observe this Direct mode operation:

```
pi! - 3.14159265359    (Double precision number is assigned to
Ok                        a single precision variable)
PRINT pi!
 3.141593              (Single precision is printed)
Ok
_
```

Use care when using type declaration characters with variables and the numbers assigned to them. Remember, GW-BASIC assumes a number with fewer than eight digits to be single precision by default. Notice the results printed by the following short program:

```
210 x# = .1
220 y# = .1#
230 PRINT "x# ="; x#, "y# ="; y#
RUN
x# = .1000000014901161        y# = .1
Ok
_
```

The printed value of x# contains a single precision round-off error due to the single precision value (.1) assigned to it. The printed value of y# contains no round-off error due to the double precision type declaration character assigned to its value (.1#). Actually, there is a small round-off error, but it is in the 17th decimal digit and does not appear in the rounded value that is printed.

Double precision numbers are indeed more precise than single precision numbers or integers, but they use more memory space and require longer calculation time. Single precision numbers are adequate for most calculations. Although seven digits are printed, the seventh digit of single precision numbers may be inaccurate. Integers require the least amount of storage space and calculation time. However, be careful not to use integers when a programming task requires single or double precision input or output.

In most demonstration programs in this book, the DEFINT A-Z statement is used near the beginning of the program. When some other variable type is needed, an individual type declaration character is used to override the general declaration. This assures that any variable without a type declaration character uses the smallest possible amount of memory and executes in the least amount of time.

Array Variables

An *array* is a group of values that share a common name. A single member of the array is called an *element* of the array. An element is referenced by the array name and an appended subscript (an integer) enclosed in parentheses. If an array is not dimensioned in a program, the default dimension value allows for these subscripts: 0, 1, 2, 3, 4, 5, 6, 7, 8, 9, and 10. For example, the element that is assigned a subscript of 5 in a one-dimensional array named City$ is referred to as:

City$(5)

An array named City$ could have the elements shown in Table 5-6. The fifth element of the array is City$(5), and its value is Keokuk.

A *dimension statement* is used to specify the maximum value for array subscripts. If you try to reference an element of an undimensioned array with a subscript greater than 10, a "Subscript out of range" error will occur. The same message will appear if you try to reference an element beyond the maximum subscript specified in a dimensioned array.

A DIM statement, in addition to specifying the maximum value for array subscripts, sets the value of all elements of a numeric array to zero and all elements of a string array to null.

```
DIM City$(7)     (Dimensions the array and sets the values
                  of all elements to null strings)
```

The minimum value for a subscript is zero (0), unless you execute an OPTION BASE 1 statement making the smallest subscript equal to 1.

Arrays may be multidimensional. The maximum number of dimensions is 255, and the maximum number of elements per dimension is 32767. Subscripts of multidimensional arrays are separated by commas.

Table 5-6.

Subscript	Value of Element
1	Austin
2	Boston
3	Chicago
4	Detroit
5	Keokuk
6	Nantucket
7	Sacramento

Elements of City$ Array

Table 5-7 shows elements of a two-dimensional array that has been dimensioned with the following:

```
DIM RowCol%(3, 4)      (Dimensioned for rows 0-3 and
                        columns 0-4)
```

This array is an abbreviated table of class test scores containing information for three students. Here are some specific elements of the RowCol% array.

RowCol%(1, 3) = 95 (row 1, column 3)
RowCol%(3, 2) = 80 (row 3, column 2)
RowCol%(1, 4) = 95 (row 1, column 4)
RowCol%(2, 1) = 90 (row 2, column 1)

☞ **REMEMBER** Numbering of rows and columns for a two-dimensional array begins with zero, unless otherwise specified by an OPTION BASE statement. You do not have to use row 0 or column 0, but they are available. They are often used to store values that are calculated from other elements of the array. For example, if the values of Table 5-7 were stored in memory, you could execute a loop to add the values of each column for each row and store them in column 0 of each row.

Table 5-7.

Column	0	1	2	3	4
Row 0	0	0	0	0	0
Row 1	0	85	100	95	95
Row 2	0	90	85	70	80
Row 3	0	75	80	85	70

Elements of RowCol% Array

Program 5-2, Total Scores and Store Average, reads the scores of Table 5-7 into the RowCol% array. It then adds the scores in

Program 5-2.

```
1 REM ** Total Scores and Store Average **
2 ' GW-BASIC Reference, Chapter 5.  File: GWRF0502.BAS

100 REM ** Initialize **
110 CLS: KEY OFF: DEFINT A-Z
120 DIM RowCol!(3, 4)

200 REM ** Read in student scores **
210 FOR row = 1 TO 3
220    FOR col = 1 TO 4
230      READ RowCol!(row, col)
240    NEXT col
250 NEXT row
260 DATA 85, 100, 95, 95, 90, 85, 70, 80
270 DATA 75, 80, 85, 70

300 REM ** Sum rows, average and store **
310 FOR row = 0 TO 3
320    Total! = 0
330    FOR col = 1 TO 4
340      Total! = Total! + RowCol!(row, col)
350      Average! = Total! / 4
360    NEXT col
370    RowCol!(row, 0) = Average!
380 NEXT row

400 REM ** Print table **
410 LOCATE 2, 5: PRINT "Column"; TAB(19); "0"; TAB(27); "1";
420 PRINT TAB(32); "2"; TAB(37); "3"; TAB(42); "4": PRINT
430 FOR row = 1 TO 3
440    PRINT TAB(5); "Student"; row; TAB(17); RowCol!(row, 0); TAB(25);
450    PRINT RowCol!(row, 1); TAB(30); RowCol!(row, 2); TAB(35);
460    PRINT RowCol!(row, 3); TAB(40); RowCol!(row, 4)
470 NEXT row

500 REM ** Wait for keypress, then restore screen and end **
510 akey$ = INPUT$(1)
520 CLS: KEY ON: END
```

Total Scores and Store Average (GWRF0502.BAS)

Figure 5-5.

```
Column       0     1    2    3    4

Student 1   93.75  85  100  95   95
Student 2   81.25  90   85  70   80
Student 3   77.5   75   80  85   70
```

Table of student scores and averages resulting from Program 5-2

each row (one student's scores), averages the scores, and stores the student's average in column 0 of the table. The table is then printed out with its new values, as shown in Figure 5-5.

Variable Storage and Type Conversion

Different types of variables require different amounts of memory space to store their values. These amounts can be important to you if you have a limited amount of memory or need very large arrays. Table 5-8 shows the amount of memory allotted to different types of variables.

Under certain conditions, GW-BASIC will automatically convert numeric constants from one type to another. When this is necessary, the conversions are carried out according to the following rules:

1. If a numeric constant of one type is assigned to a numeric variable of another type, the constant is stored as the type declared by the variable name. Look at the results of a run of

the following two-line program:

```
110 Amount% = 49.71      (Single precision constant assigned
120 PRINT Amount%            to an integer variable)
RUN
 50                       (Constant is rounded to nearest
Ok                           integer, stored and printed)
_
```

2. If an expression is being evaluated, all of the numbers involved in an arithmetic or relational operation (called *operands*) are converted to the same degree of precision—that of the most precise operand. The result of the operation is returned at the converted degree of precision. However, once again the final factor is the variable type to which the result is assigned. Enter and run the following short program:

```
110 Amount# = 16# / 17!
120 Amount! = 16# / 17%
130 Amount% = 16! / 17%
140 PRINT Amount#; Amount!; Amount%
```

Table 5-8.

Type of Variable	Bytes Used
Simple variables	
Integer	2
Single precision	4
Double precision	8
Array variables	
Integer	2 per element
Single precision	4 per element
Double precision	8 per element
Strings	3 for overhead plus 1 for each character in the string

Memory Used to Store Variables

Type: **RUN**
and press ENTER.
The computer prints:

```
.9411764705882353  .9411765  1
```

In the first two calculations (lines 110 and 120), the result is calculated as a double precision value. For Amount#, the result is stored and printed as double precision. For Amount!, the result is stored and printed as single precision. In the third calculation (line 130), the result is calculated as a single precision value. However, because Amount% is an integer type, the result is stored and printed as an integer.

3. If a single precision value is assigned to a double precision variable, only the first seven digits (rounded) of the converted number are valid. A result cannot be more precise than the data supplied. The absolute value of the difference between the converted result and the original value is very small. Enter the following program and run it:

```
110 AmtSingle! = 4.15
120 AmtDouble# = AmtSingle!
130 PRINT AmtSingle!; AmtDouble#
```

Type: **RUN**
and press ENTER.
The computer prints:

```
4.15  4.150000095367432
```

The very small difference between the two numbers printed is approximately $9.5E-08$.

Arithmetic, Relational, and Logical Operations

Mathematical, relational, or logical operations are performed when an operation symbol, called an *operator,* is executed.

- *Arithmetic operations* include subtraction, addition, multiplication, division, integer division, negation, exponentiation, and modulus arithmetic.
- *Relational operations* include equality, inequality, less than, greater than, less than or equal to, and greater than or equal to.
- *Logical operations* include NOT, AND, OR, XOR, EQV, and IMP.

These operations and their operators are explained in the following sections.

Arithmetic Operators

The arithmetic operators recognized by GW-BASIC are shown in Table 5-9, along with the operations they perform. When more than one operation occurs in an expression, the operations within parentheses are performed first. Otherwise, the operations are performed in the order in which they appear in the table. Any two consecutive operators must be separated by parentheses.

Table 5-10 shows examples of each type of arithmetic, along with comments on each operation.

Exponentiation   Exponentiation raises an expression to a specified power. The expression to the left of the exponential symbol (^) is used as a factor in multiplication. The expression to the right of the exponential symbol tells how many times the factor is to be used.

Table 5-9.

Operator	Operation
^	Exponentiation
–	Negation
*	Multiplication
/	Division
\	Integer division
MOD	Modulus arithmetic
+	Addition
–	Subtraction

Arithmetic Operators

Negation   Negation (–) is the symbol used to indicate negative numbers.

Multiplication   Multiplication is performed as in textbook arithmetic. However, a different symbol (*) is used to avoid conflicts with the use of the letter *x*.

Division   Division is performed as in textbook arithmetic. The operator is the slash (/) symbol.

Integer Division (\)   This is similar to textbook division, but returns an integer result. The remainder (or decimal part) is discarded. If the operands (expressions used in integer division) are nonintegers, they are rounded to integers before the division.

Modulus Arithmetic   This uses the MOD operator to return the remainder of an integer division.

Addition (+) and Subtraction (–)   These operations are performed in the same way as textbook addition and subtraction.

Table 5-10.

Operation	Comment
2 ^ 3	Raise the factor 2 to the third power. (2 * 2 * 2 = 8)
(3 + 1) ^ 2	Raise the result of 3 + 1 to the second power. (4 * 4 = 16)
−2	Negate the number 2.
3 + (−2)	Add positive 3 to negative 2. Parentheses separate the two operations. (3 + (−2) = 1)
3 * 4	Multiply 3 times 4. (3 * 4 = 12)
(−3) * (4 + 2)	Negate 3, add 4 and 2, then multiply the results. ((−3) * 6 = −18)
5 / 2	Divide 5 by 2. (5 / 2 = 2.5)
(−12) / (3 − 1)	Negate 12, subtract 1 from 3, then divide. ((−12) / 2 = −6)
5.3 \ 2	Change 5.3 to integer 5, and use integer division. (5 \ 2 = 2)
(12 − 3) \ 4	Subtract 3 from 12, and use integer division. (9 \ 4 = 2)
5.7 \ 3.9	Round 5.7 to 6, round 3.9 to 4, and use integer division. (6 \ 4 = 1)
5 MOD 2	Get remainder of integer division. (5 MOD 2 = 1)
19.2 MOD 4	Change 19.2 to integer (19), and get remainder of integer division. (19 MOD 4 = 3)
5 + 3	Add 5 and 3. (5 + 3 = 8)
−5 + (−3)	Add negative 5 to negative 3. (−5 + (−3) = −8)
5 − 3	Subtract 3 from 5. (5 − 3 = 2)
5 − (−3)	Subtract negative 3 from 5. (5 − (−3) = 8)

Arithmetic Examples

Relational Operators

Relational operators compare two quantities, either numbers or strings. Numbers are evaluated by their magnitude. Strings are evaluated by taking one character at a time from each string and comparing the ASCII values of the characters. If the ASCII values differ, the character with the lower code is considered less than the other character. If both strings are the same, they have an equal value. If one string is longer than the other, but both strings are the same up to the end of the shorter string, the shorter string is considered to be less than the longer one.

When two values are compared, the relational operators return a result of -1 (true) or 0 (false). The relational operators recognized by GW-BASIC are shown in Table 5-11. Examples of each operation are shown in Table 5-12.

Logical Operators

Logical operators available in GW-BASIC are AND, OR, XOR, EQV, IMP, and NOT. Logical operators are primarily used to test the combination of Boolean expressions. Each expression is either

Table 5-11.

Operator	Operation
=	Equality
< >	Inequality
<	Less than
>	Greater than
< =	Less than or equal to
> =	Greater than or equal to

Relational Operators

Table 5-12.

Direct Statement	Result	Comment
PRINT 2 = 2	-1	True
PRINT 3 = 2	0	False
PRINT "Hello" = "hello"	0	False, H = ASCII 72, h = ASCII 104
PRINT 5 <> 5	0	False, 5 = 5
PRINT "Hello" <> "hello"	-1	True, H = ASCII 72, h = ASCII 104
PRINT (3 + 2) < 6.18	-1	True, 5 < 6.18
PRINT "this" < "this"	0	False, "this" = "this"
PRINT 5 > 5	0	False, 5 = 5
PRINT "today" > " today"	-1	True, t = ASCII 116, ASCII blank space = 32
PRINT 4 <= 5	-1	True, 4 < 5
PRINT "SMALL" <= "LARGE"	0	False, "SMALL" > "LARGE"
PRINT 4 >= 4	-1	True, 4 = 4
PRINT "Big" >= "Little"	0	False, "Big" < "Little"

Relational Operations

true or false. When the logical operation is performed on the expressions, the result is also either true or false. Table 5-13 shows possible operands (expressions operated on) and the result of their logical combination. Such a table is called a *truth table*.

Logical operators are often embedded in the IF clause of an IF/THEN statement. With the AND operator, you can test whether a number is within a given range, like this:

```
110 IF number < 200 AND number >= 100 THEN PRINT number
```

The number is first tested to see if it is less than 200. If it is, that expression is true; if not, it is false. Then the number is tested to see if it is greater than or equal to 100. If it is, the second

Table 5-13.

Operation	First Expression	Second Expression	Result
AND	True	True	True
	True	False	False
	False	True	False
	False	False	False
OR	True	True	True
	True	False	True
	False	True	True
	False	False	False
XOR	True	True	False
	True	False	True
	False	True	True
	False	False	False
EQV	True	True	True
	True	False	False
	False	True	False
	False	False	True
IMP	True	True	True
	True	False	False
	False	True	True
	False	False	True
NOT	True	-----	False
	False	-----	True

AND, OR, and XOR Truth Table

expression is true; otherwise it is false. If both expressions are true, the operation (the entire IF clause) is true. If either or both expressions are false, the operation is false. The number will be printed only if both expressions are satisfied (the operation is true).

The AND, OR, XOR (exclusive or), EQV (equivalent), and IMP (implication) operators are called *binary operators* because they test two expressions, or operands.

- If both operands of an AND operation are true, the AND operation is true. If either or both operands are false, the AND operation is false.

- If either or both operands of an OR operation are true, the OR operation is true. If both operands are false, the OR operation is false.

- If one operand of an XOR operation is true *and* the other is false, the XOR operation is true. If both operands are true *or* if both operands are false, the XOR operation is false.

- A test for equivalency is made by the EQV operator. If the two expressions of the operation are the same, the EQV operator returns a result of true. Therefore, a result of the EQV operation is true if both operands are true. The result is also true if both operands are false. If the two expressions of the operation are different, the EQV operator returns a result of false.

- A test for implication is made by the IMP operator. The only case resulting in a false result from the IMP operator is if the first expression (the one on the left of the operator) is true, and the second expression (the one on the right of the operator) is false. In all other cases, IMP returns a result of true.

- NOT is a unary operation—it acts on only one expression. If the expression is true, the NOT operator gives a result of false. If the expression is false, the NOT operator gives a result of true. Enter and run the following three program lines:

```
110 number = 5
120 PRINT number < 10 AND number > 0
130 PRINT NOT (number < 10 AND number > 0)
```

Type: **RUN**
and press ENTER.
The computer prints:

```
-1              (The statement of line 120 is true)
 0              (The statement of line 130 is false)
Ok
_
```

Use Program 5-3, Logical Operations Test, to test the AND operation. The two tested conditions are

```
number < 100
number / 2 = INT(number / 2)
```

Program 5-3.

```
1 REM ** Logical Operations Test **
2 ' GW-BASIC Reference, Chapter 5.  File: GWRF0503.BAS

100 REM ** Initialize **
110 CLS: KEY OFF: DEFINT A-Z
120 PRINT "Logical AND"

200 REM ** Print prompt, then get number and test **
210 LOCATE 25, 1: PRINT "Enter negative number to exit loop";
220 LOCATE 2, 1
230 WHILE number > -.1
240    INPUT "Enter an integer"; number
250    PRINT (number < 100) AND (number / 2 = INT(number / 2))
260 WEND

300 REM ** Wait for keypress, then restore screen and end **
310 LOCATE 25, 1: PRINT "Now, press any key to quit        ";
320 akey$ = INPUT$(1)
330 CLS: KEY ON: END
```

Logical Operations Test (GWRF0503.BAS)

Enter and run Program 5-3. Enter an integer at the prompt. The computer prints -1 (minus one) when the AND operation of line 250 is true, and 0 (zero) when the operation is false. Figure 5-6 shows successive entries of 50, 51, 102, and 101 for the AND operation. These numbers test all possible truth values for the two operands. Remember, the AND operation is true if -1 is the result, and false if 0 is the result.

You can test the OR, XOR, EQV, and IMP operations in the same way, by simply changing two lines of Program 5-3 as shown in Table 5-14. Make the changes listed in the table, one at a time, and try each revision.

Logical operators are also used to merge two bytes of numbers in their binary form. The difference of upper- and lowercase ASCII codes for letters A-Z is 32. For example, the ASCII code for the letter *a* is 97, and the ASCII code for the letter *A* is 65. Figure 5-7 shows how the ASCII code for an uppercase letter *A* is ORed with 32 to get the ASCII code for a lowercase letter *a*.

Figure 5-6.

```
Logical AND
Enter an integer? 50
-1                    (True; both expressions are true)
Enter an integer? 51
 0                    (False; less than 100 but odd)
Enter an integer? 102
 0                    (False; even but greater than 100)
Enter an integer? 101
 0                    (False; greater than 100 and odd)
Enter an integer? _
```

Output of Program 5-3 using AND

Table 5-14.

Operation	Change
OR	120 PRINT "Logical OR"
	250 PRINT (num < 100) OR ((num / 2) = INT(num / 2))
XOR	120 PRINT "Logical XOR"
	250 PRINT (num < 100) XOR ((num / 2) = INT(num / 2))
EQV	120 PRINT "Logical EQV"
	250 PRINT (num < 100) EQV ((num / 2) = INT(num / 2))
IMP	120 PRINT "Logical IMP"
	250 PRINT (num < 100) IMP ((num / 2) = INT(num / 2))

Changes to Test Logical Operations

Figure 5-7.

```
ASCII code for "a" = 97      ASCII code for "A" = 65

In binary, ASCII code for "a" = 1100001 (64 + 32 + 1)
In binary, ASCII code for "A" = 1000001 (64 + 1)

                  32 = 0100000 binary
ASCII code for "A"  = 65 = 1000001 binary
          -----------------------------------
                  32 OR 65 = 1100001 binary (64 + 32 + 1)

ASCII code for "A" OR 32 = 97 = ASCII code for "a"
```

OR operation on ASCII codes

Here is a short program that changes uppercase letters to lowercase letters using an OR operation.

```
210 PRINT "Enter a letter";
220 letter$ = INPUT$(1)
230 number = ASC(letter$) OR 32
240 PRINT ASC(letter$); number; CHR$(number)
```

Enter the program and run it. Enter any uppercase letter and see it changed to lowercase. Try entering lowercase letters, or characters other than letters.

Summary

This chapter described strings and numbers and how they are used in GW-BASIC expressions. Strings are composed of alphanumeric characters, usually contained within double quotation marks. A string can be assigned to a variable.

Numeric constants were classified as integer, single precision, or double precision. Each type was defined, and examples of each were shown. Integers may be negative or positive, but they contain no decimal part. Single and double precision decimal numbers sometimes appear in fixed-point form and sometimes in floating point notation. They can also be negative or positive. Here are some examples of the number types:

Integers:	23	44	13952
Single precision:	1.394238	4.1935E+07	
Double precision:	398.1245678	5.12373589D+03	

Hexadecimal and octal number systems were also discussed.

GW-BASIC has limits on the magnitude of the numbers it can use. Integers can range from -32768 to $+32767$. Negative and positive single and double precision numbers of very large absolute value cause an overflow. Negative and positive single and double precision numbers of very small absolute value are treated as zero.

You learned that GW-BASIC reserved words cannot be used as variable names. String and numeric variables can be declared a specific variable type by means of an appended type character.

Type	Character
String	$
Integer	%
Single precision	!
Double precision	#

You can also declare a specific alphabetic range to be a specific type, for example,

- DEFINT A-C defines all variables whose names begin with A, B, or C to be integer variables.

- DEFSNG D-E defines all variables whose names begin with D or E to be single precision variables.

- DEFDBL F-H defines all variables whose names begin with F, G, or H to be double precision variables.

- DEFSTR L-N defines all variables whose names begin with L, M, or N to be string variables.

You can also specify the dimensions of variable arrays and assign subscripts to elements of the arrays. Arrays may have up to 255 dimensions, and each dimension may have up to 32767 elements.

The chapter also described how GW-BASIC handles arithmetic expressions. Relational operations that compare two expressions were explained. Relational operators include the following:

=	Equality
<	Less than

>   Greater than
< >   Inequality
< =   Less than or equal to
> =   Greater than or equal to

The chapter closed with a discussion of Boolean logic operators, and the truth table for these binary logic operators:

AND   OR   XOR   NOT   EQV   IMP

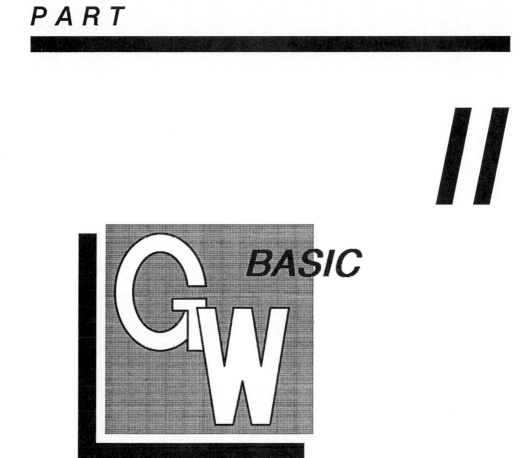

The GW-BASIC Language

Part I gave you some informal background on how BASIC began, and a review of how GW-BASIC performs its tasks. Part II is a more formal, detailed presentation. It shows you the formal syntax of each GW-BASIC statement, command, and function.

These essential parts of the BASIC language are grouped into chapters according to subject. Individual items covered by a chapter are listed near the beginning of the chapter. Related items are discussed in close proximity to each other to provide continuity. Each statement, command, and function has its own formal syntax box.

If you wish to find a particular statement, command, or function, turn to Appendix A, "GW-BASIC Keywords," to find the chapter in which it is discussed. You can locate individual references to an item in the book's index.

CHAPTER

6

Assignment and Program Flow

A *program* is a sequence of statements that tells the computer what to do and when to do it. The statements are normally executed in the order of their line numbers; however, there are times when you want to interrupt the normal flow. GW-BASIC includes statements that tell the computer when to make these interruptions, as well as where to find statements for continuing the program sequence. These statements are called *control structures*.

This chapter discusses control structures, their syntax, and their use. Also included are statements that make assignments to variables from within a program. The following statements are discussed in this chapter:

DATA	IF/THEN/ELSE	READ
FOR/NEXT	LET	RESTORE
GOSUB/RETURN	ON . . . GOSUB	WHILE/WEND
GOTO	ON . . . GOTO	

LET Statement

The LET statement was used in earlier versions of BASIC to assign values to variables. It is seldom (if ever) used, but is included in GW-BASIC to ensure compatibility with previous versions of BASIC that required it. The keyword LET is optional and is usually omitted when assigning values to variables.

LET   **Statement**

Syntax: [LET] *variable* = *expression*

Purpose: Assigns the value of an expression to a variable.

Notes: The keyword LET is optional. When assigning a value to a variable, only the variable, the equal sign, and the expression are necessary.

Parameters: *variable* is any valid numeric or string variable; *expression* is any valid numeric or string expression.

One of the following examples uses LET, and the other omits it. Both forms print the number 65.

```
120 LET ascii = 65          (LET keyword used)
130 PRINT ascii

120 ascii = 65              (LET keyword omitted)
130 PRINT ascii
```

Since the LET keyword is optional, it will not be used hereafter in this book.

DATA and READ Statements

DATA and READ statements provide another way to include information that will be used in a program. When you have previous knowledge of the information that will be used, you can place the information in a list included in a DATA statement. At the appropriate location in your program, place a READ statement that tells the computer to get one or more pieces of information from the list in your DATA statement. Data items are read from the list in the order listed. An internal "pointer" keeps track of the item in the list that is next in line.

The two statements, DATA and READ, are used together. You can't have one without the other.

READ   **Statement**

Syntax: READ *variable1*[, *variable2*] . . .

Purpose: Reads values from a DATA statement and assigns them to variables.

Notes: See also DATA and RESTORE in this chapter. Each variable in the READ statement accesses one item from the DATA list. One READ statement may access one or more DATA statements. Several READ statements may access the same DATA statement. If a READ statement is executed after all items in DATA statements have been used, an "Out of data" message is printed. To reuse items in DATA statements, include a RESTORE statement to reset the internal pointer to the beginning of the DATA list.

Parameters: *variable1, variable2,* and so on indicate one or more numeric or string variables.

DATA statements are used, not executed, by the computer. You can place DATA statements anywhere in your programs; however, your program will be easier to read, understand, and edit if DATA statements appear as near as possible to their associated READ statements.

DATA   **Statement**

Syntax: DATA *constant1*[, *constant2*] . . .

Purpose: Stores numeric and string constants in the order they are accessed by READ statements.

Notes: See also READ and RESTORE in this chapter. String constants do not always have to be enclosed within double quotation marks when used in DATA statements. However, if the string constant contains commas, colons, leading spaces, or trailing spaces, double quotation marks are needed.

Parameters: *constant1, constant2,* and so on indicate one or more numeric or string constants.

Program 6-1, READ from DATA Statement, shows the use of READ and DATA statements. It reads and prints the abbreviations for the first six months of a year. Each month abbreviation is printed on a separate line, with one line space between each month. This format could be used to label the bars of a horizontal bar graph.

The abbreviations are read in by line 220. The program tabs to position six of each line before printing the abbreviation (line

Program 6-1.

```
1 REM ** READ from DATA Statement **
2 ' GW-BASIC Reference, Chapter 6.  File: GWRF0601.BAS

100 REM ** Initialize **
110 CLS: KEY OFF: DEFINT A-Z

200 REM ** Read and print data **
210 FOR month = 1 TO 6
220    READ MonthAbbr$
230    PRINT TAB(6); MonthAbbr$
240    PRINT
250 NEXT month
260 DATA JAN, FEB, MAR, APR, MAY, JUNE

300 REM ** Wait for keypress, then end **
310 akey$ = INPUT$(1)
320 CLS: KEY ON: END
```

READ from DATA Statement (GWRF0601.BAS)

Figure 6-1.

```
JAN

FEB

MAR

APR

MAY

JUNE
```

Output of Program 6-1

230). Line 240 provides the blank line between consecutive months. A run of the program is shown in Figure 6-1.

RESTORE Statement

In certain situations, you may want to use the same data more than once. The RESTORE statement moves the internal DATA pointer to the beginning of the first DATA statement. If a line number is appended to RESTORE, the pointer is moved to the beginning of the DATA statement at that line number. You can use this latter option when you want to repeat only a part of a DATA list.

RESTORE   **Statement**

Syntax: RESTORE [*line number*]

Purpose: Allows DATA statements to be reused.

Notes: If a line number is specified, the next READ statement reads the first item in the DATA statement at that line number. If no line number is specified, the next READ statement reads the first item in the first DATA statement.

Parameters: *line number* is an integer. The line number must exist in the program and must be a DATA statement.

Program 6-2, RESTORE DATA Pointer, uses a RESTORE statement along with DATA and READ statements. In the previous program (6-1), the abbreviations for six months were printed horizontally, one month to a row. In this program, they are printed vertically, one month to a column. The program tells the

Program 6-2.

```
1 REM ^^ RESTORE DATA Pointer  **
2 ' GW-BASIC Reference, Chapter 6.  File: GWRF0602.BAS

100 REM ** Initialize **
110 CLS: KEY OFF: DEFINT A-Z

200 REM ** Read and print data **
210 FOR row = 1 TO 3
220   FOR month = 1 TO 6
230     READ MonthAbbr$: Pick$ = MID$(MonthAbbr$, row, 1)
240     PRINT TAB(6 * month); Pick$;
250   NEXT month
260   PRINT
270   RESTORE
280 NEXT row
290 DATA JAN, FEB, MAR, APR, MAY, JUNE

300 REM ** Wait for keypress, then end **
310 akey$ = INPUT$(1)
320 CLS: KEY ON: END
```

RESTORE DATA Pointer (GWRF0602.BAS)

computer to print one letter from each month in each row of each column. This process could be used to label bars of a vertical bar graph.

Line 230 reads in one of six months listed in the DATA statement. The MID$ statement picks out one letter of the month (the letter is determined by the value of the row variable). Line 240 tabs six times the value of the month variable and prints the letter that was picked. The semicolon at the end of line 240 tells the computer to stay on the same line for further printing. After the first letter of each month is printed, the PRINT statement of line 260 tells the computer to move to the next row. Line 270 restores the pointer to the beginning of the DATA statement in line 290. The computer then goes on to the next row and repeats the process for the second letter of each month. When this is completed, the data pointer is restored and the process is repeated for the third letter.

Here is the result of a run of Program 6-2.

```
J    F    M    A    M    J
A    E    A    P    A    U
N    B    R    R    Y    N
```

FOR and NEXT Statements

Just as DATA and READ statements go together, the FOR and NEXT statements are used as a matched pair. The FOR statement uses a variable to specify the initial and final values of the loop and optionally a STEP parameter as an increment to the variable on each pass through the loop. The series of statements executed by the loop are between the FOR and the NEXT statement.

FOR   **Statement**

Syntax: FOR *variable* = *first* TO *final* [STEP *increment*]

Purpose: Specifies the beginning and end values for the loop and, optionally, the increment used to step between those values.

Notes: Each FOR statement must have an accompanying NEXT statement. If the STEP option is not used, the variable is incremented 1 for each pass through the loop. FOR/NEXT loops may be nested. Variables may be used as the beginning (*first*) and ending (*final*) values in the loop. Negative values may be used for STEP. See also NEXT.

Parameters: *variable* is a numeric variable; *first* is a numeric expression, the initial value of the *variable*; *final* is also a numeric expression, the final value of the *variable*; *increment* is a numeric expression also.

It is possible that the final value of the variable of a FOR/NEXT loop never occurs. For example:

```
FOR row = 1 TO 10 STEP 2
```

In this example, the values of the row variable that would be used are: 1, 3, 5, 7, and 9. The next value, 11, is beyond the final value. A value of 10 is not used.

If the initial value of *variable* times the SGN of the STEP increment is greater than the final value of *variable* times the SGN of the STEP increment, the body of the loop is not executed at all. The GW-BASIC function SGN returns +1 if the argument is positive, 0 if the argument is zero, and −1 if the argument is negative. The argument in this case is the STEP increment. Here are two examples of FOR statements whose loops would not be executed.

```
FOR a = 8 to 2 STEP 2      (STEP positive, 8 > 2)

FOR b = 2 TO 4 STEP -2     (STEP negative, -2 > -4)
```

Program 6-1 used a FOR/NEXT loop to read and print the abbreviations for the first six months of a year. Here is another FOR/NEXT loop that prints ASCII codes 33 through 122, along with the characters they represent.

```
110 CLS
210 FOR ascii = 33 TO 122
220   PRINT CHR$(ascii); " "; ascii
230 NEXT ascii
```

The characters and codes are printed as pairs in adjacent columns so that you can easily identify the code for each character. Enter and run this four-line program to see the codes and their associated characters.

The NEXT statement at line 230 of the program increases the value of ascii by 1 each time through the loop. If the new value is less than or equal to 122, the execution of the loop continues. When the value of ascii reaches 123, the program exits from the loop and ends.

NEXT   **Statement**

Syntax: NEXT [*variable*]

Purpose: Marks the end of a FOR/NEXT loop.

Notes: A FOR statement must be executed before each NEXT statement. See also FOR.

Parameters: The use of *variable* is optional. If it is used, it must be the same *variable* used in the matching FOR statement.

FOR/NEXT statements may be nested. That is, one FOR/NEXT loop may lie within another. Nested loops are executed in a manner similar to sets of parentheses in a numeric expression. The inside loop is executed first, and then the computer works outward through each existing loop. The NEXT statement of the inner loop must appear before the NEXT statement of the outer loop. Each loop must use a unique variable name. Program 6-2 uses nested FOR/NEXT loops.

The program shown in Figure 6-2 uses nested loops to display foreground and background color combinations for SCREEN 0. Press any key to change colors. You cannot see the text when the foreground and background color numbers are the same, such as foreground = 0 (black) and background = 0 (black).

If there are no statements between two NEXT statements, as in Figure 6-2, you may use one NEXT statement, as long as it contains the variables of the loops in the appropriate order.

Figure 6-2.

```
110 SCREEN 0: CLS: KEY OFF: DEFINT A-Z
210 FOR back = 0 TO 7
220   FOR text = 0 TO 15
230     akey$ = INPUT$(1)
240     COLOR text, back: CLS
250     PRINT "Text"; text, "Background"; back
260   NEXT text
270 NEXT back
310 COLOR 7, 0: CLS: END
```

A program that displays SCREEN 0's colors

Remember, the order of the variables is important. For example, the previous nested loops could be written like this:

```
210 FOR back = 0 TO 7
220   FOR text = 0 TO 15
230     akey$ = INPUT$(1)
240     COLOR text, back: CLS
250     PRINT "Text"; text, "Background"; back
260 NEXT text, back
```

If you want to exit from a loop before the final value of the variable in the FOR statement is reached, set the variable to that value and use a GOTO statement to the NEXT statement, as in the following example. This frees up the memory that was set aside to hold the values of the increment and the beginning and final values of the variable in the FOR statement.

```
220   FOR text = 0 TO 15
230     akey$ = INPUT$(1)
235     IF akey$ = CHR$(27) THEN text = 15: GOTO 260
240     COLOR text, back: CLS
250     PRINT "Text"; text, "Background"; back
260   NEXT text
```

When you press the ESC key, the loop variable (text) is set to 15 at line 235. Then GOTO 260 is executed, text is increased to 16, and the program exits from the loop.

Decimal values can be used for STEP, as well as integers. Use care when using single or double precision values for STEP, because round-off errors can occur that may affect the result of the program. Run the following short program that prints single precision numbers and their squares. The numbers increase in steps of 0.1, from 1 to 3.

```
110 CLS: KEY OFF: DEFSNG A-Z    (Single precision variables)
210 FOR number = 1 TO 3 STEP 0.1
220   PRINT number; TAB(12); number ^ 2
230 NEXT number
```

The result of a run of this program is shown in Figure 6-3. The value of .1, used as the increment, is a single precision number and cannot be stored exactly as a finite binary number. Notice the resulting round-off errors from 1.5^2 through 2.1^2 and from 2.5^2 through 3^2. A round-off error even appears in the last number (3), which is printed as 2.999999 before it is squared.

WHILE and WEND Statements

The WHILE/WEND loop is a program control structure that allows execution of a block of a program to be repeated as long as

Figure 6-3.

```
1          1
1.1        1.21
1.2        1.44
1.3        1.69
1.4        1.96
1.5        2.250001
1.6        2.560001
1.7        2.890001
1.8        3.240001
1.9        3.510001
2          4.000001
2.1        4.410001
2.2        4.64
2.3        5.29
2.4        5.76
2.5        6.249999
2.6        6.759999
2.7        7.289998
2.8        7.839998
2.9        8.409996
2.999999   8.999996
```

Round-off errors in the output of a program

a specified condition is satisfied. Using WHILE/WEND, you can avoid the cluttered appearance of programs that contain GOTO statements.

WHILE   **Statement**

Syntax: WHILE *expression*

Purpose: Specifies the beginning of a loop that is executed as long as the condition specified by *expression* is satisfied.

Notes: If a WHILE statement is not matched with a WEND statement, a "WHILE without WEND" error message is printed.

Parameters: *expression* is any expression that can be evaluated to true or false. A value of zero is considered false. A nonzero value is considered true. The "standard" value for true is −1. Expressions commonly represent relationships between numbers or between strings.

Several different types of WHILE statements are shown in Table 6-1.

Just as a FOR statement is always paired with a NEXT statement, so is a WHILE statement always paired with a WEND statement. The WEND statement marks the end of a WHILE/ WEND loop.

Table 6-1.

Statement	*Comment*
WHILE 1 = 1	Always true
WHILE 1 = 2	Always false
WHILE 1	Always true
WHILE 0	Always false
WHILE Letter$ <= "M"	Truth depends on Letter$
WHILE number <= 10	Truth depends on number

Examples of WHILE Statements

WEND   **Statement**

Syntax: WEND

Purpose: Marks the end of a WHILE/WEND loop.

Notes: If a WEND statement is not matched with a WHILE statement, a "WEND without WHILE" error statement is displayed. Only one WEND statement can be used in a WHILE/WEND loop.

Parameters: None

A WHILE/WEND loop is similar to a FOR/NEXT loop. The FOR/NEXT loop is normally used when you want to execute a block of code a known number of times. A WHILE/WEND loop is used when you want to execute a loop while a known condition is true.

Here is a WHILE/WEND loop that reads strings from a DATA list and prints them. It uses the last string in the WHILE statement to trigger an exit from the loop.

```
310 WHILE astring$ <> "Santa Rosa"
320    READ astring$: PRINT astring$
330 WEND
340 DATA Sebastopol, Bodega Bay, Santa Rosa
```

Earlier in this chapter, the following FOR/NEXT loop was discussed:

```
110 CLS
210 FOR ascii = 33 TO 122
220    PRINT CHR$(ascii); " "; ascii
230 NEXT ascii
```

The actions of this FOR/NEXT loop can be duplicated by the following WHILE/WEND loop, which uses a numeric value to trigger an exit from the loop.

```
110 CLS: ascii = 33
210 WHILE ascii <= 122
220    PRINT CHR$(ascii); " "; ascii
230    ascii = ascii + 1
240 WEND
```

In comparing these two loops, notice that the desired number of executions is known; therefore, the FOR/NEXT loop is more suitable than the WHILE/WEND. However, there are cases where you want to execute a block of statements until some known condition changes, and you do not know how many loop executions will be needed. That is the time to use a WHILE/WEND loop. For example, you may want to delay a given amount of time between program actions. Although you could write a FOR/NEXT loop that counted to a value that consumed the desired time delay on your computer, many different computers operate at different speeds. A WHILE/WEND loop would be more suitable in this case.

The WHILE/WEND loop can produce a time delay that is independent of the speed of your computer. Computers have a built-in clock, and GW-BASIC has a TIMER function that reads the number of seconds since midnight (or since system reset) in single precision. By reading the TIMER, you can make a time delay that is quite accurate, and entirely independent of the speed of the computer being used. Here is a "do nothing but pass the time" delay that you can use to test various length delays.

```
310 INPUT "Delay in seconds "; delay!
320 start! = TIMER: WHILE TIMER < start! + delay!: WEND
```

Program 6-3, Colors with Time Delay, uses the foregoing one-line time delay between the changes of SCREEN 0 text colors. If no time delay is used, the colors will flash on and off so fast that you can't distinguish them. An INPUT$(1) statement could be used between color changes, as in the short program shown previously in Figure 6-2. However, in that program, you have to press a key for each color change. If the time delay is used, you don't have to press a key between color changes. You can sit back and watch as the colors are automatically changed.

IF/THEN/ELSE Statement

GW-BASIC can use relational operators to create a condition that will cause different actions based on decisions resulting from an IF/THEN/ELSE statement. THEN and ELSE are *not* GW-BASIC statements; they are only used as conjunctions in an IF statement.

Program 6-3.

```
1 REM ** Colors with Time Delay **
2 ' GW-BASIC Reference, Chapter 6.  File: GWRF0603.BAS
3 ' Demonstrates SCREEN 0 colors with time delay

100 REM ** Initialize **
110 SCREEN 0: CLS: KEY OFF: DEFINT A-Z
120 delay! = .5

200 REM ** Change foreground and background colors **
210 FOR back = 0 TO 7
220   FOR text = 0 TO 15
230     COLOR text, back: CLS
240     PRINT "Text"; text, "Background"; back
250     start! = TIMER: WHILE TIMER < start! + delay!: WEND
260   NEXT text
270 NEXT back
280 COLOR 7, 0: CLS: END
```

Colors with Time Delay (GWRF0603.BAS)

 REMEMBER   You can use the ALT key shortcuts to produce the keywords THEN and ELSE. ALT+T prints THEN, and ALT+E prints ELSE.

IF   **Statement**

Syntax:

IF *condition* [,] THEN *statements* [[,] ELSE *statements*]
IF *condition* [,] GOTO *line number* [[,] ELSE *statements*]
IF *condition* [,] THEN *line number* [[,] ELSE *line number*]
IF *condition* [.] THEN *statements* [[,] ELSE *line number*]

Purpose: Performs an action or changes program flow, based on the result of the condition in the IF clause.

Notes: Because IF/THEN/ELSE is all one statement, it must be contained on one logical line (no more than 255 characters). THEN and ELSE may be followed by either a line number for branching, or one or more statements. GOTO is always followed by a line number. A comma is allowed before THEN, GOTO, and ELSE.

Parameters: *condition* is an expression that evaluates to true or false; *statement* is a valid GW-BASIC statement; and *line number* (an integer) used with GOTO, THEN, and ELSE must exist in the program.

The IF clause specifies a condition that will evaluate to nonzero (true) or zero (false). If the result is true, the THEN or GOTO *line number* clause is executed. If the result is false, the THEN or GOTO clause is ignored. Relational operators =, >, <, and so on are often used in the expression that specifies the condition of the IF statement.

Program 6-4, IF/THEN Test, uses an IF/THEN statement in its simplest form to determine whether the number you enter is negative, positive, or zero. Enter and run the program to see how IF/THEN works. Press CTRL+BREAK when you have tested enough numbers. Figure 6-4 shows typical results.

You can add a colon and another statement on the same program line as the IF/THEN statement. For example, lines 310, 320, and 330 of Program 6-4 could be changed to

```
310 IF number# < 0 THEN PRINT number#; neg$: GOTO 210
320 IF number# = 0 THEN PRINT number#; zer$: GOTO 210
330 IF number# > 0 THEN PRINT number#; pos$: GOTO 210
```

Program 6-4.

```
1 REM ** IF/THEN Test **
2 ' GW-BASIC Reference, Chapter 6.  File: GWRF0604.BAS
3 ' Demonstrates simple IF/THEN statements

100 REM ** Initialize **
110 CLS: KEY OFF: DEFINT A-Z
120 neg$ = "is negative": pls$ = "is positive": zer$ = "is zero"

200 REM ** Get number **
210 PRINT : INPUT "Number, please "; number#

300 REM ** Determine number kind **
310 IF number# < 0 THEN PRINT number#; neg$
320 IF number# = 0 THEN PRINT number#; zer$
330 IF number# > 0 THEN PRINT number#; pls$

400 REM ** Get new number **
410 GOTO 210
```

IF/THEN Test (GWRF0604.BAS)

Figure 6-4.

```
Number, please ? 3.5691234
 3.5691234 is positive

Number, please -3.14159
-3.14159 is negative

Number, please ? 0
 0 is zero

Number, please ? 0.00001
 .00001 is positive

Number, please ? _
```

Output of Program 6-4

One, and only one, of the IF clauses will be true. After the THEN clause of the true IF statement is executed, the GOTO statement of that line will be executed. When an IF statement is false, neither the THEN clause nor the subsequent GOTO statement is executed.

With these three lines revised as shown, there is no need for lines 400 and 410; they can be deleted. Program 6-5, IF/THEN Test - Version 2, is the new version. If you enter the same numbers when you run the revised program, the results will be the same as shown previously in Figure 6-4.

Every IF statement must have a THEN or a GOTO clause, but the ELSE clause is optional. If an ELSE clause is included, it adds a second action that will be carried out when the condition in the IF CLAUSE is false.

```
IF condition THEN act1 ELSE act2
                      /         \
                IF true,    IF false,
                do this     do this
```

Program 6-6, IF/THEN with ELSE, is another version of Program 6-4. This time the 400 block of code is changed to include an ELSE clause in an IF statement.

```
400 REM ** Quit or new number? **
410 PRINT: PRINT "Press ENTER for new number, ESC to quit"
420 akey$ = INPUT$(1)
430 IF akey$ = CHR$(27) THEN END ELSE GOTO 210
```

The ASCII code for the ESC key is 27. If you press the ESC key at line 420, the THEN clause will be executed and the program will end. If you press any other key (including the ENTER key), the IF

Program 6-5.

```
1 REM ** IF/THEN Test - Version 2 **
2 ' GW-BASIC Reference, Chapter 6.  File: GWRF0605.BAS
3 ' Demonstrates simple IF/THEN statements

100 REM ** Initialize **
110 CLS: KEY OFF: DEFINT A-Z
120 neg$ = "is negative": pls$ = "is positive": zer$ = "is zero"

200 REM ** Get number **
210 PRINT: INPUT "Number, please "; number#

300 REM ** Determine number kind and get new number **
310 IF number# < 0 THEN PRINT number#; neg$: GOTO 210
320 IF number# = 0 THEN PRINT number#; zer$: GOTO 210
330 IF number# > 0 THEN PRINT number#; pls$: GOTO 210
```

IF/THEN Test - Version 2 (GWRF0605.BAS)

Program 6-6.

```
1 REM ** IF/THEN with ELSE **
2 ' GW-BASIC Reference, Chapter 6.  File: GWRF0606.BAS
3 ' Demonstrates IF/THEN/ELSE statement

100 REM ** Initialize **
110 CLS: KEY OFF: DEFINT A-Z
120 neg$ = "is negative": pls$ = "is positive": zer$ = "is zero"

200 REM ** Get number **
210 PRINT: INPUT "Number, please "; number#

300 REM ** Determine number kind **
310 IF number# < 0 THEN PRINT number#; neg$
320 IF number# = 0 THEN PRINT number#; zer$
330 IF number# > 0 THEN PRINT number#; pls$

400 REM ** Quit or new number? **
410 PRINT: PRINT "Press ENTER for new number, ESC to quit"
420 akey$ = INPUT$(1)
430 IF akey$ = CHR$(27) THEN END ELSE GOTO 210
```

IF/THEN with ELSE (GWRF0606.BAS)

clause is false, and therefore the ELSE clause will be executed
(GOTO 210). This returns you to the prompt for a new number.
Figure 6-5 shows typical entries and results for Program 6-6.

There are many ways to combine IF, THEN, and ELSE, since
more than one IF clause can exist in a given statement. The
problem with long, complex IF statements is the confusion that
may result. Try to keep IF statements limited to 80 characters or
fewer, so that they will be visible on one physical line of the screen.
Longer statements are hard to read and understand. If you must
use them, Figure 6-6 gives a few examples of more complex IF
statements.

Figure 6-5.

```
Number, please ? 3.5691234
 3.5691234 is positive

Press ENTER for new number, ESC to quit

Number, please ? -3.14159
-3.14159 is negative

Press ENTER for new number, ESC to quit

Number, please ? 0
 0 is zero

Press ENTER for new number, ESC to quit

Number, please ? 0.0001
 .00001 is positive

Press ENTER for new number, ESC to quit
Ok

 _
```

Output of Program 6-6

Figure 6-6.

```
210 INPUT "Enter an integer"; n
310 IF n > 0 THEN IF n / 2 = INT(n / 2) THEN PRINT "Even and positive"


210 INPUT "Enter an integer"; n
310 IF n >= 0 THEN PRINT "Positive or zero" ELSE IF n < 0 THEN PRINT "Negative"


210 INPUT "Enter an integer"; n
310 IF n > 0 THEN PRINT "Positive" THEN IF n / 2 = INT(n / 2) THEN PRINT ", even
" ELSE PRINT ", odd"
```

Complex IF/THEN statements

GOTO Statement

There are times when you want to branch to a section of a program that is not in the normal line number sequence. This can be accomplished with a GOTO statement.

GOTO   **Statement**

Syntax: GOTO *line number*

Purpose: Branches unconditionally from the current sequence of line number execution to a specified *line number*.

Notes: *line number* must be a line number within the program. If the line with the specified *line number* is an executable statement, it and the lines following it are executed. If it is not an executable statement, execution proceeds at the next executable statement following *line number*. GOTO statements should be avoided whenever possible, as they interrupt the program flow and make programs difficult to read and understand.

Parameters: *line number* is the number of a line contained in the program and is an integer.

GOTO is often used in an IF statement, as in line 430 of Program 6-6.

```
430 IF akey$ = CHR$(27) THEN END ELSE GOTO 210
```

If you press a key other than ESC, the GOTO in the ELSE clause sends the computer back to line 210 for another entry.

You can also use GOTO in the Direct mode. You can use it when you are developing programs; it lets you bypass long routines so you can test new parts of the program. If you have a program in memory, you can use a direct GOTO statement as a debugging tool. For example, you could assign a value to a variable in the Direct mode, then GOTO a specified line number in the program, to test the program from that line with the known variable value.

GOSUB and RETURN Statements

GOSUB and RETURN are two more GW-BASIC statements that work as a pair. Every subroutine that is called by a GOSUB statement from the main part of the program must have a RETURN statement. The RETURN statement in the subroutine passes control back to the main program when the subroutine has been completed.

GOSUB   **Statement**

Syntax: GOSUB *line number*

Purpose: Branches to a subroutine.

Notes: Although subroutines can appear at any point in a program, the computer must be able to distinguish the subroutine from the main program.

Parameters: *line number* is either the first line of the subroutine, or the number of the first executable line of the subroutine.

A subroutine must be clearly distinguishable from the main program that calls it. You can accomplish this by placing all subroutines at the end of your main program. Then place a STOP, END, or GOTO statement before the subroutine to prevent GW-BASIC from entering the subroutine when the end of the main program is reached. Alternatively, you can place all subroutines at the beginning of a program—this way, there is no danger of running into a subroutine from the main program. However, you would need to begin the program with a GOTO to skip over the subroutines. Generally, a program will run faster if the subroutines are placed at the beginning, although this method is used infrequently because it tends to distract from the main program.

Program 6-3 used a time delay between color changes in SCREEN 0. You could also use a subroutine to provide the time delay. To do this, replace the time delay at line 250 with the following GOSUB statement:

```
250 GOSUB 1010
```

Then add the following subroutine to the program:

```
1000 REM ** SUBROUTINE: Half-second time delay **
1010 start! = TIMER: WHILE TIMER < start! + pause!: WEND
1020 RETURN
```

The subroutine contains the half-second time delay. You should now have the program shown in Figure 6-7. Run the program in this form, and the results will be the same as those of Program 6-3.

Notice line 280. The COLOR and CLS statements restore the screen so that you are in the default colors when the END statement is executed. The END statement assures that the

Figure 6-7.

```
1 REM ** Colors with Time Delay Subroutine**
2 ' GW-BASIC Reference, Chapter 6.  File: GWRF0603.BAS
3 ' Demonstrates subroutine

100 REM ** Initialize **
110 SCREEN 0: CLS: KEY OFF: DEFINT A-Z
120 pause! = .5

200 REM ** Change foreground and background colors **
210 FOR back = 0 TO 7
220   FOR text = 0 TO 15
230     COLOR text, back: CLS
240     PRINT "Text"; text, "Background"; back
250     GOSUB 1010
260   NEXT text
270 NEXT back
280 COLOR 7, 0: CLS: END

1000 REM ** SUBROUTINE: Half-second time delay **
1010 start! = TIMER
1020 WHILE TIMER < start! + pause!: WEND
1030 RETURN
```

Colors with time delay subroutine

computer does not inappropriately enter the subroutine at the end of the main program.

Run the program as it is. Then remove the END statement from line 280 and run it again. When the END statement is removed, the computer enters the subroutine after the screen is cleared by line 280, and you get a "RETURN without GOSUB" error message. Put the END statement back in line 280 before saving the program in ASCII format.

The RETURN statement with no *line number* argument causes GW-BASIC to branch back to the statement following the last executed GOSUB statement.

RETURN   **Statement**

Syntax: RETURN [*line number*]

Purpose: Returns from a subroutine.

Notes: A RETURN without a *line number* causes a return to the statement following the GOSUB statement that called the subroutine.

Parameters: The optional *line number* is used when you want to return from the subroutine to the specified line.

The time delay subroutine uses a RETURN statement without the optional *line number* value. Therefore, the program returns to line number 260, the NEXT statement of the FOR/NEXT loop.

The *line number* option is primarily intended for use with *event trapping*. It is used to send the event trapping routine back to the GW-BASIC program at the specified line number. See Chapter 20, "Commands for Ports, Joystick, Light Pen, and Function/Cursor Keys," for more information on this use. Use the *line number* option with care.

A subroutine may contain more than one RETURN statement, to accommodate returns from different places in the subroutine. For example, in the following lines of code, a subroutine is called to change the foreground color of the text screen:

```
410 CLS
420 PRINT "Enter a number less than 0 to quit"
430 INPUT "Text color number "; kolor
440 IF kolor < 0 THEN 460
450 GOSUB 1010: GOTO 420
460 COLOR 7: CLS: KEY ON: END
```

If a negative color number is entered, the program flow goes from line 440 to line 460, where the default foreground is set and the program ends. If a positive color number (*Kolor*) is entered, the following subroutine is called.

```
1000 REM ** SUBROUTINE: Change text colors **
1010 IF kolor > 31 THEN RETURN
1020 COLOR kolor: CLS
1030 RETURN
```

If a positive color number is too large (> 31), a RETURN occurs at line 1010 without changing the text colors. If the positive number is less than or equal to 31, the screen is cleared to the new colors. After returning from the subroutine, line 450 sends control back to line 420. This is another variation that can be used to experiment with foreground colors in SCREEN 0.

ON. . .GOSUB and ON. . .GOTO

The ON . . . GOSUB statement provides decision-making to branch to one of several subroutines whose beginning lines are specified in the statement. ON . . . GOTO provides similar branching capabilities to program lines that are specified by the statement.

ON . . . GOSUB   Statement

Syntax: ON *expression* GOSUB *line1, line2, . . .*

Purpose: Provides a choice of subroutines to call.

Notes: If the value of *expression* is zero or is greater than the number of specified *line* numbers, the program does not branch to any of the *line* numbers—instead, it continues to the next executable statement. If the value of *expression* is negative or greater than 255, an "Illegal function call" error message is printed. If the value of *expression* is a noninteger, it is rounded.

Parameters: *expression* is any expression that will evaluate to a number, preferably an integer in the range of the specified *line* numbers. The specified line numbers (*line1, line2, . . .*) should be the first executable lines of subroutines.

The expression in an ON . . . GOSUB statement is usually a numeric variable the value of which ranges from 1 to the number of line numbers following the keyword GOSUB. If the value of the expression is a noninteger, it is rounded to the nearest integer.

Program 6-7, ON . . . GOSUB Demonstration, allows you to enter a number. Try entering all kinds of numbers: negative, zero, and positive numbers in the range 1 through 3; positive numbers greater than 3; and numbers greater than 255. Look at the notes in the foregoing boxed text for an explanation of any questionable results. Figure 6-8 shows some possible results.

ON . . . GOTO is to GOTO as ON . . . GOSUB is to GOSUB — it provides a choice of line numbers to which the computer can branch, depending on the value of the line number following the keyword GOTO. The ON . . . GOTO syntax and restrictions are similar to those of ON . . . GOSUB.

Program 6-7.

```
1 REM ** ON...GOSUB Demonstration **
2 ' GW-BASIC Reference, Chapter 6.  File: GWRF0607.BAS
3 ' Demonstrates choice of subroutines

100 REM ** Initialize **
110 CLS: KEY OFF: DEFINT A-Z
120 number = 1

200 REM ** Pick a Subroutine **
210 WHILE number > 0 AND number < 4
220   INPUT "1 for date, 2 for time, 3 for date and time "; number
230   ON number GOSUB 1010, 2010, 3010
240 WEND
250 KEY ON: END

1000 REM ** SUBROUTINE 1: Date **
1010 PRINT DATE$
1020 RETURN

2000 REM ** SUBROUTINE 2: Time **
2010 PRINT TIME$
2020 RETURN

3000 REM ** SUBROUTINE 3: Date and Time **
3010 PRINT DATE$; "  "; TIME$
3020 RETURN
```

ON . . . GOSUB Demonstration (GWRF0607.BAS)

Figure 6-8.

```
1 for date, 2 for time, 3 for date and time ? 1
12-23-1990
1 for date, 2 for time, 3 for date and time ? 2
15:12:10
1 for date, 2 for time, 3 for date and time ? 3
12-23-1990  15:12:19
1 for date, 2 for time, 3 for date and time ? 4
Ok
_
```

Output of Program 6-7

ON . . . GOTO   **Statement**

Syntax: ON *expression* GOTO *line1, line2, . . .*

Purpose: Provides a choice of branching paths.

Notes: If the value of *expression* is zero or is greater than the number of specified *line* numbers, the program does not branch to any of the *line* numbers—instead, it continues to the next executable statement. If the value of *expression* is negative or greater than 255, an "Illegal function call" error message is printed.

Parameters: *expression* is any expression that will evaluate to a number, preferably an integer in the range of the number of specified *line* numbers; *line1, line2,* and so on are a series of line numbers to which a branch can be made.

One of the popular games in the early days of BASIC was "Guess My Number." It picked a random number and asked for your guess. The guess you entered was compared with the random number. There were three possible results: too big, too small, or just right. Program 6-8, Guess My ASCII Code, is a variation of this game based on the ASCII codes for the uppercase letters of the alphabet. The program uses an ON...GOTO statement.

Program 6-8.

```
1 REM ** Guess My ASCII Code **
2 ' GW-BASIC Reference, Chapter 6. File: GWRF0608.BAS
3 ' Demonstrates ON . . .GOTO

100 REM ** Initialize **
110 CLS: KEY OFF: DEFINT A-Z
120 RANDOMIZE TIMER

200 REM ** Computer picks a number **
210 Pick = INT(26 * RND) + 65
220 CLS
230 LOCATE 5, 2: INPUT "Which letter did I pick "; letter$
240 IF ASC(letter$) > 90 THEN letter$ = CHR$(ASC(letter$) - 32)
250 Guess = ASC(letter$)

300 REM ** Decide on the GOTO and do it **
310 ON SGN(Pick - Guess) + 2 GOTO 320, 330, 340
320 PRINT " Too big": GOTO 350
330 PRINT " You guessed it": GOTO 350
340 PRINT " Too small"
350 PRINT: PRINT " Press ESC to quit, or"
360 PRINT " press a different key to try again."
370 akey$ = INPUT$(1)
380 IF akey$ = CHR$(27) THEN 410 ELSE GOTO 220

400 REM ** Restore screen and end **
410 CLS: KEY ON: END
```

Guess My ASCII Code (GWRF0608.BAS)

The random number is picked by this line:

```
210 Pick = INT(26 * RND) + 65        (Range = 65 - 90)
```

The printed result is determined by whether the quantity Pick − Guess is negative, positive, or zero. The expression SGN(Pick − Guess) + 2 is used as the decision-maker.

The GW-BASIC SGN function returns

−1 if the expression in parentheses is negative
0 if the expression in parentheses is zero
1 if the expression in parentheses is positive

Therefore, SGN(Pick - Guess) + 2 evaluates to

1 if SGN(Pick − Guess) is −1   (*Guess too big*)
2 if SGN(Pick − Guess) is 0   (*Guess just right*)
3 if SGN(Pick − Guess) is +1   (*Guess too small*)

One of three messages is delivered as a result of the ON . . . GOTO statement:

```
310 ON SGN(Pick - Guess) GOSUB 320, 330, 340
```

The possible messages are:

Too big
You guessed it
Too small

Run the program, and make your guesses.

Explore

Here are two programs to conclude this chapter. You can run them to experiment with the statements discussed so far.

Program 6-9, SCREEN 0 Color Selections, requests color number entries for the screen's foreground, background, and border colors of the text mode. The range of numbers that you can use is given in the INPUT prompts. When you have made all three entries, the color combinations are displayed as a miniature screen in the center-right portion of the text screen, as shown in Figure 6-9.

Program 6-10, Code Encryption by ASCII, requests you to type in a message. As you type, the program looks at the ASCII code of each character. The ASCII code numbers are converted to string format and joined together to make one long string. When you have finished typing your message, press the ESC key. The screen clears, and the string of ASCII codes appears.

As a run of the program begins, the following message is printed.

```
Type the message to be encoded
```

The following three-line message was entered for demonstration purposes.

```
This is my message.
Beware of typing mistakes.
There is no way to correct them.
```

If the ESC key is pressed at the end of the third sentence, the screen clears. The codes are then displayed as shown in Figure 6-10.

Program 6-9.

```
1 REM ** SCREEN 0 Color Selections **
2 ' GW-BASIC: The Reference, Chapter 6.  File: GWRF0609.BAS
3 ' Enter foreground, background and border colors
4 ' See a sample miniature screen

100 REM ** Initialize **
110 CLS: KEY OFF: DEFINT A-Z

200 REM ** Enter desired colors **
210 LOCATE 2, 37: PRINT SPACE$(3);
220 LOCATE 2, 5: PRINT "Enter foreground color (0-31)";
230 LOCATE 2, 36: INPUT fore
240 IF fore < 0 OR fore > 31 GOTO 210
250 LOCATE 4, 37: PRINT SPACE$(3);
260 LOCATE 4, 5: PRINT "Enter background color (0-7)";
270 LOCATE 4, 36: INPUT back:
280 IF back < 0 OR back > 7 THEN 250
290 LOCATE 6, 37: PRINT SPACE$(3);
300 LOCATE 6, 5: PRINT "Enter border color (0-15)";
310 LOCATE 6, 36: INPUT border
320 IF border < 0 OR border > 15 GOTO 290

400 REM ** Draw a miniature screen with selected colors **
410 LOCATE 8, 5: PRINT "Here is how your screen would look"
420 FOR lyne = 8 TO 20
430    COLOR back: LOCATE lyne, 44: PRINT STRING$(30, 219)
440 NEXT lyne
450 COLOR fore, back: LOCATE 14, 57: PRINT "TEXT";
460 COLOR border: LOCATE 8, 45: PRINT STRING$(29, 223)
470 LOCATE 20, 45: PRINT STRING$(29, 220)
480 FOR lyne = 8 TO 20
490    LOCATE lyne, 44: PRINT CHR$(219)
500    LOCATE lyne, 74: PRINT CHR$(219)
510 NEXT lyne

600 REM ** Go again?  If not, restore screen and end **
610 akey$ = INPUT$(1)
620 COLOR 7, 0, 0: CLS
630 IF akey$ <> CHR$(27) THEN COLOR 7, 0, 0: GOTO 210
640 KEY ON: END
```

SCREEN 0 Color Selections (GWRF0609.BAS)

Figure 6-9.

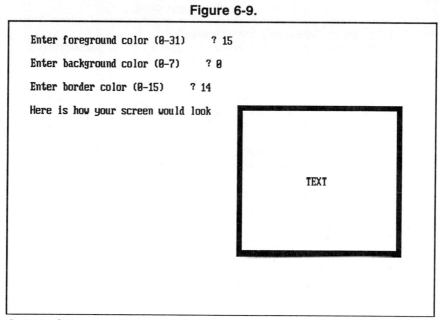

```
Enter foreground color (0-31)    ? 15

Enter background color (0-7)     ? 0

Enter border color (0-15)    ? 14

Here is how your screen would look


                                        TEXT
```

Output of Program 6-9

Experiment with these two programs. Feel free to edit them as you wish. Write a program to convert a string of ASCII codes back into characters, to use as a companion to Program 6-10.

Program 6-10.

```
1 REM ** Code encryption by ASCII *
2 ' GW-Basic: The Reference, Chapter 6. File: GWRF0610.BAS
3 ' Prints ASCII codes for characters typed

100 REM ** Initialize **
110 CLS : KEY OFF: DEFINT A-Z
120 astring$ = ""

200 REM ** Get entries until ESC key is pressed
210 LOCATE 2, 1: PRINT "Type the message to be encoded"
220 LOCATE 4, 1
230 WHILE akey$ <> CHR$(27)
240    akey$ = INPUT$(1): PRINT akey$;
250    ascii = ASC(akey$)
260    astring$ = astring$ + STR$(ascii) + " "
270 WEND

300 REM ** Clear the screen and print ASCII codes **
310 CLS : PRINT : PRINT astring$
320 LOCATE 23, 1: PRINT "Press ESC key to end or"
330 PRINT "press a different key for another message entry";
340 akey$ = INPUT$(1): IF akey$ <> CHR$(27) THEN 110
350 END
```

Code Encryption by ASCII (GWRF0610.BAS)

Figure 6-10.

```
84   104   105   115   32   105   115   32   109   121   32   109   101   115   115   97   103
101   46   13   66   101   119   97   114   101   32   111   102   32   116   121   112   105
110   103   32   109   105   115   116   97   107   101   115   46   13   84   104   101   114
101   32   105   115   32   110   111   32   119   97   121   32   116   111   32   99   111   11
4   114   101   99   116   32   116   104   101   109   46   27
```

```
Press ESC key to end or
press a different key for another message entry
```

Code output of Program 6-10

Remarks, Constants, Variables, and Expressions

The fundamental parts of the statements and functions in a GW-BASIC program are *constants, variables,* and *expressions.* Program *comments* (remarks) are also essential for reading and understanding programs. This chapter covers these parts, as well as the statements and functions that make *type conversions* and *type definitions.*

Some of the following statements and functions have been used in earlier chapters. Here they will be discussed more formally.

ASC	CHR$	CDBL	CINT
CSNG	DEFDBL	DEFINT	DEFSNG
DEFSTR	HEX$	OCT$	REM

REM Statement

REM (REMark) statements have been used periodically in earlier chapters in all but short demonstration programs. Remarks contain comments on the purpose of the program and on what it is doing at various stages. These comments can be used to clearly identify functional blocks of programs.

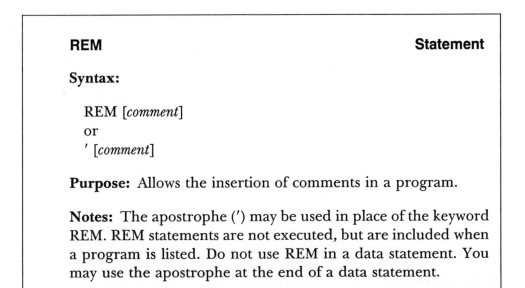

REM   **Statement**

Syntax:

REM [*comment*]
or
' [*comment*]

Purpose: Allows the insertion of comments in a program.

Notes: The apostrophe (') may be used in place of the keyword REM. REM statements are not executed, but are included when a program is listed. Do not use REM in a data statement. You may use the apostrophe at the end of a data statement.

Parameters: Since REM statements are not executed, *comment* may include any keyboard character.

When a REM statement is encountered, GW-BASIC ignores everything that follows on the line where the REM occurs. For example, a CLS statement follows a REM in line 220 of this example:

```
210 INPUT "Enter your name "; naym$
220 REM Clear screen and continue: CLS
230 PRINT "Hello "; naym$
240 GOTO 210
```

When this block of code is executed, the screen is *not* cleared by line 220, because everything on the line is considered part of the REM. To clear the screen, place the CLS *before* the REM statement in line 220, as in either of the following examples:

```
220 CLS      'Clear screen and continue
```

```
220 CLS: REM Clear screen and continue
```

Although you may branch to a REM statement from either a GOSUB or GOTO statement, a program will run faster if the branch is to the first executable statement following the REM. Programs in this book avoid branching to REM statements, and you should avoid this in your programs, too. Not only do you speed up your program by avoiding branching to REMs, you may want to eliminate some REM statements in the final version of the program. If branching to REM statements has been avoided, the program will still run correctly when remarks have been removed.

If you want quick program execution, you should also avoid placing REM statements in a loop that will be executed many times, since REM statements slow the execution of a program slightly.

Remarks may be added to the end of an executable line, if the apostrophe (') is used in place of REM, as in the following lines:

```
330 average! = total! / number    'Average the scores
340 PRINT average!                 'Print the result
```

You can use any number of remarks in a program. Use them, for example, to identify a program and its author. Even though the lines are not executed, they are printed by the LIST command. Here is how a program might be identified by REM statements.

```
4 REM     o o o o o o o o o o o o o o o o o o o o o
5 REM     o                                       o
6 REM     o     Fancy Program by Albert Outlander  o
7 REM     o                                       o
8 REM     o o o o o o o o o o o o o o o o o o o o o
```

The Notes section in the REM syntax box states that you should not use REM in a DATA statement. If REM is used as data that is being assigned to a numeric variable, you will get a "Syntax error" message. However, if REM occurs in a DATA statement that is read into a string variable, REM will be assigned as a valid string. For example, enter and run this four-line program:

```
250 FOR number = 1 to 4
260    READ naym$: PRINT naym$,
270 NEXT number
280 DATA John, Bob, REM, Don
```

Here is the output.

```
John          Bob          REM          Don
```

REM statements are a great aid; while you are developing a program, use lots of them. You can remove superfluous REM statements after the program is finalized.

ASC and CHR$ Functions

You got a preview of the ASC and CHR$ functions in Chapter 6. A more formal description follows in this section. ASC and CHR$

are the inverse of each other. ASC is used to get the ASCII code that represents a character, and CHR$ is used to get the character represented by an ASCII code.

ASC Function

ASC is frequently used to get the ASCII codes of numeric digits, uppercase letters, and lowercase letters. These characters have the following ranges of codes.

Characters	ASCII Code Range
Digits 0 to 9	48 to 57
Uppercase letters *A* to *Z*	65 to 90
Lowercase letters *a* to *z*	97 to 122

ASC **Function**

Syntax: ASC (*string*)

Purpose: Returns the numeric ASCII code for the first character of *string*.

Notes: If *string* is the null string (""), an "Illegal Function Call" error is returned. See also CHR$ function. See Appendix B for a list of ASCII character codes.

Parameters: *string* is any valid string expression.

Both ASC and CHR$ were used in Chapter 6 in Program 6-10. The ESC key has an ASCII code of 27, and in the program ASC is used to detect the character whose key has been pressed. CHR$ is used to detect when the ESC key has been pressed. This provides an escape from the WHILE/WEND loop.

```
230 WHILE akey$ <> CHR$(27)
240    akey$ = INPUT$(1): PRINT akey$
250    ascii = ASC(akey$)
```

The program then changes the value of the ascii variable to string form by using the STR$ function. Each time a key is pressed, the string form of the ascii code is joined to the astring$ variable, along with an appended blank space, like this:

```
260    astring$ = astring$ + STR$(ascii) + " "
270 WEND
```

CHR$ Function

CHR$ is the inverse function of ASC. It converts an ASCII code to the character it represents. CHR$ is also used to send codes to a device such as a printer or modem. Check your printer or modem user manual for the appropriate parameters.

CHR$ **Function**

Syntax: CHR$(*expression*)

Purpose: Converts an ASCII code to the character it represents.

Notes: Some ASCII codes have special meaning when sent to a printer or modem. Use these with care. See Appendix B for a list of ASCII codes.

> **Parameters:** *expression* may be an integer, a variable, or an expression; *expression* must evaluate to a number from 0 to 255; *expression* is enclosed in parentheses.

Since double quotation marks are used to mark the beginning and end of a string, you cannot use double quotation marks within a string. CHR$ is used to get around this limitation. Here is what happens when you try to include a double quotation mark in a string.

```
A$ = "Don't enclose double quotation marks (") in strings."
Syntax error
Ok
_
```

To avoid this error, break the string into two parts: one part that is to the left of the double quotation mark that you want printed, and one part that is to the right.

    Part 1: Don't enclose double quotation marks (
    Part 2:) in strings.

Assign each part to a separate variable. Then use CHR$(34) between the two variables in a PRINT statement, as shown here.

```
A$ = "Don't enclose double quotation marks ("
Ok
B$ = ") in strings."
Ok
PRINT A$ CHR$(34) B$_
```

When this PRINT statement is executed, the string you want will be printed.

```
Don't include double quotation marks (") in strings.
Ok
_
```

Some ASCII codes cause special things to happen. Enter and run the following four-line program:

```
220 FOR number = 1 TO 4
230   PRINT CHR$(7)
240   start! = TIMER: WHILE TIMER < start! + 1: WEND
250 NEXT number
```

Line 230, PRINT CHR$(7), sounds a beep on the computer's speaker, just like a BEEP statement does. Either beep is fairly long, but the one-second time delay of line 240 prevents the four beeps from overlapping into one long tone. Try removing line 240, and then run the remaining three lines of the program again. You should hear one long beep instead of four shorter ones.

Some ASCII codes should be used with care. For example, some codes have specific meanings when sent to your printer or modem by the CHR$ function, causing these devices to perform in special ways. See your printer or modem user manual for specific examples, because the codes may vary from device to device.

CHR$ is often used to insert nonkeyboard characters into strings. Some of these are control characters and some are displayable characters. Program 7-1, Draw Box and Insert Characters, uses some graphics characters and other displayable characters that are not on the keyboard. You'll see smiling faces, happy musical notes, and playing card suit shapes. Try it out. Figure 7-1 shows the output.

HEX$ and OCT$ Functions

These two functions are used to return a string that represents the hexadecimal (HEX$) and octal (OCT$) values of a number. The

Program 7-1.

```
1 REM ** Draw Box and Insert Characters **
2 ' GW-BASIC: The Reference, Chapter 7. File: GWRF0701.BAS
3 ' Displays Characters Using CHR$

100 REM ** Initialize **
110 CLS: KEY OFF: DEFINT A-Z

200 REM ** Draw the box **
210 ' Top, then bottom
220 LOCATE 10, 24
230 PRINT CHR$(218); STRING$(32, 196); CHR$(191);
240 LOCATE 10, 24
250 PRINT CHR$(192); STRING$(32, 196); CHR$(217);
260 ' Sides
270 FOR lyne = 11 TO 14
280    LOCATE lyne, 24: PRINT CHR$(179);      'Left side
290    LOCATE lyne, 57: PRINT CHR$(179);      'Right side
300 NEXT lyne

400 REM ** Print characters, wait for key press, end **
410 LOCATE 11, 26: PRINT CHR$(3); SPACE$(28); CHR$(4);
420 LOCATE 12, 32
430 PRINT "Smile !!   "; CHR$(1); SPACE$(2); CHR$(1);
440 LOCATE 13, 32
450 PRINT "Be happy !!  "; CHR$(14); SPACE$(2); CHR$(14);
460 LOCATE 14, 26: PRINT CHR$(6); SPACE$(28); CHR$(5);
470 akey$ = INPUT$(1): CLS: END
```

Draw Box and Insert Characters (GWRFO701.BAS)

use of HEX$ is quite common, but OCT$ has fallen into disuse—
partly because of its cumbersome format for large numbers.

HEX$ Function

The hexadecimal number system has a base of 16 and uses the
symbols 0, 1, 2, 3, 4, 5, 6, 7, 8, 9, A, B, C, D, E, and F. See the
"Integers" section of Chapter 5 for more information on hexa-

Figure 7-1.

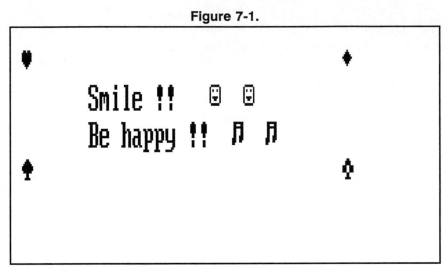

Output of Program 7-1

decimal numbers and their symbols. Table 5-4 shows the decimal equivalents of these symbols.

HEX$ was used in Chapter 5 to demonstrate how broken lines can be drawn in graphics mode. HEX$ is also used to designate segments of memory. For this use, see DEF SEG, Chapter 17, "Memory Access and Control."

HEX$ **Function**

Syntax: HEX$(*expression*)

Purpose: Returns a string that represents the hexadecimal value of a number.

Notes: HEX$ converts decimal values in the range of −32768 to 65535 into a string expression in hexadecimal format that has a range of 0 to FFFF. See Appendix E, "Decimal/Octal/Hexa-decimal Equivalents."

Parameters: *expression* is any numeric expression that evaluates to a decimal number in the range −32768 to 65535. The number is rounded to an integer before HEX$ is evaluated. If the integer is negative, the binary 2's complement form is used.

A detailed discussion of the binary number system and the 2's complement form is beyond the scope of this book. Refer to a book on assembly or machine language for further information.

If the number being converted to a hexadecimal string is greater than 65535 or less than −32768, an "Overflow" error message results.

```
PRINT HEX$(65536)
Overflow
Ok
_
```

You can even use a hexadecimal number as the *expression*.

```
PRINT HEX$(&HFFFF)
FFFF
Ok
PRINT HEX$(&H1234)
1234
Ok
_
```

Unfortunately, GW-BASIC does not have a function to convert a hexadecimal string back to a decimal number. However, you can write such a program yourself. Program 7-2, Convert Hex String to Decimal, will do this task. It uses the VAL function (see Chapter 13, "String Manipulation"), along with the &H prefix, to evaluate the hexadecimal string.

The program opens with the prompt

```
Enter a hex string (4 characters or less) _
```

Enter any hexadecimal string of four characters or less, and its decimal value is printed. Here is an example.

```
Enter a hex string (4 characters or less) A2B
A2B = decimal value of  2603
```

Program 7-2.

```
1 REM **Convert Hex String to Decimal **
2 ' GW-BASIC: The Reference, Chapter 7.  File: GWRFO702.BAS
3 ' Displays Decimal Equivalent of Hex String

100 REM ** Initialize **
110 CLS: KEY OFF: DEFINT A-Z

200 REM ** Enter Hex String and Convert **
210 INPUT "Enter hex string (4 characters or less) ", Hexstr$
220 DecNum! = VAL("&H" + Hexstr$)

300 REM ** Print decimal value of input **
310 LOCATE 3, 2: PRINT Hexstr$; " = decimal value of"; DecNum!
320 akey$ = INPUT$(1)
330 IF akey$ <> CHR$(27) THEN CLS: GOTO 210
340 CLS: KEY ON: END
```

Convert Hex String to Decimal (GWRFO702.BAS)

Press the ESC key to quit, or any other key to enter another decimal string. Here is a second example.

```
Enter a hex string (4 characters or less) FFFF
FFFF = decimal value of  65535
```

OCT$ Function

The octal number system has a base of eight, and uses the symbols 0, 1, 2, 3, 4, 5, 6, and 7.

OCT$ **Function**

Syntax: OCT$(*expression*)

Purpose: Returns a string that represents the octal value of a numeric expression.

Notes: OCT$ converts decimal values in the range −32768 to 65535 into a string expression in octal format in the range 0 to 177777.

Parameters: *expression* is a numeric expression that is rounded to an integer before OCT$ is evaluated. If the integer is negative, the binary 2's complement form is used.

Test OCT$ in the Direct mode to see how it works. Here are entries for its negative decimal value limits.

```
PRINT OCT$(-32768)
10000
Ok
PRINT OCT$(-32769)
Overflow
Ok
_
```

You can also evaluate a hexadecimal or octal expression.

```
PRINT OCT$(&HA4C)
5114
Ok
PRINT OCT$(&O172)
172
Ok
_
```

The following list shows the octal strings for numbers at or near zero.

Decimal Value	Octal Representation
2	2
1	1
0	0
−1	177777
−2	177776

Here are direct PRINT outputs for decimal values near or over the maximum decimal value.

```
PRINT OCT$(65535)
100000
Ok
PRINT OCT$(65536)
Overflow
Ok
_
```

If the number is negative and greater than -32768, OCT$(*number*) is the same as OCT$(65536 + *number*).

```
PRINT OCT$(-1000)
176030
Ok
PRINT OCT$(65536 + (-1000))
176030
```

Program 7-3, Convert Octal String to Decimal, is similar to the last program (Program 7-2) that converted hex strings to decimal, except that it takes an octal string as input. It uses the VAL function, along with the &O prefix, to evaluate the octal string, and outputs a decimal value of the octal string.

DEFINT, DEFSNG, DEFDBL, and DEFSTR Statements

The default numeric type used by GW-BASIC is single precision. The DEFtype statements (DEFINT, DEFSNG, DEFDBL, and DEFSTR) are used to declare a range of variables as to their type: integer, single precision, double precision, or string. You can also declare individual variables, separating them by commas.

Program 7-3.

```
1 REM ** Convert Octal String to Decimal
2 ' GW-BASIC: The Reference, Chapter 7.  File: GWRF0703.BAS
3 ' Displays Decimal Equivalent of Octal String

100 REM ** Initialize **
110 CLS: KEY OFF: DEFINT A-Z

200 REM ** Enter Hex String and Convert **
210 INPUT "Enter a four character octal string "; astring$
220 DecNum! = VAL("&O" + astring$)

300 REM ** Print decimal value of input **
310 LOCATE 3, 2: PRINT astring$; " = decimal value of"; DecNum!
320 akey$ = INPUT$(1)
330 IF akey$ <> CHR$(27) THEN CLS: GOTO 210
340 CLS: KEY ON: END
```

Convert Octal String to Decimal (GWRF0703.BAS)

DEFINT Statement

DEFINT is used to declare a group of variables as integers. The first letters of the variables are appended to the keyword DEF-INT.

DEFINT   **Statement**

Syntax:

> DEFINT *letter1 —letter2*
> or
> DEFINT *letter1, letter2,* . . .

Purpose: Declares a group of variables (whose names begin with a letter in the specified range) to be integers.

Notes: A variable is single precision by default, if no DEFtype statement or type declaration character is used. A type declaration character (%, !, #, or $) always takes precedence over a DEFINT statement.

Parameters: *letter1* is the first letter and *letter2* is the last letter of the range of names. Individual *letters* can also be used, separated by commas if there is more than one letter, as in

```
DEFINT A, B, C
```

You may have noticed that most of the named and numbered programs in this book have a DEFINT statement in the initialization block.

```
100 REM ** Initialize **
110 CLS: KEY OFF: DEFINT A-Z
```

This defines *all* variables to be of integer type. Type declaration characters are used when a different type of variable is desired.

DEFSNG Statement

DEFSNG is used to declare a group of variables as single precision. The first letters of the variables are appended to the keyword DEFSNG.

DEFSNG   **Statement**

Syntax:

DEFSNG *letter1* —*letter2*
or
DEFSNG *letter1, letter2,* . . .

Purpose: Declares a group of variables (whose names begin with a letter in the specified range) to be single precision.

Notes: A variable is single precision by default, if no DEFtype statement or type declaration character is used. A type declaration character (%, !, #, or $) always takes precedence over a DEFSNG statement.

Parameters: *letter1* is the first letter and *letter2* is the last letter of the range of names. Individual *letters* can also be used, separated by commas if there is more than one letter, as in

```
DEFSNG X, Y, Z
```

 REMEMBER If you have not used a DEFtype statement in a program, any variables that do not have a type character attached will be single precision by default.

DEFDBL Statement

DEFDBL is used to declare a group of variables as double precision. The first letters of the variables are appended to the keyword DEFDBL.

DEFDBL **Statement**

Syntax:

DEFDBL *letter1 —letter2*
or
DEFDBL *letter1, letter2,* ...

Purpose: Declares a group of variables (whose names begin with a letter in the specified range) to be double precision.

Notes: A variable is single precision by default, if no DEFtype statement or type delcaration character is used. A type declaration character (%, !, #, or $) always takes precedence over a DEFDBL statement.

Parameters: *letter1* is the first letter and *letter2* is the last letter of the range of names. Individual *letters* can also be used, separated by commas if there is more than one letter, as in

```
DEFDBL D, E, F
```

DEFSTR Statement

DEFSTR is used to declare a group of variables as strings. The first letters of the variables are appended to the keyword DEFSTR.

DEFSTR   **Statement**

Syntax:

DEFSTR *letter1 —letter2*
or
DEFSTR *letter1, letter2,* . . .

Purpose: Declares a group of variables (whose names begin with a letter in the specified range) to be strings.

Notes: A variable is single precision by default, if no DEFtype statement or type declaration character is used. A type declaration character (%, !, #, or $) always takes precedence over a DEFSTR statement. GW-BASIC strings can be from 0 to 255 characters long.

Parameters: *letter1* is the first letter and *letter2* is the last letter of the range of names. Individual *letters* can also be used, separated by commas if there is more than one letter, as in

DEFSTR S, T, U

Other Comments on DEFtype

Here are some ways that you can use DEFtype.

Statement	Variables Declared
DEFINT A-Z	All variables are integers
DEFSNG A-E	All variables beginning with A, B, C, D, or E are single precision
DEFDBL M, N, O	All variables beginning with M, N, or O are double precision

DEFSTR S, V-Y   All variables beginning with S, V,
                       W, X, or Y are strings

DEFtype statements are usually placed near the beginning of a program. It is becoming standard programming practice to define all variables as integers, and then override this declaration for other types of variables, using type declaration characters (%, !, #, or $).

For example, consider a biker who is accelerating at the rate of 2.5 meters per second.

```
110 DEFINT A-Z
250 acceleration! = 2.5
```

In this example, even though all variables were defined as integers in line 110, the type character attached to acceleration (!) makes it single precision.

DEFtype statements can also apply to array variables. In the following example, all elements of the Address array will be treated as strings.

```
DEFSTR A-Z
DIM Address(15)
```

You can use the same letter in more than one DEFtype statement. However, if that letter appears in the second DEFtype statement, all variables beginning with the letters of the second statement are reinitialized to zero. For example:

```
110 DEFINT A-Z
210 number = 32: PRINT "number ="; number
220 DEFSNG N: PRINT "number ="; number
```

The results of this three-liner will appear as follows.

```
number = 32
number = 0
```

DEFtype statements are no longer in effect after any of these statements are executed:

```
CHAIN, CLEAR, LOAD, NEW, or MERGE
```

DEFtype statements do remain in effect after a CHAIN MERGE statement.

CINT, CSNG, and CDBL Functions

The CINT, CSNG, and CDBL functions are used to convert expressions to the desired degree of precision. Suppose you want to add two measurements: one measured to the nearest inch, and a second one measured to the nearest hundredth of an inch. The sum of these measurements can be no more precise than the least precise of the two. You should therefore convert the second measurement to an integer before adding the two together. Another reason for converting one type of number to another is that arithmetic operations are performed faster when the numbers being operated on are the same degree of precision.

CINT Function

Integers require less memory space than single or double precision numbers. Arithmetic operations on integers are performed faster than on single or double precision numbers. Therefore, you will probably use the CINT function more often than its companions.

CINT   **Function**

Syntax: CINT(*expression*)

Purpose: Converts a single or double precision expression to an integer.

Notes: If *expression* does not evaluate to a number in the range −32768 to 32767, an "Overflow" error occurs. See also FIX and INT in Chapter 12, "Numeric Functions and Machine Language Subroutines."

Parameters: *expression* is any valid numeric expression that will evaluate to a number that lies within GW-BASIC's integer range (−32768 to 32767).

Use the following short program to experiment with converting single precision numbers to integers.

```
110 CLS: KEY OFF: DEFINT A-Z
210 INPUT "Enter a single precision number"; number!
220 PRINT number!,
230 ConvSNG = CINT(number!): PRINT ConvSNG
240 PRINT: GOTO 210
```

After experimenting with single precision numbers, change lines 210, 220, and 230 to

```
210 INPUT "Enter a double precision number"; number#
220 PRINT number#,
230 ConvDBL = CINT(number#): PRINT ConvDBL
```

With these changes, experiment some more by entering double precision numbers. Figure 7-2 shows some examples of each version: single precision and double precision.

CSNG Function

This function converts integers and double precision numbers to single precision. Double precision numbers require more memory space than single precision. Both space and execution time can be saved by converting double precision values to single precision.

CSNG   **Function**

Syntax: CSNG(*expression*)

Purpose: Converts an integer or a double precision expression to a single precision number.

Notes: The number being converted must be greater than $-1.7E+38$ and less than $+1.7E+38$, or an overflow will occur. Numbers between $-3.0E-39$ and $+3.0E-39$ will be converted to zero.

Parameters: *expression* is any valid numeric expression that will evaluate to the range of single precision numbers given in the foregoing Notes.

If the diameter of a circle is measured to three significant figures (single precision), and you know the value of pi to double precision, convert pi to a single precision number before calculating the circumference of a circle (Circumference = pi * diameter).

Figure 7-2.

Single precision entries

```
    Enter single precision number? 3.14159
     3.14159        3

    Enter single precision number? 2.58
     2.58           3

    Enter single precision number? 32767.4
     32767.4        32767

    Enter single precision number? 32767.5
     32767.5
Overflow in 230
Ok
 _


Double precision entries

    Enter double precision number? 3.14159265358979
     3.14159265358979          3

    Enter double precision number? -2.5800001
    -2.5800001     -3

    Enter double precision number? -32768.499
    -32768.499     -32768

    Enter double precision number? -32768.511
    -32768.511
Overflow in 230
Ok
 _
```

Examples using CINT

```
220 diameter! = 5.31
230 pi# = 3.14159265358979
240 Circumference! = diameter! * CSNG(pi#)
250 PRINT diameter!; CSNG(pi#), Circumference!
```

A run of this four-line program prints the circumference as

```
5.31   3.141593              16.68186
```

As you can see, the value of pi# is converted to single precision before the circumference is calculated.

CDBL Function

This function converts integers and single precision numbers to double precision numbers. Double precision numbers require more space than single precision, but they can represent values with up to 16 digits.

CDBL   **Function**

Syntax: CDBL(*expression*)

Purpose: Converts an integer or a single precision expression to double precision.

Notes: The number being converted must be greater than −1.7E+38 and less than +1.7E+38, or an overflow will occur. Numbers between −3.0E−39 and +3.0E−39 will be converted to zero.

Parameters: *expression* is any valid expression that will evaluate to the range of double precision numbers given in the foregoing Notes.

If a number is first specified as single precision, it generally will not be more precise than six digits. Converting a single precision number to double precision does not make the number more accurate. The only single precision constants that can be converted with increased precision by CDBL are those that are an integer power of two, or that can be expressed as the sum of a finite number of powers of 2 (for example, $.875 = 2^{-1} + 2^{-2} + 2^{-3}$). This is because the computer uses binary format for storage and to perform its computations.

When you use CINT, CSNG, or CDBL on a numeric expression, the expression is evaluated first, then converted to the specified precision. For example, consider these two conversions:

```
110 CLS: KEY OFF: DEFINT A-Z
220 number1# = CDBL(5 / 3)
230 number2# = CDBL(5# / 3)
240 PRINT "number 1 ="; number1#
250 PRINT "number 2 ="; number2#
```

If these four lines were executed, the output would be

```
number 1 = 1.666666626930237
number 2 = 1.666666666666667
```

In line 220, the number 5 is treated as a single precision number. This introduces a single precision round-off error in the printed value of number 1. In line 230, the number 5 is treated as double precision because of the type declaration character (#). Therefore, the result is rounded to true double precision. Use care in appending type declaration characters to variables and constants.

8

Terminal I/O

This chapter discusses the statements and functions that give you control of your keyboard, screen, and printer. You have seen some terminal input and output features in previous chapters. Now you will get a closer look at their formal syntax. Here are the statements and functions covered in this chapter.

CLS	COLOR	CSRLIN	INKEY$
INPUT	INPUT$	KEY	LINE INPUT
LOCATE	LPOS	LPRINT	LPRINT USING
POS	PRINT	PRINT USING	SCREEN
SPACE$	SPC	TAB	WIDTH
WRITE	VIEW PRINT		

CLS and KEY Statements

In the previous chapters, the CLS statement has been used to clear the text screen. KEY OFF and KEY ON have been used to turn off and on the function key description line at the bottom of the screen.

CLS Statement

The CLS statement is used to make sure the screen is cleared before anything is displayed.

```
110 CLS: KEY OFF: DEFINT A-Z
```

Use a line like the following one to restore the original screen before the program ends.

```
510 CLS: KEY ON: END
```

CLS   **Statement**

Syntax: CLS

Purpose: Clears the display screen.

Notes: The screen may also be cleared by pressing CTRL+HOME, CTRL+L, or by changing screen modes with a SCREEN or WIDTH statement. See WIDTH, later in this chapter. If a graphics VIEW statement has been used, CLS clears only the last viewport specified. See VIEW PRINT, later in this chapter.

Parameters: None.

A CLS statement clears the screen and puts the cursor in the upper-left corner. The last graphics point referenced is set to the center of the screen.

KEY Statement

A KEY statement can turn the function key line off or on, change the assignment of a function key, or display a list of function key assignments. You saw all these uses in Chapter 2.

KEY   **Statement**

Syntax:

```
KEY ON
KEY OFF
KEY LIST
KEY number, string
KEY number, CHR$(hex code) + CHR$(scan code)
```

Purpose: Turns the key line off or on; lists the assignments of the function keys; or assigns a string (up to 15 characters) to a function key to provide quick entry of often-used terms.

Notes: If a string that is longer than 15 characters is assigned to a key, only the first 15 characters are used. KEY OFF does not disable the function keys, but simply turns off the function key descriptions on line 25 of the screen. To disable a function key, you must assign a null string to the key.

Parameters: *number* may be any valid function key number; *string* is any valid string expression. The *hex code* parameter is the hexadecimal code assigned to the key, from Appendix C. Hex codes may be added, such as &H03, which is either SHIFT key. The *scan code* parameter is the code number defining the key you want to trap. (See Appendix C, "Key HEX Codes and Scan Codes.")

SCREEN, WIDTH, and COLOR Statements

These three closely related statements control the appearance of the display screen, and are often used on the same program line.

SCREEN Statement

Use the SCREEN statement to select a screen mode that is appropriate to your computer's hardware configuration. There are many different kinds of graphics hardware; therefore, GW-BASIC provides many screen modes. This discussion applies to computers that have the graphics capabilities that GW-BASIC supports. See Appendix H, "Screen Descriptions and Colors." To be absolutely certain which screen modes work with your monitor and graphics adapter, study the user manual for your computer.

SCREEN   **Statement**

Syntax: SCREEN [*mode*][,[*colorswitch*]][,[*apage*]][,[*vpage*]]

Purpose: Sets the characteristics of the display screen.

Notes: GW-BASIC supports MDPA (IBM Monochrome Display and Printer Adapter) with screen mode 0; CGA (Color Graphics Adapter) with screen modes 0, 1, and 2; and EGA (Enhanced Graphics Adapter) with screen modes 0, 1, 2, 7, 8, 9, and 10. Modes 9 and 10 require an IBM-compatible Enhanced Color Display. Adapters with higher resolutions can use any of the supported modes. Some computers, such as the Tandy 1000 series, support additional modes.

Parameters: *mode* must be an integer expression with values 0, 1, 2, 7, 8, 9, or 10. Your computer hardware must be able to handle the selected mode. The *colorswitch* parameter is used to enable or disable color in SCREEN 0 or SCREEN 1. In all modes except mode 0, a value of zero (false) disables color, and any nonzero value (true) enables color. In SCREEN mode 0, the meaning of *colorswitch* is inverted. The parameter *apage* (active page) is the area of memory where graphics information is written. The parameter *vpage* (visual page) is the area of memory that is being displayed. The *apage* and *vpage* parameters are useful when producing animated graphics.

Do not confuse this SCREEN *statement* with the SCREEN *function* discussed later in this chapter.

Screen modes 0, 1, and 2 are demonstrated in this book because monitors and adapters of higher capabilities can also produce graphics in these modes. CGA monitors and adapters cannot produce graphics in screen modes other than 0, 1, and 2.

WIDTH Statement

The WIDTH statement sets the line width, in characters-per-line, for either the screen or a line printer. Only a 40- or 80-column line screen width is allowed for most computers. The Tandy 1000 series also allows a 20-column line. When GW-BASIC is first accessed, SCREEN 0 with WIDTH 80 is automatically set.

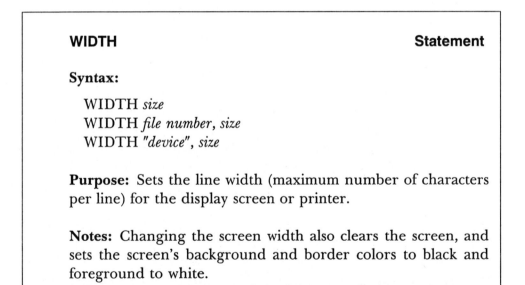

WIDTH   **Statement**

Syntax:

> WIDTH *size*
> WIDTH *file number, size*
> WIDTH *"device", size*

Purpose: Sets the line width (maximum number of characters per line) for the display screen or printer.

Notes: Changing the screen width also clears the screen, and sets the screen's background and border colors to black and foreground to white.

Parameters: *size* is an integer in the range 1 to 255 for a printer or file, but is either 40 or 80 for the screen. (It may be 20, also, for Tandy 1000 series screens.) The *file number* parameter is the number of the open file in use. The *device* parameter is a valid device, like SCRN:, LPT1:, LPT2:, LPT3:, COM1:, or COM2, whose width can be set.

Here are two ways to set the screen width to 40 in SCREEN 0.

```
WIDTH 40
WIDTH "SCRN:", 40
```

You can also assign a string such as "LPT1:" or "SCRN:" to a variable such as *device$,* and use the variable as follows:

```
device$ = "SCRN:"
Ok
WIDTH device$, 40
```

The WIDTH value must be compatible with the SCREEN mode being used. In SCREEN 1, WIDTH is automatically 40 characters per line. In SCREEN 2, WIDTH is automatically 80 characters per line. Use WIDTH statements only in modes that allow more than one width. See SCREEN in Appendix H, "Screen Descriptions and Colors."

The following WIDTH statement sets the printer to WIDTH 60:

```
WIDTH "LPT1:", 60
```

The next WIDTH statement example opens file #1 to the line printer and sets the printer to 48 characters per line for printing records to the file. The capabilities of your printer must be considered when setting the number of characters per line.

```
330 OPEN "LPT1:" FOR OUTPUT AS #1
340 WIDTH #1, 48
```

COLOR Statement

The syntax used for the COLOR statement depends upon the SCREEN mode that is active. In general, COLOR allows you to select foreground and background colors for the screen. In SCREEN 0, the screen's border color can also be set. In SCREEN 1, no foreground color is selected. Instead, a palette is selected for use by graphics statements. If you have an EGA or VGA adapter, see also the PALETTE statement in Chapter 15, "Graphics."

COLOR   **Statement**

Syntax:

COLOR [*foreground*][,[*background*][,*border*]]
COLOR [*background*][,[*palette*]]
COLOR [*foreground*][,[*background*]]

Purpose: Selects display colors for the display screen.

Notes: COLOR allows you to select the foreground and background for all screen modes except SCREEN 1. Graphics statements (such as LINE and CIRCLE) are used to set foreground colors in SCREEN 1 from one of two palettes. In SCREEN 0, the border color can also be set. COLOR has no effect in SCREEN 2. See Appendix H, "Screen Descriptions and Colors," for colors. Also see COLOR, SCREEN, and PALETTE in Chapter 15, "Graphics."

Parameters: *foreground* is an expression that evaluates to an integer in the range 0 to 31; *background* is an expression that evaluates to an integer in the range 0 to 7; *border* is an expression that evaluates to an integer in the range 0 to 15; *palette* is an odd or even integer expression (usually 0 and 1 are used).

If you make the foreground color the same as the background color, the printed characters will be invisible. The default background is black (number 0) for all screen modes.

Program 8-1, A Rainbow of Colors, shows eight lines of text in SCREEN 0, each with a different background color. Unless the screen is cleared after the background color is set each time, only the background of the text displayed after the COLOR statement is changed. Therefore, this program gives each text line a uniquely colored background while the rest of the screen remains blue.

After a short time delay, the text screen is cleared and a display of color-filled circles in random patterns is shown in SCREEN 1. SCREEN, CLS, KEY, WIDTH, and COLOR statements are all used in the program.

LOCATE Statement; TAB, SPC, and SPACE$ Functions

These statements control cursor positioning, skipping spaces, and printing spaces.

Program 8-1.

```
1 REM ** A Rainbow of Colors **
2 ' GW-BASIC: The Reference, Chapter 8.  File: GWRF0801.BAS
3 ' Displays text in SCREEN 0, then circles in SCREEN 1

100 REM ** Initialize **
110 SCREEN 0: CLS: KEY OFF: WIDTH 40: DEFINT A-Z

200 REM ** Print title **
210 LOCATE 12, 6, 0: PRINT "BACKGROUND COLORS IN SCREEN 0"
220 start! = TIMER: WHILE TIMER < start! + 2: WEND

300 REM ** Print colored text in SCREEN 0, WIDTH 80 **
310 WIDTH 80: COLOR 15, 1, 0: CLS
320 FOR kolor = 0 TO 7
330   COLOR , kolor: READ ColorName$: LOCATE 2 * kolor + 4, 26
340   PRINT "Background color"; kolor; ColorName$
350 NEXT kolor
360 DATA black, blue, green, cyan, red, magenta, brown, white
370 start! = TIMER: WHILE TIMER < start! + 5: WEND
380 COLOR 7, 0: CLS

400 REM ** Colored circles in SCREEN 1 **
410 SCREEN 1: COLOR 0, 1: CLS
420 LOCATE 2, 5: PRINT "CIRCLES IN SCREEN 1"
430 LOCATE 24, 5: PRINT "Press ESC to quit";
440 WHILE INKEY$ <> CHR$(27)
450   col = INT(300 * RND) + 10: row = INT(142 * RND) + 24
460   radius = INT(8 * RND) + 3: kolor = INT(4 * RND)
470   CIRCLE (col, row), radius, 3
480   PAINT (col, row), kolor, 3
490   start! = TIMER: WHILE TIMER < start! + .3: WEND
500 WEND

600 REM ** Restore screens and end **
610 CLS: SCREEN 0: WIDTH 80: KEY ON: END
```

A Rainbow of Colors (GWRF0801.BAS)

LOCATE Statement

The LOCATE statement has already been used in many programs. It is used four times in Program 8-1.

```
210 LOCATE 12, 6: PRINT "BACKGROUND COLORS IN SCREEN 0"
330 COLOR , kolor: READ ColorName$: LOCATE 2 * kolor + 4, 26
420 LOCATE 2, 5: PRINT "CIRCLES IN SCREEN 1"
430 LOCATE 24, 5: PRINT "Press ESC to quit";
```

LOCATE   **Statement**

Syntax: LOCATE [*row*][,[*column*][,[*cursor*][,[*start*][,*stop*]]]]

Purpose: Moves the cursor to a specified position on the screen, and selects appropriate parameters for the cursor.

Notes: When LOCATE moves the cursor to the specified position, printing begins at that position. You may make the cursor invisible, as well as change its size.

Parameters: *row* is a numeric expression that evaluates to an integer—a screen line number in the range 1 to 25. The *column* parameter is a numeric expression that evaluates to an integer in the range 1 to 40, or 1 to 80, depending on WIDTH. This is the screen column number. The *cursor* parameter is a Boolean value 0 (invisible) or nonzero (visible) in SCREEN 0. The *start* parameter is a numeric expression in the range 0 to 31—the start scan line for the cursor; and *stop* is a numeric expression in the range 0 to 31—the stop scan line for the cursor. Start and stop scan lines determine the size of the cursor. Only the *row* and *column* parameters have an effect in graphics modes.

Figure 8-1.

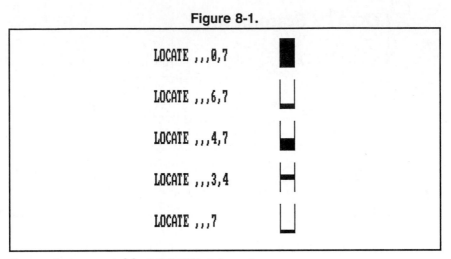

Cursor shapes created by LOCATE statements

You can use LOCATE to modify the cursor's shape. For most graphics devices, the cursor has eight scan lines, numbered 0 to 7. By default, GW-BASIC uses line 7 alone in the Overwrite text mode, and lines 4 through 7 in the Insert text mode. Figure 8-1 shows five cursor shapes and the LOCATE statements that create them. Only the horizontal lines shown in the figure are displayed; the vertical lines merely indicate the relative position of the scan lines within the maximum possible cursor shape. Program 8-2, Change Cursor Shape, allows you to select different start and stop scan lines to create various cursor shapes. Lines 250 and 280 insure that the scan lines entered are within range (0 to 7).

TAB Function

The TAB function is used in PRINT statements to move the cursor to a specified column (print position) on the current line.

Program 8-2.

```
1 REM ** Change Cursor Shape **
2 ' GW-BASIC: The Reference, Chapter 8.  File: GWRF0802.BAS
3 ' Enter scan lines for cursor, display cursor shape

100 REM ** Initialize **
110 SCREEN 0: CLS: KEY OFF: WIDTH 40: DEFINT A-Z

200 REM ** Enter scan lines **
210 WHILE akey$ <> CHR$(27)
220    CLS
230    LOCATE 2, 2, 1: PRINT SPACE$(32);: LOCATE 2, 2
240    INPUT "Enter start scan line (0-7): ", start
250    IF start < 0 OR start > 7 GOTO 230
260    LOCATE 3, 2: PRINT SPACE$(32);: LOCATE 3, 2
270    INPUT "Enter stop scan line (0-7) : ", finis
280    IF finis < 0 OR finis > 7 GOTO 260

300    REM ** Locate cursor and display new shape **
310    LOCATE 10, 1: PRINT "Press ESC to quit"
320    LOCATE , , , start, finis
330    PRINT "Press space bar to continue";
340    akey$ = INPUT$(1)
350 WEND

400 REM ** Restore screen and end **
410 CLS: WIDTH 80: KEY ON: END
```

Change Cursor Shape (GWRF0802.BAS)

TAB   **Function**

Syntax: TAB(*expression*)

Purpose: Spaces to the specified column on the screen or printer.

Notes: Column 1 is the leftmost column. The rightmost column is 40 or 80, depending on the value you assign to screen WIDTH. If the current print position is beyond the value of this number, TAB goes to the specified column on the next line. See also SPC function.

Parameters: *expression* is a numeric expression that evaluates to an integer in the range 1 to 255. Nonintegers are rounded. TAB(1) is used if the number is less than 1.

TAB may be used only in PRINT, LPRINT, or PRINT# statements. If TAB is at the end of a list of data items to be printed, the cursor does not return to the next line. It is as if TAB had an implied semicolon following it.

SPC Function

The SPC function also provides spacing in PRINT, LPRINT, and PRINT# statements. As TAB moves the cursor *to* a specific column, SPC moves the cursor *to the right* a specified number of columns, skipping over any text in those columns.

SPC   **Function**

Syntax: SPC(*expression*)

Purpose: Skips a specified number of spaces.

Notes: A semicolon is assumed to follow the SPC function. If the specified number of spaces is greater than the width of the printer or screen, the value will be *number* MOD *width*. See also the SPACE$ function.

Parameters: *expression* is a numeric expression that evaluates to an integer in the range 0 to 255.

SPC can only be used with PRINT, LPRINT, and PRINT# statements. Figure 8-2 contains a short program where the SPC function separates the color numbers of palette 0 from the names of the colors. The program's output is also shown.

Figure 8-2.

```
Program

110 CLS: KEY OFF
210 FOR number = 0 TO 3
220    READ naym$: LOCATE 3 + number, 5
230    PRINT number; SPC(5); naym$
240 NEXT number
250 DATA background, green, red, brown


Run of Program

RUN
     0        background
     1        green
     2        red
     3        brown
Ok

_
```

Demonstration of the SPC function

SPACE$ Function

The SPACE$ function differs from SPC in that it inserts a specified number of spaces in a PRINT, LPRINT, or PRINT# statement.

SPACE$ **Function**

Syntax: SPACE$(*expression*)

Purpose: Returns a string of spaces equal to the value of the specified number.

Notes: The value of the specified number is rounded to an integer.

Parameters: *expression* is a numeric expression that evaluates to an integer in the range 0 to 255.

Program 8-3, A Table of Colors for SCREEN 1, uses LOCATE, TAB, SPC, and SPACE$. LOCATE is used in line 210 to place the cursor at row 2, column 23 before printing the title of the table. The value of the *cursor* parameter (0) makes the cursor invisible.

```
210 LOCATE 2, 23, 0: PRINT "FOREGROUND COLORS IN SCREEN 1"
```

LOCATE and SPC are used in block 300 of the program to print the table's subheadings. The TAB function is used in block 400 to provide required spacing for the first two lines in the body of the table. SPC and SPACE$ are used in block 500 to provide spacing in the last two lines of the table. Figure 8-3 shows the output of Program 8-3.

Program 8-3.

```
1 REM ** A Table of Colors for SCREEN 1 **
2 ' GW-BASIC: The Reference, Chapter 8.  File: GWRF0803.BAS
3 ' Demonstrates LOCATE, TAB, SPC, and SPACE$

100 REM ** Initialize **
110 SCREEN 0: CLS: KEY OFF: DEFINT A-Z

200 REM ** Print title with LOCATE **
210 LOCATE 2, 23, 0: PRINT "FOREGROUND COLORS IN SCREEN 1"

300 REM ** Print headings with LOCATE and SPC **
310 LOCATE 5, 17: PRINT "Color"; SPC(10); "Palette"; SPC(11);
320 PRINT "Palette"
330 LOCATE 6, 17: PRINT "Number"; SPC(12); "0"; SPC(17); "1"

400 REM ** Print two lines using TAB **
410 PRINT: PRINT TAB(19); "0"; TAB(31); "background"; TAB(49);
420 PRINT "background"
430 PRINT TAB(19); "1"; TAB(33); "green"; TAB(51); "cyan"

500 REM ** Print two lines using SPC and SPACE$ **
510 PRINT SPC(18); "2"; SPACE$(13); "red"; SPACE$(15); "magenta"
520 PRINT SPC(18); "3"; SPACE$(13); "brown"; SPACE$(13); "white"

600 REM ** Wait, then restore screen and end **
610 akey$ = INPUT$(1)
620 CLS: KEY ON: END
```

A Table of Colors for SCREEN 1 (GWRF0803.BAS)

Figure 8-3.

```
              FOREGROUND COLORS IN SCREEN 1


      Color           Palette           Palette
      Number             0                 1


        0            background        background
        1              green             cyan
        2              red               magenta
        3              brown             white
```

Output of Program 8-3

CSRLIN, POS, LPOS, and SCREEN Functions

The CSRLIN function is used to determine the line on which the cursor resides. POS and LPOS provide the column position of the cursor for the screen and printer, respectively. The SCREEN function is used to return the ASCII code or the color of a character at a specified position on the screen.

CSRLIN Function

CSRLIN can be used in a PRINT statement for a display, or assigned to a variable. It returns the number of the row in which the cursor resides on the screen.

CSRLIN   **Function**

Syntax: CSRLIN

Purpose: Returns the current line number position of the cursor.

Notes: An integer—the row number in which the cursor resides on the active page of the screen—is returned. CGA supports 25 rows. Advanced graphics cards support 30, 43, 50, or even 60 rows.

Parameters: None.

Here is a FOR/NEXT loop that locates the cursor at line 1, uses CSRLIN to determine the line number, and prints it. The cursor moves to each successive line, printing its line number.

```
310 FOR row = 1 TO 25
320   LOCATE row, 2, 0: CurLine = CSRLIN: PRINT CurLine;
330   start! = TIMER: WHILE TIMER < start! + .5: WEND
340 NEXT row
350 akey$ = INPUT$(1)
```

POS Function

The POS function returns the column number of the cursor's position on the screen.

POS   **Function**

Syntax: POS(*number*)

Purpose: Returns the current cursor position (column number) on a screen line.

Notes: The leftmost position is column 1, and the rightmost position is the same number as the current screen width. The value returned is an integer.

Parameters: *number* is a dummy argument. Some value must be used, but its value is irrelevant. Zero is a good choice.

A FOR/NEXT loop can move a point (dot) along a row, printing the value of the cursor's column position as each point is printed.

```
310 FOR column = 1 to 80
320    LOCATE 2, column: col = POS(column): PRINT "."
330    LOCATE 5, 2: PRINT col;: start! = TIMER
340    WHILE TIMER < start! + .3: WEND: CLS
350 NEXT column
360 akey$ = INPUT$(1)
```

LPOS Function

LPOS is similar to POS, but returns the current column number position of the printer head, rather than the cursor.

LPOS   **Function**

Syntax: LPOS(*number*)

Purpose: Returns an integer that is the current position (column number) of the printer head within the printer buffer.

Notes: LPOS does not necessarily give the physical position of the printer head. If the printer has less than a 132-characters-per-line capability, it may issue internal line feeds and not inform the computer's internal printer buffer. If this happens, the integer value returned by LPOS may be incorrect.

Parameters: *number* is a dummy argument. Some value must be used, but its value is irrelevant. Zero is a good choice.

LPOS counts the number of printable characters since the last line feed.

SCREEN Function

Do not confuse the SCREEN function with the SCREEN statement. The SCREEN *statement* is used to set the screen mode. The SCREEN *function* returns either the ASCII code or the color of the character at the current cursor position.

SCREEN　　　　　　　　　　　　　　　　　　　**Function**

Syntax: SCREEN(*row, column* [, *expression*])

Purpose: Returns the ASCII code (0 to 255) for the character at the specified row and column on the screen, if the *expression* parameter is not given. If *expression* is specified, an integer is returned, from which the color number of the character can be calculated (see explanation following syntax box).

Notes: Any out-of-range values entered will result in an "Illegal function call" error. Row 25 may be referenced only if the function key line is off.

Parameters: *row* is a numeric expression in the range 1 to 25; *column* is a numeric expression in the range 1 to 40 or 1 to 80, depending on the screen width; *expression* is any expression that evaluates to zero or a positive number when rounded. A negative value for *expression* results in an "Illegal function call."

When you omit the *expression* parameter, ASCII codes are returned. When you use a numeric *expression* that evaluates to zero or a positive number, the color number returned is calculated as follows:

Foreground a nonblinking color:
number = (B * 16) + F

Foreground a blinking color:
number = (B * 16) + F + 112

In both cases, B is the background color number of the character, and F is the foreground color of the character.

Tables 8-1A and 8-1B show examples of both uses for the SCREEN function. Table 8-1A shows PRINT statements using SCREEN functions that produce the ASCII codes for the letters of the word "SCREEN," which is displayed beginning at row 5, column 5. The *expression* parameter is not used in these SCREEN functions. Table 8-1B shows foreground and background color numbers and the resulting colors used to print letters of the word "SCREEN" at row 5, column 5. The PRINT statement used was PRINT SCREEN(5, 5, 1). Refer to Appendix H, "Screen Descriptions and Colors," to see which number is assigned to which color.

Table 8-1A.

PRINT Statement Containing SCREEN Function	Number Printed	ASCII Code Definition
PRINT SCREEN(5, 5)	83	S
PRINT SCREEN(5, 6)	67	C
PRINT SCREEN(5, 7)	82	R
PRINT SCREEN(5, 8)	69	E
PRINT SCREEN(5, 10)	78	N

Examples of Uses for the SCREEN Function

Table 8-1B.

PRINT Colors Foreground	Background	Number Printed	Calculation
7	0	7	$(16 * 0) + 7 = 7$
7	1	23	$(16 * 1) + 7 = 23$
7	2	39	$(16 * 2) + 7 = 39$
15	3	63	$(16 * 3) + 15 = 63$
17†	0	129	$(16 * 0) + 17 + 112 = 129$
31†	4	207	$(16 * 4) + 31 + 112 = 207$

NOTE: † denotes blinking color

Color Number Calculations for the SCREEN Function

Program 8-4.

```
1 REM ** Read ASCII Codes with SCREEN Function **
2 ' GW-BASIC: The Reference, Chapter 8.  File: GWRF0804.BAS
3 ' Demonstrates SCREEN Function

100 REM ** Initialize **
110 SCREEN 0: CLS: KEY OFF: DEFINT A-Z

200 REM ** Print title with LOCATE **
210 LOCATE 2, 5, 0: PRINT "Test SCREEN Function"
220 column = 5: row = 2: right = 1: lyne = 4

300 REM ** Look at one letter at a time **
310 WHILE column < 25
320    LOCATE column, 2: number = SCREEN(row, column)
330    LOCATE lyne, 7 * right
340    PRINT number; CHR$(number);
350    IF number = 32 THEN lyne = lyne + 1: right = 0
360    column = column + 1: right = right + 1
370    start! = TIMER: WHILE TIMER < start! + .5: WEND
380 WEND

500 REM ** Wait, then restore screen and end **
510 akey$ = INPUT$(1): CLS: KEY ON: END
```

Read ASCII Codes with SCREEN Function (GWRF0804.BAS)

Program 8-4, READ ASCII Codes with SCREEN Function, prints three words: "Test SCREEN Function." It then looks at one letter of the string at a time, and prints the letter and its ASCII code. Try it; Figure 8-4 shows the output.

Figure 8-4.

```
TEST SCREEN Function

    84 T    101 e  115 s  116 t  32
    83 S    67 C   82 R   69 E   69 E   78 N   32
    70 F    117 u  110 n  99 c   116 t  105 i  111 o  110 n
```

Output of Program 8-4

INKEY$ and INPUT$ Functions; INPUT and LINE INPUT Statements

The INKEY$ and INPUT$ functions and the INPUT and LINE INPUT statements accept input information from the keyboard.

INKEY$ Function

The INKEY$ function looks for keyboard entries. If a key is pressed, INKEY$ will place the key's ASCII code in a special area of memory called the keyboard buffer, which will hold up to 15 characters. The INKEY$ function does not cause the computer to wait for a keypress, as does the INPUT$ function.

INKEY$ **Function**

Syntax: INKEY$

Purpose: Returns one or two characters that have been read from the keyboard.

Notes: INKEY$ does not produce a prompt or question mark. Two characters are returned for extended codes, such as those for the cursor movement arrow keys: UP ARROW, DOWN ARROW, LEFT ARROW, and RIGHT ARROW. The first character is zero for extended codes. INKEY$ does not display characters on the screen.

Parameters: None.

If no character is in the keyboard buffer, INKEY$ returns the null string (" "). If several characters are in the buffer, only the first is returned. The INKEY$ function allows you to detect keypresses in a running program without unwanted prompts or question marks. You can alter program flow without stopping execution. The INPUT$ function is more appropriate at places where program execution can be naturally interrupted.

INPUT$ Function

The INPUT$ function returns a string of specified length from the keyboard or from a specified file number. A running program is interrupted until the specified number of characters have been read.

INPUT$ **Function**

Syntax: INPUT$(*expression* [,[#] *file number*])

Purpose: Returns a string of characters from the keyboard or from the *file number*. The length of the string is equal to the value of *expression*.

Notes: If a string is entered from the keyboard, characters are returned but not displayed. All control characters are returned.

Parameters: *expression* is a numeric expression that evaluates to an integer—the number of characters to be read; *file number* specifies a file to be read.

The INPUT$ function is preferred over INPUT and LINE INPUT for reading communications files, because INPUT causes input from a communications file to stop when a comma or carriage return is communicated, and because LINE INPUT terminates input from the file when a carriage return is communicated.

INPUT Statement

The INPUT statement accepts values from the keyboard for a specified list of variables. In addition, INPUT can display a string to prompt for the type of information needed.

INPUT   **Statement**

Syntax:

> INPUT [;][*prompt*;] *variable list*
> INPUT [;][*prompt*,] *variable list*

Purpose: Accepts input from the keyboard and assigns it to one or more specified variables.

Notes: The prompt must be enclosed in double quotation marks. If you specify more than one variable, separate them with commas. Keyboard entries are assigned to variables in the variable list and must match the variable list in number of items.

Parameters: *prompt* is a string requesting data to be entered; *variable list* contains variables used to store the data.

The variable names in the list may be numeric or string, but the type of data entered must agree with the type specified in the variable list. Too many entries, too few entries, or the wrong type of entry all result in a "?Redo from start" error message. No assignments to variables are made until an acceptable entry is received.

Either a comma or a semicolon must be used after the prompt parameter. When a comma is used, it suppresses the question mark. Thus this line:

```
310 INPUT "Enter a color number ", kolor
```

causes this input prompt to appear.

```
Enter a color number _
```

When a semicolon is used after the prompt string, like this:

```
310 INPUT "Enter a color number "; kolor
```

a question mark follows the prompt, as shown here.

```
Enter a color number ? _
```

You can place a semicolon before the prompt string also.

```
310 INPUT; "Enter a color number "; kolor
320 PRINT kolor
```

If the prompt string is preceded by a semicolon, no carriage return is made when you press the ENTER key. Your keyboard entry is displayed along with data from the next PRINT statement. In this example, the next PRINT statement was in line 320.

```
Enter a color number ? 3 3
```

Strings assigned to a string variable in an INPUT statement do not have to be enclosed in double quotation marks unless they contain commas, or leading or trailing blanks. You may, however, use the quotation marks if you wish.

LINE INPUT Statement

The LINE INPUT statement allows you to enter up to 255 characters from the keyboard. It assigns the character string to a string variable.

LINE INPUT   **Statement**

Syntax: LINE INPUT [;][*prompt*;] *variable$*

Purpose: Accepts an entire line (up to 255 characters) from the keyboard into a string variable.

Notes: LINE INPUT ignores delimiters, even reading quotation marks. If the LINE INPUT statement is immediately followed by a semicolon, the cursor will not move to the next line when you press ENTER.

Parameters: *prompt* is a string requesting that data be entered; *variable$* is a string variable that accepts the input from the prompt string, until a carriage return occurs (trailing blanks are ignored).

When LINE INPUT is used, a question mark is not printed unless it is included in the prompt string. Enter the following lines:

```
330 LINE INPUT; astring$
340 PRINT astring$
```

Run these two lines. Notice that no question mark is printed. Make the keyboard entry shown below (in bold print), and watch your entry immediately printed—with comma, apostrophe, and period, just as you entered it.

```
RUN
Now, let's try some punctuation.
Now, let's try some punctuation.
Ok
_
```

You can escape from a LINE INPUT by pressing CTRL+BREAK. This returns you to the command level. Enter **CONT** to resume execution at the line containing the LINE INPUT statement.

PRINT, PRINT USING, WRITE, LPRINT, and LPRINT USING Statements

All of the statements discussed in this section are used to display information on the screen, or to send information to your printer. PRINT USING and LPRINT USING provide a format string used to define the format to be used for printing.

PRINT and LPRINT Statements

PRINT has been used in almost every program you have seen so far. It is the "workhorse" for putting information on the screen. LPRINT is the same as PRINT, except it sends information to a printer.

PRINT and LPRINT   **Statements**

Syntax:

PRINT [*list*][;]
or
? [*list*][;]
LPRINT [*list*][;]

Purpose: Outputs data to the screen (PRINT or ?) or to a printer (LPRINT).

Notes: If no *list* parameter is specified, a blank line is displayed. A question mark may be used in place of the word "PRINT." In this case, when the program is listed, the question mark is replaced by the word "PRINT." You may use the ALT+P combination to display the word "PRINT." LPRINT statements assume an 80-characters-per-line printer. See also WIDTH, PRINT USING, and LPRINT USING.

Parameters: *list* is a list of numeric and/or string expressions to be printed; the optional semicolon represses the normal carriage return/line feed after the last item in the list is printed. A separator (comma, blank space, or semicolon) is used between expressions in the list. Strings in a list must be enclosed in double quotation marks.

WRITE Statement

WRITE is similar to the PRINT statement, but it displays all strings with double quotation marks around them. It also displays a comma between items in the WRITE list. Table 8-2 shows examples of differences between uses of PRINT and WRITE.

Table 8-2.

Statement and Output	Comments
PRINT "Celsius:", 146 Celsius: 146	Comma separator. Space to next expression.
WRITE "Celsius:", 146 "Celsius:",146	Comma separator. Comma printed; no space.
PRINT "Celsius:"; 146 Celsius: 146	Semicolon separator. Leading blank space before 146.
WRITE "Celsius:"; 146 "Celsius:",146	Semicolon separator. Comma printed; no space.
PRINT "Celsius:" 146 Celsius: 146	One space separator. Leading blank space before 146.
WRITE "Celsius:" 146 "Celsius:" Syntax error	One space separator. Space not accepted as a separator.
PRINT "Celsius:"; SPC(5); 146 Celsius: 146	SPC(5) as separator. 5 spaces plus one before 146.
WRITE "Celsius:"; SPC(5); 146 "Celsius:", Syntax error	SPC(5) as separator. Comma as separator, but SPC not recognized.
PRINT "Celsius:"; SPACE$(5); 146 Celsius: 146	SPACE$(5) as separator. 5 spaces plus one before 146.
WRITE "Celsius:"; SPACE$(5); 146 "Celsius:," ",146	SPACE$(5) as separator. 5 spaces printed within double quotes; commas as separators.

Differences Between PRINT and WRITE Statements

WRITE   **Statement**

Syntax: WRITE [*list*]

Purpose: Outputs data to the screen.

Notes: If no *list* parameter is specified, a blank line is displayed.
When items in the list are printed, a comma separates each one.
Strings are enclosed in double quotation marks when printed.
After the last item in the list is printed, a carriage return/line
feed is inserted.

Parameters: *list* is a list of numeric and/or string expressions to
be printed. A separator (comma or semicolon) is used between
each expression in the list. Strings in a list must be enclosed in
double quotation marks.

PRINT USING and LPRINT USING Statements

PRINT USING is similar to the PRINT statement, but PRINT
USING provides a template for formatting information when it is
displayed on the screen. LPRINT USING is the same as PRINT
USING, except the information is sent to your printer.

PRINT USING and LPRINT USING   **Statements**

Syntax:

    PRINT USING *format string*; *list*[;]
    LPRINT USING *format string*; *list*[;]

Purpose: Prints information, using a specified format, to the screen (PRINT USING) or to a printer (LPRINT USING).

Notes: Three characters may be used to format a string field, as shown in Table 8-3. Special characters used to format a numeric field are shown in Table 8-4. LPRINT USING assumes an 80-characters-per-line printer. See also WIDTH, PRINT, and LPRINT.

Parameters: *format string* is a string constant or string variable consisting of special formatting characters. The *list* parameter is a list of string or numeric expressions, separated by semicolons. The optional semicolon at the end represses the normal carriage return/line feed after the last item in the list is printed.

Table 8-3.

Format Character	Result
!	Only the first character of a string is printed.
\n spaces\	2 + n characters from the string are printed. If backslashes are used with no value for n, two characters are printed. If the string is longer than the field, the extra characters of the string are ignored. If the field is longer than the string, the string is left-justified in the field, and spaces fill in the field to the right of the string.
&	Specifies a variable-length field. The string is output exactly as input.

Characters for Formatting String Fields in PRINT USING Statements

Table 8-4.

Format Character	Result
#	Represents each digit position in the number. If the number has fewer digits than positions specified, the number is right-justified in the field, and spaces fill in the field to the left of the number. A decimal point may be inserted at any position in the field. Numbers are rounded if necessary.
+	Used at the beginning *or* end of the format string. Causes the sign of the number (+ or −) to be printed before or after the number.
−	Used at the end of the format string. Causes negative numbers to be printed with a trailing minus sign (−).
**	Used at the beginning of the format string. Causes leading spaces in the field to be filled with asterisks. Also specifies positions for two more digits.
$$	Used at the beginning of the format string. Causes a dollar sign to be printed to the immediate left of the number. Also specifies positions for two more digits, one of which is the dollar sign. Numbers in exponential format cannot be used. Negative numbers cannot be used unless they have a trailing minus sign.
**$	Used at the beginning of a format string. Fills leading spaces with asterisks *and* prints a dollar sign before the number. The combined symbols specify positions for three more digits, one of which is the dollar sign.
,	A comma to the *left* of the decimal point in the format string causes a comma to be displayed to the left of every third digit to the left of the decimal point. A comma at the *end* of the format string is printed as part of the string.

Characters for Formatting Numeric Fields in PRINT USING Statements (continued on next page)

Table 8-4.

^^^^	Four carets placed after the digit position characters specify exponential format. They allow space for E + *nn* to be printed. Any decimal point must be specified. Significant digits are left-justified, with an adjustment to the exponent. One digit position is used to the left of the decimal point to print a space or minus sign, unless a leading or trailing plus sign, or a trailing minus sign is specified.
_	An underscore causes the next character to be output as a literal character. The literal character itself may be made an underscore by placing "_" in the format string.
%	A percent sign is displayed in front of the formatted number if the number is larger than the specified field. If rounding causes a number to exceed the field, the % sign is printed in front of the rounded number.

Characters for Formatting Numeric Fields in PRINT USING Statements

Table 8-5 shows some strings formatted by PRINT USING, and Table 8-6 shows some numbers formatted by PRINT USING. Experiment with PRINT USING to fully investigate the possibilities of the characters shown in Tables 8-3 and 8-4.

VIEW PRINT Statement

The VIEW PRINT statement is used to reserve an area of the text screen. You can print information that you want to be

Table 8-5.

Expressions used in these direct statements:	A\$ = "Print"
	B\$ = "Strings"

Statement	*Output*
PRINT USING "!"; A$; B$	PS
PRINT USING "\\\\"; A$; B$	PrSt
PRINT USING "\ \"; A$; B$	PrintStrin
PRINT USING "\ \"; A$; B$	Print Strings
PRINT USING "\ \"; A$; B$; "!"	Print Strings!
PRINT USING "&"; A$; B$	PrintStrings
PRINT USING "&"; A$; B$; "&\!"	PrintStrings&\!

Examples of Strings Formatted with PRINT USING Statements

Table 8-6.

Numbers used in these direct statements:	n = 3.14159
	d = 15487.8

Statement	*Output*
PRINT USING "##.##"; n / 10	0.31
PRINT USING "##.###"; d	%15487.800
PRINT USING "+#####.#"; n; d	+3.1+15487.8
PRINT USING "#####.##"; d	15487.80
PRINT USING "-#.#####"; n	-3.14159
PRINT USING "**###.##"; n	****3.14
PRINT USING "$$#####,.##"; d	$15,487.80
PRINT USING "##.###^^^^"; n	3.142E+00
PRINT USING "#####.##^^^^"; d	1548.78E+01
PRINT USING "##.#####^^^^"; d	1.54878E+04
PRINT USING "_$#####,.##"; d	$15,487.80

Examples of Numeric Strings Formatted with PRINT USING Statements

undisturbed in one section of the screen. Then define a second area of the screen as a window, with VIEW PRINT. The window can be accessed in subsequent PRINT statements, but the lines in the reserved area cannot be accessed by the cursor and do not scroll.

VIEW PRINT   **Statement**

Syntax: VIEW PRINT [*top line* TO *bottom line*]

Purpose: Sets boundaries for the text window, so that subsequent PRINT statements do not disturb the rest of the screen.

Notes: If the *top line* and *bottom line* parameters are not specified, the entire screen area becomes the text window. Lines 1 to 24 are considered the entire screen by default. Line 25 is not normally used.

Parameters: *top line* is an expression that evaluates to a positive integer greater than or equal to 1 — the first line of the defined text window; *bottom line* — the last line of the text window — is an expression that evaluates to a positive integer greater than or equal to the value of the top line.

Any CLS, LOCATE, PRINT, or SCREEN statements used after a VIEW PRINT statement has been executed will affect only the text window defined by VIEW PRINT. Scrolling and cursor movement are limited to the defined text window.

In the following example, instructions to the user are printed on lines 22 and 23 of the screen. The VIEW PRINT statement then sets the text window for lines 1 through 20. Subsequent printing takes place in this text window, leaving the instructions undisturbed.

```
210 LOCATE 20, 2: PRINT STRING$(78, 205)
220 LOCATE 22, 1
230 PRINT "Enter a one-line string at the prompt"
240 PRINT "Press ENTER without a string to quit"
310 VIEW PRINT 1 TO 19
```

A VIEW PRINT statement with no parameters defines the entire screen as the text window. Scrolling and cursor movement are then active in the entire screen. The following line redefines the text window to be the entire screen, so that lines 22 and 23 in the foregoing example are again available for printing:

```
510 VIEW PRINT
```

You can only execute a VIEW PRINT statement when in SCREEN 0, the Text mode.

Program 8-5, Using VIEW PRINT and LINE INPUT, prints instructions for its use near the bottom of the screen. It draws a double line separator above the instructions. A VIEW PRINT statement (line 310) sets lines 1 through 19 as a text window. Your text entries are accepted by a LINE INPUT statement (line 330) and printed. A WHILE/WEND loop repeatedly accepts your entries and prints them until you press the ENTER key without typing a string. This creates a null string (""), and an exit is made from the loop. Only the text window is cleared at line 410. The computer waits at this line for another keypress before restoring the entire screen as the text window at line 510. The entire screen is cleared by line 520, and the program ends.

Program 8-5.

```
1 REM ** Using VIEW PRINT and LINE INPUT **
2 ' GW-BASIC: The Reference, Chapter 8.  File: GWRF0805.BAS
3 ' Demonstrates VIEW PRINT and LINE INPUT Statements

100 REM ** Initialize **
110 SCREEN 0: CLS: KEY OFF: DEFINT A-Z

200 REM ** Print instructions in protected area **
210 LOCATE 20, 2: PRINT STRING$(78, 205)
220 LOCATE 22, 1
230 PRINT "Enter a one-line string at the prompt"
240 PRINT "Press ENTER without a string to quit"

300 REM ** Define text window and input strings **
310 VIEW PRINT 1 TO 19: astring$ = "1"
320 WHILE astring$ <> ""
330   LINE INPUT astring$: PRINT astring$
340   PRINT
350 WEND

400 REM ** Clear text window; wait for keypress **
410 CLS: akey$ = INPUT$(1)

500 REM ** Restore full text screen and end **
510 VIEW PRINT
520 CLS: KEY ON: END
```

Using VIEW PRINT and LINE INPUT (GWRF0805.BAS)

Figure 8-5 shows a full text window just before the ENTER key is pressed at the end of an entry. Figure 8-6 shows the screen when the text scrolls up after the entry on screen line 19. When a null string is entered, the text window is cleared, leaving the double line separator and instructions at the bottom of the screen.

Enter and run the program, and type in the strings of your choice.

Figure 8-5.

```
This is the first string
This is the first string

Now, let's try one with some punctuation.
Now, let's try one with some punctuation.

LINE INPUT accepts commas and other punctuation marks.
LINE INPUT accepts commas and other punctuation marks.

Let's see if it will accept double quotes, "Will it?"
Let's see if it will accept double quotes, "Will it?"

Yes, it did.
Yes, it did.

Now, we're getting near the boundary of the text window.
Now, we're getting near the boundary of the text window.

Will it scroll this time?_
_____

Enter a one-line string at the prompt
Press ENTER without a string to quit
```

Screen from Program 8-5 before scrolling

Figure 8-6.

```
Now, let's try one with some punctuation.
Now, let's try one with some punctuation.

LINE INPUT accepts commas and other punctuation marks.
LINE INPUT accepts commas and other punctuation marks.

Let's see if it will accept double quotes, "Will it?"
Let's see if it will accept double quotes, "Will it?"

Yes, it did.
Yes, it did.

Now, we're getting near the boundary of the text window.
Now, we're getting near the boundary of the text window.

Will it scroll this time?
Will it scroll this time?

Yes, it did.  Our instructions are protected._
_____

Enter a one-line string at the prompt
Press ENTER without a string to quit
```

Screen from Program 8-5 after scrolling

Program Control

This chapter contains the GW-BASIC statements and commands that control loading, running, interrupting, and ending programs. Also included are statements and commands that display programs and filenames, and the ones that provide a connecting link between programs or program parts. The following statements and commands are included.

CALL	END	LLIST	MOTOR	SAVE
CHAIN	FILES	LOAD	NEW	SHELL
COMMON	LIST	MERGE	RUN	

END and MOTOR Statements

The END statement has been used in most of the named programs in this book. It marks the end of a program. MOTOR is listed as a reserved word but is no longer used in BASIC programs.

END Statement

An END statement may be placed anywhere in a program, but it is normally used at the end of a program. An END statement terminates a program and closes all open files.

END   **Statement**

Syntax: END

Purpose: Terminates a program and closes all files.

Notes: GW-BASIC returns to the command level after an END statement is executed.

Parameters: None.

An END statement at the end of a program is optional. However, if a subroutine follows the main part of the program, an END statement should be used after the main part of the program to prevent it from continuing into the subroutine without a GOSUB statement being executed.

After executing an END statement, GW-BASIC returns to the command level.

MOTOR Statement

MOTOR was used to turn a cassette on and off, when cassette tapes were used for saving and loading programs. Since MOTOR is no longer used, its syntax is not given.

NEW, SAVE, and FILES Commands

If you have a program in memory and want to use it at a later time, use the SAVE command before you give a NEW command. The NEW command deletes any program in memory and clears all variables. It wipes the slate clean, ready for a new program. The FILES command lets you look (from GW-BASIC) at the names of files on a disk in the specified drive.

NEW Command

NEW is entered at the GW-BASIC command level as a direct command. It clears the computer's memory in preparation for receiving a new program. It also clears numeric variables to zero and string variables to null strings. In general, NEW removes information previously set by all statements except DEF SEG and DEF USR. NEW doesn't affect the result of commands such as SCREEN or COLOR, even though it does reset the effects of program statements. Executing a NEW statement from within a program terminates that program.

NEW   **Command**

Syntax: NEW

Purpose: Deletes any program in memory and clears all variables.

Notes: NEW is entered at the command level. GW-BASIC remains at the command level after a NEW command is executed.

Parameters: None.

Access the GW-BASIC command level. Use the NEW command. Then enter the program shown in Figure 9-1. This program will be used later to demonstrate the MERGE command. Do not run the program yet, because the subroutine called at line 120 has not been added to the program. When you have entered the program, save it in ASCII format to a blank, formatted disk under the name STOCK.TEM (TEM indicates a temporary, incomplete program). Use whatever disk drive designation is appropriate to your computer, but do not forget the ASCII format designation (, A).

```
SAVE "C:\PROG\STOCK.TEM", A
```

or

```
SAVE "B:STOCK.TEM", A
```

Also, copy the subroutine file (GWRF0403.SUB) from Chapter 4 to the same disk as the temporary program (STOCK.TEM) created earlier. It is easier to merge the two programs if they are on the same disk.

Figure 9-1.

```
1 REM ** Stock Report **
2 ' GW-BASIC Reference, Chapter 9. File: GWRF0901.BAS
3 ' Use date and time stamp stock holdings

100 REM ** Initialize **
110 CLS: KEY OFF: DEFINT A-Z
120 GOSUB 1010

200 REM ** Enter data and print stock worth **
210 LOCATE 23, 2
220 PRINT "Press ENTER for new stock, ESC to quit"
230 VIEW PRINT 4 TO 20
240 WHILE akey$ <> CHR$(27)
250    akey$ = INPUT$(1)
260    IF akey$ = CHR$(27) GOTO 330
270    INPUT "Name of stock"; Stock$
280    INPUT "Number of shares "; shares#
290    INPUT "Value per share "; value#
300    worth# = shares# * value#
310    PRINT "Worth of "; Stock$; ": ";
320    PRINT USING "$$#######,.##"; worth#: PRINT
330 WEND
340 VIEW PRINT: CLS: END
```

STOCK.TEM program

SAVE Command

The SAVE command is used to save a file to a floppy disk or hard disk. Various kinds of SAVE commands were discussed in Chapter 3, "The Program Mode." Programs in memory can be run and edited, but they must be saved to disk to be made available for future use.

SAVE   **Command**

Syntax:

   SAVE *filename* [, A]
   SAVE *filename* [, P]

Purpose: Saves a program currently in memory to disk.

Notes: SAVE is entered at the command level. GW-BASIC remains at the command level after a SAVE command is executed. If neither the A nor the P option is specified, the file is saved in compressed binary format. The keyword SAVE can also be entered by pressing the F4 function key.

Parameters: filename is a string in double quotation marks (*quoted string*) or a string variable that follows DOS file-naming conventions. The *filename* specifies an optional disk drive, the name of the file, and an optional extension; the ,A option specifies that the file is to be saved in ASCII format; the ,P option specifies the file is to be saved in encoded binary format as a protected file.

After a SAVE command, a program remains in memory; therefore, you can continue to edit it. It is good practice to save programs frequently while developing and editing them, so that you always have a recent copy.

A file saved with the ASCII option (A) takes more space on a disk than the other two types of files. However, some GW-BASIC commands (such as MERGE) and some DOS commands (such as TYPE) require that the file be in ASCII format.

A file saved with the protect option (P) cannot be listed or edited.

If the extension is omitted from the filename, the extension BAS is automatically appended. If you specifically want no extension, type a period immediately following the filename.

```
SAVE "B:NOEXTEN.", A
```

DOS does not distinguish between upper- and lowercase characters in a filename. The case.bas, Case.BAS, and CASE.BAS filenames are all considered the same name. However, filenames are always displayed in uppercase.

If a file with the same name as the filename specified in the SAVE command is already in use on the disk to which the file is being saved, the existing file will be overwritten. Before saving a new program, use the GW-BASIC FILES command to check the disk for possible filename duplication.

FILES Command

The FILES command displays the names of files (in all uppercase characters) residing on the specified disk drive, as well as the number of bytes free on the disk.

FILES   **Command**

Syntax: FILES [*pathname*]

Purpose: Displays the files on the specified disk drive.

Notes: If no pathname is given, FILES displays all files in the current directory of the default drive. Subdirectories are denoted by <DIR> following the directory name. FILES is entered at the command level. GW-BASIC remains at the command level after a FILES command is executed.

Parameters: *pathname* specifies the disk drive desired and may contain question marks (?) to match any character in the filename or extension. An asterisk (*) may be used as the first character of the filename or extension to match any file or any extension.

Let's say the FILES command is executed with no parameters on a hard drive:

```
FILES
```

The hard disk in use has so many files on it that the screen is filled and scrolls by many of the first files in the list. The following FILES command will narrow down the filename search to only files with an EXE extension:

```
FILES "*.EXE"
```

Figure 9-2 shows the file list produced. Other examples of formats for the FILES command are given in Table 9-1.

The FILES command format specifying disk drive B would give the following result:

```
FILES "B:"
B:\
GWRF0403.SUB        STOCK.TEM
 360448 Bytes free
```

Figure 9-2.

```
Ok
FILES "*.EXE"
C:\
ATTRIB  .EXE        BASIC   .EXE     FC      .EXE      FIND    .EXE
JOIN    .EXE        REPLACE .EXE     SORT    .EXE      SUBST   .EXE
XCOPY   .EXE        AUTOFMT .EXE     EXE2BIN .EXE      LIB     .EXE
LINK    .EXE        SHARE   .EXE
 24795136 Bytes free

Ok
_
```

File list produced by a FILES ".EXE" command*

Table 9-1.

Command	Resulting List
FILES	All files on the current directory of the current drive.
FILES "*.EXE"	All files with extension EXE on the current directory of the current drive.
FILES "A:"	All files on drive A.
FILES "A:*.*"	All files on drive A.
FILES "C:\WORD\PW*.*"	All files in PW subdirectory of WORD subdirectory on drive C.
FILES "B:*.BAS"	All files in current directory of drive B that have a BAS extension.
FILES "B:GWRF090?.BAS"	All files in current directory of drive B that have a BAS extension and begin with GWRF090.

Examples of the FILES Command

Only two files are listed, because a new disk was prepared for the demonstrations in this chapter. We will be using these two files in the "LOAD, MERGE, and RUN Commands" section of this chapter to demonstrate merging programs.

LOAD, MERGE, and RUN Commands

LOAD is used to copy a file from disk into memory. MERGE is used to merge an ASCII file with a program in memory. RUN is used to execute a program. We will use these three commands with the two files STOCK.TEM and GWRF0403.SUB.

LOAD Command

The LOAD command is used to load a program from a disk file into memory. Optionally, you can add a parameter to run the program immediately after it is loaded.

LOAD   **Command**

Syntax: LOAD *filename* [, R]

Purpose: Loads a file from disk into memory.

Notes: LOAD is entered at the command level. GW-BASIC remains at the command level after a LOAD command (without the R option) is executed. If the R option is specified, the program is run immediately after it is loaded into memory.

Parameters: *filename* is a quoted string that follows DOS file-naming conventions. It specifies an optional disk drive, the name of the file, and an optional extension; if the extension is omitted, BAS will be used. The R option is used with LOAD to run the program immediately after it is loaded; all data files remain open while the program runs.

LOAD with the R option lets you chain programs or segments of a program together. Information can be passed between programs using disk data files. For example, the following command loads and runs the program GWRF0701.BAS. An extension is unnecessary since the file has a BAS extension. All open files and variables from the program previously used would be preserved.

```
LOAD "GWRF0701", R
```

LOAD without the R option closes all open files and deletes all variables and programs currently residing in memory before it loads the specified program. LOAD the GWRF0403.SUB file that you saved in ASCII format in Chapter 4. LOAD it without the R option, and insert the appropriate disk drive specification. The following example uses drive B:

```
LOAD "B:GWRF0403.SUB"
```

Figure 9-3 shows a LIST of the program after it is loaded. If you wish, you can delete the remarks lines 60001 through 60100 with the DELETE command.

```
DELETE 60001-60100
```

Then renumber the lines so that they match the GOSUB statement of STOCK.TEM that you saved in ASCII format earlier in this chapter. Figure 9-4 shows the renumbered subroutine. Leave the subroutine in memory until you have read the next section about the MERGE command.

Figure 9-3.

```
LIST
60000 REM ** SUBROUTINE: Date and Time Stamp **
60001 ' GW-BASIC Reference, Chapter 4. File: GWRF0403.SUB
60002 ' Saved in ASCII format.
60003 ' Use to send the date and time to the screen.
60004 ' Renumber the subroutine to fit the program
60005 ' being used.

60100 REM ** Send date and time to screen **
60110 PRINT DATE$
60120 PRINT TIME$
60130 RETURN
Ok
_
```

LIST of GWRF0403.SUB file

Figure 9-4.

```
LIST
1000 REM ** SUBROUTINE: Date and Time Stamp **
1010 PRINT DATE$
1020 PRINT TIME$
1030 RETURN
Ok
_
```

LIST of renumbered subroutine GWRF0403.SUB

MERGE Command

MERGE can be used to merge a program from a disk into the program in memory, as long as the program on disk was saved in ASCII format. Before performing the merge, make sure that no lines in the program to be merged have the same number as those of the program in memory. If any lines in the two programs have the same number, the line of the program being merged will replace the line of the program in memory.

MERGE   **Command**

Syntax: MERGE *filename*

Purpose: Merges the lines from an ASCII file into the program in memory.

Notes: MERGE is entered at the command level. After the programs are merged, GW-BASIC returns to the command level.

Parameters: *filename* is a quoted string that follows DOS file-naming conventions. It specifies an optional disk drive, the name of the file, and an optional extension. If the extension is omitted, BAS will be used.

When the MERGE command is executed, the specified disk is searched for the specified filename. When found, the program lines of the file are merged with the program lines in memory. If any lines in the file to be merged are numbered the same as those of the program in memory, the lines from the file to be merged replace the corresponding lines in memory.

If you try to merge a file that was not saved in ASCII format, you get a "Bad file mode" error. The program in memory remains unchanged.

With the renumbered subroutine (GWRF0403.SUB) in memory, merge the STOCK.TEM program with it. When the merge is complete, you have Program 9-1, Stock Report. This program allows you to display a date- and time-stamped report of your current stock holdings, which you can use to prepare periodic reports. Save it as GWRF0901.BAS. You will use it after reading about the RUN command.

RUN Command

The RUN command is used to execute a program currently in memory, or to load and run a file from a specified disk.

Program 9-1.

```
1 REM ** Stock Report **
2 ' GW-BASIC Reference, Chapter 9.  File: GWRF0901.BAS
3 ' Use date and time stamp stock holdings

100 REM ** Initialize **
110 CLS : KEY OFF: DEFINT A-Z
120 GOSUB 1010

200 REM ** Enter data and print stock worth **
210 LOCATE 23, 2
220 PRINT "Press ENTER for new stock, ESC to quit"
230 VIEW PRINT 4 TO 20
240 WHILE akey$ <> CHR$(27)
250    akey$ = INPUT$(1)
260    IF akey$ = CHR$(27) GOTO 330
270    INPUT "Name of stock      "; Stock$
280    INPUT "Number of shares "; shares#
290    INPUT "Value per share   "; value#
300    worth# = shares# * value#
310    PRINT "Worth of "; Stock$; ": ";
320    PRINT USING "$$#######,.##"; worth#: PRINT
330 WEND
340 VIEW PRINT: CLS: KEY ON: END

1000 REM ** SUBROUTINE: Date and Time Stamp **
1010 PRINT DATE$
1020 PRINT TIME$
1030 RETURN
```

Stock Report (GWRF0901.BAS)

RUN   **Command**

Syntax:

> RUN [*line number*][, R]
> RUN *filename* [, R]

Purpose: Executes the program currently in memory, optionally from a specified line number, or loads a file (program) from a disk into memory and runs it.

Notes: Both RUN and RUN *line number* start the program currently in memory. RUN *filename* closes all open files and deletes the current memory contents before loading the specified program from disk into memory and running it. The R option keeps all data files open.

Parameters: *line number* specifies at what line the program execution is to begin; if omitted, execution begins at the lowest line number of the program. The *filename* parameter is a quoted string that follows DOS file-naming conventions; it specifies an optional disk drive, the name of the file, and an optional extension. If the extension is omitted, BAS will be used. The R option keeps all data files open.

If you are using the speaker on the computer, executing a RUN command turns off any sound that is currently running. It also resets the PEN and STRIG statements to OFF.

Load Program 9-1 if it isn't already in memory. This program clears the screen and calls the subroutine to print the date and time on lines 1 and 2 of the screen. It then prints instructions for the use of the program on line 23 of the screen. After the instructions are printed, the VIEW PRINT statement at line 230 sets up a text window from lines 4 through 20, where you make your entries. This leaves the date, time, and instructions undisturbed by the scrolling area of the screen.

When you press the ENTER key, you are prompted for the name of a stock. Enter the name, and you are prompted for the number of shares. When you enter this, a final prompt asks for the price of the stock. The worth of this stock holding is then printed. Press ENTER at this point, and you get to enter information on another stock. If you press the ESC key, the text window becomes the full screen at line 340 because of a new VIEW PRINT statement. The screen is cleared, and the program ends. Figure 9-5 shows a sample output of the program.

The CHAIN and COMMON Statements

The CHAIN and COMMON statements are often used together. The CHAIN statement allows you to link two programs together,

Figure 9-5.

```
12-20-90
12:23:54

Name of stock ?     Johnson & Smith
Number of shares ? 1100
Value per share ?  13.5
Worth of Johnson & Smith:     $14,850.00

Name of stock ?     Burnam Bros.
Number of shares ? 2200
Value per share ?  13.125
Worth of Burnam Bros.:     $28,875.00

Name of stock?     Kolburn & Sons
Number of shares ? 2215
Value per share ?  9.875
Worth of Kolburn & Sons:     $21,873.13




Press ENTER for new stock, ESC to quit
```

Output of Program 9-1

and the COMMON statement lets you pass variables to a chained program.

The CHAIN Statement

If you have a very large program that will not fit into available memory, you can break it up into separate parts, under different filenames. The first part of the program can contain a CHAIN statement that will load and run the second part. The CHAIN MERGE version of the CHAIN statement allows you to alter a program during its operation.

CHAIN   **Statement**

Syntax: CHAIN [MERGE] *filename* [,[*line*][,[ALL] [,DELETE *range*]]]

Purpose: Transfers control to the program that is chained, and passes variables to it from the current program.

Notes: The program that is chained (called) must be in ASCII format if it is to be merged (see MERGE command).

Parameters: The MERGE option overlays (merges) the current program with the called program. The *filename* is the name of the program to be chained. The *line* is a line number (or expression that evaluates to a line number) in the chained program, where execution of the chained program starts; if *line* is omitted, execution begins at the first line of the chained

---

program. ALL specifies that every variable in the current program is chained to the called program; if ALL is omitted, the current program must contain a COMMON statement to list the variables that are passed. DELETE is used to delete lines that have been executed and will no longer be needed.

Use caution when using the RENUM command with a chained program. The *line* parameter in the CHAIN statement is not changed by the RENUM command, but all line numbers in the range specified by RENUM are affected.

CHAIN executes a RESTORE for the pointer in DATA statements before it runs the chained program. A READ statement in the chained program will get the first item in a DATA list. Reading *does not* then resume where it left off in the original program.

When MERGE is used in the CHAIN statement, files are left open and the current OPTION BASE setting (the lowest subscript for arrays, 0 or 1) is preserved. If MERGE is omitted, the OPTION BASE setting is also preserved.

CHAIN preserves no variable types or user-defined functions for use by the chained program. Any DEFtype or DEF FN statements containing shared variables must be restated for use in the chained program. Place user-defined functions before any CHAIN MERGE statements in the original program, or the user-defined functions will be undefined after the merge is complete.

The COMMON Statement

The COMMON statement is only used when a program is being called by the CHAIN statement.

COMMON   **Statement**

Syntax: COMMON *variable list*

Purpose: Passes variables to a chained program.

Notes: The COMMON statement is uscd along with CHAIN. The pair may appear anywhere in a program, but it is best to place them near the beginning of a program.

Parameters: *variable list* is one or more variables to be passed to the chained program; use commas to separate the variables in the list.

Any number of COMMON statements may appear in a program. However, the same variable cannot appear in more than one COMMON statement. Omit COMMON statements if you are using the ALL option in the CHAIN command.

To pass array variables, place parentheses after the variable name to indicate an array. In the following example, Fox( ) indicates that the complete array named Fox is to be passed to the called program—GWRF0909 on a disk in drive A.

```
450 COMMON alpha, beta, Fox()
460 CHAIN "A:GWRF0909"
```

After the COMMON statement specifies the individual variables (alpha and beta) and the array variables (Fox( )), the CHAIN statement is executed. It calls the file GWRF0909.BAS from disk A. Table 9-2 shows other possible forms for the CHAIN statement.

Program 9-2, Stock Entries, uses CHAIN and COMMON statements. You enter stock data (name, shares, and value per

Table 9-2.

Command and Result

CHAIN "A:GWRF0907"
  Chains file GWRF0907 from disk drive A, replacing the program
  in memory.

CHAIN "A:GWRF0906", 110
  Chains file GWRF0906 from disk drive A, replacing the program
  in memory; execution begins at line 110 of the chained program.

CHAIN "A:GWRF0909", , ALL
  Chains file GWRF0909 from disk drive A, replacing the program
  in memory; all variables are passed to the chained program.

CHAIN MERGE "A:GWRF0907", , , DELETE 210-290
  Chains file GWRF0907 from disk drive A, merging it with the program currently in memory; lines 210-290 of the original program
  are deleted from the merged program.

CHAIN MERGE "A:GWRF0903", 210, ALL, DELETE 330
  Chains file GWRF0903 from disk drive A, merging it with the program currently in memory; execution of the merged program begins at line 210; all variables are passed to the chained program;
  line 330 is deleted from the merged program.

Examples of the CHAIN Command

share) in this program. Figure 9-6 shows entries for three stocks.
The program uses COMMON at line 320 to specify three arrays
that are to be passed to the chained program.

   Program 9-3, Stock Output, uses the arrays to calculate and
print the value of each stock holding, and the total value of the
stock portfolio. Figure 9-7 shows the output of the program using
the three entries (Figure 9-6) that were made in Program 9-2.

   When the entries have been made in Program 9-2, the CHAIN
statement in line 330 automatically replaces Program 9-2 with

Program 9-2.

```
1 REM ** Stock Entries **
2 ' GW-BASIC Reference, Chapter 9.  File: GWRF0902.BAS
3 ' Create arrays of stock names, shares, and value

100 REM ** Initialize **
110 CLS: KEY OFF: DEFINT A-Z

200 REM ** Enter data **
210 INPUT "How many stocks to enter "; number
220 DIM Stock$(number), shares#(number), value#(number)
230 FOR StockNumber = 1 TO number
240    INPUT "Name of stock     "; Stock$(StockNumber)
250    INPUT "Number of shares "; shares#(StockNumber)
260    INPUT "Value per share  "; value#(StockNumber)
270    PRINT
280 NEXT StockNumber

300 REM ** Clear screen, share variables, & chain **
310 CLS
320 COMMON number, Stock$(), shares#(), value#()
330 CHAIN "B:GWRF0903"

400 REM ** Restore original screen, end **
410 CLS: KEY ON: END
```

Stock Entries (GWRF0902.BAS)

Figure 9-6.

```
How many stocks to enter ? 3
Name of stock     ? Johnson & Johnson
Number of shares ? 2045
Value per share  ? 23.5

Name of stock     ? Burnam & Sons
Number of shares ? 1050
Value per share  ? 12.675

Name of stock     ? Filbert Corp.
Number of shares ? 950
Value per share  ? 9.875
```

Entries of stock data made in Program 9-2

Program 9-3.

```
1 REM ** Stock Output **
2 ' GW-BASIC Reference, Chapter 9.  File: GWRF0903.BAS
3 ' Scan arrays of stock names, shares, and value

100 REM ** Initialize **
110 CLS: KEY OFF: DEFINT A-Z

200 REM ** Get and print data **
210 Total# = 0
220 FOR StockNumber = 1 TO number
230    worth# = shares#(StockNumber) * value#(StockNumber)
240    PRINT Stock$(StockNumber); TAB(25); shares#(StockNumber);
250    PRINT "shares"; TAB(40); "value:"; SPC(2); worth#
260    PRINT
270    Total# = Total# + worth#
280 NEXT StockNumber
290 PRINT "Total stock value: ";
300 PRINT USING "$$########,.##"; Total#
310 PRINT: PRINT "Press ENTER to continue"
320 akey$ = INPUT$(1)

400 REM ** Restore screen, end **
410 CLS: KEY ON: END
```

Stock Output (GWRF0903.BAS)

Program 9-3, which prints the final results. Since CHAIN is used without MERGE in line 330, Program 9-2 is effectively erased before Program 9-3 is called. However, the values of the variables

Figure 9-7.

```
Johnson & Johnson    2045 shares    value:    48057.5
Burnham & Sons       1050 shares    value:    13308.75
Filbert Corp.         950 shares    value:    9381.25
Total stock value: $70,747.50
Press ENTER to continue
```

Output of Program 9-3

are passed from Program 9-2 to Program 9-3 because of the COMMON statement in line 320.

There is another way to pass the variables from Program 9-2 to Program 9-3. You can eliminate the COMMON statement (line 320), and change line 330 to

```
330 CHAIN "A:GWRF0903", , ALL
```

The ALL option causes all variables (including arrays) to be passed from a program to a chained program. This is a convenient way to pass variables. However, there may be many variables in the original program that are not used in the chained program. A COMMON statement is more appropriate when the chained program only needs a few variables from the original program.

LIST and LLIST Commands and SHELL Statement

The LIST command is used to list all or part of the program currently in memory to the screen. LLIST lists all or part of the program currently in memory to a printer. The SHELL statement causes a temporary exit from GW-BASIC to DOS. You can return to GW-BASIC with an EXIT command from DOS.

LIST Command

LIST is used from the command level to list all or any part of a program to the screen, printer, or a file. You will use it often while developing, editing, and reviewing programs.

LIST   **Command**

Syntax:

LIST [*line number*][*-line number*][*,filename*]
LIST [*line number-*][*,filename*]

Purpose: Lists all or part of a program.

Notes: GW-BASIC returns to the command level after a LIST command is executed. If the *filename* parameter is omitted, the specified program lines are listed to the screen. A hyphen is used to specify a line range.

Parameters: *line number* is a valid line number within the program currently in memory; *filename* is a valid DOS filename or device name.
   If the line range is omitted, the entire program is listed. The *line number-* format lists the specified line and all higher-numbered lines. The *-line number* format lists lines from the beginning of the program through the specified line. A period (.) can be used instead of *line number* to indicate the current line. Any listing can be interrupted with CTRL+BREAK.

The LIST command with no parameters lists Program 9-2 as shown in Figure 9-8, provided the program is in memory.
   Table 9-3 illustrates possible forms of the LIST command.

LLIST Command

LLIST is similar to LIST but lists all or part of the program currently in memory to a printer.

Figure 9-8.

```
LIST
1 REM ** Stock Entries **
2 ' GW-BASIC Reference, Chapter 9.  File: GWRF0902.BAS
3 ' Create arrays of stock names, shares, and value
100 REM ** Initialize **
110 CLS: KEY OFF: DEFINT A-Z
200 REM ** Enter data **
210 INPUT "How many stocks to enter "; NUMBER
220 DIM STOCK$(NUMBER), SHARES#(NUMBER), VALUE#(NUMBER)
230 FOR STOCKNUMBER = 1 TO NUMBER
240   INPUT "Name of stock     "; STOCK$(STOCKNUMBER)
250   INPUT "Number of shares "; SHARES#(STOCKNUMBER)
260   INPUT "Value per share  "; VALUE#(STOCKNUMBER)
270   PRINT
280 NEXT STOCKNUMBER
300 REM ** Clear screen, share variables, & chain **
310 CLS
320 COMMON NUMBER, STOCK$(), SHARES#(), VALUE#()
330 CHAIN "B:GWRF0903"
400 REM ** Restore original screen, end **
410 CLS: KEY ON: END
```

LIST of Program 9-2

LLIST   **Command**

Syntax:

LLIST [*line number*][*-line number*]
LLIST [*line number-*]

Purpose: Lists all or part of a program to the printer.

> **Notes:** GW-BASIC returns to the command level after a LLIST command is executed. A hyphen is used to specify a line range.
>
> **Parameters:** *line number* is a valid line number within the program currently in memory.

The LLIST command with no parameters lists the program in memory to the printer.

Possible forms of the LLIST (along with those of LIST) command are shown in Table 9-3.

SHELL Statement

Use the SHELL statement with no parameters to exit ("shell out") from GW-BASIC to DOS, where you can execute any valid DOS command. When your DOS chores are completed, return to GW-BASIC by entering the DOS EXIT command. You can also use SHELL to load and execute another program or a batch file.

> **SHELL**   **Statement**
>
> **Syntax:**   SHELL [*string*]
>
> **Purpose:**   Loads and executes another program or batch file.
>
> **Notes:**   The program name in the string may have any extension that the DOS COMMAND.COM file supports. If no extension is given, COMMAND.COM looks for a COM file, then an

EXE file, and finally a BAT file. If a matching filename is not found with any of these extensions, a "File not found" error occurs. Any text separated from the program name by at least one space will be processed by COMMAND.COM as program parameters.

Parameters: *string* is a string expression containing the name of the program to run and (optionally) command arguments.

Table 9-3.

LIST Command	*LLIST Command*	*Listed Portion of the Program in Memory*
LIST	LLIST	Entire program.
LIST 150	LLIST 150	Line 150.
LIST 100-150	LLIST 100-150	Lines 100 to 150.
LIST 150-	LLIST 150-	Line 150 to the highest numbered line.
LIST -100	LLIST -100	From the beginning line to and including line 100.
LIST .	LLIST .	The most recently displayed line.
LIST .-200	LLIST .-200	From the most recently displayed line to and including line 200.
LIST 100-.	LLIST 100-.	From line 100 to and including the most recently displayed line.
LIST -.	LLIST -.	From the first line through the most recently displayed line.
LIST .-	LLIST .-	From the most recently displayed line through the last line.

NOTE: LIST can also be used with a device designator, as in LIST ,"SCRN:" to send the listing to the screen, and as in LIST ,"LPT1:" to send the listing to the printer.

NOTE: LLIST can be replaced with LIST if the printer device designator is appended, as in LIST 100-150, "LPT1:".

Examples of the LIST and LLIST Commands

GW-BASIC remains in memory while the SHELL command is in effect. If you use a string to load and execute another program (called a *child process*), GW-BASIC continues at the statement that follows the SHELL statement, when the child process finishes. If you use SHELL with no string, control is passed to DOS; there you may carry out any action that COMMAND.COM allows. To return to GW-BASIC, enter an EXIT command from DOS.

Suppose you have just loaded Program 9-2 (GWRF0902.BAS) and want to see if Program 9-3 (GWRF0903.BAS) is on the same disk. First, enter SHELL as a direct statement with no string.

```
SHELL
```

After the SHELL command is entered, a DOS message and prompt are displayed.

```
Microsoft(R) MS-DOS(R)  Version 3.20
(C)Copyright Microsoft Corp 1981-1986

C:\>_
```

Tell DOS to list the files on disk drive B.

```
C:\>DIR B:
```

After the directory is displayed, the DOS prompt appears again. If the directory did not include Program 9-3 (filename GWRF0903.BAS), look at another disk. When the disk containing Program 9-3 is found and is in the desired drive, you can return to GW-BASIC and run Program 9-2, which chains Program 9-3. The EXIT command returns you to GW-BASIC.

```
C:\> EXIT
```

SHELL can also be used as a statement within a program. In a program that reads in data from a disk file, you might want to first examine the directory of the disk drive to make sure the correct disk is in the drive. To do this, you could include a line in the program to "shell out" to DOS and look at the directory of the disk currently in the drive.

```
510 SHELL "DIR A:"
520 akey$ = INPUT$(1)
530 IF akey$ = "R" THEN 510
```

When these lines are executed, the GW-BASIC program is interrupted, and the directory of the disk in drive A is displayed. Then control is immediately returned to the GW-BASIC program. The program waits for a keypress at line 520. If the correct disk is not in the drive, you can switch disks while the program is halted. Press the R key to execute line 510 again, and look at the files on the new disk. Repeat the process until the correct disk is found. Then continue by pressing a key other than R.

The CALL Statement

Some tasks can be performed more efficiently in machine language than in GW-BASIC. One such task is the manipulating of individual bits or complete bytes of information stored in memory. GW-BASIC includes a CALL statement that allows you to access a machine language subroutine. The machine language subroutine must be in memory at the time it is called. The subroutine must include a machine language return instruction that will pass control back to the GW-BASIC program that called it.

CALL   **Statement**

Syntax: CALL *startvar* [(*variable1*), (*variable2*), (*variable3*), . . .]

Purpose: Calls an assembly or machine language subroutine.

Notes: You may alter strings in a machine language routine, but their lengths must not be changed. GW-BASIC cannot correctly erase strings if their lengths are modified by external routines. See also DEF SEG and VARPTR (Chapter 17).

Parameters: *startvar* is the starting memory location of the subroutine being called (as an offset to the current segment). *variable1*, *variable2*, and *variable3* are the variables or constants that are passed to the routine. These variables are separated by commas and enclosed in parentheses.

Program 9-4, Rotate Bits, includes a FOR/NEXT loop that reads each machine language instruction byte from the DATA statements (in hexadecimal format) and pokes it into memory. When you enter an integer at the prompt, the subroutine is called. It rotates the bits of the lower byte one place to the right. The upper byte of the integer remains as it was. The last machine language instruction returns control to the main program at the instruction following the CALL statement.

One parameter (*Anumber*) is passed to the subroutine. The machine language subroutine is stored in the bytes reserved for the array named Rotate. The starting address of this array is obtained from VARPTR(Rotate(0)). See Chapter 17, "Memory Access and Control," for more information on VARPTR. Line 320 calls the Rotate subroutine, passing *Anumber,* which is your entry.

Program 9-4.

```
1 REM ** Rotate Bits **
2 ' GW-BASIC Reference, Chapter 9.  File: GWRF0904.BAS
3 ' Enters and runs a machine language program

100 REM ** Initialize **
110 CLS: KEY OFF: DEFINT A-Z
120 Anumber = 0: Bite = 0: count = 0
130 DEF SEG : DIM ByteHold(7)
140 Rotate = VARPTR(ByteHold(0))

200 REM ** Read and store subroutine **
210 FOR count = 0 TO 15
220    READ Bite: POKE Rotate + count, Bite
230 NEXT count
240 DATA &H55, &H8B, &HEC, &H8B
250 DATA &H76, &H06, &H8B, &H04
260 DATA &HD0, &HC8, &H89, &H04
270 DATA &H5D, &HCA, &H02, &H00

300 REM ** Enter, rotate, and print integer, then end **
310 INPUT "Enter an integer (between 1 and 255): "; Anumber
320 CALL Rotate(Anumber)
330 PRINT "The result is: "; Anumber
340 END
```

Rotate Bits (GWRF0904.BAS)

Program 9-4 uses a CALL statement to access the simple machine language subroutine. The subroutine rotates (to the right) the lower eight bits of an integer stored in memory. The rightmost bit is rotated to the leftmost position of the lower eight bits. Integers are stored (in binary format) in memory as two bytes. This program requests an entry between 1 and 255, so that the upper eight bits of the two bytes will be zero. If the number entered is an even integer in this range, rotating the lower bits one place to the right in effect divides the number by two.

For example, the number 50 is stored in binary format as

Upper byte   Lower byte
00000000   00110010

            / \ \
          32   16   2

Decimal equivalent = 32 + 16 + 2 = 50

After the subroutine has rotated the lower eight bits, the integer is changed to

Upper byte   Rotated lower byte
00000000   00011001

            / \ \
        16   8   1

Decimal equivalent = 16 + 8 + 1 = 25

A run of Program 9-4 verifies the old and new values of the integer that is entered.

```
RUN
Enter an integer: 50
The result is: 25
Ok
_
```

If you enter an odd integer, the results may seem very strange to you. Enter 25; the result of this entry is 140. The binary form of the decimal number 25 has a 1 in the rightmost position, as shown in the preceding result. This bit will be rotated to the leftmost position. The other seven bits in the lower byte move to the right one place.

Before rotation, this is expressed as

Upper byte   Lower byte
00000000   00011001

                    / \ \
                16 8 1

Decimal equivalent = 16 + 8 + 1 = 25

After rotation, this changes to

Upper byte   Rotated lower byte
00000000   10001100

            / / \
       128 8   4

Decimal equivalent = 128 + 8 + 4 = 140

The result (when 25 is entered) is 140, because the rotation of the bits is interpreted as 128 + 8 + 4.

The computer performs arithmetic by manipulating bits in this and other ways. Machine language algorithms that perform arithmetic are complicated, and assembly and machine language are not discussed in detail in this book. Appendix F, "Assembly Language Use," gives some assembly language subroutine uses.

It is beyond the scope of this book to describe in detail how the computer handles numbers. Whenever possible, experiment with formats for GW-BASIC statements and functions until you feel comfortable using them. Use Program 9-4 to experiment with rotating the lower bits of an integer. Try integers outside the suggested range (2-255). If you get some strange results, try converting the decimal results to binary. Also try entering negative integers, and even nonintegers.

10

Editing

This chapter discusses the commands and statements that allow you to create and edit your programs. You saw several of these in Chapter 4, but they are presented more formally in this chapter. Here are the commands and statements covered in this chapter.

AUTO	DELETE	RENUM	TROFF
CONT	EDIT	STOP	TRON

While typing a program line (before pressing the ENTER key), you can make small editing changes with the BACKSPACE and then the DELETE key, or with the CTRL+H key combination. You can move the cursor to the position of the error and make the necessary changes. Both these techniques were described in Chapter 4.

Table 4-1 of that chapter listed shortcuts for cursor movements, and Table 4-2 listed other editing shortcuts. You also learned to use the EDIT command in Chapter 4. Its formal syntax is given in this chapter.

Table 10-1 lists methods for deleting and inserting characters in the Overtype and Insert edit modes.

Sometimes you will want to delete an entire line or several lines. A single line can be deleted by entering only its line number and pressing the ENTER key. GW-BASIC's DELETE command can delete a single line, several consecutively numbered lines, or even a complete program.

Table 10-1.

Action	Method
Replace characters	Type over the characters in the Overtype edit mode.
Delete characters to left of cursor	Use BACKSPACE key or CTRL+H in Overtype or Insert edit mode.
Delete characters at the cursor	Use DELETE key in Overtype or Insert edit mode.
Delete characters to the end of a program line	Move cursor to desired position and press CTRL+END (or CTRL+E and then ENTER) in Overtype or Insert edit mode.
Insert characters at the cursor	Type while in Insert edit mode.
Add characters at the end of a program line	Move cursor to end of line and type while in Overtype or Insert edit mode.

Replacing, Deleting, and Inserting Characters

DELETE and EDIT Commands

The DELETE command is used to delete an entire line or several lines. It has a variety of possible forms. The EDIT command is used to display a single line that you want to edit, but not delete.

DELETE Command

The DELETE command is used to remove an entire line, or a range of lines, or an entire program.

Although DELETE is usually executed in the Direct mode, it can be used in a program. When it is executed in a program, the specified lines are deleted. Then the program is terminated, and cannot be restarted by a CONT command. Table 10-2 lists various forms of DELETE.

DELETE   **Command**

Syntax:

DELETE [*line number1*][*—line number2*]
DELETE *line number*

Purpose: Deletes a range of program lines or a single line.

Notes: GW-BASIC returns to the command level after a DE-LETE command is given. A period (.) may be used in place of either line number to specify the last displayed line.

Parameters: *line number1* is the first line to be deleted; *line number2* is the last line to be deleted; *line number* is the only line to be deleted.

If the parameter *line number1* is greater than the parameter *line number2,* an "Illegal function call" error occurs. The parameter *line number2* must correspond to a line number in the program. The DELETE keyword can be displayed by pressing ALT+D.

Table 10-2.

Command	*Lines Deleted*
DELETE	The entire program in memory
DELETE 210	Only line 210
DELETE .	The most recently displayed line
DELETE 240—310	All lines from 240 through 310; line 310 must exist
DELETE 250—	All lines from 250 through the end of the program
DELETE —450	All lines from the lowest-numbered line through line 450

NOTE: A period may be used in place of a line number in all these examples to specify the last line displayed.

DELETE Command Examples

EDIT Command

You can edit a single line by using LIST followed by the desired line number, moving the cursor back to the displayed line, and making your edit. The EDIT command displays the desired line with the cursor already at the first digit of the line number.

The EDIT command is usually used in the Direct mode, but can be used in a program. When it is executed in a program, the specified line is displayed. The program is terminated, and cannot be restarted by a CONT command.

If the program contains no line with the specified number, an "Undefined line number" error occurs. If a dot is used in the EDIT command in place of a line number, the most recently displayed line is printed, ready for editing.

EDIT   **Command**

Syntax:

    EDIT *line number*
    EDIT .

Purpose: Displays a program line with the cursor positioned under the first digit of the line number, ready for editing.

Notes: GW-BASIC returns to the command level after an EDIT command is given.

Parameters: *line number* is the number of the line to be displayed and edited; a period indicates the last displayed line number.

Program 10-1, Random Characters, will be used to demonstrate some uses of DELETE and EDIT. This version of the program places alphabetic and numeric characters randomly about the screen. Enter and run the program. The characters are not only randomly chosen by ASCII code, but their color and position on the screen are also randomly selected.

```
220    char$ = CHR$(INT(RND * 68) + 33)
230    kolor = INT(RND * 16)
240    row = INT(RND * 23) + 1: col = INT(RND * 39) + 1
```

Program 10-1.

```
1 REM ** Random Characters **
2 ' GW-BASIC: The Reference, Chapter 10.  File: GWRF1001.BAS
3 ' Displays random characters in SCREEN 0

100 REM ** Initialize **
110 CLS: KEY OFF: WIDTH 40: DEFINT A-Z

200 REM ** Pick random values **
210 WHILE INKEY$ <> CHR$(27)
220    char$ = CHR$(INT(RND * 68) + 33)
230    kolor = INT(RND * 16)
240    row = INT(RND * 23) + 1: col = INT(RND * 39) + 1

300    REM ** Place characters **
310    COLOR kolor: LOCATE row, col, 0: PRINT char$;
320    start! = TIMER: WHILE TIMER < start! + .25: WEND
330 WEND

400 REM ** Restore screens and end **
410 CLS: WIDTH 80: KEY ON: END
```

Random Characters (GWRF1001.BAS)

The ranges of numbers produced by these lines are

Expression	Number Range
(INT(RND * 68) + 33)	33-100
INT(RND * 16)	0-15
INT(RND * 23) + 1	1-23
INT(RND * 39) + 1	1-39

After running Program 10-1, use the following EDIT command to display line 240 for editing:

```
EDIT 240
240   row = INT(RND * 23) + 1: col = INT(RND * 39) + 1
```

Move the cursor to the *I* of INT in the expression for the row variable.

```
240   row = INT(RND * 23) + 1: col = INT(RND * 39) + 1
```

Type the number 24. Then delete all characters up to the colon.

```
240   row = 24: col = INT(RND * 39) + 1
```

Use the EDIT command again to display line 310.

```
310   COLOR kolor: LOCATE row, col: PRINT char$;
```

Move the cursor to the end of the line by pressing the END key (or CTRL+N), and delete the semicolon.

With these two changes, run the revised program. This time, the random characters are printed at line 24. Since you removed the semicolon following the PRINT statement in line 310, the characters on the screen scroll up one line each time a new character is printed. The characters seem to rise to the top of the screen and disappear.

To see a little faster action, delete line 320.

```
DELETE 320
```

This removes the time delay at line 320. Now run the program again, and watch the characters literally fly upward.

AUTO and RENUM Commands

Both of these commands were discussed previously—AUTO in Chapter 3, "The Program Mode," and RENUM in Chapter 4, "Editing and Merging Programs." AUTO is useful in creating a new program because it makes typing line numbers unnecessary. RENUM is useful when editing programs. It renumbers lines and also makes the necessary line number reference changes in statements like GOTO and GOSUB.

AUTO Command

AUTO begins numbering at the specified line number. It increments each line number by the value of the specified increment. The default value for both parameters is 10.

AUTO   **Command**

Syntax:

    AUTO [*line number*][,[*increment*]]
    AUTO .[,[*increment*]]

Purpose: Generates and increments line numbers each time you press the ENTER key.

Notes: AUTO is terminated by pressing CTRL+BREAK or CTRL+C. Then GW-BASIC returns to the command level. The period can be used in place of a line number to specify the current line number as the line on which the AUTO command begins.

Parameters: *line number* is the first line to be generated; *increment* is the number to be added to the current line number to generate the next line number.

If you follow the *line number* parameter of an AUTO command with a comma, and omit the increment, the last specified increment is used. ALT+A can be used to display the AUTO keyword. If AUTO is used in a program, the program terminates when AUTO is executed. Table 10-3 shows some examples of the AUTO command.

RENUM Command

It is good programming practice to number lines with a constant increment. However, you may find it necessary to insert a new line between two existing lines, thus voiding the constant increment. Use the RENUM command to renumber the program lines so the constant increment is restored.

RENUM   **Command**

Syntax: RENUM [*new number*],[*old number*][,*increment*]

Purpose: Renumbers program lines.

Notes: RENUM also changes all line number references following ELSE, GOTO, GOSUB, THEN, ON . . . GOTO, ON . . . GOSUB, RESTORE, RESUME, and ERL statements that specify the new line numbers.

Parameters: *new number* is the first line number to be used in the new sequence; *old number* is the number of the line in the current program where the renumbering is to start; *increment* is the increment to be used in the new sequence.

A RENUM command will not be executed if the renumbering would result in a line number greater than 65529. To demonstrate this, enter the following short program:

```
10 CLS
20 PRINT "Use RENUM"
30 END
```

Table 10-3.

Command	Starting Point and Increment
AUTO	Line 10; increment by 10
AUTO 200	Line 200; increment by 10
AUTO 300.	Line 300; increment by current value
AUTO, 5	Line 0; increment by 5
AUTO.	Current line; increment by current value
AUTO., 10	Current line; increment by 10
AUTO 100, 20	Line 100; increment by 20

NOTE: A period may be used in place of a line number in all these examples to specify the last line displayed.

AUTO Command Examples

Renumber the program with this command:

```
RENUM 65527, 10, 1
```

The program lines are renumbered as follows:

```
65527 CLS
65528 PRINT "Use RENUM"
65529 END
```

Now try to renumber beyond 65529 by entering

```
RENUM 65528, 65527, 1
Illegal function call
```

Notice that an "Illegal function call" occurs. The program is not renumbered because the third line would be 65530—out of the valid range.

Table 10-4 shows several examples of the RENUM command.

Table 10-4.

Command	*Comment*	*Result*
	Original program	5 CLS
		6 PRINT "RENUM"
		7 END
RENUM	No parameters	10 CLS
		20 PRINT "RENUM"
		30 END
RENUM 20,,5	First line 20, renumber from start, increment 5	20 CLS
		25 PRINT "RENUM"
		30 END
RENUM 400,25,15	First line 400, renumber from 25, increment 15	20 CLS
		400 PRINT "RENUM"
		415 END

RENUM Command Examples (continued on next page)

Table 10-4.

Command	Comment	Result
RENUM,,20	Same first line, renumber from start, increment 20	20 CLS 40 PRINT "RENUM" 60 END
RENUM 1010	First line 1010, renumber all lines, default increment 10	1010 CLS 1020 PRINT "RENUM" 1030 END

NOTE: Commands made and results obtained in the order in which they appear in the table.

RENUM Command Examples

STOP Statement and CONT Command

The STOP statement and CONT command are often used together. STOP interrupts a running program, and CONT continues the program's execution. In between the two, you can perform various actions.

STOP Statement

When a STOP statement is executed, open files are not closed. After STOP is invoked, you can display the values of variables, make changes to those values, and make calculations.

STOP   **Statement**

Syntax: STOP

Purpose: Interrupts a running program and returns to the command level.

Notes: STOP statements may be used anywhere in a program to interrupt a program's execution. When STOP is executed, the message "Break in line *nnnn*" is printed, where *nnnn* is the line number where the interruption occurred.

Parameters: None.

After any of these actions, you can resume the program by using a CONT command. However, if you enter or delete a program line or execute a CLEAR, MERGE, or CHAIN MERGE statement, you cannot use CONT to continue execution of the program.

You can continue the program's execution by using RUN *nnnn*, GOTO *nnnn*, or GOSUB *nnnn* (where *nnnn* is a program line number). These statements continue the program's execution at the specified line number. A RUN statement with no line number runs the program from the beginning. When a RUN or RUN *nnnn* command is used after a STOP statement, variables lose the value they had when STOP was executed. They retain their current values, however, when either the CONT command or GOTO *nnnn* is used to resume program execution after a STOP.

CONT Command

The CONT command resumes execution of a program that has been interrupted by CTRL+BREAK, a STOP or END statement, or an error. In case of an error, the error must first be corrected (without changing the program) before the program can continue.

CONT   **Command**

Syntax: CONT

Purpose: Continues program execution after an interruption.

Notes: Execution of the program continues at the point where the interruption occurred. If the interruption occurred during an INPUT statement, execution continues after the input prompt is reprinted.

Parameters: None.

CONT is useful in debugging (finding and correcting errors in programs), because it allows you to continue execution of a program interrupted by a STOP statement. STOP lets you interrupt a program at predefined points. When the interruption occurs, you can examine variables with direct PRINT statements. You can then modify variables as desired, using direct statements. Then you can continue execution at the point where the interruption took place, using CONT. You can also continue at a specified line number by using a GOTO statement with an appended line number.

If a program is modified at an interruption, the CONT command will not work.

Program 10-2, PRINT Characters, displays ASCII codes in the range 34 to 255 and the characters or shapes they represent. Without a STOP statement, so many codes would scroll quickly by on the screen that you wouldn't be able to determine what they were. A STOP statement interrupts the program after a block of 20 codes and shapes is displayed. A "Break in line 300" message

Program 10-2.

```
1 REM ** PRINT Characters **
2 ' GW-BASIC: The Reference, Chapter 10.  File: GWRF1002.BAS
3 ' Displays ASCII codes and their characters
4 ' 20 at a time using STOP between groups

100 REM ** Initialize **
110 CLS: KEY OFF: WIDTH 40: DEFINT A-Z

200 REM ** Outer loop codes 34 to 255 **
210 FOR code = 34 TO 234 STEP 20
220   CLS: LOCATE 2, 5: lyne = 2
230   PRINT "Code"; SPC(3); "Char"; SPC(10);
240   PRINT "Code"; SPC(3); "Char"
250   FOR number = code TO code + 20 STEP 2
260     LOCATE lyne + 2, 5
270     PRINT number; TAB(13); CHR$(number);
280     PRINT TAB(26); number + 1; TAB(34); CHR$(number + 1)
290     lyne = lyne + 1
300   NEXT number
310   PRINT: PRINT: STOP
320 NEXT code

400 REM ** Restore screens and end **
410 CLS: WIDTH 80: KEY ON: END
```

PRINT Characters (GWRF1002.BAS)

is displayed when the STOP statement is executed. By entering a CONT command you can resume execution of the program and display the next set of 20 codes and shapes.

Figure 10-1 shows the opening screen of Program 10-2, and Figure 10-2 shows the final screen. When the CONT command is entered after the final screen, the screen is cleared and the program ends.

STOP and CONT can be used to debug programs. In Program 10-3, Temperature Conversion, the following FOR/NEXT loop

Figure 10-1.

Code	Char		Code	Char
34	"		35	#
36	$		37	%
38	&		39	'
40	(		41	)
42	*		43	+
44	,		45	–
46	.		47	/
48	0		49	1
50	2		51	3
52	4		53	5
54	6		55	7

```
Break in 310
Ok
–
```

First display of Program 10-2

reads Fahrenheit temperatures from a DATA statement and converts them to centigrade temperatures.

```
210 FOR day = 1 TO 7
220    READ TempF!
230    TempC! = (TempF! - 32) * 5 / 9
240    GOSUB 1010          'Use TempC! in a subroutine
250 NEXT day
```

The following DATA statement supplies values for the temperatures.

```
260 DATA 68.3, 72.9, 73.5, 71.8, 69.3, 69.8, 66.7
```

Figure 10-2.

Code	Char	Code	Char
234	Ω	235	δ
236	∞	237	∅
238	∈	239	∩
240	≡	241	±
242	≥	243	≤
244	⌠	245	⌡
246	÷	247	≈
248	°	249	·
250	·	251	√
252	ⁿ	253	²
254	■	255	

```
Break in 310
Ok
-
```

Last display of Program 10-2

Program 10-3.

```
1 REM ** Temperature Conversion **
2 ' GW-BASIC: The Reference, Chapter 10.  File: GWRF1003.BAS
3 ' Reads Fahrenheit temperatures and
4 ' Converts them to Centigrade

100 REM ** Initialize **
110 CLS: KEY OFF: DEFINT A-Z

200 REM ** Read Fahrenheit, convert to Centigrade **
210 FOR day = 1 TO 7
220    READ TempF!
230    TempC! = (TempF! - 32) * 5 / 9
240    GOSUB 1010
250 NEXT day
260 DATA 68.3, 729, 73.5, 71.8, 69.3, 69.8, 66.7
270 LOCATE 24, 2: PRINT "Press a key to end";
280 akey$ = INPUT$(1)
290 CLS: KEY ON: END

1000 REM ** SUBROUTINE: Print day and temperatures **
1010 PRINT day; TempC!
1020 RETURN
```

Temperature Conversion (GWRF1003.BAS)

You can use the calculated centigrade values in the subroutine called at line 240. The subroutine merely prints the day and centigrade temperature:

```
1000 REM ** SUBROUTINE: Print day and temperatures **
1010 PRINT day; TempC!
1020 RETURN
```

Suppose you were getting results that you knew were not correct, and suspected the temperature conversion calculations were at fault. You could interrupt the program with a STOP statement inserted just after the calculation at line 230.

```
235 STOP
```

Now run the program again. It stops at line 235 and delivers its prompt, "Break in 235."

In the Direct mode, print the day and each temperature.

```
Break in 235
Ok
PRINT day; TempF!; TempC!
 1  68.3  20.16667
Ok
_
```

These values look correct. Enter the CONT command in the Direct mode and repeat the process.

```
CONT
 1  20.156667          (Printed from subroutine)
Break in 235
Ok
PRINT day; TempF!; TempC!
 2  729  387.2222
Ok
_
```

Wow! That's pretty hot. There must be some mistake. The Fahrenheit temperature from which the calculation was made is too large. Check the DATA statement (line 260) while the program is stopped.

```
LIST 260
260 DATA 68.3, 729, 73.5, 71.8, 69.3, 69.8, 66.7
Ok
_
```

Note that the second value in the DATA statement is missing a decimal point. It should be 72.9, not 729. Correct the DATA statement. Because you have altered a program line, you cannot use the CONT statement at this point. Since the DATA statement now looks reasonable, however, you can remove the STOP statement at line 235, by entering the line number and pressing ENTER.

A GOTO 250 could have been used as a direct statement in place of the CONT command. GOTO 250 would skip over the subroutine call at line 240 and cause the NEXT statement of line 250 to be executed.

Leave the corrected Program 10-3 in memory, or SAVE it. It will be used again in the next section.

TRON and TROFF Commands

These two statements are used together. TRON (trace on) causes each line number to be printed as it is executed. Line numbers are printed as each line is executed until a TROFF (trace off) command is executed, or a NEW, LOAD, or CHAIN command is entered. Pressing F7 (TRON) will turn on a trace. Pressing F8 (TROFF) will turn off the trace.

TRON and TROFF   **Commands**

Syntax:

    TRON
    TROFF

Purpose: Traces the flow of program lines as they are executed.

Notes: If a trace has been activated by TRON, it is deactivated if a NEW command is executed. The line numbers are enclosed in square brackets when they are printed.

Parameters: None.

When a TRON command is executed, each line number is printed as it is executed. The line numbers are enclosed in square brackets. TRON may be executed in either the Direct or Program mode.

Load Program 10-3 again if it is not already in memory. Then add the following program line:

```
120 TRON
```

Run the program with the TRON statement at line 120. Figure 10-3 shows the output. Each line number is printed as its line is executed. Notice that the day and centigrade temperatures are printed after line 1010, which contained a PRINT statement. Also, notice that line 290 (containing the END statement) was not printed.

Run the program again. The line numbers still appear unless you have executed a TROFF statement. This can be done as a direct statement.

```
TROFF
```

Remove line 120 from the program for the next experiment.

If you suspect an error in a specific part of the program, you can place TRON and TROFF at strategic places in the program to report the program flow. If you suspect the subroutine is not being executed, for example, you can place TRON just before the subroutine is called and TROFF after the return from the subroutine.

```
235 TRON
240 GOSUB 1010
245 TROFF
```

Run the program with these additions. Figure 10-4 shows the output. Notice that only line numbers 240, 1010, 1020, and 245 are printed. The trace is not turned on until line 235 is executed. The trace is not turned off until after line number 245 has been printed and the line executed.

Figure 10-3.

```
[200] [210] [220] [230] [240] [1010] 1  20.16667
[1020] [250] [220] [230] [240] [1010] 2  22.72222
[1020] [250] [220] [230] [240] [1010] 3  23.05556
[1020] [250] [220] [230] [240] [1010] 4  22.11111
[1020] [250] [220] [230] [240] [1010] 5  20.72222
[1020] [250] [220] [230] [240] [1010] 6  21
[1020] [250] [220] [230] [240] [1010] 7  19.27778
[1020] [250] [260] [270]




Press a key to end[280]_
```

Output of Program 10-3 with TRON at line 120

You can also interrupt a running program with CTRL+BREAK, and then turn the trace on or off. Use Program 10-3 (or any other program) to experiment with TRON, TROFF, STOP, and CONT.

Figure 10-4.

```
[240][1010] 1  20.16667
[1020][245][240][1010] 2  22.72222
[1020][245][240][1010] 3  23.05556
[1020][245][240][1010] 4  22.11111
[1020][245][240][1010] 5  20.72222
[1020][245][240][1010] 6  21
[1020][245][240][1010] 7  19.27778
[1020][245]




                                  Press a key to end_
```

Output of Program 10-3 with TRON at line 235 and TROFF at line 245

CHAPTER

11

Arrays

In previous chapters, you have used simple numeric and string variables. You will learn more about *arrays* and *array variables* in this chapter. An array is a set, or collection, of related array variables. Each individual array variable is called an *element* (or *member*) of the array. An array has a name. An array variable consists of the name of the array followed by a *subscript*.

An array can be compared to a human family. A family has a last name. Members of the family (elements of the array) are named by a unique first name (subscript) and a common last name (name of the array).

The following GW-BASIC statements are discussed and used in this chapter.

DIM   ERASE   OPTION BASE   SWAP

Array Structure

You learned about numbers, strings, and variables in Chapter 5. That chapter also included a bit about array variables. You learned that an integer requires two bytes of memory for storage, a single precision number requires four bytes, a double precision number requires eight, and a string requires three bytes for overhead plus one byte for each character in the string.

Integer arrays require two bytes of memory per array element, *single precision arrays* require four bytes per array element, and *double precision arrays* require eight bytes per array element. Each element of a *string array* requires the number of characters in the string plus three bytes.

Think of an array as being stored in drawers of a cabinet. The cabinet represents the array, and each drawer in the cabinet represents one element of the array. A cabinet for single precision arrays would have drawers that hold twice as much as the drawers of a cabinet for integers. Figure 11-1 shows representations of cabinets for storing integers and single precision arrays. The arrays in the figure have five elements with subscripts 0 through 4.

A cabinet for double precision arrays would need drawers that hold twice as much as a cabinet for single precision arrays.

The arrays shown in Figure 11-1 are one-dimensional arrays. However, arrays may have more than one dimension. Figure 11-2 represents a two-dimensional array as a cabinet made up of three columns of drawers. Each row of drawers represents a row of a two-dimensional array, and each drawer in a given row represents a column of the two-dimensional array. To specify a given element, you must state both its row and its column. Therefore, these elements have two subscripts, as represented here.

ArrayName(row subscript, column subscript)

Figure 11-1.

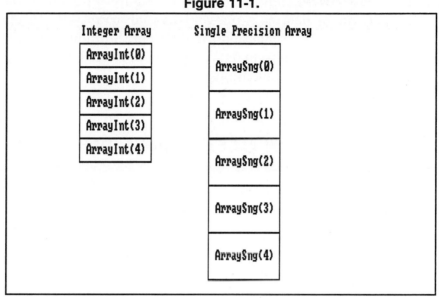

One-dimensional array

Figure 11-2.

Two-dimensional Array

Row 0, Col 0	Row 0, Col 1	Row 0, Col 2
Row 1, Col 0	Row 1, Col 1	Row 1, Col 2
Row 2, Col 0	Row 2, Col 1	Row 2, Col 2
Row 3, Col 0	Row 3, Col 1	Row 3, Col 2
Row 4, Col 0	Row 4, Col 1	Row 4, Col 2

Two-dimensional array

The two-dimensional array of Figure 11-2 holds the same amount of data as a one-dimensional array with 15 elements; however, the organization is different. Multidimensional arrays allow you to represent data as groups of related items. Arrays may have up to 255 dimensions.

DIM and OPTION BASE Statements

A DIM statement is used to tell the computer the maximum subscript value that an array can have. The OPTION BASE statement tells the computer whether to start numbering the elements with 0 (zero) or 1 (one). If a DIM statement is not used to dimension an array, the maximum subscript value (the default value) for the array is 10. The default value for the starting subscript (OPTION BASE) is 0 (zero).

DIM Statement

The DIM statement not only specifies the maximum subscript value that can be used for an array, but it also allocates memory space for the specified elements.

It is good practice to DIM arrays even if the default value of 10 is large enough for an array that you intend to use. With all the arrays dimensioned, you can quickly determine all the arrays that are being used in a program. Place the DIM statement near the beginning of a program. In this book, DIM statements are usually placed in the program block that initializes the screen, turns the key line off, defines the default variable type, and other house-keeping chores.

DIM **Statement**

Syntax: DIM *variable(subscripts)*[, *variable(subscripts)*]. . .

Purpose: Specifies the maximum value for array variable subscripts and allocates storage accordingly.

Notes: If an array variable is used without a DIM statement, the maximum value of its subscript is 10. If a subscript greater than the maximum value is used, a "Subscript out of range" error occurs. The DIM statement initializes all elements of numeric arrays to zero and string arrays to null.

Parameters: *variable* is the name of the array being dimensioned; *subscripts* are numerical expressions that evaluate to an integer, indicating the maximum value to be used for the subscripts.

Dimensioning One-Dimensional Arrays The following short program sets the dimension of a one-dimensional array to 5. Therefore, it can hold six elements with the subscript 0, 1, 2, 3, 4, and 5. The array is used to hold the names and phone numbers that you enter.

```
110 CLS: KEY OFF: DEFINT A-Z
120 max = 5
130 DIM Phone$(max)
140 FOR row = 0 TO 5
150   LINE INPUT "Name and phone ? "; Phone$(row)
160 NEXT row
```

The maximum subscript (5) is assigned to the max variable at line 120. It is used to dimension the array at line 130. Each element is entered at line 150.

Enter the program and run it. Here are some sample fictitious entries.

```
Name and phone ? Thomas, Bill      123-4567
Name and phone ? Outlander, Albert 890-1234
Name and phone ? Excelaunt, Jim    567-8901
Name and phone ? Claude, Irwin     234-5678
Name and phone ? Zurbot, Zeke      901-2345
Name and phone ? Culbert, Sonny    678-9012
```

After running the program, GW-BASIC's Ok prompt and cursor reappear. At the cursor,

Type: **FOR n = 0 TO 5: PRINT n; Phone$(n): NEXT n**
and then press ENTER

These six names and phone numbers were printed for our sample.

```
0 Thomas, Bill      123-4567
1 Outlander, Albert 890-1234
2 Excelaunt, Jim    567-8901
3 Claude, Irwin     234-5678
4 Zurbot, Zeke      901-2345
5 Culbert, Sonny    678-9012
```

Once a DIM statement has been executed for an array, you cannot re-dimension the array with another DIM statement unless you first execute a CLEAR or ERASE statement. CLEAR is discussed in Chapter 17, "Memory Access and Control." ERASE is discussed later in this chapter.

For example, use the DIM statement from line 130 again by adding this line to the sample program.

```
170 max = 10: GOTO 130
```

When you run the program with this addition, you can enter the first six names and numbers as before. However, when line 170 is executed, control returns to line 130 for a second attempt at dimensioning the array. The following message appears, and the program is terminated.

```
Duplicate Definition in 130
```

Dimensioning Multidimensional Arrays An array may have more than one dimension. Continuing with our example, you could use a DIM statement to define a two-dimensional array that would contain the names as one dimension and the phone numbers as the second dimension.

Program 11-1, Using a Two-Dimensional Array, creates and prints elements of a two-dimensional array of names and phone numbers. Figure 11-3 shows a sample of both input and output

Program 11-1.

```
1 REM ** Using a Two-dimensional Array **
2 ' GW-BASIC: The Reference, Chapter 11.  File: GWRF1101.BAS
3 ' Creates and prints a two-dimensional array

100 REM ** Initialize **
110 CLS: KEY OFF: DEFINT A-Z
120 max1 = 5: max2 = 2: DIM Phone$(max1, max2)

200 REM ** Create array **
210 FOR row = 0 TO 5
220   strng$ = "Name ? "
230   FOR column = 1 TO 2
240     PRINT strng$;
250     LINE INPUT; Phone$(row, column)
260     PRINT: strng$ = "Phone ? "
270   NEXT column
280 NEXT row
```

Using a Two-Dimensional Array (GWRF1101.BAS) (continued on next page)

Program 11-1.

```
300 REM ** Print array **
310 CLS
320 FOR row = 0 TO 5
330    FOR column = 1 TO 2
340       PRINT Phone$(row, column); SPC(2);
350    NEXT column
360    PRINT
370 NEXT row

400 REM ** Wait; restore screen and end **
410 akey$ = INPUT$(1)
420 CLS: KEY ON: END
```

Using a Two-Dimensional Array (GWRF1101.BAS)

for Program 11-1. The program clears the screen between the input and output stages.

As you recall, arrays may have up to 255 dimensions. The maximum number of elements for each dimension is an integer. Since the maximum size of an integer is 32767, this value is the maximum value of each dimension.

Figure 11-3.

Input	*Output*
Name ? **Thomas, Bill**	Thomas, Bill 123-4567
Phone ? **123-4567**	Outlander, Albert 890-1234
Name ? **Outlander, Albert**	Excelaunt, Jim 567-8901
Phone ? **890-1234**	Claude, Irwin 234-5678
Name ? **Excelaunt, Jim**	Zurbot, Zeke 901-2345
Phone ? **567-8901**	Culbert, Sonny 678-9012
Name ? **Claude, Irwin**	
Phone ? **234-5678**	
Name ? **Zurbot, Zeke**	
Phone ? **901-2345**	
Name ? **Culbert, Sonny**	
Phone ? **678-9012**	

Input and output samples of Program 11-1

OPTION BASE Statement

The OPTION BASE statement specifies whether subscript values for an array will begin at 0 or 1. The default value is 0. All arrays in a program have the same minimum subscript value (0 or 1).

OPTION BASE **Statement**

Syntax: OPTION BASE *number*

Purpose: Specifies the minimum value for array variable subscripts.

Notes: The default OPTION BASE value is 0. An array subscript may never have a negative value. If you try to change the option base after any arrays are in use, an error results. Chained programs may contain an OPTION BASE statement, as long as the specified value does not change the initial setting of the program that invoked the chain.

Parameters: *number* is either 0 or 1.

The examples used so far have not had an OPTION BASE statement; therefore, the minimum subscript value for all arrays was 0. Even when the minimum subscript is zero, you do not have to use the zero subscript element. For example, the array named Phone$ in Program 11-1 did not use an OPTION BASE statement. The minimum default subscript value was 0. Thus the zero subscript was used for the row subscript but not for the column subscript.

Try placing this OPTION BASE statement at line 130:

```
130 OPTION BASE 1
```

Now run the revised program. You are immediately confronted with this error message:

```
Duplicate Definition in 130
```

If you use an OPTION BASE statement, it must be executed *before* an array is defined or used. Since the Phone$ array is dimensioned in line 120 and no OPTION BASE statement preceded the DIM statement, the default value of 0 is invoked when the program runs. Therefore, the OPTION BASE statement in the added line 130 is an attempt to change the option base, which is not allowed.

Next, delete line 130.

```
130
Ok
_
```

Move the OPTION BASE statement to the end of line 110 so that it will be executed before the DIM statement in line 120.

```
110 CLS: KEY OFF: DEFINT A-Z: OPTION BASE 1
```

Run the revised program. This time, the prompt for the first name is printed by line 240. However, the error message "Subscript out of range in 250" also appears, and the program terminates. The error has occurred at line 250, when an attempt is made to input an entry for Phone$(0,1). Since line 110 calls for the minimum subscript to be 1, the row subscript (0) is out of range.

The subscripts used to implement an array must be greater than or equal to the minimum value of the option base. They must also be less than or equal to the maximum value declared by the DIM statement.

SWAP Statement

The SWAP statement allows you to exchange the values of two variables of the same type. You may not realize the power of this statement until you attempt to write a sort routine for an array or data file.

SWAP   **Statement**

Syntax: SWAP *variable1*, *variable2*

Purpose: Exchanges the values of two variables.

Notes: Variables must be of the same type (integer, single precision, double precision, or string).

Parameters: *variable1* and *variable2* are the variables whose values are to be swapped.

As mentioned in the notes of the syntax box, any type of variable may be swapped, provided the two variables being exchanged are of the same type. If you try to swap the variables of different types, a "Type mismatch" error occurs.

Enter and run the following program segment:

```
210 Array$(1) = "Jimson": Array$(2) = "Billson"
220 PRINT "Before swap: Array$(1) = "; Array$(1);
230 PRINT SPC(2); "Array$(2) = "; Array$(2)
240 SWAP Array$(1), Array$(2)
250 PRINT "After swap: Array$(1) = "; Array$(1);
260 PRINT SPC(2); "Array$(2) = "; Array$(2)
```

This short program enters two elements into the array named Array$. It prints out the elements in the order they were entered. Next it swaps the elements, and then prints them in their new order.

When you run these six lines, the printed results are

```
Before swap: Array$(1) = Jimson  Array$(2) = Billson
After swap: Array$(1) = Billson  Array$(2) = Jimson
```

You can see that the values held by the subscripted array elements have been swapped.

Program 11-2, Sorting a Small Array, uses READ and DATA statements to enter data into a two-dimensional array named Phone$. The program uses OPTION BASE 1 to set the minimum subscript value for the elements to 1. The DIM statement specifies the variables max1 (6) and max2 (3) as the maximum subscripts that can be used for the Phone$ array.

```
120 OPTION BASE 1: max1 = 6: max2 = 3
130 DIM Phone$(max1, max2)
```

The data used in Program 11-2 is the same data used in previous examples. This time each row of the array contains three columns: last name (with an appended comma), first name, and phone number. Row 1, for example, will contain

Column 1	Column 2	Column 3
Thomas,	Bill	123-4567

After the data is read into the array, the elements are printed in their unsorted order by the following FOR/NEXT loop.

Next, the array is printed.

```
310 FOR row = 1 TO 6
320   PRINT Phone$(row, 1); SPC(2); Phone$(row, 2);
330   PRINT TAB(22); Phone$(row, 3)
340 NEXT row
```

Program 11-2.

```
1 REM ** Sorting a Small Array **
2 ' GW-BASIC: The Reference, Chapter 11.  File: GWRF1102.BAS
3 ' Creates and sorts a three-column array

100 REM ** Initialize **
110 CLS: KEY OFF: DEFINT A-Z
120 OPTION BASE 1: max1 = 6: max2 = 3
130 DIM Phone$(max1, max2)

200 REM ** Create array **
210 FOR row = 1 TO 6
220    READ Phone$(row, 1), Phone$(row, 2), Phone$(row, 3)
230 NEXT row
240 DATA "Thomas,", "Bill", "123-4567", "Outlander,", "Albert"
250 DATA "890-1234", "Excelaunt,", "Jim", "567-8901", "Claude,"
260 DATA "Irwin", "234-5678", "Zurbol,", "Zeke", "901-2345"
270 DATA "Culbert,", "Sonny", "678-9012"

300 REM ** Print unsorted array **
310 FOR row = 1 TO 6
320    PRINT Phone$(row, 1); SPC(2); Phone$(row, 2);
330    PRINT TAB(22); Phone$(row, 3)
340 NEXT row

400 REM ** Sort array **
410 top = 1: bottom = max1
420 WHILE top < bottom
430    FOR pr = bottom TO top + 1 STEP -1
440      IF Phone$(pr, 1) < Phone$(pr - 1, 1) THEN GOSUB 1010
450    NEXT pr
460    top = top + 1
470 WEND

500 REM ** Print sorted array **
510 PRINT
520 FOR row = 1 TO 6
530    PRINT Phone$(row, 1); SPC(2); Phone$(row, 2);
540    PRINT TAB(22); Phone$(row, 3)
550 NEXT row
```

Sorting a Small Array (GWRF1102.BAS) (continued on next page)

Program 11-2.

```
600 REM ** Wait; restore screen and end **
610 akey$ = INPUT$(1)
620 CLS: KEY ON: END

1000 REM ** SUBROUTINE: Swap elements **
1010 FOR col = 1 TO 3
1020   SWAP Phone$(pr, col), Phone$(pr - 1, col)
1030 NEXT col
1040 RETURN
```

Sorting a Small Array (GWRF1102.BAS)

The printed results are shown at the top of Figure 11-4.

After the array is printed, it is sorted alphabetically using the last name of each person. Thus the sort key for the sort is the person's last name. The array is sorted by an algorithm called a *bubble sort*. A bubble sort is not very efficient, but it works well on small arrays like this one. This sort gets its name from the way the

Figure 11-4.

```
Unsorted:
Thomas,   Bill        123-4567
Outlander,  Albert    890-1234
Excelaunt,  Jim       567-8901
Claude,   Irwin       234-5678
Zurbot,   Zeke        901-2345
Culbert,  Sonny       678-9012

Sorted:
Claude,   Irwin       234-5678
Culbert,  Sonny       678-9012
Excelaunt,  Jim       567-8901
Outlander,  Albert    890-1234
Thomas,   Bill        123-4567
Zurbot,   Zeke        901-2345
```

Array before and after swap

elements "bubble up" to their proper sorted position as the sort progresses. Elements are compared, two at a time. If two compared elements are already in their correct respective positions, a swap does not take place. If the two compared elements are reversed from their correct respective positions, a subroutine is called to swap the two elements.

The sort begins with a value of 1 for the variable named top and a value of 6 for the variable named bottom. A pointer (the variable pr) is used to access rows of the array. Only the last names (first column of the array) are compared.

```
420 WHILE top < bottom
430   FOR pr = bottom to top + 1 STEP -1
440     IF Phone$(pr, 1) < Phone$(pr - 1, 1) THEN GOSUB 1010
450   NEXT pr
460   top = top + 1
470 WEND
```

The swaps take place in the following subroutine lines:

```
1010 FOR col = 1 TO 3
1020   SWAP Phone$(pr, col), Phone$(pr - 1, col)
1030 NEXT col
1040 RETURN
```

Although only the last names are compared, all three columns are exchanged by the FOR/NEXT loop containing the SWAP statement.

Table 11-1 shows the order in which the element swaps take place. After the array is sorted, the final order is printed by the program as shown in Figure 11-4. To change the sort key from the person's last name to the person's first name, change line 440 to:

```
440    IF Phone$(pr, 2) < Phone$(pr-1, 2) THEN GOSUB 1010
```

Table 11-1.

Original Order	After 1st Swap	After 2nd Swap	After 3rd Swap
Thomas	Thomas	Thomas	Thomas
Outlander	Outlander	Outlander	**Claude**
Excelaunt	Excelaunt	**Claude**	**Outlander**
Claude	Claude	**Excelaunt**	Excelaunt
Zurbot	**Culbert**	Culbert	Culbert
Culbert	**Zurbot**	Zurbot	Zurbot

After 4th Swap	After 5th Swap	After 6th Swap	After 7th Swap
Claude	Claude	Claude	Claude
Thomas	Thomas	Thomas	**Culbert**
Outlander	Outlander	**Culbert**	**Thomas**
Excelaunt	**Culbert**	**Outlander**	Outlander
Culbert	**Excelaunt**	Excelaunt	Excelaunt
Zurbot	Zurbot	Zurbot	Zurbot

After 8th Swap	After 9th Swap	After 10th Swap
Claude	Claude	Claude
Culbert	Culbert	Culbert
Thomas	**Excelaunt**	Excelaunt
Excelaunt	**Thomas**	**Outlander**
Outlander	Outlander	**Thomas**
Zurbot	Zurbot	Zurbot

NOTE: Swapped pairs are in boldface.

Order of Swaps in Progam 11-2

ERASE Statement

The ERASE statement eliminates arrays so that the memory space used for the arrays may be used for other purposes. After an array has been erased, the name of the previous array may be used in a DIM statement and a new array created.

ERASE   **Statement**

Syntax: ERASE *list of names*

Purpose: Eliminates arrays from memory.

Notes: Arrays may be re-dimensioned (by a new DIM statement) after they are erased. If you attempt to re-dimension an array without erasing it first, an error occurs.

Parameters: *list of names* contains the names of the arrays to be erased.

The ERASE statement eliminates all array variables specified in the ERASE list. Several arrays can be erased by listing the arrays, separated by commas.

```
ERASE A                 (Erases the array named A)
ERASE Phone$, Address$  (Erases both Phone$ and Address$)
```

Program 11-3, Erasing an Array, creates a temporary array of numbers—in our example, the sales of the people in the previous

Program 11-3.

```
1 REM ** Erasing an Array **
2 ' GW-BASIC: The Reference, Chapter 11.  File: GWRF1103.BAS
3 ' Creates a two-dimensional and a one-dimensional array
4 ' Erases the one-dimensional array

100 REM ** Initialize **
110 CLS: KEY OFF: DEFINT A-Z
120 OPTION BASE 1: max1 = 6: max2 = 4
130 DIM Phone$(max1, max2), ArrayTemp!(max1)

200 REM ** Create array **
210 FOR row = 1 TO 6
220    READ Phone$(row, 1), Phone$(row, 2), Phone$(row, 3)
230 NEXT row
240 DATA "Thomas,", "Bill", "123-4567", "Outlander,", "Albert"
250 DATA "890-1234", "Excelaunt,", "Jim", "567-8901", "Claude,"
260 DATA "Irwin", "234-5678", "Zurbot,", "Zeke", "901-2345"
270 DATA "Culbert,", "Sonny", "678-9012"

300 REM ** Get one-dimensional array elements **
310 sum! = 0
320 FOR row = 1 TO 6
330    READ ArrayTemp!(row)
340    sum! = sum! + ArrayTemp!(row)
350 NEXT row
360 DATA 50545, 123760, 422555, 678720, 32768, 4120
370 GOSUB 2010
380 ERASE ArrayTemp!

400 REM ** Sort array **
410 top = 1: bottom = max1
420 WHILE top < bottom
430    FOR pr = bottom TO top + 1 STEP -1
440      IF Phone$(pr, 1) < Phone$(pr - 1, 1) THEN GOSUB 1010
450    NEXT pr
460    top = top + 1
470 WEND

500 REM ** Print sorted array **
510 PRINT
520 FOR row = 1 TO 6
```

Erasing an Array (GWRF1103.BAS) (continued on next page)

Program 11-3.

```
530   PRINT Phone$(row, 1); SPC(2); Phone$(row, 2);
540   PRINT TAB(22); Phone$(row, 3); TAB(32); Phone$(row, 4)
550 NEXT row

600 REM ** Wait; restore screen and end **
610 akey$ = INPUT$(1)
620 CLS: KEY ON: END

1000 REM ** SUBROUTINE: Swap elements **
1010 FOR col = 1 TO 4
1020   SWAP Phone$(pr, col), Phone$(pr - 1, col)
1030 NEXT col
1040 RETURN

2000 REM ** SUBROUTINE: Add column to Phone$ **
2010 FOR row = 1 TO 6
2020   Add$ = STR$(INT(ArrayTemp!(row) * 1000 / sum!) / 10#)
2030   Phone$(row, 4) = Add$
2040 NEXT row
2050 RETURN
```

Erasing an Array (GWRF1103.BAS)

Phone$ array. The percentage sold by each person is calculated and placed in column four of an expanded Phone$ array. The temporary array is then erased to free up the memory space it occupied.

Program 11-3 is obtained by making a few changes to Program 11-2. The REM lines 1, 2, and 3 are modified to reflect what the new program does. Line 4 adds further description.

```
1 REM ** Erasing an Array **
2 ' GW-BASIC: The Reference, Chapter 11.  File: GWRF1103.BAS
3 ' Creates a two-dimensional and a one-dimensional array
4 ' Erases the one-dimensional array
```

Line 120 increases the maximum number of columns in the Phone$ array. Line 130 adds the dimension of the temporary array, ArrayTemp!, that will be used to temporarily hold the sales values. These values will then be placed in the new column 4 of the Phone$ array.

```
120 OPTION BASE 1: max1 = 6: max2 = 4
130 DIM Phone$(max1, max2), ArrayTemp!(max1)
```

The complete 300 block of Program 11-2 is replaced by the block shown in Figure 11-5. This new block reads the values into ArrayTemp!.

Line 1010 is changed, as shown next, to swap data in the fourth column.

```
1010 FOR col = 1 TO 4
```

A new subroutine is inserted to calculate the percentage of sales for each person and add it to the Phone$ array.

```
2000 REM ** SUBROUTINE: Add column to Phone$ **
2010 FOR row = 1 TO 6
2020    Add$ = STR$(INT(ArrayTemp!(row) * 1000 / sum!) / 10#)
2030    Phone$(row, 4) = Add$
2040 NEXT row
2050 RETURN
```

Figure 11-6 shows the output of Program 11-3.

Figure 11-5.

```
300 REM ** Get one-dimensional array elements **
310 sum! = 0
320 FOR row = 1 TO 6
330    READ ArrayTemp!(row)
340    sum! = sum! + ArrayTemp!(row)
350 NEXT row
360 DATA 50545, 123760, 422555, 678720, 32768, 4120
370 GOSUB 2010
380 ERASE ArrayTemp!
```

Block 300 code for Program 11-3

Figure 11-6.

```
Claude,   Irwin      324-5678   51.7
Culbert, Sonny       678-9012   .3
Excelaunt, Jim       567-8901   32.1
Outlander, Albert    890-1234   9.4
Thomas, Bill         123-4567   3.8
Zurbot, Zeke         901-2345   2.4
```

Output of Program 11-3

The discussion of arrays in this chapter should prepare you to learn to use data files, discussed in Chapter 14, "File and Device I/O." Most of the arrays used here have been string arrays. Numeric arrays may also be used, as in the temporary array of Program 11-3. However, when using GW-BASIC random acccss files, numeric data must be made into strings before being placed in a file. This is done with an MKD\$, MKI\$, or MKS\$ function as explained in Chapter 14.

You may search through an array for items. Program 11-4, Searching an Array, uses the array of names and phone numbers from Program 11-2. The array is created with READ and DATA statements in block 200, as before, but the blocks that printed the entire array have been omitted. The array is sorted, then a prompt is displayed to tell you how to either exit from the program or make a search. A viewport is specified in line 430 to protect the prompt information.

```
400 REM ** Search array for item **
410 LOCATE 23, 1: PRINT "Press ESC to quit, ";
420 PRINT "any other key for search.";
430 VIEW PRINT 1 TO 20
```

You are then allowed to select whether you want to search the array by last name, first name, or phone number. One subroutine is called from within a WHILE/WEND loop to change the search

Program 11-4.

```
1 REM ** Searching an Array **
2 ' GW-BASIC: The Reference, Chapter 11.  File: GWRF1104.BAS
3 ' Creates a two-dimensional and sorts it
4 ' Searches array for your entry

100 REM ** Initialize **
110 CLS: KEY OFF: DEFINT A-Z
120 OPTION BASE 1: max1 = 6: max2 = 3
130 DIM Phone$(max1, max2)
140 VIEW PRINT

200 REM ** Create array **
210 FOR row = 1 TO 6
220   READ Phone$(row, 1), Phone$(row, 2), Phone$(row, 3)
230 NEXT row
240 DATA "Thomas,", "Bill", "123-4567", "Outlander,", "Albert"
250 DATA "890-1234", "Excelaunt,", "Jim", "567-8901", "Claude,"
260 DATA "Irwin", "234-5678", "Zurbot,", "Zeke", "901-2345"
270 DATA "Culbert,", "Sonny", "678-9012"

300 REM ** Sort array **
310 top = 1: bottom = max1
320 WHILE top < bottom
330   FOR pr = bottom TO top + 1 STEP -1
340     IF Phone$(pr, 1) < Phone$(pr - 1, 1) THEN GOSUB 1010
350   NEXT pr
360   top = top + 1
370 WEND

400 REM ** Search array for item **
410 LOCATE 23, 1: PRINT "Press ESC to quit, ";
420 PRINT "any other key for search.";
430 VIEW PRINT 1 TO 20
440 WHILE akey$ <> CHR$(27)
450   PRINT "1 Last name, 2 First name, 3 Phone"
460   INPUT "Which column 1, 2, or 3"; look
470   INPUT "Enter search to match: ", Search$
480   word$ = Search$: GOSUB 2010
490   SearchU$ = wordU$: GOSUB 3010
500   akey$ = INPUT$(1)
510 WEND
```

Searching an Array (GWRF1104.BAS) (continued on next page)

Program 11-4.

```
600 REM ** Wait; restore screen and end **
610 CLS: KEY ON: END

1000 REM ** SUBROUTINE: Swap elements **
1010 FOR col = 1 TO 3
1020    SWAP Phone$(pr, col), Phone$(pr - 1, col)
1030 NEXT col
1040 RETURN

2000 REM ** SUBROUTINE: Change to upper case **
2010 wordU$ = ""
2020 FOR n = 1 TO LEN(word$)
2030    cd = ASC(MID$(word$, n, 1))
2040    IF cd < 123 AND cd > 96 THEN cd = cd - 32
2050    wordU$ = wordU$ + CHR$(cd)
2060 NEXT n
2070 RETURN

3000 REM ** SUBROUTINE: Check for match **
3010 flag = 0
3020 FOR row = 1 TO 6
3030    Match$ = LEFT$(Phone$(row, look), LEN(Search$))
3040    word$ = Match$: GOSUB 2010
3050    MatchU$ = wordU$
3060    IF MatchU$ = SearchU$ THEN GOSUB 4010
3080 NEXT row
3090 IF flag = 0 THEN PRINT "Match not found"
3100 PRINT
3110 RETURN

4000 REM ** SUBROUTINE: Print matching row **
4010 FOR column = 1 TO 3
4020    PRINT Phone$(row, column); SPC(2);
4030    flag = 1
4040 NEXT column
4050 PRINT : RETURN
```

Searching an Array (GWRF1104.BAS)

keyword to uppercase characters. Another subroutine is called to
conduct the search. The WHILE/WEND loop is shown in Figure
11-7.

Figure 11-7.

```
440 WHILE akey$ <> CHR$(27)
450   PRINT "1 Last name, 2 First name, 3 Phone"
460   INPUT "Which column 1, 2, or 3"; look
470   INPUT "Enter search to match: ", Search$
480   word$ = Search$: GOSUB 2010
490   SearchU$ = wordU$: GOSUB 3010
500   akey$ = INPUT$(1)
510 WEND
```

WHILE/WEND loop of Program 11-4

If no match for your entry is found in the "Check for search" subroutine, the message "Match not found" is displayed after the search terminates, as a result of this line:

```
3090 IF flag = 0 THEN PRINT "Match not found"
```

If a match *is* found in the subroutine, all three columns of information associated with the array row are printed, as a result of these lines:

```
4010 FOR column = 1 TO 3
4020   PRINT Phone$(row, column); SPC(2);
4030   flag = 1
4040 NEXT column
```

You do not have to enter the complete name or number. The program will match a partial entry in whichever column is selected for the search.

Some typical search request entries and search results are shown in Figure 11-8. Notice that any of the three columns (last name, first name, or phone number) may be used for the search. Your entries may be in uppercase, lowercase, or mixed upper- and lowercase. Matches can occur when an entry is not complete. Look at the third entry; the letter *C* is entered for the last name. Both last names, Claude and Culbert, are found.

Figure 11-8.

```
1 Last name, 2 First name, 3 Phone
Which column 1, 2, or 3? 1
Enter search to match: Thomas
Thomas,  Bill  123-4567

1 Last name, 2 First name, 3 Phone
Which column 1, 2, or 3? 2
Enter search to match: JIM
Excelaunt,  Jim  567-8901

1 Last name, 2 First name, 3 Phone
Which column 1, 2, or 3? 1
Enter search to match: C
Claude,  Irwin  234-5678
Culbert,  Sonny  678-9012

1 Last name, 2 First name, 3 Phone
Which column 1, 2, or 3? 3
Enter search to match: 345
Match not found

1 Last name, 2 First name, 3 Phone
Which column 1, 2, or 3? 3
Enter search to match: 901
Zurbot,  Zeke  901-2345

1 Last name, 2 First name, 3 Phone
Which column 1, 2, or 3? 2
Enter search to match: Outlander
Match not found
```

Typical search requests and results of Program 11-4

Alter the DATA statements and array sizes to create, sort, and search your own arrays. You can also use INPUT statements to enter the array data. If you happen to have a data file that is appropriate, read the data from that file into an array, and sort and search it.

Numeric Functions and Machine Language Subroutines

Functions related to numeric expressions are discussed in this chapter. You have already seen a few of them (such as INT and RND) used in programs in other chapters. In addition to these numeric functions, user functions and machine language subroutines are also discussed. Here are the functions and machine language subroutine statements used in this chapter.

ABS	DEF USR	LOG	SIN
ATN	EXP	RANDOMIZE	SQR
COS	FIX	RND	TAN
DEF FN	INT	SGN	USR

GW-BASIC has a rich repertoire of built-in functions: *numeric functions* and *string functions*. A *function* is a keyword that, when used, returns a value; this value is the result that has been computed by the function. The value of a numeric function is a number; the value of a string function is a string. In other words, a numeric function returns a numeric value, and a string function returns a string value. String function names, like string variable names, end with a dollar sign ($).

Numeric functions return a number in single precision form, unless you have used the /d switch when starting up GW-BASIC. To produce double precision results for these functions, enter the name of your GW-BASIC at the command line, and follow it with **/d**.

```
C:\>GW-BASIC /d
```

Approximately 3000 bytes of additional memory space is used to provide double precision results for ATN, COS, EXP, LOG, SIN, SQR, and TAN. If a program requires the /d switch, the requirement should be well documented in the program's REM statements and/or the opening display screen.

Some functions require arguments; others do not. An *argument* is a number or string on which the function operates to produce the value of the function.

The simplest type of function is one that does not require an argument. You have already used this type of function. For example, TIMER is a numeric function that does not require an argument. INKEY$ is a string function that does not require an argument. RND is a numeric function that can be used with or without an argument. SQR is a numeric function that requires an argument.

SQR Function

The SQR function returns the square root of a numeric expression. The numeric expression is the argument. Consider this example:

If 3 ^ 2 = 9, then SQR(9) = 3

In this example, 9 is the argument of SQR, and 3 is the result produced. Here is the SQR function using the symbolism of mathematics.

$$\sqrt{9} = 3$$

SQR   **Function**

Syntax: SQR(*expression*)

Purpose: Returns the square root of its argument, which is a numerical expression.

Notes: The value of *expression* must be greater than or equal to zero. A negative argument causes an "Illegal function call" error message. SQR is calculated to single precision unless the /d switch is used at GW-BASIC startup.

Parameters: *expression* is a numeric expression greater than or equal to zero.

A typical use of the SQR function is to find the length of a line. If one end of a line has the coordinates x1, y1, and the other end has the coordinates x2, y2, then the length of the line is calculated as follows:

length of line = SQR((x2 − x1) ˆ 2 + (y2 − y1) ˆ 2)

Here is a line in the x −y plane used in mathematics. The line has the endpoints (x1, y1) and (x2, y2).

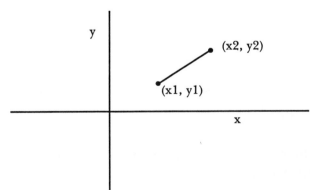

You can calculate the length of the line with the following short program:

```
10 CLS
20 x1 = 14: y1 = 8: x2 = 38: y2 = 24
30 PRINT "Length ="; SQR((x2 - x1) ^ 2 + (y2 - y1) ^ 2)
```

RND Function and RANDOMIZE Statement

The RND function produces a *random number* with a value between 0 and 1. A numeric expression can be used as an argument to produce random numbers in different sequences. When used with the RND function, the RANDOMIZE statement allows you to produce different sequences of random numbers each time a program is run.

RND Function

RND is a numeric function. Its value is a random number between zero and one. The numbers generated by the RND function are not truly random, as are numbers obtained, for example, by rolling dice. Rather, RND generates pseudorandom numbers. To see the difference between truly random and pseudorandom numbers, run the following short program at least twice:

```
10 CLS
20 PRINT RND, RND, RND, RND
```

The numbers printed by two runs are shown below. Notice that both runs produced the same set of numbers.

First run:

.1213501   .651861   .8688611   .7297625

Second run:

.1213501   .651861   .8688611   .7297625

This program uses RND without an argument. RND generates the same sequence of numbers each time you run the program. These numbers are pseudorandom; if RND generated truly random numbers, the numbers produced would be unpredictable.

RND   **Function**

Syntax: RND [*expression*]

Purpose: Returns a random number between 0 and 1.

Notes: GW-BASIC maintains a sequence of randomly ordered numbers between 0 and 1. If the *expression* parameter is omitted, the same sequence of random numbers is generated each time a program is run. The sequence can be altered by various values used for the *expression* parameter.

Parameters: *expression* is a numeric expression.

You can avoid the replication of so-called random numbers by using the RANDOMIZE statement with the TIMER function, as shown in the program that follows. RANDOMIZE TIMER is needed only once in each program. It starts the computer's random number generator at a place determined by the value of TIMER, which, as you know, is constantly changing. Thus you will see a different sequence of numbers when you run the program at different times.

```
10 CLS
20 RANDOMIZE TIMER
30 PRINT RND, RND, RND, RND
```

The results of two runs of this program are shown next. Notice that these two runs produced different sets of random numbers.

First run:

.5256403   .9975232   .9377611   .456812

Second run:

.4028528   .8815107   .8949388   .6939488

The RND function generates a random number between 0 and 1, but never 0 or 1. That is, RND is a random number greater than 0 and less than 1, or

$$0 < RND < 1$$

You can obtain random numbers in other ranges of values by multiplying RND by an appropriate number. For example, 10 * RND is a random number between 0 and 10, but never 0 or 10. That is, 10 * RND is a random number greater than 0 and less than 10, or

$$0 < 10 * RND < 10$$

Program 12-1, Random Music, makes random sounds with frequencies between 37Hz and 2037Hz. Run it several times to hear different sounds produced by a SOUND statement, discussed in Chapter 16, "Sound."

RANDOMIZE Statement

The RANDOMIZE statement used in Program 12-1 causes GW-BASIC's random number generator to start with a new number in its sequence of random numbers. This process is called *reseeding* the random number generator. When the random number generator is reseeded, the RND function produces a new sequence of random numbers.

RANDOMIZE   **Statement**

Syntax: RANDOMIZE [*expression*]

Purpose: Provides a seed value to the random number generator.

Notes: If the *expression* parameter is omitted, program execution is suspended and a prompt is displayed, asking you to provide a number.

Parameters: *expression* is a numeric expression.

If you omit the argument, the program being executed is interrupted. The computer asks you for a value to be used in the reseeding process, as shown here.

```
Random number seed (-32768 to 32767)?_
```

Entering a number that has been previously used for reseeding will repeat the previous sequence. This can be used to advantage

Program 12-1.

```
1 REM ** Random Music **
2 ' GW-BASIC: The Reference, Chapter 12.  File: GWRF1201.BAS
3 ' Plays random notes

100 REM ** Initialize **
110 CLS: KEY OFF: DEFINT A-Z
120 RANDOMIZE TIMER
130 PRINT "Random music.  Press ESC to stop."

200 REM ** Choose random frequency, play notes **
210 WHILE INKEY$ <> CHR$(27)
220    frequency = (2000 * RND) + 37    'Between 37 and 2037
230    duration = (2 * RND) + 1         'Between 1 and 3
240    SOUND frequency, duration
250 WEND

300 REM ** Restore screen and end **
310 CLS: KEY ON: END
```

Random Music (GWRF1201.BAS)

when you are debugging a program. It allows you to test the program with the same values until you find the bugs.

You can enter a number directly to avoid the prompt, as in

```
RANDOMIZE 1
```

A convenient way to automatically produce a new sequence each time a program is run (without having to enter a random number seed) is to use the TIMER function as the expression to provide the seed. This was done in Program 12-1.

```
120 RANDOMIZE TIMER
```

Program 12-2, Printing in Random Colors, uses a RANDOM-IZE TIMER statement to provide a new sequence of numbers for a COLOR statement used to change printing colors.

```
120 RANDOMIZE TIMER: OPTION BASE 1: DIM KolorWord$(15)
```

A color number from 1 through 15 is selected randomly using the RND and INT functions.

```
330    kolor = INT(RND * 15) + 1: COLOR kolor: LOCATE row, 2
```

Program 12-2.

```
1 REM ** Printing in Random Colors **
2 ' GW-BASIC: The Reference, Chapter 12.  File: GWRF1202.BAS
3 ' Prints sentences in random colors

100 REM ** Initialize **
110 CLS: KEY OFF: DEFINT A-Z
120 RANDOMIZE TIMER: OPTION BASE 1: DIM KolorWord$(15)

200 REM ** Read color names into array **
210 FOR number = 1 TO 15
220    READ KolorWord$(number)
230 NEXT number
240 DATA blue, green, cyan, red, magenta, brown, white
250 DATA gray, light blue, light green, light cyan
260 DATA light red, light magenta, yellow, bright white

300 REM ** Pick random color and print **
310 CLS
320 FOR row = 1 TO 20
330    kolor = INT(RND * 15) + 1: COLOR kolor: LOCATE row, 2
340    PRINT "The random color chosen was ";
350    PRINT KolorWord$(kolor); "."
360    start! = TIMER: WHILE TIMER < start! + .25: WEND
370 NEXT row

400 REM ** Restore normal color, go again ? **
410 COLOR 7
420 LOCATE 22, 9: PRINT "Press ESC to quit";
430 LOCATE 23, 1: PRINT "Press space bar for new selection";
440 akey$ = INPUT$(1): IF akey$ <> CHR$(27) THEN 310

500 REM ** Restore screen and end **
510 CLS: KEY ON: END
```

Printing in Random Colors (GWRF1202.BAS)

The random number produced by (RND * 15) will be between 0 and 14.99999. The INT function changes this to integers ranging from 0 through 14. Color number 0 is black. Since the background is black, a value of 1 is added to change the color number range to 1 through 15.

Instead of printing the color numbers, this program uses an array of color number names assigned to the array variables KolorWord$(number).

```
210 FOR number = 1 TO 15
220   READ KolorWord$(number)
230 NEXT number
240 DATA blue, green, cyan, red, magenta, brown, white
250 DATA gray, light blue, light green, light cyan
260 DATA light red, light magenta, yellow, bright white
```

The subscripts of the KolorWord$ elements allow the computer to pair the correct color name with the selected color number. Figure 12-1 shows a display of typical colors selected. You can't see their color in this book, but you can tell what the color is by the color name printed at the end of each line.

You saw previously that using RND with no argument and with no RANDOMIZE statement produces the same sequence of random numbers. Now, try using a zero as the argument with RND, like this:

```
10 CLS
20 FOR number = 1 TO 5
30   PRINT RND(0);
40 NEXT number
```

Run the program. Here are the numbers of a typical run.

```
.3116351   .3116351   .3116351   .3116351   .3116351
```

Using zero as the argument produces the same random number each time the RND function is executed.

Figure 12-1.

```
The random color chosen was white.
The random color chosen was blue.
The random color chosen was red.
The random color chosen was bright white.
The random color chosen was brown.
The random color chosen was red.
The random color chosen was light red.
The random color chosen was green.
The random color chosen was yellow.
The random color chosen was cyan.
The random color chosen was light magenta.
The random color chosen was light cyan.
The random color chosen was green.
The random color chosen was light red.
The random color chosen was light blue.
The random color chosen was bright white.
The random color chosen was yellow.
The random color chosen was light blue.
The random color chosen was gray.
The random color chosen was white.


           Press ESC to quit
  Press space bar for new selection
```

Results of Program 12-2

To experiment with negative values for the argument, enter and run the following program:

```
110 CLS
210 FOR num = 1 TO 20
220    ex = -1 * num: PRINT "number ="; num, "ex = "; ex;
230    PRINT TAB(25); RND(ex)
240 NEXT num
```

Table 12-1 shows the output of this program when the RND statement in line 230 uses different negative values for the *expression* parameter. Notice that when the absolute value of

Table 12-1

Output of RND Function			*See Note*
number = 1	ex = -1	.65086	(a)
number = 2	ex = -2	.65086	(a)
number = 3	ex = -3	.90086	(b)
number = 4	ex = -4	.65086	(a)
number = 5	ex = -5	.27586	(c)
number = 6	ex = -6	.90086	(b)
number = 7	ex = -7	.52586	(d)
number = 8	ex = -8	.65086	(a)
number = 9	ex = -9	.46336	(e)
number = 10	ex = -10	.27586	(c)
number = 11	ex = -11	8.836001E-02	
number = 12	ex = -12	.90086	(b)
number = 13	ex = -13	.71336	
number = 14	ex = -14	.52586	(d)
number = 15	ex = -15	.33836	
number = 16	ex = -16	.65086	(a)
number = 17	ex = -17	.55711	
number = 18	ex = -18	.46336	(e)
number = 19	ex = -19	.36961	
number = 20	ex = -20	.27586	(c)

NOTE: (a) *expression* is a power of 2
      (b) *expression* is 3 times a power of 2
      (c) *expression* is 5 times a power of 2
      (d) *expression* is 7 times a power of 2
      (e) *expression* is 9 times a power of 2

Using Negative Expressions with RND

expression is a multiple of an integer power of two, repetitions occur in the random numbers produced. When the absolute value of *expression* is not a power of two, a different random number is produced.

As you have seen, the RANDOMIZE statement can produce different sequences of random numbers more conveniently than changing the value of the expression parameter in RND.

ABS and SGN Functions

The ABS and SGN functions are closely related. The ABS function returns the *absolute value* of its argument (its *magnitude*). The SGN function returns an indication of the sign of the number.

ABS Function

The ABS function returns the magnitude of the number. In mathematical symbolism, vertical bars are used to indicate absolute value, like this:

$|number|$

If *expression* $>=$ 0 then ABS(*expression*) $=$ *expression*
If *expression* $<$ 0 then ABS(*expression*) $=$ $-expression$

For example, the ABS(7.9) equals 7.9, and the ABS(-7.9) $=$ 7.9.

ABS   **Function**

Syntax: ABS(*expression*)

Purpose: Returns the absolute value of an expression (number).

Notes: The absolute value of a number is its magnitude, regardless of whether it is positive or negative.

Parameters: *expression* is a numeric expression.

Here is a short program that allows you to enter a number. It prints the absolute value of the number and returns to line 20 for another entry. Press CTRL+BREAK to quit.

```
10 CLS
20 INPUT "Enter a number: ", number#
30 PRINT "Absolute value of"; number#; "=";
40 PRINT ABS(number#): PRINT
50 GOTO 20
```

Figure 12-2 shows results of some negative numbers, some positive numbers, and even zero.

The argument for ABS can be either a number or a numeric expression as shown here.

```
PRINT ABS(2 * 3.5)
 7
Ok
PRINT ABS(-3.5 + 1.125)
 2.375
```

Figure 12-2.

```
Enter a number: -3.5
Absolute value of -3.5 = 3.5

Enter a number: -1000
Absolute value of -1000 = 1000

Enter a number: -0.00002
Absolute value of -.00002 = .00002

Enter a number: 3.5
Absolute value of  3.5 = 3.5

Enter a number: 1000
Absolute value of  1000 = 1000

Enter a number: 0.00002
Absolute value of   .00002 = .00002

Enter a number: 0
Absolute value of  0 = 0
```

ABS function examples

SGN Function

The SGN function returns an indication of the sign of its argument. The argument can be any valid numeric expression. Thus:

If *expression* < 0, then SGN(*expression*) $= -1$
If *expression* $= 0$, then SGN(*expression*) $= 0$
If *expression* > 0, then SGN(*expression*) $= 1$

SGN   **Function**

Syntax: SGN(*expression*)

Purpose: Returns an indication of the sign of the expression.

Notes: SGN returns 1 if *expression* is positive, 0 if zero, or −1 if negative.

Parameters: *expression* is a numeric expression.

Here is a short program that you can use to experiment with the SGN function.

```
10 CLS
20 INPUT "Enter a number: ", number#
30 PRINT "The sign of"; number#; "=";
40 PRINT SGN(number#): PRINT
50 GOTO 20
```

Figure 12-3 shows some results of this program.

FIX and INT Functions

FIX and INT both return an integer for the value of a specified numeric expression. They return the same value for expressions that evaluate to zero or to a positive value, but they return different values for negative expressions.

Figure 12-3.

```
Enter a number: -3.5
The sign of -3.5 = -1

Enter a number: -1000
The sign of -1000 = -1

Enter a number: -0.00002
The sign of -.00002 = -1

Enter a number: 3.5
The sign of  3.5 =  1

Enter a number: 1000
The sign of  1000 =  1

Enter a number: 0.00002
The sign of  .00002 =  1

Enter a number: 0
The sign of  0 = 0
```

SGN function examples

If the expression evaluates to a negative number, INT returns an integer that is one less than the integer part of the evaluated expression. FIX merely truncates the number at the decimal point.

$$\text{FIX}(-5.9) = -5 \qquad\qquad \text{INT}(-5.9) = -6$$
$$\text{FIX}(-5.2) = -5 \qquad\qquad \text{INT}(-5.2) = -6$$

INT Function

INT is the function known in mathematics as the *greatest integer function*. It returns the greatest integer that is less than or equal to the value of the argument. In mathematics terminology, square brackets are used as the greatest integer function.

Math symbolism: [*number*]
GW-BASIC syntax: INT(*number*)

INT   **Function**

Syntax: INT(*expression*)

Purpose: Returns the greatest integer value of an expression.

Notes: The integer value of a number is equal to the value of *expression* if *expression* evaluates to an integer. Otherwise, the integer value is the nearest integer that is less than the value of *expression*.

Parameters: *expression* is a numeric expression.

FIX Function

The FIX function truncates the decimal part of a number and returns the integer part. When the expression is a division, the FIX function produces the same result as the MOD operator. For example:

FIX(15/4) = 3   15 MOD 4 = 3
FIX(−15/4) = −3   −15 MOD 4 = −3

FIX   **Function**

Syntax: FIX(*expression*)

Purpose: Truncates the value of an expression.

Notes: The FIX function differs from the INT function in that it merely chops off any noninteger part of the value of the expression. The only difference between the results of INT and FIX occur when *expression* evaluates to a negative number.

Parameters: *expression* is a numeric expression.

Use the following short program to experiment with the INT and FIX functions:

```
10 CLS
20 INPUT "Enter a number: ", number#
30 PRINT "INT(number) = "; INT(number#)
40 PRINT "FIX(number) = "; FIX(number#)
50 PRINT
60 GOTO 20
```

Figure 12-4 compares INT and FIX examples, using this program.

Program 12-3, Student Scoreboard, lets you enter scores for a class of students. You can choose the class size at line 210. In line 220, arrays are dimensioned to hold student names and scores.

```
210 INPUT "Number in class "; ClassSize
220 DIM Student$(ClassSize), Score!(ClassSize)
```

Figure 12-4.

```
Enter a number: -3.5
INT(number) = -4
FIX(number) = -3

Enter a number: -1000
INT(number) = -1000
FIX(number) = -1000

Enter a number: -0.00002
INT(number) = -1
FIX(number) =  0

Enter a number: 3.5
INT(number) =  3
FIX(number) =  3

Enter a number: 1000
INT(number) =  1000
FIX(number) =  1000

Enter a number: 0.00002
INT(number) =  0
FIX(number) =  0

Enter a number: 0
INT(number) =  0
FIX(number) =  0
```

INT and FIX function examples

As names and scores are entered, a running total of the scores is compiled, using sum! as a variable. The average of all scores is then computed at line 280.

```
280 Ave! = sum! / ClassSize
```

The difference between each student's score and the class average is then calculated. The SGN function is thus used to find

Program 12-3.

```
1 REM ** Student Scoreboard **
2 ' GW-BASIC: The Reference, Chapter 12.  File: GWRF1203.BAS
3 ' Prints student names, scores and deviation from average

100 REM ** Initialize **
110 CLS: KEY OFF: DEFINT A-Z
120 sum! = 0

200 REM ** Get data and calculate average **
210 INPUT "Number in class "; ClassSize
220 DIM Student$(ClassSize), Score!(ClassSize)
230 FOR num = 1 TO ClassSize
240   INPUT "Name "; Student$(num)
250   INPUT "Score "; Score!(num)
260   sum! = sum! + Score!(num)
270 NEXT num
280 Ave! = sum! / ClassSize
290 CLS

300 REM ** Calculate deviation, print results **
310 FOR num = 1 TO ClassSize
320   diff! = Score!(num) - Ave!: sign = SGN(diff!)
330   PRINT Student$(num); TAB(12); Score!(num); TAB(20);
340   IF sign = -1 THEN PRINT USING "###.#"; diff!;
350   PRINT
360 NEXT num

400 REM ** Wait, restore screen, end **
410 akey$ = INPUT$(1): CLS: END
```

Student Scoreboard (GWRF1203.BAS)

whether a student is below the average. The teacher could use this information to decide if students with scores below the class average might need special tutoring. When a student's score is below average, the difference between that student's score and the average is added to the name and score information that is printed.

```
320    diff! = Score!(num) - Ave!: sign = SGN(diff!)
330    PRINT Student$(num); TAB(12); Score!(num); TAB(20);
340    IF sign = -1 THEN PRINT USING "###.#"; diff!;
350    PRINT
```

Figure 12-5 shows the entries for a small class of ten students. Figure 12-6 shows the printed output of names, scores, and, for below-average students, the difference between the scores and the average.

Figure 12-5.

```
Number in class ? 10
Name ? Mary
Score ? 85
Name ? John
Score ? 78
Name ? Eileen
Score ? 95
Name ? Shorty
Score ? 88
Name ? Carmen
Score ? 92
Name ? Kenneth
Score ? 68
Name ? Carla
Score ? 100
Name ? Phillip
Score ? 84
Name ? Harry
Score ? 80
Name ? Sheryl
Score ? 92
```

Student name and score entries for Program 12-3

Figure 12-6.

```
Mary       85    -  1.2
John       78    -  8.2
Eileen     95
Shorty     88
Carmen     92
Kenneth    68    - 18.2
Carla     100
Phillip    84    -  2.2
Harry      80    -  6.2
Sheryl     92
```

Student score results

LOG and EXP Functions

The LOG and EXP functions are based on a system of *logarithms*. The logarithm of a number is defined in terms of a *base* and a *power*. For example:

3 to the 2nd power = 9. (*In GW-BASIC terms 3 ^ 2 = 9*)

The logarithm of 9 to the base 3 = 2.

The exponent of 2 with base 3 = 9.

There are two systems of logarithms in common use. One system is called *common* (or *Briggs*) *logarithms*, and uses a base of 10. The other system is called *natural* (or *Naperian*) *logarithms*. It uses a base denoted by the letter *e*. The numeric value of *e* is approximately 2.718282. GW-BASIC uses the natural system of logarithms based on *e*.

LOG Function

The LOG function returns the natural logarithm (base *e*) of the specified numeric expression. The numeric expression must evaluate to a number greater than zero.

LOG   **Function**

Syntax: LOG(*expression*)

Purpose: Returns the natural logarithm of an expression.

Notes: The logarithm is calculated in single precision, unless the /d switch option is used at GW-BASIC startup. The logarithm is computed to the base *e*, where *e* is approximately 2.718282.

Parameters: *expression* is a numeric expression greater than zero. A negative argument causes an "Illegal function call" error message.

The value returned by LOG(*expression*) is the power to which the value of *e* (the base of natural logarithms) must be raised to obtain the expression. For example:

```
PRINT LOG(100)
4.60517
```

This indicates that the value of *e* (approximately 2.718282) must be raised to the power of 4.60517 to obtain the value of 100 (*e* ^ 4.60517 = 100).

```
PRINT 2.718282 ^ 4.60517
99.99996
```

The value of *expression* must be a positive number, or an "Illegal function call" will occur.

```
PRINT LOG(0)
Illegal function call
Ok
PRINT LOG(-1)
Illegal function call
```

Even though GW-BASIC's LOG function uses base *e*, you can calculate the logarithm of a number to a different base. If *b* is the base of the logarithm desired,

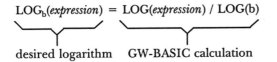

$$\mathrm{LOG}_b(\textit{expression}) = \mathrm{LOG}(\textit{expression}) / \mathrm{LOG}(b)$$

desired logarithm   GW-BASIC calculation

For example, to find the common logarithm (base 10) of 100,

$$\mathrm{LOG}\ (100) = \log(100) / \log(10)$$
$$= 4.60517 / 2.302585$$
$$= 2$$

Tables of logarithms can be found in trigonometry textbooks or in handbooks of mathematical tables and formulas. Table 12-2

Table 12-2.

LOG Statement	*Printed Result*
PRINT LOG(.001)	–6.907755
PRINT LOG(.01)	–4.65017
PRINT LOG(.1)	–2.302585
PRINT LOG(1)	0
PRINT LOG(5)	1.609438
PRINT LOG(10)	2.302585
PRINT LOG(50)	3.912023
PRINT LOG(100)	4.60517
PRINT LOG(500)	6.214809
PRINT LOG(1000)	6.907755

Examples of LOG Function

shows examples of GW-BASIC's LOG function. Figure 12-7 shows a graph of y = LOG(x).

Figure 12-7.

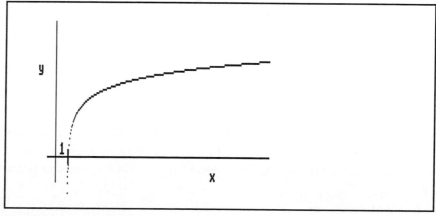

Graph of y = LOG (x)

EXP Function

The EXP function returns the value of *e* (the base used in the LOG function) to the power of the specified expression. The relationship between LOG and EXP is as follows:

LOG(*number1*) = *number2*
EXP(*number2*) = *number1*

Thus the EXP function is the inverse of the LOG function, and LOG(EXP(10)) is equal to 10.

EXP   **Function**

Syntax: EXP(*expression*)

Purpose: Returns the value of *e* raised to the power of the specified expression.

Notes: The value of *expression* must be less than 88.02969, or an "Overflow" error occurs. EXP is calculated to single precision unless the /d switch is used at GW-BASIC startup.

Parameters: *expression* is a numeric expression as described above.

The maximum value that GW-BASIC can handle is 1.701412E+38; therefore, an overflow occurs when a value greater than 88.02968 is used for the EXP *expression* parameter.

```
PRINT EXP(88.02968)
 1.701385E+38
Ok
PRINT EXP(88.02969)
Overflow
 1.701412E+38
```

To demonstrate how EXP is the inverse of LOG, try the following:

```
PRINT LOG(10)
 2.302585
Ok
PRINT EXP(2.302585)
 9.999998
```

There is a small round-off error. Here is what happens when GW-BASIC is invoked with the /d prompt. Notice that you must use the type declaration symbol (#) to declare the argument (10#) a double precision number.

```
PRINT LOG(10#)
 2.302585092994046
Ok
PRINT EXP(2.302585092994046)
 10
```

Figure 12-8 shows a graph of y = EXP(x).

Figure 12-8.

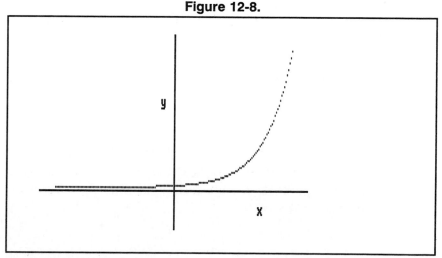

Graph of y = EXP (x)

Trigonometric Functions SIN, COS, TAN, and ATN

The trigonometric functions SIN, COS, TAN, and ATN all require that the value of the angle (used as an argument) be expressed in radians. An angle measured in degrees can be changed to radians with the following calculation:

Angle in radians = Angle in degrees * pi / 180

Thus:

pi / 180 = .01745329   (*single precision*)
         = .01745328696438513   (*double precision*)

The values returned by all these functions are single precision unless the double precision switch (/d) is used at GW-BASIC startup.

SIN Function

The sine of an acute angle in a right triangle is the ratio of the side opposite the acute angle over the hypotenuse of the triangle, as shown in Figure 12-9. This ratio is commonly written in mathematics textbooks as

$$SIN = \frac{Opp}{Hyp}$$

The value of the SIN function ranges from -1 to 1.

SIN **Function**

Syntax: SIN(*expression*)

Purpose: Returns the trigonometric sine of an angle.

Notes: The value of *expression* is an angle expressed in radians. SIN is calculated to single precision unless the /d switch is used at GW-BASIC startup.

Parameters: *expression* is a numeric expression of radian measure.

Figure 12-9.

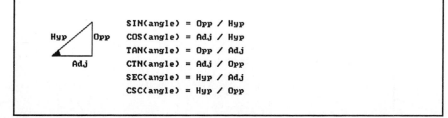

```
       /|        SIN(angle) = Opp / Hyp
 Hyp /  |Opp     COS(angle) = Adj / Hyp
    /   |        TAN(angle) = Opp / Adj
   /____|        CTN(angle) = Adj / Opp
    Adj          SEC(angle) = Hyp / Adj
                 CSC(angle) = Hyp / Opp
```

Trigonometric functions

Mathematics textbooks on trigonometry usually contain a table of sine values. See Figure 12-10 for a graph of GW-BASIC's SIN and COS functions. The two functions are scaled and plotted in the following FOR/NEXT loop:

```
210 FOR angle = -6.28 TO 6.28 STEP .025
220    sine = -(SIN(angle) * 40) + 100
230    cosine = -(COS(angle) * 40) + 100
240    col = (angle * 15) + 210
250    PSET (col, sine), 3: PSET (col, cosine), 3
260 NEXT angle
```

COS Function

The cosine of an acute angle in a right triangle is the ratio of the side adjacent to the acute angle over the hypotenuse of the triangle, as shown with the other trigonometric functions in Figure 12-9. This ratio is commonly written in mathematics textbooks as

$$COS = \frac{Adj}{Hyp}$$

Figure 12-10.

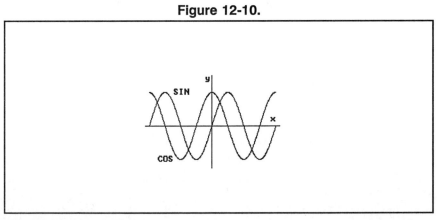

Graph of SIN and COS

The value of the COS function ranges from −1 to 1.

COS   **Function**

Syntax: COS(*expression*)

Purpose: Returns the trigonometric cosine of an angle.

Notes: The value of *expression* is an angle expressed in radians. COS is calculated to single precision unless the /d switch is used at GW-BASIC startup.

Parameters: *expression* is a numeric expression of radian measure.

Mathematics textbooks on trigonometry usually contain a table of cosine values. See Figure 12-10 for a graph of GW-BASIC's COS function.

TAN Function

The tangent of an acute angle in a right triangle is the ratio of the side opposite the acute angle over the side adjacent to the acute angle of the triangle, as shown with the other trigonometric functions in Figure 12-9. This ratio is commonly written in mathematics textbooks as

$$TAN = \frac{Opp}{Adj}$$

The value of the TAN function ranges from the minimum value to the maximum value that GW-BASIC can handle. Theoretically, the tangent of an angle can range from positive infinity to negative infinity. Therefore, an overflow can occur when the TAN function is used. See Notes in the syntax box.

TAN   **Function**

Syntax: TAN(*expression*)

Purpose: Returns the trigonometric tangent of an angle.

Notes: The value of *expression* is an angle expressed in radians. TAN is calculated to single precision unless the /d switch is used at GW-BASIC startup. If use of TAN causes an overflow, the "Overflow" error message occurs.

Parameters: *expression* is a numeric expression of radian measure.

Mathematics textbooks on trigonometry usually contain a table of tangent values. See Figure 12-11 for a graph of GW-BASIC's TAN function.

Other commonly used trigonometric functions used in mathematics are cotangent (CTN), secant (SEC), and cosecant (CSC). GW-BASIC does not contain these functions, but they can be calculated from other functions in the following way:

cotangent(*angle*) = 1 / TAN(*angle*)

secant(*angle*) = 1 / COS(*angle*)

cosecant(*angle*) = 1 / SIN(*angle*)

Figure 12-11.

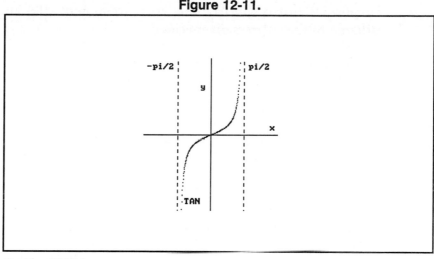

Graph of TAN

ATN Function

The ATN (arctangent) is the inverse function of TAN. The arctangent is an angle whose tangent is the specified expression. Thus:

    If TAN(*angle*) = *value*, then ATN(*value*) = *angle*

The angle returned by the ATN function ranges from −pi / 2 radians to pi / 2 radians.

ATN   **Function**

Syntax: ATN(*expression*)

Purpose: Returns the trigonometric arctangent (the angle in radians) of the expression specified.

Notes: The value of *expression* is a numeric expression. ATN is calculated to single precision unless the /d switch is used at GW-BASIC startup.

Parameters: *expression* is a numeric expression.

Mathematics textbooks on trigonometry usually contain a table of tangent values. You can look up a given angle inside these tables and find the angle that has the given tangent value.

The sine, cosine, secant, and cosecant functions also have an arc function, even though GW-BASIC does not implement them.

If SIN(*angle*) = *value*, then arcsine(*value*) = *angle*
If COS(*angle*) = *value*, then arccos(*value*) = *angle*
If SEC(*angle*) = *value*, then arcsec(*value*) = *angle*
If CSC(*angle*) = *value*, then arccsc(*value*) = *angle*
If CTN(*angle*) = *value*, then arcctn(*value*) = *angle*

Program 12-4, Random SIN and COS Starbursts, uses the SIN and COS functions to draw rays from the centers of colorful starbursts, randomly located on the screen. You can end the program by pressing the ESC key, causing an exit from the WHILE/WEND loop that produces the starbursts.

```
210 WHILE AKEY$ <> CHR$(27)
```

The INKEY$ function in line 300 also allows you to change the background color of the screen while the program is running. Press the *B* key for "Background."

```
300   akey$ = INKEY$: IF akey$ = "b" or akey$ = "B" then 120
```

Program 12-4.

```
1 REM ** Random SIN and COS Starbursts **
2 ' GW-BASIC: The Reference, Chapter 12.  File: GWRF1204.BAS
3 ' Uses SIN and COS functions to draw lines

100 REM ** Initialize **
110 SCREEN 1: CLS : KEY OFF: DEFINT A-Z: RANDOMIZE TIMER
120 BackColor = INT(RND * 15): COLOR BackColor

200 REM ** Draw Starbursts **
210 WHILE akey$ <> CHR$(27)
220    kolor = INT(RND * 4): radius = INT(RND * 5) + 3
230    col = INT(RND * 288) + 20: row = INT(RND * 158) + 20
240    StepSize! = 3.14159 / 4: finis! = 7 * StepSize!
250    FOR angle! = 0 TO finis! STEP StepSize!
260       rowpt = radius * SIN(angle!) + row
270       colpt = radius * COS(angle!) + col
280       LINE (col, row)-(colpt, rowpt), kolor
290    NEXT angle!
300    akey$ = INKEY$: IF akey$ = "b" OR akcy$ = "B" TIIEN 120
310 WEND

400 REM ** Restore screens and end **
410 CLS : WIDTH 80: CLS : KEY ON
```

Random SIN and COS Starbursts (GWRF1204.BAS)

Figure 12-12 shows typical starbursts.

DEF FN Statement

You can use the DEF FN statement to define single-line functions of your own. The DEF FN statement must define the function before it is called.

Figure 12-12.

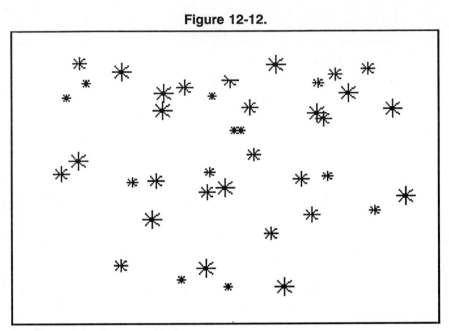

Starbursts from Program 12-4

DEF FN   **Statement**

Syntax: DEF FN*name[arguments](expression)*

Purpose: Names and defines a function that you write.

Notes: The *expression* is limited to one statement. If there is more than one argument, the arguments are separated by commas.

Parameters: *name* is a valid variable name (the name of the function); *arguments* are variable names used in the function that are to be replaced by some value when the function is called; *expression* is an expression that performs the operation of the function.

Here is a function defined by DEF FN.

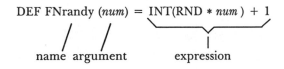

DEF FNrandy *(num)* = INT(RND * *num*) + 1

name argument   expression

This function would return a random integer in the range 1 through the value of the variable (num) used in the calling statement. After the function is defined by a DEF FN statement, it can be called by a statement that uses a variable to replace the argument. In our example, DEF FNrandy could be used to determine whether a coin toss is heads or tails.

```
350 HeadOrTail = FNrandy(2)
360 IF HeadOrTail = 1 then PRINT "Heads" ELSE PRINT "Tails"
```

The number 2 replaces the argument (num) in the DEF FN, and the result of the DEF FN expression, INT(RND * num) + 1, is assigned to the variable HeadOrTail.

A roll of a six-sided die could be simulated by

```
350 Face = FNrandy(6)
```

Here is a user-defined function named DEF FNcnt# that uses SGN, INT, and ABS to round off an amount of money (m#) to dollars and cents.

```
DEF FNcnt#(m#) = SGN(m#) * INT(100 * ABS(m#) + .5) / 100
```

Experiment with this function by entering and running the following short program:

```
10 CLS
20 DEF FNcnt#(m#) = SGN(m#) * INT(100 * ABS(m#) + .5) / 100
30 INPUT "Enter a number"; m#
```

```
40 PRINT FNcnt#(m#)
50 PRINT: GOTO 30
```

DEF USR Statement and USR Function

The DEF USR statement and USR function used together provide a way to call a machine language subroutine that currently resides in memory. DEF USR and USR are retained in GW-BASIC to provide compatibility with previous versions of BASIC. The CALL statement (discussed in Chapter 9, "Program Control") is more versatile.

DEF USR Statement

The DEF USR statement specifies the starting address of a machine language subroutine that is to be called by a statement containing a USR function.

DEF USR   **Statement**

Syntax: DEF USR[*integer*] = (*address*)

Purpose: Specifies the starting address of a machine language subroutine.

Notes: The current segment value is added to *address* to get the starting address of the user routine. See also CALL in Chapter 9, "Program Control."

Parameters: *integer* may be any digit from 0 through 9, corresponding to the digit used in the USR function; *address* is the offset address of the USR routine. If the *integer* parameter is omitted, the default is DEF USR0.

If more than ten user routines are required, a number may be reused to redefine the starting address of a previously used routine.

When a machine language subroutine is called, the GW-BASIC program execution pauses as control is passed to the subroutine. When the subroutine has finished execution, control is returned to the GW-BASIC program at the point of interruption.

The address of the machine language subroutine is given by two statements, as shown here.

```
250 DEF SEG = 0
260 DEF USR0 = 32000
```

Specifying a memory location for the computer is a complicated process. GW-BASIC addresses a memory location (called an *absolute location*) in two parts: a *segment* (or *block*) value and an *offset* value. The combination of the two gives the absolute location. You tell the computer the segment desired by using the DEF SEG statement. Zero is often used as the segment value. The offset is given in the DEF USR statement. In the above example, the offset is 32000.

USR Function

The USR function calls a machine language subroutine at the address specified in the associated DEF USR statement.

USR   **Function**

Syntax: *variable* = USR[*integer*](*argument*)

Purpose: To call a machine language subroutine.

Notes: The USR function can pass only one argument to the subroutine. Arrays cannot be passed by USR. If no argument is needed by the machine language subroutine, a dummy argument (one with no actual meaning) must be specified in the statement that calls the USR function.

Parameters: *variable* is any valid variable name; *integer* is a single digit, 0 through 9; *argument* is any valid numeric or string expression (the expression type must match the type used for the *variable* parameter).

The user function named in a DEF USR statement is called by referencing the USR function.

```
340 Circum! = pi! * diameter!
350 subx! = USR0(Circum!)
```

Here, the value of the expression inside the parentheses is passed to the user routine.

The CALL statement is more versatile than the DEF USR statement and USR function combination. CALL allows more than one argument to be passed to a machine language subroutine. Unless you need to be compatible with a previous version of BASIC, use CALL rather than the DEF USR statement and the USR function. See Chapter 9, "Program Control."

String
Manipulation

Some string statements and functions have already been discussed, such as CHR$, HEX$, OCT$, and DEFSTR in Chapter 7, "Remarks, Constants, Variables, and Expressions," and INPUT$, INKEY$, SPACE$, SPC$, and PRINT USING in Chapter 8, "Terminal I/O." This chapter contains descriptions of the statements and functions that manipulate string expressions.

Here is a list of functions and statements discussed in this chapter.

CVD	LEFT$	MKD$	RSET
CVI	LEN	MKI$	STR$
CVS	LSET	MKS$	STRING$
INSTR	MID$	RIGHT$	VAL

LEN and INSTR Functions

The LEN function is used to determine the length of a string. The INSTR function allows you to search one string to find out if it contains a second string.

LEN Function

LEN is a numeric function of a string argument. It examines a specified string and returns the number of characters in the string. LEN includes nonprinting characters and blank spaces in its count.

LEN **Function**

Syntax: LEN(*string expression*)

Purpose: Returns the number of characters in a string.

Notes: Nonprinting characters and blanks are counted. The value returned is an integer in the range 0 to 255.

Parameters: *string expression* is any valid string expression.

Enter and run the following program lines:

```
110 City1$ = "Bodega Bay, CA"
120 PRINT LEN(City1$)
```

The printed result reveals that there are 14 characters in the "Bodega Bay, CA" string.

Here is a harder one for the LEN function to handle.

```
130 City2$ = "Sebastopol," + SPACE$(2) + "California"
140 PRINT LEN(City2$)
```

City2$ is formed by catenating the "Sebastopol," string with two spaces and the "California" string. This results in one long string—"Sebastopol, California"—that has 23 characters, counting the two spaces provided by SPACE$(2).

Table 13-1 shows several examples of the LEN function.

Table 13-1.

PRINT Statement Using LEN	Printed Result	Comment
PRINT LEN("")	0	The null string
PRINT LEN(" ")	1	One space
A$ = "Count my length."		
PRINT LEN(A$)	16	16 characters counted in A$
PRINT LEN(SPACE$(255))	255	SPACE$ prints spaces

NOTE: Strings may be from 0 to 255 characters in length. Try executing this statement:

```
PRINT LEN(SPACE$(256))
```

The error message "Illegal function call." is printed.

Examples of the LEN Function

INSTR Function

INSTR is a numeric function of mixed string and numeric arguments. It has two string arguments: a "base" string that is searched, and a second string (substring) that INSTR looks for as it conducts the search. Optionally, you can specify a numeric position within the base string for starting the search.

INSTR   **Function**

Syntax: INSTR([*numeric expression,*] *string exp1, string exp2*)

Purpose: Searches for the first occurrence of *string exp2* in *string exp1* and returns the position in *string exp1* where *string exp2* is found.

Notes: The *numeric expression* must have a value in the range 1 through 255. If it is out of this range, an "Illegal function call" occurs. INSTR returns 0 if the value of *numeric expression* is greater than the length of *string exp1*, or *string exp1* is null, or *string exp2* cannot be found. If *string exp2* is null, INSTR returns the value of the *numeric expression,* or a value of 1 if no expression is specified.

Parameters: *numeric expression* (default 1), the position for beginning the search, is optional; *string exp1* is the string being searched; *string exp2* is the string sought. *string exp1* and *string exp2* may be string variables, string expressions, or string literals.

Table 13-2 shows several examples of the INSTR function.

Program 13-1, Searching Strings for Strings, allows you to input two strings. It also requests the position in the first string at which the search is to begin. The program prints the length of both strings and the result of the search.

The INSTR function is first used in line 340 to search the base string for the substring, starting at the position you entered. The value returned is assigned to the variable called found.

```
340 found = INSTR(start, BaseString$, SubString$)
```

The INSTR function is also used to determine a correct keypress in response to the prompt "Another search (Y or N) ?"

Table 13-2.

The variable String1$ is used as a base string in these examples.

```
String1$ = "This is a base string."
```

PRINT Statement Using INSTR	*Printed Result*
`PRINT INSTR(String1$, "his")`	2
`PRINT INSTR(String1$, "as")`	12
`PRINT INSTR(String1$, "ring")`	18
`PRINT INSTR(String1$, "is")`	3
`PRINT INSTR(4, String1$, "is")`	6
`PRINT INSTR(7, String1$, "is")`	0

NOTE: You cannot start a search at a position less than 1 or greater than 255. Try executing these statements:

```
PRINT INSTR(0, String1$, "is")
```

```
PRINT INSTR(256, String1$, "is")
```

In both cases, the error message "Illegal function call." is printed.

Examples of the INSTR Function

Program 13-1.

```
1 REM ** Searching Strings for Strings **
2 ' GW-BASIC Reference, Chapter 13. File: GWRF1301.BAS
3 ' Searches a base string for a substring

100 REM ** Initialize **
110 CLS: KEY OFF: DEFINT A-Z

200 REM ** Get strings **
210 PRINT "Enter the string to be searched."
220 LINE INPUT; BaseString$
230 PRINT: PRINT "Enter the substring to look for."
240 LINE INPUT; Substring$: PRINT
250 INPUT "What position to start search"; start

300 REM ** Conduct search and report **
310 PRINT: PRINT "Length of the base string is";
320 PRINT LEN(BaseString$)
330 PRINT "Length of substring is"; LEN(Substring$)
340 found = INSTR(start, BaseString$, Substring$)
350 IF found = 0 THEN PRINT "Substring not found."
360 IF found <> 0 THEN PRINT Substring$; " found at"; found

400 REM ** Go Again? **
410 akey$ = "a": PRINT: PRINT "Another search (Y or N) ? "
420 WHILE INSTR("YyNn", akey$) = 0: akey$ = INPUT$(1): WEND
430 IF INSTR("yY", akey$) <> 0 THEN GOTO 210

500 REM ** Restore screen and end **
510 CLS: KEY ON: END
```

Searching Strings for Strings (GWRF1301.BAS)

Execution of the WHILE/WEND loop at line 420 is repeated until your keypress is one of the four acceptable letters: Y, y, N, or n. The INSTR function in line 430 determines whether or not to go back for another search.

```
400 REM ** Do Again? **
410 akey$ = ""
```

```
420 WHILE INSTR("YyNn", akey$) = 0: akey$ = INPUT$(1): WEND
430 IF INSTR("Yy", akey$) <> 0 THEN 210
```

Enter the program and experiment with string searches. Figure 13-1 shows the results of two searches.

STR$ and VAL Functions

In some cases, the STR$ and VAL functions complement each other. STR$ returns the string representation of a number, and VAL returns the numeric value of a number that is in string form.

Figure 13-1.

```
Enter the string to be searched.
This is the base string that is to be searched.
Enter the substring to look for.
ring
What position to start search? 1

Length of the base string is 47
Length of the substring is 4
ring found at 20

Another search (Y or N) ?
Enter the string to be searched.
This is the base string that is to be searched.
Enter the substring to look for.
ring
What position to start search? 21

Length of the base string is 47
Length of the substring is 4
Substring not found.

Another search (Y or N) ?
```

Sample output of Program 13-1

However, the string upon which the VAL function operates may contain characters that are not numeric.

STR$ Function

STR$ is a string function of a numeric argument. It returns a string representation of the value of the specified numeric argument.

STR$ **Function**

Syntax: STR$(*numeric argument*)

Purpose: Returns a string representation of the value of the numeric argument.

Notes: STR$ is the complementary function of VAL(astring$), discussed in the next section.

Parameters: *numeric argument* is any valid numeric expression.

Table 13-3 shows some examples of the STR$ function. Notice that positive printed results have a leading blank space. Negative printed results have a leading minus (−) sign.

VAL Function

VAL is a numeric function of a string argument. It returns the numeric value of a number that is in string form; when used in this way, VAL is the complement of the STR$ function. If the first

Table 13-3.

PRINT Statement Using STR$	Printed Result	Length of Result and Comment
PRINT STR$(1)	1	2 characters; leading blank space and number
PRINT STR$(-1)	-1	2 characters; minus sign and number
PRINT STR$(255-24)	231	4 characters; leading blank space and difference
PRINT STR$(1E23)	1E+23	6 characters; leading blank space and exponential number
PRINT STR$(1.23 * 2)	2.46	5 characters; leading blank space and product
PRINT STR$(23) + "."	23.	4 characters; leading blank space, number, and decimal point

Examples of the STR$ Function

character of the string is not numeric, the VAL function returns a zero. If a string begins with a number but contains characters that are not numeric, VAL evaluates the string until it comes to a nonnumeric character and returns only the value of the numeric portion.

VAL   **Function**

Syntax: VAL(*string argument*)

Purpose: Returns the numeric value of a string.

Notes: The VAL function strips any leading blanks, tab, and line feed characters from the string argument. The string argument is then evaluated from left to right until a character is reached that is not numeric. If the leading character is not numeric, a zero is returned.

Parameters: *string argument* is the string expression whose value is returned.

Table 13-4 shows some examples of the VAL function.

You can catenate (join) two strings together by placing a plus sign (+) between them, but you cannot perform arithmetic operations on strings. You can, however, perform arithmetic operations on the values of the strings if the VAL function is used to obtain their numeric value, as in the next short program. The

Table 13-4.

PRINT Statement Using VAL	*Printed Result*
PRINT VAL("9 inches")	9
PRINT VAL("-10 degrees")	−10
PRINT VAL("The number is 14")	0
PRINT VAL("6 inches = .5 feet")	6
PRINT VAL("234567")	234567
PRINT VAL("234"); VAL("567")	234 567
PRINT VAL("234") + VAL("567")	801

Examples of the VAL Function

STR$ function is used to change the sum of the two values back to a string for printing.

```
310 A$ = "234"; B$ = "567"
320 sum = VAL(A$) + VAL(B$)
330 PRINT "A$ + B$ equals "; A$ + B$
340 PRINT "VAL("; A$; ") + VAL("; B$; ") equals";
350 PRINT STR$(sum); "."
```

The first line printed is the catenation of the strings A$ and B$. The second line printed is the arithmetic sum of VAL(A$) and VAL(B$).

```
A$ + B$ equals 234567.
VAL("234") + VAL("567") equals 801.
```

LEFT$, MID$, and RIGHT$ Functions

LEFT$, MID$, and RIGHT$ are string functions of mixed string and numeric arguments. They are used to extract all or portions of a string. Their names describe the string portions that are extracted.

LEFT$ Function

The LEFT$ function returns a substring made up of the specified number of leftmost characters in a string.

LEFT$ **Function**

Syntax: LEFT$(*string expression, numeric expression*)

Purpose: Returns a string containing the specified number (numeric expression) of leftmost characters in a string expression.

Notes: Nonprinting characters and blanks are counted. If the value of the *numeric expression* is greater than the length of the *string expression,* the entire string is returned. If the value of the *numeric expression* is zero, the null string is returned. See also the MID$ and RIGHT$ functions that follow this section.

Parameters: *string expression* is any valid string expression whose leftmost characters are returned; the value of the *numeric expression* must evaluate to an integer within the range 0 to 255, or an "Illegal function call" error message occurs.

In the following example, the LEFT$ function returns the four leftmost characters of the string assigned to A$.

```
A$ = "$140 is the cost."
Ok
PRINT LEFT$(A$, 4)
$140
```

MID$ Function and Statement

MID$ can be used as a function to extract a portion of a string, or as a statement to replace a portion of a string.

MID$ **Function/Statement**

Syntax:

MID$(*string expression, numericexp1*[*,numericexp2*])
MID$(*BaseStrExp, numericexp1*[*,numericexp2*]) = *RepStrExp*

Purpose: As a function, returns a string of characters (of length *numericexp1*) from *string expression,* beginning with the character *numericexp2*. As a statement, replaces characters in one string (*BaseStrExp*) with the specified characters from another string (*RepStrExp*).

Notes: MID$ can be used as a function with the arguments *string expression, numericexp1,* and (optionally) *numericexp2*. It can also be used as a statement to replace part of a specified string. See also the LEFT$ and RIGHT$ functions.

Parameters: *string expression* is the string from which characters are obtained; *numericexp1* is a numeric expression that evaluates to a value within the range 1 to 255; *numericexp2* is a numeric expression that evaluates to a value within the range 0 to 255; *BaseStrExp* is the string whose characters are replaced; *RepStrExp* is a string containing characters that will replace characters in *BaseStrExp*.

The following conditions apply when MID$ is used as a function:

- If the *numericexp2* parameter is omitted, or there are fewer characters than the value of *numericexp2* to the right of the value of *numericexp2*, all the rightmost characters beginning with *numericexp1* are returned.

- If *numericexp1* is greater than the length of *stringexpression,* or *numericexp2* evaluates to zero, a null string is returned.

- If either *numericexp1* or *numericexp2* is out of range, an "Illegal function call" error occurs.

Here is an example of MID$ used as a function. The function has three arguments: A$, 4, and 23.

```
10 CLS
20 A$ = "GW-BASIC is a good programming language."
30 PRINT MID$(A$, 4, 23)
```

Enter and run these lines. The MID$ function returns a substring of 23 characters from A$, starting with the fourth character.

```
BASIC is a good program
```

When MID$ is used as a statement, the following conditions apply.

- Characters in *BaseStrExp* are replaced, beginning with character *numericexp1,* by the first *numericexp2* characters of *RepStrExp.*

- If *numericexp2* is omitted, all the characters of *RepStrExp* are used when there is enough room in *BaseStrExp* to accommodate them.

To see MID$ used as a statement, as well as a function, add two lines to the previous three-line program.

```
10 CLS
20 A$ = "GW-BASIC is a good programming language."
30 PRINT MID$(A$, 4, 23)
40 MID$(A$, 15, 4) = "fine"
50 PRINT A$
```

Run this modified version to see the MID$ function return the same substring as before, and the MID$ statement replace the 15th through 18th characters of A$ (the word "good") with the word "fine."

```
BASIC is a good program
GW-BASIC is a fine programming language.
```

RIGHT$ Function

The RIGHT$ function returns a substring made up of the specified number of rightmost characters in a string.

RIGHT$ **Function**

Syntax: RIGHT$(*string expression, numeric expression*)

Purpose: Returns the number (specified by the value of *numeric expression*) of rightmost characters in a string (*string expression*).

Notes: If the value of *numeric expression* is equal to or greater than the length of the string, the entire string is returned. If the value of *numeric expression* equals zero, the null string is returned. See also the LEFT$ and MID$ functions.

Parameters: *string expression* is the string from which the rightmost characters are returned; *numeric expression* is a valid numeric expression that evaluates to an integer.

The following Direct mode example prints three substrings extracted from A$:

```
A$ = "GW-BASIC is a fine programming language."
Ok
PRINT LEFT$(A$, 9); MID$(A$, 10, 5); RIGHT$(A$, 21)
GW-BASIC is a programming language.
Ok
_
```

The three functions in the PRINT statement each return a substring of A$ as illustrated here.

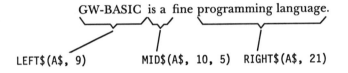

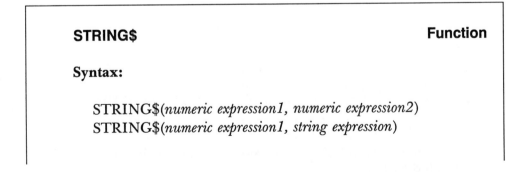

STRING$ Function

The STRING$ function returns a string of specified length whose characters all have the specified ASCII code, or returns the first character of a string a specified number of times.

STRING$ **Function**

Syntax:

STRING$(*numeric expression1, numeric expression2*)
STRING$(*numeric expression1, string expression*)

Purpose: Returns a string with a length equal to the value of *numeric expression1* whose characters all have the ASCII code of *numeric expression2*. Or returns the ASCII code of the first character of *string expression* the number of times specified by the value of *numeric expression1*.

Notes: STRING$ is useful for printing borders or shapes using ASCII codes greater than 127.

Parameters: *numeric expression1* and *numeric expression2* must evaluate to an integer in the range 0 to 255; *string expression* is a string from which an ASCII code is returned.

Enter and run Program 13-2, Print with STRING$, to see the results of each of the two uses of STRING$. The program first uses ASCII codes to draw a rectangle, and then places a string of A's from the word "Abraham" within the rectangle.

Figure 13-2 shows the output of Program 13-2. The top and bottom lines are formed by ASCII codes at lines 210 and 260, using the STRING$ function. The sides of the rectangle are formed by ASCII codes at lines 230 and 240 of the FOR/NEXT loop, using the CHR$ function. The string of letter A's is formed from the first character of the word "Abraham" in line 310.

LSET and RSET Statements

GW-BASIC random-access files accept data only in string format. The LSET and RSET statements are primarily used to left- or

Program 13-2.

```
1 REM ** Print with STRING$ **
2 ' GW-BASIC Reference, Chapter 13. File: GWRF1302.BAS
3 ' Demonstrates two uses of the STRING$ function

100 REM ** Initialize **
110 CLS: WIDTH 40: KEY OFF: DEFINT A-Z

200 REM ** Print border **
210 LOCATE 5, 5: PRINT STRING$(24, 220)
220 FOR row = 6 TO 8
230   LOCATE row, 5: PRINT CHR$(221)
240   LOCATE row, 28: PRINT CHR$(222)
250 NEXT row
260 LOCATE 9, 5: PRINT STRING$(24, 223)

300 REM ** Print 1st character of "Abraham" **
310 LOCATE 7, 10: PRINT STRING$(14, "Abraham");

400 REM ** Restore screen and end **
410 akey$ = INPUT$(1): CLS: WIDTH 80: KEY ON: END
```

Print with STRING$ (GWRF1302.BAS)

right-justify strings within a previously defined field. LSET and
RSET can also be used to format data for printing purposes.

Figure 13-2.

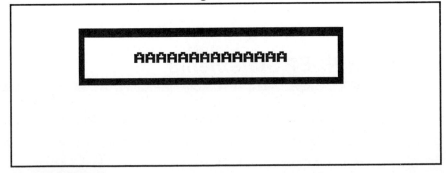

Using STRING$

LSET and RSET   **Statements**

Syntax:

LSET *string variable* = *string expression*
RSET *string variable* = *string expression*

Purpose: Left- or right-justifies a string in a specified field.

Notes: The LSET and RSET statements are primarily used on data from memory, in preparation for moving the data into a random-access file with a PUT statement. LSET and RSET may also be used with a string variable to left-justify a string in a specified field. You can use LSET and RSET as an aid in formatting printed output.

Parameters: *string variable* is any valid variable name; *string expression* is the data to be justified.

The use of LSET and RSET to left- or right-justify the data of random-access files is discussed in the next chapter. Their use to adjust data when printing fields is discussed here.

The following lines define two string fields (A$ and B$). In addition, two strings are defined: "Candy" and "Peanuts."

```
10 CLS
20 A$ = SPACE$(10): B$ = SPACE$(15)     (Two fields)
30 string1$ = "Candy"
40 string2$ = "Peanuts"
```

Now, add line 50 to left-justify "Candy" in one field (A$) and "Peanuts" in the other field (B$). Add line 60 to print the formatted data.

```
50 LSET A$ = string1$: LSET B$ = string2$
60 PRINT A$; B$
```

Line 50 places each of the two strings in the specified fields and left-justifies them. The PRINT statement (line 60) specifies the variables A$ and B$. Since A$ now contains "Candy" in its 10-character field, and B$ contains "Peanuts" in its 15-character field, the data is printed as follows.

```
RUN
Candy      Peanuts
```

"Candy" followed by 5 spaces occupies the 10-character field, A$. "Peanuts" followed by 8 spaces occupies the 15-character field, B$.

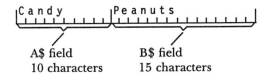

Other formatting arrangements can be obtained by adding the following lines:

```
70 LSET A$ = string1$: RSET B$ = string2$
80 PRINT A$; B$
90 RSET A$ = string1$: LSET B$ = string2$
100 PRINT A$; B$
110 RSET A$ = string1$: RSET B$ = string2$
120 PRINT A$; B$
```

The output of the completed program is

```
Candy      Peanuts            (from lines 50 and 60)
Candy             Peanuts     (from lines 70 and 80)
     CandyPeanuts             (from lines 90 and 100)
     Candy         Peanuts    (from lines 110 and 120)
```

MKI$, MKS$, and MKD$ Functions

Numeric values placed with an LSET or RSET statement in a random-access file buffer (a special area of memory used to handle data going to or from a disk file) must be converted to a specific string format. The MKI$, MKS$, and MKD$ functions are used to convert a numeric value to that format. These functions differ from the STR$ function, and are used only when preparing numeric data for use in a random-access file.

MKI$, MKS$, and MKD$ **Functions**

Syntax:

MKI$(*integer expression*)
MKS$(*single precision expression*)
MKD$(*double precision expression*)

Purpose: Converts numeric values to string format in preparation for their use in random-access files.

Notes: Any numeric value must be converted to a string before being sent to a random-access file. See also CVI, CVS, and CVD in the next section.

Parameters: *integer expression* evaluates to an integer; *single precision expression* evaluates to a single precision number; *double precision expression* evaluates to a double precision number.

MKI$ converts an integer to a 2-byte string, MKS$ converts a single precision number to a 4-byte string, and MKD$ converts a double precision number to an 8-byte string.

As an example, the following lines of a program segment prepare and send data to random-access file #1:

```
210 amount! = price! + tax!
220 FIELD #1, 8 AS A$, 16 AS B$    (Defines file record fields)
230 LSET A$ = MKS$(amount!)        (Single precision to string)
240 LSET B$ = name$                (Already in string form)
250 PUT #1
```

Line 210 defines the fields used for the file records. Line 230 converts the single precision value (amount!) string format and left-justifies it in the field A$. Line 240 left-justifies the string (name$) associated with the amount.

The use of files and these functions are demonstrated in more detail in Chapter 14, "File and Device I/O."

CVI, CVS, and CVD Functions

Numeric values read from a random-access disk file must be converted from the string format used in the file back into numbers if they are to be used in arithmetic operations. The CVI, CVS, and CVD functions differ from the VAL function, and are used only when converting numeric data from a random-access file.

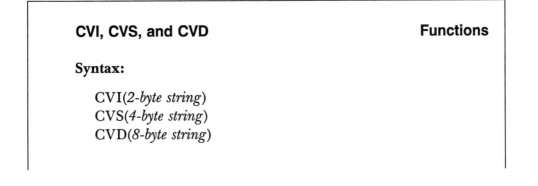

CVI, CVS, and CVD   **Functions**

Syntax:

CVI(*2-byte string*)
CVS(*4-byte string*)
CVD(*8-byte string*)

Purpose: Converts string values to numeric values.

Notes: Numeric values read from a random-access disk file must be converted back into numbers if they are to be used in arithmetic operations. See also the MKI$, MKS$, and MKD$ functions.

Parameters: *2-byte string* is an integer in string format; *4-byte string* is a single precision number in string format; *8-byte string* is a double precision number in string format.

CVI converts a 2-byte string to an integer, CVS converts a 4-byte string to a single precision number, and CVD converts an 8-byte string to a double precision number.

As an example, the following lines of a program segment read a record from a file and convert a single precision number in string format to numeric format, in preparation for the number's use in an arithmetic operation.

```
310 FIELD #1, 8 AS A$, 16 AS B$   (Defines file record fields)
320 GET #1                        (Get a file record)
330 amount! = CVS(A$)             (Convert to number)
```

Line 310 defines the fields used for the file records. Line 320 reads a record from file #1. Line 320 converts the string data from field A$ to a single precision number and assigns it to the amount! variable.

The use of files and these functions will be demonstrated in more detail in Chapter 14, "File and Device I/O."

14

File and Device I/O

A file is a collection of information. The information contained in a file can be on any topic and organized in the way you choose. There are several kinds of computer files, including program files and data files. This chapter describes data files, used to store information, and *device input/output*.

There are two types of *data files*: *sequential* and *random access*, and data is stored in them differently. If a file is created as a sequential file, you cannot access it as a random access file, and vice versa.

The following commands, statements, and functions are covered in this chapter:

CLOSE	GET	LOC	MKS$	RESET
CVD	INPUT#	LOCK	NAME	RSET
CVI	IOCTL	LOF	OPEN	UNLOCK
CVS	IOCTL$	LSET	PRINT#	WIDTH
EOF	KILL	MKD$	PRINT# USING	WRITE#
FIELD	LINE INPUT#	MKI$	PUT	

Sequential Files

The statements and functions discussed in this section apply to sequential files. A *sequential file* is a file made up of units called *records*. The records in a sequential file must be accessed sequentially; that is, to read the fifth record in a sequential file, records one through four must be accessed first. The following statements and functions are discussed in this section:

Statements: CLOSE, INPUT#, LINE INPUT#, OPEN, PRINT#, PRINT# USING, and WRITE#

Functions: EOF and LOF

You create sequential files by

1. Opening the file with an OPEN statement

2. Writing data to the file with PRINT#, PRINT# USING, or WRITE#

3. Closing the file with a CLOSE statement

You access the data in a sequential file by

1. Opening the file with an OPEN statement

2. Reading data from the file with INPUT# or LINE INPUT#

3. Closing the file with a CLOSE statement

OPEN and CLOSE Statements

These two statements control access to a sequential data file. OPEN opens access to the file. CLOSE closes access to a file after it has been opened.

OPEN   **Statement**

Syntax:

OPEN *mode*, [#] *file expression*, *file name* [*record length*]
or
OPEN *file name* [FOR *mode*] AS [#] *file expression*
[LEN = *record length*]

Purpose: Opens a file for input/output.

Notes: When you open a sequential file, you must declare the kind of access mode: INPUT, OUTPUT, or APPEND.

Parameters: In the first syntax form, *mode* is a string expression with one of these characters: *O* (uppercase letter *O*, for sequential output), *I* (for sequential input), or *A* (for position to end of file and append). In the second syntax form, *mode* is either INPUT (for sequential input), OUTPUT (for sequential output), or APPEND (for position to end of file and append). The *file name* parameter is the name of the file; *file expression* is a numeric expression that evaluates to a number between 1 and the maximum number of files allowed; *record length* is optional. If used, *record length* is 128 bytes by default and cannot exceed the value specified (maximum 32767) if the /s switch is used for setting the *record length* when loading GW-BASIC.

Here are two examples that open a sequential file (#1, for output). One example is given for each syntax form.

```
OPEN "O", #1, "A:TEMP.DAT"          (First syntax)
OPEN "A:TEMP.DAT" FOR OUTPUT AS #1  (Second syntax)
```

After you have completed use of an open file, it must be closed.

CLOSE   **Statement**

Syntax: CLOSE [[#] *file number* [,[#] *file number*]. . .]

Purpose: Closes an open file when input/output is complete.

Notes: The END, NEW, RESET, SYSTEM, or RUN and LOAD (without the R option) statements always close all files or devices automatically. STOP does not close files.

Parameters: *file number* is the number under which the file was opened.

The association between a file and its file number terminates when the file is closed. The file can then be reopened using the same or a different number. Here are some examples of CLOSE statements and the action they perform.

```
CLOSE              (Closes all open files)
CLOSE 2            (Closes file #2)
CLOSE #1, #2       (Closes files #1 and #2)
CLOSE 1, #3        (Closes files #1 and #3)
```

WRITE#, PRINT#, and PRINT# USING Statements

These three statements are used to send data from memory to a sequential file. (You will note we have included a space following the given command and # sign, denoting number, in syntax and program statements.)

WRITE#   **Statement**

Syntax: WRITE #*file number, expression list*

Purpose: Writes information to a sequential file.

Notes: After the last item in the *expression list* is written, a carriage return/line feed is inserted.

Parameters: *file number* is the number under which the file was opened for output; *expression list* is a list of string and/or numeric expressions separated by commas or semicolons.

The WRITE# statement inserts commas between items as they are written and delimits strings with quotation marks. WRITE#

does not put a blank space in front of a positive number. For example, an unstructured sequential file could consist of records that are strings with up to 255 characters. The records could be entered and written to the file by these lines:

```
310 LINE INPUT; record$    (Enters a string from keyboard)
320 WRITE #1, record$      (Writes the string to file #1)
```

A WRITE# statement can have more than one expression. You might structure the sequential file into fields (items in the *expression list*) by using the LEFT$ function described in Chapter 13. If a sequential file has been opened as #1, the following lines will produce a sequential file with records made up of two 38-character fields.

```
410 LINE INPUT "Japanese? "; Japanese$    (Get first field)
420 LINE INPUT "English ? "; English$     (Get second field)
430 Japanese$ = LEFT$(Japanese$, 38)      (38-character limit)
440 English$ = LEFT$(English$, 38)        (38-character limit)
450 WRITE #1, Japanese$, English$         (Send record to file)
```

Line 450 writes one record consisting of two strings to the file statement. The WRITE# statement encloses each string in quotation marks and inserts a comma between the two strings. Therefore, one record consists of the first string enclosed in quotation marks, a comma, the second string enclosed in quotation marks, and two end-of-record characters (CR, a carriage return, and LF, a line feed).

PRINT# and PRINT# USING can also be used to write a record to a sequential file. These statements also write the end-of-record characters, CR (carriage return) and LF (line feed), after each record.

PRINT# and PRINT# USING   Statements

Syntax: PRINT *#file number,* [USING *string expression;*] *expression list*

Purpose: Writes information to a sequential file.

Notes: PRINT# writes an image of the information to the disk, just as it would be printed on the screen by a PRINT statement. Be sure to delimit the data sent to the disk so that it can be input correctly later from the disk.

Parameters: *file number* is the number under which the file was opened; *string expression* consists of the formatting characters described under PRINT USING in Chapter 8, "Terminal I/O"; *expression list* consists of the numeric and/or string expressions to be written to the file, separated by semicolons.

Double quotation marks are used as delimiters for numeric and/or string expressions, but do not appear in the disk image of the file. For example, if

```
A$ = "Albert Outlander"
B$ = "(800) 123-4567"
```

then the PRINT# statement will be

```
PRINT #1, A$; ","; B$
```

The disk image of the record will be

```
Albert Outlander,(800) 123-4567
```

Program 14-1, Create a NotePad.TXT File, creates an unstructured sequential file of records that you enter from the keyboard. The default record length (128 characters) is specified in line 210. Each record is sent to the file with a PRINT# statement. (A WRITE# statement could also be used. The disk image of a WRITE# statement would include double quotation marks at the beginning and end of each record.)

Enter and run Program 14-1. You can scan the file it creates later in the chapter, following the discussion of the INPUT# and LINE INPUT# statements. The > symbol signifies where to begin typing a record. When you press the ENTER key, the record is terminated. Figure 14-1 shows some sample string inputs.

Program 14-1.

```
1 REM ** Create a NotePad.TXT File **
2 ' GW-BASIC: The Reference, Chapter 14.  File:GWRF1401.BAS
3 ' Creates an unstructured sequential file

100 REM ** Initialize **
110 CLS: KEY OFF: DEFINT A-Z

200 REM ** Open file and enter data **
210 OPEN "A:NotePad.TXT" FOR OUTPUT AS #1 LEN = 128
220 LINE INPUT "> "; record$        'Enter a string
230    IF record$ = "" THEN 310     'Exit if no string input
240    PRINT #1, record$            'Send string to file
250 GOTO 220

300 REM ** Close file, restore screen, and end **
310 CLOSE #1
320 CLS: KEY ON: END
```

Create a NotePad.TXT File (GWRF1401.BAS)

Figure 14-1.

```
> This is the NotePad.TXT file.
> It is an unstructured sequential file.
> Each record is one string, up to 128 characters.
> Use the file for notes of any kind.
> Doctor appt. 10:30 AM
> Meet Kit for lunch 12:30 PM
> _
```

Entries made in Program 14-1

INPUT# and LINE
INPUT# Statements

These statements are used to read data from a sequential file and assign them to variables, so the data can be used in a program.

INPUT#   **Statement**

Syntax: INPUT #*file number, variable list*

Purpose: Reads data items from an open sequential file and assigns them to variables.

Notes: The variable type of the variables in the *variable list* must match the data type of the item assigned from the file.

Parameters: *file number* is the number under which the file was opened; *variable list* contains the variable names to be assigned the values of the items of the file.

INPUT# can also be used for random access files.

- *For numeric values*   The first character encountered (not a space or line feed) is assumed to be the start of the number. The number terminates on a space, carriage return, line feed, or comma.

- *For string values*   If the first character is a double quotation mark ("), the string will consist of all characters read between the first and the second double quotation mark. If the first character is not a double quotation mark, the string terminates when a comma, carriage return, or line feed is encountered, or when 255 characters have been read.

For example, consider the difference in the way a string is stored by PRINT# and WRITE# statements. Assuming a sequential notepad file has been opened, as in Program 14-1, the following note is entered at the LINE INPUT statement (line 220):

```
> This is a notepad file.
```

At line 240 of the program, the PRINT# statement stores the data in the file as

```
This is a notepad file.<CR/LF>
```

with <CR/LF> representing a carriage return and line feed, marking the end of the record.

When the INPUT# statement reads the record, it interprets the first character as the beginning of the record. It reads all characters, from the first character to the <CR/LF>, as the record.

If a WRITE# statement were used in place of PRINT# at line 240, the data would be stored in the file as

```
"This is a notepad file."<CR/LF>
```

When the INPUT# statement reads the record, it interprets the first double quotation mark as the beginning of the record. It reads all characters between that double quotation mark and the next double quotation mark as the record.

LINE INPUT#   **Statement**

Syntax: LINE INPUT *#file number, string variable*

Purpose: Reads an entire record (up to the CR and LF end-of-record characters) from an open sequential file and assigns it to a string variable.

Notes: LINE INPUT# is especially useful when each record of a data file has been stored in fields, or if a GW-BASIC program file (saved in ASCII format) is being read as data by another program.

Parameters: *file number* is the number under which the file was opened; *string variable* is a valid string variable name to which the line read will be assigned.

Program 14-2, Scan the NotePad.TXT File, uses the sequential data file created previously. When you run the program, the NotePad.TXT file is opened, and the first record is read and displayed. Each time you press a key, the next record is displayed. After the last record is displayed (the end of the file is reached), the number of characters (bytes) in the file is displayed. The EOF (end-of-file) and LOF (length-of-file) functions are discussed in the next section.

Program 14-2.

```
1 REM ** Scan the NotePad.TXT File **
2 ' GW-BASIC: The Reference, Chapter 14.  File:GWRF1402.BAS
3 ' Scans a previously created unstructured sequential file

100 REM ** Initialize **
110 CLS: KEY OFF: DEFINT A-Z

200 REM ** Open file and read data **
210 OPEN "A:NotePad.TXT" FOR INPUT AS #1
220 WHILE EOF(1) = 0                  'Loop until end of file
230    LINE INPUT #1, record$        'Read a file record
240    PRINT record$                 'Print the record
250    akey$ = INPUT$(1)             'Wait for a key press
260 WEND

300 REM ** Print file size, close file, and end **
310 PRINT: PRINT "NotePad.TXT has"; LOF(1); "bytes"
320 PRINT "Press a key to close file and end"
330 akey$ = INPUT$(1)
340 CLOSE #1: CLS: KEY ON: END
```

Scan the NotePad.TXT File (GWRF1402.BAS)

Figure 14-2 shows a scan of the file. Each record of a sequential file is accessed, in turn, from the beginning to the end of the file.

Figure 14-2.

```
This is the NotePad.TXT file.
It is an unstructured sequential file.
Each record is one string, up to 128 characters.
Use the file for notes of any kind.
Doctor appt. 10:30 AM
Meet Kit for lunch 12:30 PM

NotePad.TXT has 210 bytes
Press a key to close file and end
```

Output of Program 14-2

EOF and LOF Functions

These functions are helpful in determining when the end of a sequential file has been reached and how long the file is. The EOF function returns a true condition (−1) when the end of a sequential file has been reached, or a false condition (0) if the end of the file has not been reached.

EOF   **Function**

Syntax: EOF(*file number*)

Purpose: Indicates whether or not the end of a sequential file has been reached.

Notes: Use EOF to prevent an attempt to input data after all records have been read.

Parameters: *file number* is the file number used when the file was opened.

The EOF function is used in Program 14-2 as the condition in the WHILE statement of the WHILE/WEND loop.

```
220 WHILE EOF(1) = 0
```

The loop reads records from the file and prints them as long as EOF(1) is false (0). When the EOF character is found at the end of the file, EOF(1) becomes true (−1), and an exit is made from the WHILE/WEND loop.

The LOF function returns the length (number of bytes) allocated to a sequential file.

LOF **Function**

Syntax: LOF(*file number*)

Purpose: Returns the length allocated to a sequential file.

Notes: The value returned includes two bytes per record for the carriage return and line feed characters used to mark the end of each record.

Parameters: *file number* is the file number used when the file was opened.

The LOF function is used in Program 14-2 to print the number of characters (bytes) in the NotePad.TXT file before it is closed.

```
310 PRINT: PRINT "NotePad.TXT" has"; LOF(1); "bytes"
```

Random Access Files

The statements and functions discussed in this section apply to *random access files*.

Statements:	CLOSE, FIELD, GET, LSET, OPEN, PUT, RSET, and INPUT#
Functions:	CVD, CVI, CVS, LOF, MKD$, MKI$, and MKS$

Random access files are highly structured, fixed-length files, in which all records in the file are the same length. You create random access files by

1. Opening the file with an OPEN statement

2. Writing data to the file with PUT

3. Closing the file with a CLOSE statement

You access the data in a random file by

1. Opening the file with an OPEN statement

2. Reading data from the file with GET or INPUT#

3. Closing the file with a CLOSE statement

OPEN and CLOSE Statements

These two statements control when access may be made to a random access data file. OPEN opens access to the file. CLOSE closes access to a file after it has been opened.

OPEN   **Statement**

Syntax:

OPEN *mode*, [#]*file number*, *file name* [*record length*]
or
OPEN *file name* [FOR *mode*] AS [#]*file number*
[LEN = *record length*]

Purpose: Opens a file for input/output.

Notes: When a random access file is opened, it may be used for either input or output.

Parameters: In the first syntax form, *mode* is a string expression with the character *R* (for random input/output). In the second syntax form, *mode* is RANDOM (for random input/output). The *file name* parameter is the name of the file; *file number* is a number between 1 and the maximum number of files allowed; *record length* is an integer in the range 1 to 32767 for random access files (128 bytes by default).

Here are two examples that open a random access file #1 for random input/output. An example is given for each syntax form.

```
OPEN "R", #1 "A:TEMP.DAT" 76              (First syntax)
OPEN "A:TEMP.DAT" FOR RANDOM AS #1 LEN = 76   (Second syntax)
```

After you have completed use of an open file, it must be closed. A random access file is closed in the same way as a sequential file. See the CLOSE statement in the "Sequential Files" section of this chapter. The syntax is the same for random access files.

FIELD Statement

A FIELD statement allocates space for variables in a random access record. The total number of bytes allocated in a FIELD statement must not exceed the record length specified when the file was opened.

FIELD   **Statement**

Syntax: FIELD [#] *file number, width* AS *string variable1*
[, *width* AS *string variable2*]. . .

Purpose: Allocates space for variables in a random access file.

Notes: Do not use a FIELD variable name (*string variable1, string variable2,. . .*) in an INPUT or LET assignment statement.

Parameters: *file number* is the number under which the file was opened; *width* is the number of characters to be allocated to the string variable; *string variable1, string variable2, . . .* are string variables that will be used.

Any number of FIELD statements may be executed for the same file, and all FIELD statements executed are in effect at the same time. FIELD only allocates space. It does not place data in the random file buffer. A FIELD statement must be executed before you can enter data with a PUT statement or get data with a GET statement.

Here is a simple FIELD statement that allocates 24 bytes for ItemF$ and 2 bytes for PageF$. The *F* at the end of these field variables is used to distinguish its use.

```
220 FIELD #1, 24 AS ItemF$, 2 AS PageF$
```

LSET and RSET Statements

These statements are used to move data from memory to a random access file buffer, and to left- or right-justify the data in preparation for a PUT statement. If the data is numeric data, the MKI\$, MKS\$, or MKD\$ functions must be used to convert the numeric data to the proper string form. (See next section.)

LSET and RSET   **Statements**

Syntax:

   LSET *string variable* = *string expression*
   RSET *string variable* = *string expression*

Purpose: Moves data from memory to a random access file buffer, and left- or right-justifies it.

Notes: LSET and RSET can also be used to justify a string in a specified field. See LSET and RSET in Chapter 13, "String Manipulation."

Parameters: *string variable* is the variable name specified in a previous FIELD statement; *string expression* is a valid string expression.

Since random access files have fixed record lengths, end-of-record characters are not necessary. If you want to add carriage return and line feed characters to each record so that the DOS TYPE command will print random access file records neatly, you can do this by adding a two-character field to the FIELD statement, as follows:

```
220 FIELD #1, 24 AS ItemF$, 2 AS PageF$, 2 AS EORF$
```

You would also need an LSET function to set the CR and LF, as follows:

```
230 LSET EORF$ = CHR$(13) + CHR$(10)
```

MKI$, MKS$, and MKD$ Functions

These functions are string functions of numeric arguments. They perform the conversion of numeric data to the string format necessary for input to a random access file. MKI$ converts integer data, MKS$ converts single precision data, and MKD$ converts double precision data.

MKI$, MKS$, and MKD$ **Functions**

Syntax:

MKI$(*integer argument*)
MKS$(*single precision argument*)
MKD$(*double precision argument*)

Purpose: Converts numeric values to string values for use in random access files.

Notes: MKI$ converts an integer to a 2-byte string; MKS$ converts a single precision number to a 4-byte string; and MKD$ converts a double precision number to an 8-byte string.

Parameters: *integer argument* is any valid integer expression; *single precision argument* is any valid single precision expression; *double precision argument* is any valid double precision expression.

If a numeric value has been assigned to a double precision variable named cost#, the following FIELD statement might be used:

```
220 FIELD #1, 24 AS ItemF$, 8 AS CostF$
```

Before the numeric data is sent to the file, it would be converted to string format and left-justified by the MKD$ function and LSET statement.

```
270 LSET CostF$ = MKD$(cost#)
```

PUT Statement

PUT, in the following syntax, is used to write a record from a random access file buffer to a random access disk file. Do not confuse this PUT syntax with the syntax used for graphics.

PUT   **Statement**

Syntax: PUT [#]*file number*[, *record number*]

Purpose: Writes a record to a random access disk file.

Notes: The PRINT#, PRINT# USING, LSET, RSET, or WRITE statements may be used to put characters in the random access file buffer before a PUT statement is executed.

Parameters: *file number* is the number under which the file was opened; *record number* is the number of the record. If *record number* is omitted, the record has the next available record number (after the last PUT statement executed).

If a random access file is being created, the following PUT statement will send to the file the record that has its number equal to RecordNum.

```
300    PUT #1, RecordNum
```

Program 14-3, Create a Random Access File, uses OPEN, FIELD, LSET, MKI$, PUT, and CLOSE to create a file with two fields: ItemF$ (length 24), and PageF$ (length 2). Each record is 26 characters long (24 + 2). The file, named Catalog.RAN, will contain information from an advertiser's catalog: item names and the page numbers where the items can be found.

A LINE INPUT statement allows you to enter an item name, and an INPUT statement allows you to enter the associated page number.

```
240    LINE INPUT "Item name ? "; item$
250    IF item$ = "" THEN 410
260    INPUT "Page number "; page
```

Line 250 provides an escape from the WHILE/WEND loop where the entries are made. When all items have been entered, you can escape from the loop by pressing ENTER without typing an item name.

Next, LSET is used to left-justify item$ in the ItemF$ field. Since the item was assigned to a string variable (item$), no conversion is necessary. LSET and MKI$ are used for the page number, since this is an integer and must be converted to string form.

```
270 LSET ItemF$ = item$
280 LSET PageF$ = MKI$(page)
```

Each time through the loop, the record number (initially zero) is increased by one before the record is sent to the file by a PUT statement.

```
290    RecordNum = RecordNum + 1
300    PUT #1, RecordNum
```

Figure 14-3 shows some sample data sent to the Catalog.RAN file. Enter Program 14-3, and type in the data shown in Figure 14-3. You will use it later to scan the file.

Program 14-3.

```
1 REM ** Create a Random Access File **
2 ' GW-BASIC: The Reference, Chapter 14.  File:GWRF1403.BAS
3 ' Creates a random access file named "Catalog"

100 REM ** Initialize **
110 CLS: KEY OFF: DEFINT A-Z
120 RecordNum = 0

200 REM ** Open file and enter data **
210 OPEN "A:Catalog.RAN" FOR RANDOM AS #1 LEN = 26
220 FIELD #1, 24 AS ItemF$, 2 AS PageF$
230 WHILE -1
240    LINE INPUT "Item name ? "; item$
250    IF item$ = "" THEN 410
260    INPUT "Page number "; page
270    LSET ItemF$ = item$
280    LSET PageF$ = MKI$(page)
290    RecordNum = RecordNum + 1
300    PUT #1, RecordNum
310 WEND

400 REM ** Close file, print length **
410 PRINT: PRINT "The file length is"; LOF(1)
420 CLOSE #1
430 PRINT: PRINT "Press a key to end"

510 REM ** Wait, restore screen, end **
520 akey$ = INPUT$(1)
530 CLS: KEY ON: END
```

Create a Random Access File (GWRF1403.BAS)

Figure 14-3.

```
Item name ? FAX machines
Page number ? 6
Item name ? Copy machines
Page number ? 8
Item name ? Computers
Page number ? 10
Item name ? Computer peripherals
Page number ? 14
Item name ? Paper
Page number ? 17
Item name ?

The file length is 130

Press a key to end
```

Entries for Program 14-3

GET Statement

The GET statement is used to get a record from a random access file.

GET   **Statement**

Syntax: GET [*#*]*file number*[, *record number*]

Purpose: Reads a record from a random access disk file.

Notes: After a GET statement, INPUT# and LINE INPUT# may be used to read characters from the random access file buffer. PRINT may be used to display a record.

Parameters: *file number* is the number under which the file was opened; *record number* is the number of the record (in the range 1 to 16,777,215). If *record number* is omitted, the next record (after the last GET) is read.

CVI, CVS, and CVD Functions

Numbers are converted to strings by MKI$, MKS$, and MKD$ to a special string format before being written to a random access file. Integers are converted to a 2-byte string, single precision numbers to a 4-byte string, and double precision numbers to an 8-byte string. The CVI, CVS, and CVD functions are used to convert these strings back to numeric form.

CVI, CVS, and CVD   **Functions**

Syntax:

CVI(*2-byte string argument*)
CVS(*4-byte string argument*)
CVD(*8-byte string argument*)

Purpose: Converts string values used in random access files to numeric values.

Notes: CVI converts a 2-byte string to an integer; CVS converts a 4-byte string to a single precision number; CVD converts an 8-byte string to a double precision number.

Parameters: *2-byte string argument* is a string (the format to which an integer was converted by MKI$); *4-byte string argument* is a string (the format to which a single precision number was converted by MKS$); *8-byte string argument* is a string (the format to which a double precision number was converted by MKD$).

LOF Function

The LOF function, when used with random access files, returns the length (number of bytes) allocated to a file.

LOF   **Function**

Syntax: LOF(*numeric argument*)

Purpose: Returns the length allocated to a random access file.

Notes: The number of records in a random access file can be found by dividing the LOF by the file's record length.

Parameters: *numeric argument* is the file number used when the file was opened.

The length of a random access file, as returned by LOF, is the length of a record times the number of records.

Program 14-4, Scan a Random Access File, uses GET to read records from the Catalog.RAN file created earlier, and CVI to convert a 2-byte string (catalog page number) to numeric form.

```
250   GET #1, RecordNum
260   PRINT ItemF$; " page:"; CVI(PageF$)
```

The LOF function is used in a PRINT statement to display the length of the file just before the file is closed.

```
310 PRINT: PRINT "The file length is"; LOF(1)
```

Program 14-4.

```
1 REM ** Scan a Random Access File **
2 ' GW-BASIC: The Reference, Chapter 14.  File:GWRF1404.BAS
3 ' Scans a random access file named "Catalog"

100 REM ** Initialize **
110 CLS: KEY OFF: DEFINT A-Z
120 RecordNum = 1

200 REM ** Open file and scan data **
210 OPEN "A:Catalog.RAN" FOR RANDOM AS #1 LEN = 26
220 FIELD #1, 24 AS ItemF$, 2 AS PageF$
230 NumRecords = LOF(1) / 26
240 WHILE RecordNum <= NumRecords
250    GET #1, RecordNum
260    PRINT ItemF$; " page:"; CVI(PageF$)
270    RecordNum = RecordNum + 1
280 WEND

300 REM ** Print file information and close file **
310 PRINT: PRINT "The file length is"; LOF(1)
320 PRINT "Number of records is"; NumRecords
330 CLOSE #1

400 REM ** Wait for keypress, then end **
410 PRINT: PRINT "Press a key to end"
420 akey$ = INPUT$(1)
430 CLS: KEY ON: END
```

Scan a Random Access File (GWRF1404.BAS)

Figure 14-4.

```
FAX machines            page: 6
Copy machines           page: 8
Computers               page: 10
Computer peripherals    page: 14
Paper                   page: 17

The file length is 130
Number of records is 5

Press a key to end
```

Output of Program 14-4

Figure 14-4 shows a scan of the Catalog.RAN file, which contains the data previously entered and shown in Figure 14-3.

Device I/O and Other Commands, Statements, and Functions

The commands, statements, and functions discussed in this section apply to general file use or to unusual uses.

Commands:	RESET, KILL, and NAME
Statements:	WIDTH, OPEN, CLOSE, LOCK, UNLOCK, and IOCTL
Functions:	LOC and IOCTL$

RESET Command

The RESET command closes all open files. If you use the CLOSE statement to close files as they are used, RESET is unnecessary.

RESET   **Command**

Syntax: RESET

Purpose: Closes all disk files and/or open devices.

Notes: Sends information currently in the buffers to the appropriate place and closes all files and devices.

Parameters: None.

KILL Command

This command is used to delete a file from a disk. It is used for all types of files. It performs the same action within GW-BASIC as the ERASE and DEL commands do in DOS.

KILL   **Command**

Syntax: KILL *file name*

Purpose: Erases a file from a disk.

Notes: You must specify the filename's extension when using KILL. Any GW-BASIC program file has the default extension BAS.

Parameters: *file name* is the name of the file to be deleted. It must be enclosed in double quotation marks.

A file that has been saved to disk can be deleted with the KILL command. For example, suppose you saved a file with:

```
SAVE "A:GWRF1304"
```

The file is now saved with a BAS extension. However, to delete the file with KILL, the correct extension must be supplied in the *file name* argument.

```
KILL "A:GWRF1304.BAS"
```

Once a file is deleted, there is no way from within GW-BASIC to recover the deleted file. However, there are utility programs available from outside sources that can restore deleted files.

A "File already open" error message occurs if you try to use the KILL command to delete a sequential or random file that is open (see OPEN later in this chapter). The KILL command will not remove a directory. This can only be done with an RMDIR command (Remove Directory; see Chapter 18, "System Routines") .

NAME Command

The NAME command allows you to change the name of a disk file. It produces the same result as the RENAME command in DOS.

NAME   **Command**

Syntax: NAME *old file name* AS *new file name*

Purpose: Changes the name of a disk file.

Notes: After a NAME command is executed, the file exists on the same disk, in the same disk location, but has a new name.

Parameters: *old file name* is the name of the file to be changed; it must be enclosed in double quotation marks and must exist on the default or the specified disk. *new file name* is the name used for renaming; it also must be enclosed in double quotation marks.

The NAME command cannot be used to create a copy of a file, or to move a file from one subdirectory to another, or from one disk to another.

To rename a file on disk A, from GWRF1303.BAS to the new name GWRF1304.BAS, use the following command:

```
NAME "A:GWRF1303.BAS" AS "A:GWRF1304.BAS"
```

If a file with the original name does not exist, a "File not found" error message occurs. If a file already exists with the same name as the *new file name* of the NAME command, an error message, "File already exists," occurs, and the file is not renamed.

LOC Function

The LOC function returns three different values, depending on how it is used: when sending or receiving a file through a communications port, with random access files, or with sequential files.

LOC   **Function**

Syntax: LOC(*numeric argument*)

Purpose: Returns the current position of a value in the file.

Notes: The number returned by the LOC function varies with the type of file in use. See the information following this syntax box.

Parameters: *numeric argument* is the file number used when the file was opened.

File buffers are used when data is transferred to or from various computer devices, including files. A file buffer is merely a temporary storage area in the computer's memory, and may be referred to as an *input buffer* (used in reading from a file) or an *output buffer* (used in writing to a file).

The number returned by the LOC function varies with the type of file in use, as follows.

- When transmitting or receiving a file through a communications port, LOC returns the number of characters in the input buffer waiting to be read.

- When used with random access files, LOC returns the record number that was just read from or written to with a GET or PUT statement. See GET and PUT statements in this chapter.

- When used with sequential files in the INPUT or OUTPUT mode, LOC returns the number of 128-byte blocks read from or written to the file since it was opened. In the APPEND mode, LOC returns the number of complete new 128-byte blocks that have been written (appended) to the file. See OPEN statement in this chapter.

If a file has been opened but no disk input/output has been performed, LOC returns zero.

WIDTH Statement for Devices

The WIDTH statement was discussed in Chapter 8, "Terminal I/O," but is also included here because it can be used with files and devices.

WIDTH   **Statement**

Syntax:

> WIDTH *file number, size*
> or
> WIDTH *"device", size*

Purpose: Sets the printed line width, in number of characters, of file or I/O device information.

Notes: Valid devices are SCRN:, LPT1:, LPT2:, LPT3:, COM1:, and COM2:.

Parameters: *file number* is the file number used to open the device or file; *size* is an integer in the range 0 to 255, the new width; *device* is a valid device described under "Notes."

You can set the width of your printer with a WIDTH statement like this:

```
210 WIDTH "LPT1:", 60
```

The printer could then be opened as a file in the same program, to recognize this stored printing-width value.

```
320 OPEN "LPT1:" FOR OUTPUT AS #1
```

While the file is open, printing conforms with the specified width. You can change the printing width with a new WIDTH statement while the file is open.

```
450 WIDTH #1, 40
```

Printing now uses the new value (40 characters per line). Valid widths for this use are 1 through 255. The maximum value possible is a function of your printer.

A value of 255 has special meaning when used with WIDTH in the device/file context. Suppose file #1 has been opened as LPT1:. Then a WIDTH #1, 255 statement is executed, as follows:

```
310 OPEN "LPT1:" AS #1
320 WIDTH #1, 255
```

This statement suppresses the line feed (producing only a carriage return). One possible use of this is to underline printed characters, as demonstrated in the short program and result shown in Figure 14-5. LPRINT is used to force a line feed at line 50. The LPRINT statement is not affected by the WIDTH statement because you aren't accessing the printer by a device number.

Figure 14-5.

```
Program:

10 OPEN "LPT1:" AS #1
20 WIDTH #1, 255
30 PRINT #1, "Go back and underline one word."
40 PRINT #1, SPC(12); STRING$(9, "_")
50 LPRINT
60 PRINT #1, "Isn't that nice?"

Output:

Go back and underline one word.
Isn't that nice?
```

Results of WIDTH #1, 255 statement

OPEN and CLOSE
Statements for Devices

The keyboard, screen, and printer devices can be opened as files in the Output mode. Data can then be sent to the specified device with PRINT# and WRITE# statements. The keyboard can be opened as a file in the Input mode. This allows INPUT# and LINE INPUT# statements to access the keyboard.

```
OPEN "SCRN:" FOR OUTPUT AS #1
OPEN "LPT1:" FOR OUTPUT AS #2
OPEN "KYBD:" FOR INPUT AS #3
```

When a device has been opened as a file, use a CLOSE statement to close the device file just as you would to close other files.

```
CLOSE #1, #2, #3
```

LOCK and UNLOCK Statements

LOCK and UNLOCK are used in a multidevice environment, often referred to as a *network* or *network environment*. The LOCK statement is used to restrict access to all or part of a file that has been opened.

LOCK   **Statement**

Syntax: LOCK [#]*n*[,[*record number1*][TO *record number2*]]

Purpose: Restricts access to all or part of an open file.

Notes: Used in a multidevice environment.

Parameters: *n* is the number assigned to the file when opened; *record number1* is the number of an individual record to be locked, or the first record number of a range of records to be locked; *record number2* is the last record number in the range of records to be locked.

UNLOCK releases locks that have been applied to an open file by LOCK statements.

UNLOCK   **Statement**

Syntax: UNLOCK [#]*n*[,[*record number1*][TO *record number2*]]

Purpose: Releases locks previously made to all or part of an open file.

Notes: Used in a multidevice (network) environment.

Parameters: *n* is the number assigned to the file when opened; *record number1* is the number of an individual record to be unlocked, or the first record number of a range of records to be unlocked; *record number2* is the last record number in the range of numbers to be unlocked.

LOCK and UNLOCK can also be used as parameters in OPEN statements, as follows:

```
OPEN file name FOR RANDOM LOCK READ AS #1 LEN = 27
```

This statement would open the specified random access file and forbid any other process from reading from the file.

Other forms of LOCK as a parameter in OPEN statements are

- LOCK WRITE forbids any other process to write to the file.
- LOCK READ WRITE forbids any other process to read from or write to the file.
- LOCK SHARED grants full access to any other process.

Since some other user may have restricted a file that you want to use, you can request the specific kind of access needed when you open a file. For example, if you want to read data from a file, open the file with

```
OPEN file name FOR RANDOM ACCESS READ AS #1 LEN = 27
```

This would open the specified file, as long as the read access has not been previously forbidden by another process.

Other ACCESS parameters are

- ACCESS WRITE opens the file, provided the write access has not been previously forbidden.

- ACCESS READ WRITE opens the file, provided the read or write access has not been previously forbidden.

When an attempt is made to open a file for a process (such as WRITE) that has been previously forbidden, the error message "Permission denied" is printed.

IOCTL Statement

The IOCTL statement allows GW-BASIC to send a control data string to a device driver after the driver has been opened.

IOCTL   **Statement**

Syntax: IOCTL [#]*file number*, *string*

Purpose: Sends a control string to a device driver.

Notes: An IOCTL string may be up to 255 bytes long, with commands in the string separated by commas.

Parameters: *file number* is the number assigned to the file when the device drive is opened; *string* is a valid string expression containing characters that control the device.

As an example, say a new driver has been installed to replace LPT2. Assuming the new driver can set the page length for printing, the following lines would open the new LPT2 device driver and set the page length to 66 lines:

```
210 OPEN "LPT2:" FOR OUTPUT AS #2
220 IOCTL #2, "PL66"
```

IOCTL$ Function

The IOCTL$ function allows GW-BASIC to read a control data string from a device driver.

IOCTL$ **Function**

Syntax: IOCTL$([#]*numeric argument*)

Purpose: Reads a control string from a device driver.

Notes: The IOCTL$ function is generally used to get an acknowledgment that an IOCTL statement was successful or unsuccessful.

Parameters: *numeric argument* is the file number assigned to the file when the device driver is opened.

If the page length assigned by the previous IOCTL statement is to be confirmed, you could use the following statement to assign the set page length to the variable PageLen:

```
PageLen = VAL(IOCTL$(2))
```

15

Graphics

You can create a wide variety of patterns, colors, and shapes with GW-BASIC graphics statements, commands, and functions. Your computer must have a graphics adapter, such as a *Color Graphics Adapter (CGA)* or an *Extended Graphics Adapter (EGA)*. Higher-resolution graphics adapters will also provide the necessary hardware for producing graphics displays.

The following graphics statements, commands, and functions are discussed in this chapter:

BLOAD	COLOR	PAINT	PMAP	PUT
BSAVE	DRAW	PALETTE	POINT	SCREEN
CIRCLE	GET	PALETTE USING	PRESET	VIEW
CLS	LINE	PCOPY	PSET	WINDOW

SCREEN, COLOR, and CLS Statements

These three statements are used to set an appropriate graphics display for the task you want to perform. There are several possible screen modes, one of which is selected by a SCREEN statement. The COLOR statement allows you to select colors to be used, and the CLS statement prepares a clean screen.

SCREEN Statement

The SCREEN statement sets specifications for the display screen. In this chapter, graphics screen modes 1, 2, 7, 8, 9, and 10 are described. SCREEN as used in the text mode (SCREEN 0) is discussed in Chapter 8, "Terminal I/O."

SCREEN   **Statement**

Syntax: SCREEN *mode*[,[*colorflag*]][,[*apage*]][,[*vpage*]]

Purpose: Sets specifications for a screen mode.

Notes: The meaning of *colorflag* for graphics modes is the reverse of its meaning in SCREEN 0, the text mode. The *apage* parameter (active page) is the area in memory where graphics are being written; *vpage* (visual page) is the area of memory being displayed on the screen.

Parameters: *mode* is the screen mode, an integer expression whose value must be 0, 1, 2, 7, 8, 9, or 10; colorflag is a numeric expression that is either true (nonzero), enabling color, or false (0), disabling color; *apage* is an integer expression denoting the "active" memory page; *vpage* is an integer expression denoting the "visual" memory page.

Table 15-1 shows the screen modes available for the most common graphics hardware. Appendix H, "Screen Descriptions and Colors," describes the attributes of available screen modes.

In its simplest form, the SCREEN statement uses only the *mode* parameter. The default value for the *colorflag* expression (true, enabling color) is used. The default condition is that the active

Table 15-1.

Display Adapter	Screen Modes Available
MDPA—Monochrome Display and Printer Adapter	0
CGA—Color Graphics Adapter	0, 1, 2
EGA—Enhanced Graphics Adapter	0, 1, 2, 7, 8
(with Enhanced Color Display)	0, 1, 2, 7, 8, 9
(with Monochrome Display)	10

NOTE: Some hardware configurations may provide other modes. For example, Tandy 1000 series computers provide modes 3 and 4.

Standard Screen Modes

page and the visual page values are the same (both equal to 1). Thus:

SCREEN 1   *(Sets the display to graphics, mode 1)*

or

SCREEN 2   *(Sets the display to graphics, mode 2)*

Text may be printed in a graphics mode. In modes 1 and 7, the text width is 40 characters. In modes 2, 8, 9, and 10, text width is 80 characters.

To produce animation in a graphics mode, the *apage* and *vpage* parameters are used to allow you to write to one area of memory (*apage*) while you are displaying another area of memory (*vpage*). For example:

SCREEN 7, , 1, 2   *(Work in page 1, display page 2)*

or

SCREEN 7, , 2, 1   *(Work in page 2, display page 1)*

COLOR Statement

COLOR is used to select display colors for the screen. The COLOR statement as used in the text mode (SCREEN 0) is discussed in Chapter 8, "Terminal I/O." Appendix H, "Screen Descriptions and Colors," describes the attributes of available screen modes.

COLOR   **Statement**

Syntax: COLOR [*color1*][,[*color2*]]

Purpose: Selects colors for the display screen.

Notes: The COLOR statement produces an "Illegal function call" error when used in SCREEN 2.

Parameters: For SCREEN 1, *color1* is an integer expression in the range 0 to 7 (the background color); *color2* is an odd or even integer expression determining the set of three colors used in addition to the background color. For SCREEN 7 through 10, *color1* is an integer expression, the foreground color number; *color2* is an integer expression, the background color number. For SCREEN 7 through 10, the range of values for *color1* and *color2* depends on the screen mode in use (see Appendix H, "Screen Descriptions and Colors").

The SCREEN and COLOR statements are usually used together to produce the appropriate display screen. Table 15-2 shows examples of SCREEN and COLOR statements.

CLS Statement

The CLS statement is described in Chapter 8, "Terminal I/O." Its syntax is included here for your convenience.

Table 15-2.

Statements	*Effect*
SCREEN 0:	
COLOR 1, 0, 8	foreground 1, background 0, border 8
SCREEN 1:	
COLOR 0, 0	background 0, palette 0
COLOR 2, 1	background 2, palette 1
COLOR 1	background 1, palette default
COLOR , 1	background default, palette 1
SCREEN 7:	
COLOR 3, 5	foreground 3, background 5
COLOR 4	foreground 4, background default
COLOR , 3	foreground default, background 3
SCREEN 8:	
COLOR 5, 7	foreground 5, background 7
SCREEN 9:	
COLOR 1, 2	foreground 1, background 2

SCREEN and COLOR Statement Examples

CLS   **Statement**

Syntax: CLS

Purpose: Clears the display screen.

Notes: The screen may also be cleared by pressing CTRL+HOME, CTRL+L, or by changing screen modes with a SCREEN or WIDTH statement. If a graphics VIEW statement (described later in this chapter) has been used, CLS clears only the last viewport specified.

Parameters: None.

The SCREEN, COLOR, and CLS statements are usually executed before any subsequent graphics statements are used.

PSET, PRESET, LINE, and CIRCLE Statements

These statements are the "building blocks" of most graphics statements. PSET turns on individual pixels on a graphics screen (sets the color of a pixel). PRESET turns off individual pixels on a graphics screen (sets a pixel to the background color). LINE draws a series of adjacent points to form a line. CIRCLE draws curved lines, or arcs, used to form all or part of a circle or an ellipse.

PSET and PRESET Statements

These two statements display a point at the intersection of a specified column and row on a graphics screen.

PSET and PRESET   Statements

Syntax:
   PSET [STEP](*xcoord, ycoord*)[, *color*]
   PRESET [STEP](*xcoord, ycoord*)[, *color*]

Purpose: Displays a point at a specified position on the screen in a specified color.

Notes: If *xcoord* or *ycoord* causes the point to be positioned beyond the edge of the screen, the point is not set. Rows (*xcoord*) and columns (*ycoord*) are numbered from 0 at the upper-left corner of the screen.

Parameters: STEP specifies that *xcoord* and *ycoord* are relative offsets for column and row with respect to the last point referenced by a graphics statement. If STEP is omitted, *xcoord* is a numeric expression designating the column of the display screen where the point is to be placed, and *ycoord* is a numeric expression designating the row of the display screen where the point is to be placed. The *color* parameter is an integer expression designating the color number to be used for coloring the point.

Here is a short program that draws a line from the upper-left corner of the screen to the point (80, 80) using PSET.

```
10 SCREEN 1: COLOR 1, 0: CLS: KEY OFF
20 FOR row = 0 to 80
30   column = row
40   PSET(column, row), 1
50 NEXT row
```

When you run the program, notice that the line is drawn in green on a blue background. The COLOR statement selected the blue background (color 1) and palette 0 (containing the 1-green, 2-red, and 3-brown colors). The PSET statement selects one of the colors (1-green) from the palette. The screen mode and colors in use remain in effect until you change them.

Add the following lines to the foregoing program:

```
80 start! = TIMER: WHILE TIMER < start! + 1: WEND
90 FOR row = 0 TO 80
100    column = row
110    PRESET(column, row)
120 NEXT row
130 start! = TIMER: WHILE TIMER < start! + 1: WEND
```

When you run the program now, the green line stays on the screen for a short time and is then erased by the PRESET statement in line 110. Since the PRESET statement specifies no color, the background color (the default value for PRESET) is used. Setting the previously colored points to the background color erases them.

The default color for PSET is color 3. You can also use PSET to erase points by using the background color number (0), as in:

```
PSET(column, row), 0
```

Program 15-1, PSET Points, allows you to enter a column and row in SCREEN 1. If the point is within the specified range (column 1 to 318, row 0 to 199), the point is plotted on the screen in white. Since a pixel turned on by PSET is so small, a cyan arrow points to the pixel.

Enter and run the program. After a point is displayed, press any key to select another point; or press ESC to quit.

LINE Statement

The LINE statement is used to draw a line between two points. With the appropriate parameters, LINE will draw a complete rectangle.

Program 15-1.

```
1 REM ** PSET Points **
2 ' GW-BASIC: The Reference, Chapter 15.  File: GWRF1501.BAS
3 ' Enter coordinates and plot points

100 REM ** Initialize **
110 SCREEN 1: CLS: KEY OFF: DEFINT A-Z
120 col = 319: row = 200

200 REM ** Get coordinates **
210 WHILE col > 318
220   INPUT "Column (1 - 318)"; col
230 WEND
240 WHILE row > 199
250   INPUT "Row (0 - 199)"; row
260 WEND

300 REM ** Plot point and draw pointer **
310 PSET (col, row), 3
320 IF row > 100 THEN sign = -1 ELSE sign = 1
330 LINE (col, row + (2 * sign))-(col, row + (8 * sign)), 1
340 PSET (col + 1, row + (3 * sign)), 1
350 PSET (col - 1, row + (3 * sign)), 1
360 akey$ = INPUT$(1)
370 CLS: IF akey$ <> CHR$(27) THEN 120

400 REM ** Restore screen and end **
410 SCREEN 0: WIDTH 80: CLS: KEY ON
420 END
```

PSET Points (GWRF1501.BAS)

LINE   **Statement**

Syntax:

   LINE [STEP][(*xcoord1, ycoord1*)] −(*xcoord2, ycoord2*)[, *options*]

where line *options* are [*color*][, [*B[F]*][, *line style*]]

Purpose: Draws lines and rectangles.

Notes: If *BF* is used with the *line style* parameter (usually specified in hexadecimal format), a "**Syntax**" error occurs.

Parameters: STEP specifies that *xcoord1* and *ycoord1* and/or *xcoord2* and *ycoord2* are relative offsets for column and row with respect to the last point referenced by a graphics statement. If STEP is omitted, *xcoord1* and *ycoord1* designate the point on the display screen for one end-point of the line, and *xcoord2* and *ycoord2* designate the row and column of the display screen for the other end-point of the line. The *color* parameter is an integer expression designating the color or intensity to be used for drawing the line; *B* draws a box with (*xcoord1, ycoord1*) and (*xcoord2, ycoord2*) as opposite corners of the box; *F* fills the interior of a box; *line style* is an expression defining a 16-bit integer specifying the style line (solid, dashed, dotted, and so on; see Table 15-3).

Table 15-3.

Line Style Value	Pixel Pattern Produced
&H0101	O O O O O O O X O O O O O O O X
&H0202	O O O O O O X O O O O O O O X O
&H0303	O O O O O O X X O O O O O O X X
&H3232	O O X X O O X O O O X X O O X O
&HF0F0	X X X X O O O O X X X X O O O O
&HE38E	X X X O O O X X X O O O X X X O

NOTE: X = pixel on
O = pixel off

Examples of LINE Styles

Table 15-4 shows examples of LINE statements. Program 15-2, Drawing Rectangles, uses PSET and several forms of the LINE statement to draw lines and a series of nested boxes. The box at the top of Figure 15-1 is drawn by PSET. The nested boxes

Table 15-4.

Statement	Result
LINE (10, 20)−(80, 60)	default color, line from (10,20) to (80, 60)
LINE −(60, 80)	default color, line from last point referenced to (60, 80)
LINE −(160, 100), 1	color 1, line from last point referenced to (160, 100)
LINE (10, 20)−(60, 60), , B	rectangle, default color, upper-left corner (10, 20), lower-right corner (60, 60)
LINE (60, 40)−(80, 70), , BF	rectangle, filled with default color, upper-left corner (60, 40), lower-right corner (80, 70)
LINE (40, 30)−(80,90), , B, &H3C3C	rectangle, upper-left corner (40, 30), lower-right corner (80, 90), dashed line
LINE STEP (20, 30)−(40, 50)	line from (last referenced x coordinate + 20, last referenced y coordinate + 30) to (40, 50)
LINE −STEP (10, 50)	line from last referenced point to (last referenced x coordinate + 10, last referenced y coordinate + 50)

LINE Statement Examples

Program 15-2.

```
1 REM ** Drawing Rectangles **
2 ' GW-BASIC: The Reference, Chapter 15.  File: GWRF1502.BAS
3 ' Demonstrates PSET and LINE

100 REM ** Initialize **
110 SCREEN 1: CLS: KEY OFF: DEFINT A-Z

200 REM ** Draw box by PSET **
210 LOCATE 5, 14: PRINT "This box by PSET"
220 row = 24
230 FOR column = 90 TO 240 STEP 5
240   PSET (column, row): PSET (column, row + 24)
250 NEXT column
260 column = 90
270 FOR row = 28 TO 48 STEP 4
280   PSET (column, row): PSET (column + 150, row)
290 NEXT row

300 REM ** Draw nested boxes by LINE **
310 LOCATE 12, 12: PRINT " Press a key to end "
320 LINE (40, 64)-(296, 116), , B
330 LINE (50, 72)-(284, 108), , B, &HEEEE
340 LINE (60, 80)-(272, 102), , B, &H2020

400 REM ** Wait for keypress, restore screen, end **
410 akey$ = INPUT$(1): CLS
420 SCREEN 0: CLS: KEY ON: END
```

Drawing Rectangles (GWRF1502.BAS)

enclosing the "Press a key to end" message are drawn by LINE statements with different line style parameters.

CIRCLE Statement

The CIRCLE statement draws all or parts (arcs) of an ellipse. If the horizontal and vertical axes of an ellipse are equal, the ellipse is a circle.

Figure 15-1.

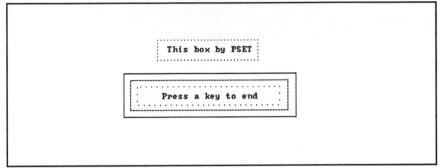

Output of Program 15-2

CIRCLE   **Statement**

Syntax:

   CIRCLE (*xcoord, ycoord*), *radius* [, *options*]

where *options* are [*color*][,[*start*][,[*end*][, *aspect*]]]

Purpose: Draws an ellipse, an arc, or a segment of a circle.

Notes: When the *start* or *end* option evaluates to a negative number, a line is connected from that point to the center of the ellipse.

Parameters: *xcoord* is a numeric expression that evaluates to an integer, the *x* coordinate of the center of the ellipse; *ycoord* is a numeric expression that evaluates to an integer, the *y* coordinate of the center of the ellipse; *radius* is a numeric expression that evaluates to an integer, the radius (along the major axis) of the ellipse; *color* is a numeric expression that evaluates to an integer, the color of the ellipse; *start* and *end* are angle measures (in radians) that specify where the drawing of an arc or segment is to start and end; *aspect* is the aspect ratio of the ellipse (the ratio of the length of the *x* axis to the length of the *y* axis).

PAINT Statement and POINT Function

The PAINT statement and POINT function both involve the individual points on the graphics screen. PAINT allows you to fill a closed graphics area with a selected color, starting at a selected point on the screen. POINT lets you retrieve the color number of a selected point on the screen, or either coordinate of the last point referenced by a graphics statement.

PAINT Statement

PAINT   **Statement**

Syntax:

PAINT (*numericexp1*, *numericexp2*)[, *color*[, *border*]]
or
PAINT (*numericexp1*, *numericexp2*)[, *tilestr*[, *border*][, *skip*]]

Purpose: Fills a closed figure with color or a tile pattern.

Notes: The second syntax form is used for filling a closed figure with a tile pattern. In special circumstances, a third option, *skip*, must be added to properly fill the figure.

Parameters: *numericexp1* and *numericexp2* are numeric expressions that evaluate to integers, the screen coordinates where painting is to begin; *color* is a numeric expression that evaluates to an integer, the color used to fill the figure; *border* is a numeric expression that evaluates to an integer, the border color of the figure; *tilestr* is a string expression defining the tile pattern optionally used when coloring the interior of a figure; *skip* is a string expression used in rare situations to solve tiling problems.

Enter and run the following short program:

```
10 SCREEN 1: CLS: KEY OFF: DEFINT A-Z
20 CIRCLE (160, 100), 20, 3
30 PAINT (160, 100), 1, 3
```

A white circle with a radius of 20 is drawn at the center of the screen, at point (160, 100). The PAINT statement in line 30 colors the interior of the circle cyan (color 1). Painting starts at the circle's center (160, 100) and continues until the border color (color 3) is encountered.

By defining a tile string and using it in the PAINT statement, a tile pattern can be used instead of a solid color. Figure 15-2 shows two short programs and the circles they draw. A different tiling pattern is used for each circle. The first program uses a simple pattern of vertical bars defined by CHR$(&H5). The second program tiles with a crosshatched pattern, formed by

Figure 15-2.

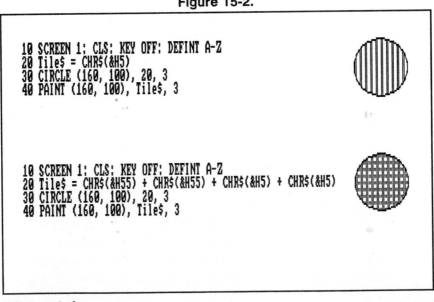

Tiling a circle

```
20 Tile$ = CHR$(&H55) + CHR$(&H55) + CHR$(&H5) + CHR$(&H5)
```

Sometimes problems arise when you try to place one tile pattern over an existing pattern. Figure 15-3 shows two more tiling programs with the tiled circles they draw. The first program fills the circle first with the same tile pattern as the first program of Figure 15-2.

```
20 Tile$ = CHR$(&H5)
```

After the circle is drawn and tiled, a two-second time delay is executed. Then a new tile pattern is defined, and the circle is retiled by a PAINT statement.

```
60 Tile$ = CHR$(&H55) + CHR$(&H55) + CHR$(&H5) + CHR$(&H5)
70 PAINT (160, 100), Tile$, 3
```

Figure 15-3.

```
10 SCREEN 1: CLS: KEY OFF: DEFINT A-Z
20 Tile$ = CHR$(&H5)
30 CIRCLE (160, 100), 20, 3
40 PAINT (160, 100), Tile$, 3
50 start! = TIMER: WHILE TIMER < start! + 2: WEND
60 Tile$ = CHR$(&H55) + CHR$(&H55) + CHR$(&H5) + CHR$(&H5)
70 PAINT (160, 100), Tile$, 3


10 SCREEN 1: CLS: KEY OFF: DEFINT A-Z
20 Tile$ = CHR$(&H5)
30 CIRCLE (160, 100), 20, 3
40 PAINT (160, 100), Tile$, 3
50 start! = TIMER: WHILE TIMER < start! + 2: WEND
60 Tile$ = CHR$(&H55) + CHR$(&H55) + CHR$(&H5) + CHR$(&H5)
70 PAINT (160, 100), Tile$, 3, CHR$(&H5)
```

Retiling a circle

As you can see from the top circle in Figure 15-3, the expected pattern did not occur. This problem sometimes happens when you are retiling a figure. If two consecutive lines of the same color as the point being painted are encountered, PAINT terminates. This problem is solved in the second program of Figure 15-3 by adding the skip parameter.

```
70 PAINT (160, 100), Tile$, 3, CHR$(&H5)
```

The skip parameter tells GW-BASIC to ignore the vertical line pattern while filling the box with the new pattern. You can also solve this problem by clearing the circle with the background color before using the new pattern.

```
65 PAINT (160, 100), 0, 3
70 PAINT (160, 100), Tile$, 3
```

POINT Function

The POINT function has two syntax forms. One form returns the color number of a specified position on the screen. The other form returns one of the coordinates of the current cursor location.

POINT   **Function**

Syntax:

POINT (*numeric expression1, numeric expression2*)
or
POINT (*integer expression*)

Purpose: Returns the color of a specified point, or returns a specified coordinate of the current cursor position.

Notes: The second syntax form returns the screen or world coordinates. In the world coordinates, the row coordinates are numbered from the bottom to the top of the screen. The world coordinate system is explained in the next section.

Parameters: *numeric expression1* is a numeric expression that evaluates to an integer, the column coordinate of the point whose color number is desired; the *numeric expression2* is a numeric expression that evaluates to an integer, the row coordinate of the point whose color is desired. The *integer expression* parameter evaluates to an integer (0, 1, 2, or 3), providing the key to the coordinate desired in the appropriate coordinate system as follows:

0 returns the column in screen coordinates
1 returns the row in screen coordinates
2 returns the column in world coordinates
3 returns the row in world coordinates

Program 15-3, Kaleidoscope, displays ever-changing circular color patterns. The patterns are produced by drawing random-sized circles at the center of the screen. The boundary color and fill color for the circles are randomly chosen. The POINT function is used in the first syntax to determine the color that exists at the center of the circle.

```
230    kolor2 = POINT (col, row): kolor3 = INT(RND * 3) + 1
```

Program 15-3.

```
1 REM ** Kaleidoscope **
2 ' GW-BASIC: The Reference, Chapter 15.  File: GWRF1503.BAS
3 ' Everchanging colored circles; uses POINT

100 REM ** Initialize **
110 SCREEN 1: CLS: KEY OFF: DEFINT A-Z
120 col = 160: row = 100: RANDOMIZE TIMER

200 REM ** Kaleidoscope loop **
210 WHILE INKEY$ <> CHR$(27)
220    radius = INT(RND * 30) + 5: kolor = INT(RND * 3)
230    kolor2 = POINT(col, row): kolor3 = INT(RND * 3) + 1
240    CIRCLE (col, row), radius, kolor3
250    IF kolor <> kolor2 THEN PAINT (col, row), kolor, kolor3
260    start! = TIMER: WHILE TIMER < start! + .0625: WEND
270 WEND

300 REM ** Restore screens and end **
310 CLS: SCREEN 0: CLS: WIDTH 80: KEY ON
320 END
```

Kaleidoscope (GWRF1503.BAS)

If this color (kolor2) is not the same as the fill color (kolor), the circle is filled with a PAINT statement.

```
250    IF kolor <> kolor2 THEN PAINT (col, row), kolor, kolor 3
```

If the color is the same as the fill color, the PAINT statement is not executed. Enter and run the program.

The POINT function is used in its second syntax in the next short program:

```
10 SCREEN 1: CLS : KEY OFF: DEFINT A-Z: RANDOMIZE TIMER
20 WHILE INKEY$ <> CHR$(27)
30    col = INT(RND * 309) + 5: row = INT(RND * 189) + 5
40    PSET (col, row), 1: CIRCLE (POINT(0), POINT(1)), 5, 3
50    start! = TIMER: WHILE TIMER < start! + .5: WEND
60 WEND
```

A point is displayed by the PSET statement in line 40. Then the POINT function is used to return the screen coordinates of that point for use in plotting the circle. Thus, the circle is drawn around that mysterious "last referenced point" that appears so often in the descriptions of graphics statements and functions.

Enter and run the program. Watch the POINT function find the random points that are set by PSET.

Selecting a Graphics Viewing Window

Pixels (picture elements) are the smallest element of graphics screens that can be turned on or off. Pixels of the default graphics screens are numbered from the upper-left corner of the screen, starting with column 0 and row 0. Column numbers increase to the right, and row numbers increase as you move down the screen, as shown in Figure 15-4. This is consistent with the way text rows and columns are numbered. However, GW-BASIC provides statements that allow you to respecify screen coordinate numbering in ways that conform to numbering coordinates in mathematics, science, and other everyday uses. The real-life numbering system is often referred to as the *world coordinate system*.

WINDOW Statement

The WINDOW statement defines a *mapping* of your chosen coordinate system to the physical coordinates of the display screen. WINDOW does not change the way GW-BASIC numbers the physical screen, but it changes the way the coordinates specified in graphics statements are interpreted.

Figure 15-4.

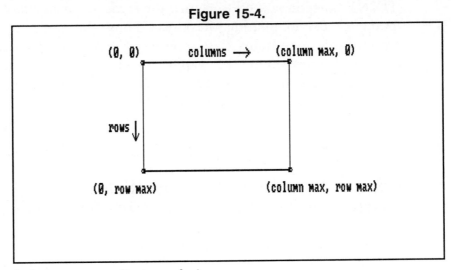

Default screen coordinate numbering

WINDOW   **Statement**

Syntax:

WINDOW[[SCREEN](*xcoord1, ycoord1*) −(*xcoord2, ycoord2*)]

Purpose: Defines the boundaries of the display screen.

Notes: GW-BASIC converts the coordinates specified in graphics statements from the world coordinates specified in the WINDOW statement to the appropriate physical coordinates of the display screen.

Parameters: SCREEN specifies numbering from (*xcoord1, ycoord1*) from the upper-left corner of the screen to (*xcoord2, ycoord2*), increasing numbers from left to right for columns and top to bottom for rows. If SCREEN is omitted, the numbering begins at the lower-left corner of the screen, and row numbering increases from bottom to top, and the (*xcoord1, ycoord1*) and (*xcoord2, ycoord2*) parameters are called *world coordinates*. They may be any valid single precision numeric expressions defining the world coordinate space that graphics statements map into the display's physical coordinate space.

Figure 15-5 shows the mapping of the graphics area defined by the following WINDOW statement to SCREEN 1:

```
WINDOW (0, 0)-(100, 100)
```

Figure 15-6 shows a graph of the SIN function in a graphics area defined by the following WINDOW statement to SCREEN 1. The points are plotted by PSET.

```
WINDOW (-6.28, -1)-(6.28, 1)
```

Program 15-4, Change WINDOWS, draws a box in SCREEN 1 with the coordinates of the following LINE statement, which is in a subroutine of the program:

```
1010 LINE (20, 30)-(80, 90), kolor, B
```

The first box is drawn in the default screen since no window has been defined at that point. The box is drawn with white (color 3 of the default palette) lines. Because the upper-left corner of the default screen has coordinates (0, 0), the box is displayed in the upper part of the screen, as shown in Figure 15-7. Follow the prompt, "Press a key to see the next window."

Figure 15-5.

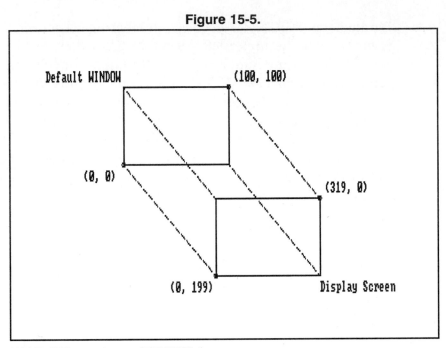

WINDOW mapping to SCREEN 1

The second box is drawn to the screen in cyan (color 1 of the default palette), with the display area defined by the following kolor assignment and WINDOW statement.

```
310 kolor = 1: WINDOW (0, 0)-(319, 199)
```

This window statement inverts the row numbering from that of the previous default screen. Therefore, the rectangle is drawn with the lower-left corner of the rectangle at (20, 30) of the new window area, as measured from the lower-left corner of the screen. The upper-right corner of the rectangle is (80, 90) as shown in Figure 15-8.

Figure 15-6.

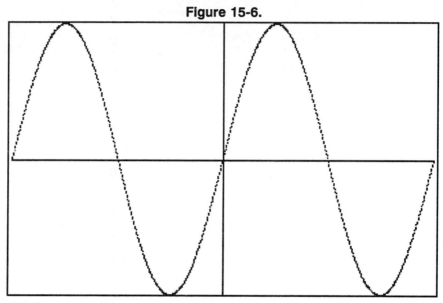

SIN for −2π *to* 2π

The third box is drawn to the screen in magenta (color 3), with the display screen defined by

```
410 kolor = 2: WINDOW SCREEN (0, 0)-(159, 99)
```

Here the use of the SCREEN option in the WINDOW statement tells the computer to number rows in the default direction (downward from the top). Since the WINDOW statement uses maximum column and row coordinates of (159, 99) this time, the rectangle appears as shown in Figure 15-9 with twice the height and twice the width as before.

WINDOW with no arguments disables a previous WINDOW statement. At the end of Program 15-4, WINDOW is used with no arguments, the graphics screen (SCREEN 1) is cleared, and then

Program 15-4.

```
1 REM ** Change WINDOWS **
2 ' GW-BASIC: The Reference, Chapter 15.  File: GWRF1504.BAS
3 ' Draw boxes using WINDOW for the display

100 REM ** Initialize **
110 SCREEN 1: CLS: KEY OFF: DEFINT A-Z

200 REM ** Draw box in default SCREEN 1 **
210 kolor = 3: GOSUB 1010
220 LOCATE 24, 2: PRINT "Press a key for next window";
230 LOCATE 15, 2: PRINT "Default SCREEN 1";
240 akey$ = INPUT$(1): CLS

300 REM ** Draw box in WINDOW (0, 0)-(319, 199) **
310 kolor = 1: WINDOW (0, 0)-(319, 199)
320 GOSUB 1010
330 LOCATE 24, 2: PRINT "Press a key for next window";
340 LOCATE 10, 2: PRINT "WINDOW (0, 0)-(319, 199)";
350 akey$ = INPUT$(1): CLS

400 REM ** Draw box in WINDOW SCREEN (0, 0)-(159, 99) **
410 kolor = 2: WINDOW SCREEN (0, 0)-(159, 99)
420 GOSUB 1010
430 LOCATE 24, 2: PRINT "Press a key to end"; SPACE$(9);
440 LOCATE 6, 2: PRINT "WINDOW SCREEN (0, 0)-(159, 99)";
450 akey$ = INPUT$(1): CLS

500 REM ** Restore screens and end **
510 WINDOW: CLS                          'Restore SCREEN 1
520 SCREEN 0: WIDTH 80: CLS: KEY ON      'Restore SCREEN 0
530 END

1000 REM ** SUBROUTINE: Draw box **
1010 LINE (20, 30)-(80, 90), kolor, B
1020 RETURN
```

Change WINDOWS (GWRF1504.BAS)

the text screen (SCREEN 0) is cleared and restored before the
program ends (lines 510, 520, and 530).

Figure 15-7.

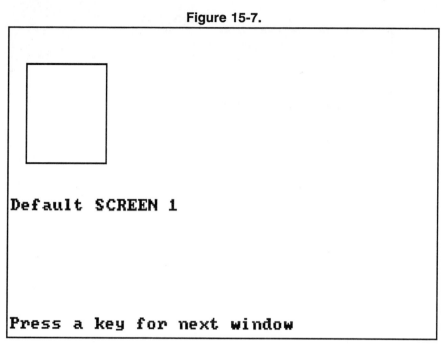

First window of Program 15-4

Figure 15-8.

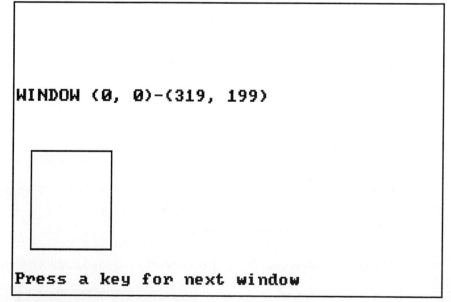

Second window of Program 15-4

Figure 15-9.

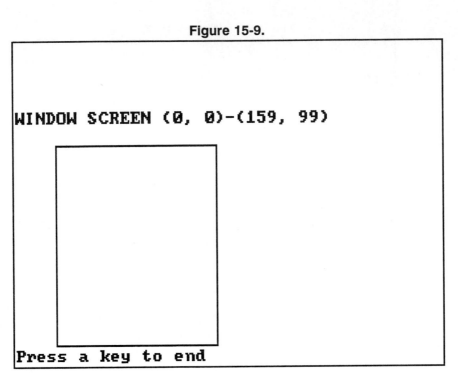

Third window of Program 15-4

PMAP Function

The PMAP function is used to map a point in world coordinates to screen coordinates, or to map a point in screen coordinates to world coordinates.

PMAP   **Function**

Syntax: PMAP *(expression, integer)*

Purpose: Maps graphic expressions to a coordinate system.

Notes: This function is valid for graphics modes only.

Parameters: *expression* is a valid numeric expression; *integer* is 0, 1, 2, or 3, describing the type of mapping desired:

0 converts *x* world system to *x* screen system
1 converts *y* world system to *y* screen system
2 converts *x* screen system to *x* world system
3 converts *y* screen system to *y* world system

If you define a world coordinate system with a WINDOW, all future graphics statements in the program will use world coordinates until a new WINDOW statement is executed. If the data you will use is in screen coordinates, you can use PMAP to convert the data to world coordinates before you plot it.

For example, suppose you want to plot a line from screen coordinates (5, 20) to (320, 100) in SCREEN 2. You are using a display screen defined by a WINDOW (0, 0)−(10, 10). Here is a short program to convert the data and plot the line.

```
10 SCREEN 2: CLS: KEY OFF: DEFINT A-Z
20 WINDOW (0, 0)-(10, 10)
30 col1 = PMAP(5, 2): row1 = PMAP(20, 3)
40 col2 = PMAP(320, 2): row2 = PMAP(100, 3)
50 LINE (col1, row1)-(col2, row2)
```

PMAP (5, 2) converts the *x* coordinate of your data (5) from screen coordinates to the window's world coordinates because of the second parameter (2). This value is assigned to col1. PMAP (20, 3) converts the *y* coordinate of your data (20) from screen coordinates to the window's world coordinates because of the second parameter (3). This value is assigned to row1. The same procedure is used for col2 and row2. These converted values are then used as the end points in the LINE statement in line 50. To see what the conversions were, use the following direct statement after you run the program:

```
PRINT col1; row1, col2; row2
 0  9         5  5
```

When converting data from world coordinates to screen coordinates, the second parameter in the PMAP statement would be 0 for the column coordinate and 1 for the row coordinate.

VIEW Statement

If you want to limit your output to a specific portion of the screen, you can create a *viewport* with the VIEW statement. All future graphics statements in the program are then limited to this viewport.

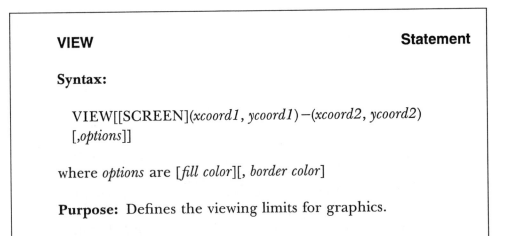

VIEW   **Statement**

Syntax:

VIEW[[SCREEN](*xcoord1*, *ycoord1*)−(*xcoord2*, *ycoord2*)
[,*options*]]

where *options* are [*fill color*][, *border color*]

Purpose: Defines the viewing limits for graphics.

Notes: The SCREEN option of VIEW has no relationship to the SCREEN option of the WINDOW statement. If the SCREEN option is omitted, the graphics points used for drawing are plotted relative to the limits of the specified viewport.

Parameters: SCREEN specifies that graphics points are to be plotted with absolute coordinates; (*xcoord1, ycoord1*) are the coordinates of one corner of the viewport; (*xcoord2, ycoord2*) are the coordinates of the opposite corner of the viewport; *fill color* is the color number used to fill the viewport; *border color* is the color number used to draw a border around the viewport.

Program 15-5, Draw In a Viewport, demonstrates some of the features of the VIEW statement in SCREEN 1. A line is drawn from (5, 5) to (85, 45), as shown in Figure 15-10a, before the VIEW statement is executed.

When you press a key, as prompted, a viewport is defined by line 310.

```
310 VIEW (25, 25)-(75, 75), 1, 3
```

The viewport is 50 pixels wide and 50 pixels high. It has a cyan background and white border, as specified by the numbers 1 (cyan) and 3 (white). The viewport overlays the line previously drawn, as shown in Figure 15-10b. All subsequent graphics statements will be relative to the viewport's limits, because no SCREEN option was used in the VIEW statement.

When you press a key at the prompt, a line is drawn within the viewport by line 410.

```
410 LINE (5, 5)-(45, 45), 2
```

Program 15-5.

```
1 REM ** Draw in a Viewport **
2 ' GW-BASIC: The Reference, Chapter 15.  File: GWRF1505.BAS
3 ' Demonstrates the VIEW statement

100 REM ** Initialize **
110 SCREEN 1: CLS: KEY OFF: DEFINT A-Z

200 REM ** Draw a line in default screen **
210 LINE (5, 5)-(85, 45), 2
220 LOCATE 13, 2: PRINT "Press a key to continue";
230 akey$ = INPUT$(1)

300 REM ** Define and display the viewport **
310 VIEW (25, 25)-(75, 75), 1, 3
320 LOCATE 13, 2: PRINT "Viewport overlays the first line."
330 LOCATE 14, 2: PRINT "Press a key to continue";
340 akey$ = INPUT$(1)

400 REM ** Draw a line inside the viewport **
410 LINE (5, 5)-(45, 45), 2
420 LOCATE 13, 2: PRINT "Magenta line is plotted relative"
430 LOCATE 14, 2: PRINT "to the viewport's lower limit."
440 LOCATE 15, 2: PRINT "Press a key to continue";
450 akey$ = INPUT$(1)

500 REM ** Draw a line that extends beyond viewport **
510 LINE (5, 25)-(100, 25), 2
520 LOCATE 13, 2: PRINT SPACE$(120);
530 LOCATE 13, 2: PRINT "This line goes beyond the viewport."
540 LOCATE 14, 2: PRINT "It is clipped off at the right edge."
550 LOCATE 15, 2: PRINT "Press a key to end";
560 akey$ = INPUT$(1)

600 REM ** Restore screens and end **
610 VIEW: CLS
620 SCREEN 0: CLS: WIDTH 80: KEY ON: END
```

Draw In a Viewport (GWRF1505.BAS)

Since the coordinates in the LINE statement are relative to the lower limits of the VIEW statement, the line begins 5 pixels to the right and 5 pixels down from the upper-left corner of the viewport. The other end-point of the line is 45 pixels to the right and 45 pixels down from the upper-left corner of the viewport. Since the viewport is 50 by 50, the line fits inside the viewport as shown in Figure 15-10c.

When you press a key at the next prompt, another line is drawn by line 510.

```
510 LINE (5, 25)-(100, 25), 2
```

This line begins within the viewport, but is drawn in a horizontal direction 95 pixels long. Since it extends beyond the viewport's limits, the end of the line is clipped (truncated) off and not displayed. Figure 15-11 shows the final display of the program. Press a key at the next prompt to end the program.

Figure 15-10.

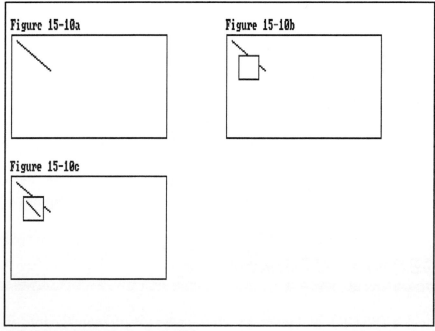

Stages in output of Program 15-5

Figure 15-11.

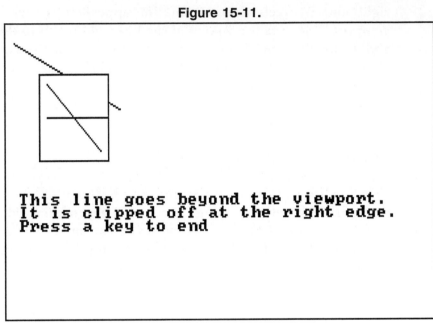

Last display of Program 15-5

If you run Program 15-5 with the SCREEN option in line 310, the results will be completely different.

```
310 VIEW SCREEN (25, 25)-(75, 75), 1, 3
```

The SCREEN option causes all the points of future graphics statements to be defined as absolute coordinates. The viewport appears as before, but the second and third lines are drawn with screen coordinates rather than relative to the viewport.

GET and PUT Statements

The GET statement is used to save a graphics image into an array. The screen information of a rectangular area that contains the image is saved. The PUT statement is used to retrieve information from an array that has been saved and to place it in a specified location on the screen.

GET Statement

Do not confuse the graphics GET statement with the GET statement for files. Their syntax, as well as the actions produced, are different. The GET statement used for graphics transfers the graphics images into an array that is specified in the statement, along with the coordinates of the upper-left and lower-right corners of a rectangular area that contains the image.

GET   **Statement**

Syntax:

   GET *(xcoord1, ycoord1)* − *(xcoord2, ycoord2), array name*

Purpose: Saves a rectangular graphics area into an array.

Notes: The array must be dimensioned large enough to hold the desired image. The amount of memory used depends on the size of the area (number of pixels) to be saved and the numeric type used to save the array; integers take much less memory space.

Parameters: *(xcoord1, ycoord1)* are the coordinates of one corner of the image to be saved; *(xcoord2, ycoord2)* are the coordinates of the opposite corner of the image to be saved; *array name* is any valid numeric variable.

The most difficult part of using GET is determining the size of the array. There are some long formulas for calculating the exact minimum size, but the following simplified formulas give an approximate array size:

colrange = columnmax − columnmin + 1
rowrange = rowmax − rowmin + 1
size = INT(colrange/8 + 1) ∗ rowrange ∗ *colorbits / arraybits* + 4

where the value of *arraybits* is

2 for integer
4 for single precision

and the value of *colorbits* is

1 for screen mode 2
2 for screen modes 1, 9 (64K EGA memory), and 10
4 for screen modes 7, 8, and 9 (more than 64K EGA memory)

For example, the following program produces a starburst at the center of the screen in SCREEN 2, using SIN and COS functions:

```
10 SCREEN 2: CLS : KEY OFF: DEFINT A-Z
20 FOR angle! = 0 TO 6.28 STEP .25
30   inc1! = COS(angle!) * 40: inc2! = SIN(angle!) * 20
40   LINE (320, 100)-(320 + inc1!, 100 + inc2!)
50   LPRINT POINT(0); POINT(1)
60 NEXT angle!
```

As each ray is plotted, LPRINT is used along with the POINT function to print the row and column positions at the end of the ray. From these values, you can determine the maximum and minimum column and row values necessary for calculating the size of the array. Here are the values obtained from the program.

column	360 359 355 349 342 333 323 313 303 295 288
values:	283 280 280 283 287 294 302 312 322 331 340
	348 354 358 360

row values:	100 105 110 114 117 119 120 120 118 116 112
	108 103 98 93 89 85 82 80 80 81 83 86 90 94 99

The maximum column value is 360; the minimum is 280. The maximum row value is 120; the minimum is 80.

To calculate the array size:

colrange = 360 − 280 + 1 = 81
rowrange = 120 − 80 + 1 = 41
array bits = 2 (integer): colorbits = 1 (SCREEN mode 2)
size = INT(81 / 8 + 1) * 41 * 1 / 2 + 4
    = 11 * 41 * .5 + 4
    = 225.5 + 4 or approximately 230

Therefore, the appropriate DIM and GET statements are

```
10 DIM burst%(230)
20 GET (280, 80)-(360, 120), burst%
```

The starburst is shown in Figure 15-12 with a border that indicates the area to be saved by a GET statement. We will use these values in the next section, to demonstrate how GET and PUT work together.

PUT Statement

Do not confuse the graphics PUT statement with the PUT statement used for files. Their syntax, as well as the actions produced, are different. The PUT statement for graphics re-

Figure 15-12.

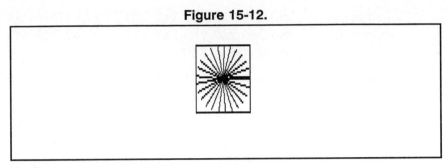

Starburst image area

trieves an array (previously saved by GET) and places it on the screen with its upper-left corner positioned at the specified coordinates.

PUT   **Statement**

Syntax: PUT *(xcoord, ycoord)*, *array name*[, *action*]

Purpose: Retrieves a graphics array from memory and places it on the screen at the specified coordinates.

Notes: PUT and GET are commonly used to transfer images to and from the screen to produce animation.

Parameters: *(xcoord, ycoord)* are the coordinates of the top-left corner of the image being retrieved; *array name* is the name under which the array was saved by GET; *action* may be any of the keywords PSET, PRESET, AND, OR, or XOR. The *action* parameter used determines the interaction between the image being retrieved and the image already on the screen in the position where the image will be placed.

Once an array has been saved with a GET statement, the image can be placed anywhere on the screen with a PUT statement. There are five different ways to do this: with PSET, PRESET, AND, OR, and XOR. A description of each of these actions is shown in Table 15-5.

Program 15-6, GET and PUT Starburst, creates the starburst described in the foregoing section about GET. The program saves the starburst with a GET statement to an array named burst%. The screen is then cleared. The starburst is placed in the upper-left corner of the screen with a PUT statement. A short time delay then allows the image to be clearly seen, before it is erased with a

Table 15-5.

Parameter Used	Result
PSET	Replaces whatever is currently on the screen.
PRESET	*In SCREEN 2*: Inverts the background and foreground colors in the image before placing it on the screen. *In other screen modes*: Colors switch around (not a true inversion).
AND	Performs an AND operation with the current background as the image is drawn.
OR	Performs an OR operation with the current background as the image is drawn.
XOR	Performs an XOR operation with the current background as the image is drawn. When you place an image at the same location a second time with PUT, the image is erased and the original background is restored. Therefore, XOR is usually used in animation when an object may pass over a complex background.

Results of action *Parameter of PUT*

Program 15-6.

```
1 REM ** GET and PUT Starburst **
2 ' GW-BASIC: The Reference, Chapter 15.  File: GWRF1506.BAS
3 ' GET starburst and move with PUT

100 REM ** Initialize **
110 SCREEN 2: CLS: KEY OFF: DEFINT A-Z
120 DIM burst%(230)

200 REM ** Creat starburst and GET it **
210 FOR angle! = 0 TO 6.28 STEP .25
220   inc1! = COS(angle!) * 40: inc2! = SIN(angle!) * 20
230   LINE (320, 100)-(320 + inc1!, 100 + inc2!)
240 NEXT angle!
250 GET (280, 80)-(360, 120), burst%: CLS
260 start! = TIMER: WHILE TIMER < start! + .5: WEND

300 REM ** Use PUT to move starburst **
310 row = 10
320 FOR col = 10 TO 530 STEP 20
330   PUT (col, row), burst%, XOR
340   start! = TIMER: WHILE TIMER < start! + .125: WEND
350   PUT (col, row), burst%, XOR
360   row = row + 5
370 NEXT col

400 REM ** Restore screens and end **
410 CLS: SCREEN 0: CLS: KEY ON
420 END
```

GET and PUT Starburst (GWRF1506.BAS)

second PUT statement. The XOR action is used with PUT, so that the second PUT statement leaves the background intact. The series of PUT statements moves the starburst from the upper-left corner of the screen to the lower-right corner.

BSAVE and BLOAD Commands

If you create a graphics image that you want to use in more than one program, use GW-BASIC's BSAVE command to save a permanent image to a disk file. You can later load the image into an array in another program with the BLOAD command.

These commands are used to save and load the contents of a memory area to a disk file. You do not need OPEN or CLOSE statements, because BSAVE and BLOAD perform those tasks automatically.

BSAVE Command

The BSAVE command saves an area of memory as a memory image to a disk file. The file is a byte-for-byte copy of the data in memory. The file also includes control information later used by the BLOAD command when the file is loaded.

BSAVE   **Command**

Syntax: BSAVE *file name*, *offset*, *length*

Purpose: Saves portions of memory to a disk file.

Notes: BSAVE is much faster than other methods of saving numeric arrays such as those from a GET statement.

> **Parameters:** *file name* is any valid filename; *offset* is a valid numeric expression, the offset into the segment declared by the last DEF SEG statement; *length* is a valid numeric expression, the length of the memory image (in bytes) to be saved.

If you find that you are frequently duplicating graphics arrays, you can build up a library of shapes and figures, with BSAVE and the files it creates. For example, the starburst shown previously in Figure 15-12 could be saved to a disk file and loaded at a later time for use in another program. Assuming you have drawn the starburst at the center of the screen, as before:

1. Use the GET statement to create the array.

2. Use a DEF SEG statement.

3. Save the array to disk with BSAVE.

```
310 GET (280, 80)-(360, 120), burst%: CLS
320 DEF SEG
330 BSAVE "B:BURST.DAT", VARPTR(burst%(0)), 460
```

Notice that the *length* parameter in the BSAVE statement is 460—twice the size used to dimension the array. Since burst% is an integer array, two bytes are needed in the file for each integer. The *offset* from GW-BASIC's DEF SEG is found by using the VARPTR function to find the location in memory where the array is stored. See Chapter 17, "Memory Access and Control," for more information on VARPTR.

BLOAD Command

The BLOAD command loads into memory an image saved with the BSAVE command. BLOAD is much faster than other methods of loading numeric arrays.

BLOAD   **Command**

Syntax: BLOAD *file name, offset*

Purpose: Transfers data saved by BSAVE from a file into memory.

Notes: The arguments of BLOAD are the same as those of BSAVE.

Parameters: *file name* is any valid filename, the same name used to BSAVE the file; *offset* is a valid numeric expression (0 to 65535), the offset into the segment declared by the last DEF SEG statement.

Since the relationship of BLOAD and BSAVE is so close, the method of loading the array into memory is almost the same as that for saving a file to disk. The beginning memory location for storing the array is specified as the offset with the VARPTR function at line 410 when loading the file. After the file is loaded, you may place the image on the screen with a PUT statement. Any valid integer array name may be used.

```
410 BLOAD "B:BURST.DAT", VARPTR(star%(0))
420 PUT (0, 0), star%, XOR
```

Program 15-7, BSAVE and BLOAD an Image, demonstrates the use of BSAVE and BLOAD with the starburst used previously. A GET statement puts the starburst into an array named burst%, and the screen is cleared at line 310. The array is saved by BSAVE at line 330. This program demonstrates that the array can be loaded with a BLOAD statement using a completely different

Program 15-7.

```
1 REM ** BSAVE and BLOAD an Image **
2 ' GW-BASIC: The Reference, Chapter 15.  File: GWRF1507.BAS
3 ' BSAVE starburst and then BLOAD it

100 REM ** Initialize **
110 SCREEN 2: CLS: KEY OFF: DEFINT A-Z
120 DIM burst%(230), star%(230)

200 REM ** Create starburst **
210 FOR angle! = 0 TO 6.28 STEP .25
220   incl! = COS(angle!) * 40: inc2! = SIN(angle!) * 20
230    LINE (320, 100)-(320 + incl!, 100 + inc2!)
240 NEXT angle!

300 REM ** GET starburst and BSAVE to a file **
310 GET (280, 80)-(360, 120), burst%: CLS
320 DEF SEG
330 BSAVE "B:BURST.DAT", VARPTR(burst%(0)), 460

400 REM ** BLOAD the file **
410 BLOAD "B:BURST.DAT", VARPTR(star%(0))
420 PUT (0, 0), star%, XOR

500 REM ** Wait, then restore screens and end **
510 akey$ = INPUT$(1): CLS: SCREEN 0: CLS: KEY ON
520 END
```

BSAVE and BLOAD an Image (GWRF1507.BAS)

array name (line 410) and put on the screen under its new name (line 420). Normally, the array would be saved by BSAVE in one program, and loaded by BLOAD into any other program desired.

Enter and run the program. Listen closely as your disk saves, then loads the BURST.DAT file. When the starburst has been loaded, you can place it anywhere on the screen with a PUT statement, erase it with a second PUT statement to the same location (using the XOR action), and move it to a new location, thus producing animation. Alternatively, you can place identical starbursts on the screen at many locations. In this example the array was saved by BSAVE and reloaded by BLOAD in the same program.

PALETTE, PALETTE USING, and PCOPY Statements

The PALETTE and PALETTE USING statements work only for systems equipped with an EGA adapter, or a VGA adapter that can produce EGA graphics modes. The PCOPY statement is only valid for screen modes 0, 7, 8, 9, and 10. For graphics screens, it is only available for graphics adapters that can utilize these modes (EGA and above).

PALETTE and PALETTE USING Statements

If you have an EGA or VGA monitor, you can change the color code of a color in the palette with the PALETTE statement. You can change the entire palette with the PALETTE USING statement.

PALETTE   **Statement**

Syntax: PALETTE [*color number, color code*]

Purpose: Changes a color in the current palette.

Notes: This statement is invalid for CGA.

Parameters: *color number* is the number of the color you want to change; *color code* is the number of the replacement color.

Here is a PALETTE statement that changes the background color (color number 0) to blue (color code 1).

```
PALETTE 0, 1
```

Here is a PALETTE statement that changes color number 2 in the current palette to yellow (color code 14).

```
PALETTE 2, 14
```

Whereas the PALETTE statement changes only one color in the current palette, the PALETTE USING statement can modify all colors in the palette.

PALETTE USING **Statement**

Syntax: PALETTE USING *array name(array index)*

Purpose: Changes all colors of the current palette.

Notes: This statement is invalid for CGA.

Parameters: *array name* is the name used to set the palette colors; *array index* specifies the subscript of the first element of *array name* to use in setting your palette.

The following program block creates an array that reverses the color codes of a 16-color palette:

```
10 FOR code% = 0 TO 15
20   newpalette%(code%) = 15 - code%
30 NEXT code%
40 PALETTE USING newpalette%
```

PCOPY Statement

This statement copies the contents of one graphics page to another. It is valid in screen mode 0, but is only valid for EGA graphics modes 7, 8, 9, and 10. Multiple pages are not possible in modes 1 and 2, or with a Monochrome Display Adapter.

PCOPY   **Statement**

Syntax: PCOPY *page1*, *page2*

Purpose: Copies one screen page to another.

Notes: PCOPY can be used in EGA graphics to smooth out the movements of animation.

Parameters: *page1* is the page being copied; *page2* is the page to which the data is being copied.

The following short program defines the active page as page 0, and the visual page as page 1. This means that any graphics statements are written to page 0, but the user only sees page 1.

Drawings taking place in the subroutine are made on page 0. When a return is made from the subroutine, the drawings are copied in their entirety to page 1 for the viewer to see.

```
110 SCREEN 7, , 0, 1
120 GOSUB 1010        (Draw on page 0; viewer can't see)
130 PCOPY 0, 1        (Copy page 0 to page 1; display)
```

DRAW Statement

The DRAW statement combines most of the capabilities of other graphics statements, using a mini-language of its own. This mini-language is made up of single-character commands that are enclosed in double quotation marks within a DRAW statement's string expression.

DRAW   **Statement**

Syntax: DRAW *string expression*

Purpose: Draws an object on the screen.

Notes: The DRAW statement is only valid in the graphics mode.

Parameters: *string expression* is a string of DRAW commands that set pixels on the screen.

The commands that may be contained in a DRAW statement's string expression are shown in Table 15-6. Here is a typical

Table 15-6.

Command	Meaning
A n	Rotation angle; n = 0 to 3
B	Blank prefix for next command
C n	Drawing color; n = color number
D n	Draw down; n = number of pixels
E n	Draw up and right; n = number of pixels
F n	Draw down and right; n = number of pixels
G n	Draw down and left; n = number of pixels
H n	Draw up and left; n = number of pixels
M x, y	Move absolute or relative; x,y = coordinates
N	Draw and return prefix for next command
P p, b	Paint; p − color number, b − border color number
S n	Scale; n = scale factor
TA n	Rotation angle; n = −360 to 360
X	Execute a substring

DRAW Statement Mini-commands

DRAW statement that draws a rectangle 40 pixels wide and 20 pixels high in the upper-left corner of SCREEN 1.

```
10 SCREEN 1: CLS: KEY OFF: DEFINT A-Z
20 DRAW "BM 10, 10; R40; D20; L40; U20"
```

The string in line 20 is divided into commands by semicolons. The commands have the following meanings:

Command	Meaning
BM 10, 10	"Blank Move"; move the cursor without drawing to the screen coordinates (10, 10).

R40   Draw a line from the current position 40 pixels to the right (R).

D20   Draw a line from the current position 20 pixels down (D).

L40   Draw a line from the current position 40 pixels to the left (L).

U20   Draw a line from the current position 20 pixels up (U).

DRAW's mini-language, shown in Table 15-6, has a wide variety of commands. Chapter 23, "The DRAW Utility," is devoted to their use.

CHAPTER

16

Sound

You can create a wide variety of sounds with a few GW-BASIC statements discussed in this chapter. These sounds are transmitted through the speaker built into your monitor. You have no control over the sound made by the BEEP statement, other than to turn it on or off. However, you can control the frequency and duration of sounds made by the SOUND and PLAY statements.

The following sound statements, commands, and functions are discussed in this chapter.

BEEP	SOUND
PLAY	ON PLAY
PLAY ON/OFF/STOP	PLAY(n)

BEEP Statement

The BEEP statement sends a sound to the speaker at 800 Hz. (Hz is an abbreviation for Hertz; 800 Hz = 800 cycles per second.) Each beep sound lasts for one-quarter of a second.

BEEP   **Statement**

Syntax: BEEP

Purpose: Sends a short 800-Hz sound to the speaker.

Notes: The sound produced by BEEP can also be produced by pressing CTRL+G, or by a PRINT CHR$(7) statement.

Parameters: None.

The BEEP statement is often used to make a sound notifying you that a long action (such as loading a file) has ended, that some error has occurred, or that some specific action should be performed (such as entering data from a keyboard). For example, when a program requires a specific data file, the BEEP statement can notify you to place the correct disk in the appropriate disk drive.

```
110 BEEP
120 PRINT "Place disk with "BURST.DAT" in drive B"
130 PRINT "Then press a key to continue"
140 akey$ = INPUT$(1)
```

There is one precaution you should observe when using BEEP. When you generate successive speaker BEEPs, the sounds may overlap. Try the following one-line program:

```
10 BEEP: BEEP
```

When you run this program, you will only hear one long beep, because the second BEEP statement in line 10 is executed before the first BEEP sound finishes. To produce two separate sounds, you can add a short time delay.

```
10 BEEP
20 start! = TIMER: WHILE TIMER < start! + .5: WEND
30 BEEP
```

SOUND Statement

The SOUND statement has two parameters—*frequency* and *duration*—that allow you to produce varied types of sounds through the speaker.

SOUND   **Statement**

Syntax: SOUND *frequency, duration*

Purpose: Sends a sound of specified frequency and duration to the speaker.

Notes: See also PLAY in the next section.

Parameters: *frequency* is a numeric expression in the range 37 to 32767, the desired frequency in Hertz (cycles per second). The *duration* parameter, the desired duration in clock ticks, is a numeric expression in the range 0 to 65535; a clock tick occurs 18.2 times per second.

Table 16-1 shows approximate frequencies of notes for four octaves with equivalent music notation. Frequencies start to be

Table 16-1.

Note	Frequency	Note	Frequency
C	131	C 3	523
C#	139	C# 3	554
D	147	D 3	587
D#	156	D# 3	622
E	165	E 3	659
F	175	F 3	698
F#	185	F# 3	740
G	196	G 3	784
G#	208	G# 3	831
A	220	A 3	880
A#	233	A# 3	932
B	247	B 3	988
C 2	262 (Middle C)	C 4	1047
C# 2	277	C# 4	1109
D 2	294	D 4	1175
D# 2	311	D# 4	1245
E 2	330	E 4	1319
F 2	349	F 4	1397
F# 2	370	F# 4	1480
G 2	392	G 4	1568
G# 2	415	G# 4	1661
A 2	440	A 4	1760
A# 2	466	A# 4	1865
B 2	494	B 4	1976

NOTE: The frequency shown for a sharp (such as C#) is also the frequency for the equivalent flat. For example, C# = D^b.

Frequencies for Musical Notes

difficult to hear around 5000 Hz, and those less than 100 Hz do not have much tone. If you set the duration to zero, any active SOUND statement is turned off.

Here is a short program that runs the scale from middle C.

```
10 FOR note = 1 TO 8
20    READ frequency: SOUND frequency, 5
30 NEXT note
40 DATA 262, 294, 330, 349, 392, 440, 494, 523
```

Now try the following short program:

```
10 WHILE INKEY$ <> CHR$(27)
20    FOR frequency = 100 TO 5000 STEP 100
30       SOUND frequency, .25
40    NEXT frequency
50 WEND
```

When you tire of that sound, press the ESC key, and add these lines between lines 40 and 50. Then rerun the program.

```
42    FOR frequency = 5000 TO 100 STEP -100
44       SOUND frequency, .25
46    NEXT frequency
```

Here is one more short program. Enter and run it. Count the notes that are played. Line 50 cuts the last sound off.

```
10 FOR note = 1 to 5
20    SOUND 523, 20
30    SOUND 698, 20
40 NEXT note
50 SOUND 100, 0
```

After running the program, insert the following two lines and run it again:

```
5 INPUT "Delay "; delay!
45 start! = TIMER: WHILE TIMER < start! + delay!: WEND
```

Try several different delay times at line 5. Listen to see when the last note is cut off. The longer the time delay, the longer the note will play.

By experimenting with the SOUND statement, you will discover some quite interesting sounds. Try generating some other sounds—bird calls, animal sounds, sounds of the city, and so on. If you are musically inclined, you may come up with some pleasing tunes. However, the PLAY statement, discussed next, is much more useful for people who can read musical notation.

PLAY Statements and Function

Two PLAY statements and a single PLAY function are described in this section. They permit more control over sounds, and use symbolism more like that encountered in musical notation.

PLAY Statement

The PLAY statement contains a macro language composed of commands that define in detail the notes to be played. The commands are contained in a string following the PLAY keyword. Notes are given in letters, as in musical notation, including symbols for flats and sharps. There are 84 available tones, giving you seven full octaves for play.

PLAY   **Statement**

Syntax: PLAY *string expression*

Purpose: Plays a string of notes through the speaker.

Notes: Arguments used with PLAY's macro commands can be constants or variables. Variables are preceded by an equal sign (=), and followed by a semicolon.

Parameters: *string expression* contains single-character macro commands (some with arguments) that define the notes to be played.

The commands used with the PLAY statement are similar to those used for the DRAW statement in Chapter 15. Table 16-2 shows a list of PLAY commands and the functions they perform.

Music produced by PLAY statements can run in either the foreground (MF, for Music Foreground), or the background (MB, for Music Background). When running in the foreground (MF), each subsequent note cannot be started until the previous note or sound is finished. Therefore, no further statements in a program can be executed until the music string has been completed. GW-BASIC uses MF by default.

When running in the background (MB), each note or sound is placed in a music buffer (an area of memory), allowing a BASIC program to continue execution while the music plays in the background. As many as 32 notes or rests can be stored in the music buffer at one time.

Here is a short program that demonstrates the difference between foreground and background music.

```
10 CLS: PLAY "MF C D E F G A B 05 C 04 B A G F E D C"
20 PRINT "That was music in the foreground."
30 PRINT "Press a key to hear background music."
40 akey$ = INPUT$(1): CLS
50 PLAY "MB C D E F G A B 05 C 04 B A G F E D C"
60 PRINT "This is music in the background.": END
```

The PLAY statement in line 10 starts with the MF command. The entire string of notes in the PLAY statement is played before

Table 16-2.

Command	Meaning
A to G [*type*]	Play specified note; *type* is # or + for sharp, − for flat.
.	(Period) Play note (3/2 times the length).
>	Play one octave higher.
<	Play one octave lower.
L *n*	Note length (*n* = 1 to 64) in one-quarter notes (L1 = 1/4 note, L4 = whole note, and so on).
MB	Music in background.
MF	Music in foreground.
ML	Music *legato* (full length).
MN	Music normal (7/8 times the length).
MS	Music *staccato* (3/4 times the length).
N *n*	Play note (*n* = 0 to 84). Note is referred to by number, rather than letter. The L command must be used with the N command.
O *n*	Play following notes in this octave (*n* = 0 to 6). Default octave is 4.
P *n*	Pause this length (*n* = 1 to 64, same lengths as for the L command).
T *n*	Music tempo (n = 32 to 255). Default is 120.
X	Execute a substring.

Commands Used with PLAY

the PRINT statements of lines 20 and 30 are executed. After the music stops, the PRINT statements are executed; the computer waits at line 40 for you to press a key. When you press a key, the screen is cleared and the PLAY string of line 50 is executed. Since this PLAY statement specifies MB, the notes are placed in the music buffer. Program execution continues at line 60 while the music is playing. The message is displayed, and the program ends. The music plays on until the music buffer is empty (all notes have been played).

Notice the letter O with the number 5, and then again with the number 4 near the middle of both PLAY command strings. The letter O specifies a change in octave. The default octave is 4. In our example, it is used for the first seven notes: C D E F G A B. Then the octave is changed to the next higher octave (5) to play the next note (C). A change is then made to octave 4 (O4) for the last seven notes: B A G F E D C. These changes result in a run up and then down the scale.

The same result could be obtained by these lines:

```
10 CLS: PLAY "MF C D F F G A B >C <B A G F E D C"
50 PLAY "MB C D E F G A B >C <B A G F E D C"
```

Here the greater than symbol (>) placed before a note means the notes that follow should be played in the next higher octave. The less than symbol (<) placed before a note means the notes that follow should be played in the next lower octave.

The letters A through G are used for notes in BASIC, just as in normal music symbolism. Sharps are produced by placing a number or plus sign (# or +) after the note. Flats are produced by placing a minus sign (−) after the note.

ON PLAY Statement

The ON PLAY statement, along with a PLAY ON/OFF/STOP statement, is used to make a background music event trap (which calls a subroutine). The ON PLAY statement defines the trap.

ON PLAY   **Statement**

Syntax: ON PLAY (*limit number*) GOSUB *line number*

Purpose: Defines a background music event trap.

Notes: The event trap must be enabled with a PLAY ON statement. (See PLAY ON/OFF/STOP in this chapter.) If you set *limit number* to zero, you will never trap the event. If you set it to one, you may get a pause before the buffer is filled. If you set it too high, you will trap the event too often and slow your program.

Parameters: *limit number* is the number of notes (in the music buffer) that triggers the event trap; *line number* is the beginning line of a subroutine that is called when the event occurs.

A sample use of ON PLAY is to refill the music buffer when it is nearly empty.

```
120 ON PLAY(2) GOSUB 1010
130 PLAY ON
```

The event trap occurs when there is one less note in the buffer than the number in parentheses in line 120. In other words, when there is only one (2−1) note left in the music buffer, the event trap (GOSUB 1010) occurs. The subroutine at line 1010 contains a PLAY statement to put more notes in the music buffer. The PLAY ON statement is necessary to enable the event trap.

The ON PLAY statement is similar to a user-defined function (DEF FN). It is executed, but its function is not carried out until the music buffer has only one note in it.

PLAY ON/OFF/STOP
Statement

The PLAY ON/OFF/STOP statement enables or disables the event trap.

PLAY ON/OFF/STOP   **Statement**

Syntax: PLAY {ON | OFF | STOP}

Purpose: PLAY ON enables the event trap; PLAY OFF disables it; PLAY STOP inhibits the event.

Notes: There is an inherent PLAY STOP statement at the start of every music event handler (the routine called when the event occurs).

Parameters: None.

The PLAY STOP statement temporarily disables the music event. If the buffer size goes below the number set by the ON PLAY statement, the event is remembered. The event will then be trapped immediately when a PLAY ON statement is encountered. With the PLAY OFF statement, the events are ignored completely (not remembered) until after the next PLAY ON statement.

PLAY Function

The PLAY function returns the number of notes in the music buffer. It has limited use when playing background music.

PLAY   **Function**

Syntax: PLAY(*dummy argument*)

Purpose: Supplies the number of notes in the music buffer.

Notes: If there is no music playing, or if the music is playing in the foreground, PLAY(*n*) will return zero.

Parameters: *dummy argument* is any valid numeric expression. It must be specified but has no effect. A value of 0 or 1 is commonly used.

A typical use of the PLAY function is to delay program execution until the music buffer is empty, as follows.

```
PLAY OFF
WHILE PLAY(0) > 0: WEND
```

Program 16-1, Play Beethoven While Circling, demonstrates background music and music event trapping. It draws random circles on the screen while playing a Beethoven melody in the background.

Lines 120 and 130 use ON PLAY to define and PLAY ON to enable the event trapping. The block of lines beginning with 200 uses the PLAY statement to play the first stanza of the music. Additional music is provided in the subroutine — two more stanzas that are alternately played.

The circles are drawn in block 300. Execution of this loop continues until you press a key, when an exit from the loop is made.

The PLAY OFF statement in line 410 then disables the event trapping. The PLAY function in line 420 allows the music to play until the buffer is empty. Then the screens are cleared and the program ends.

Remember, PLAY can use both music foreground (MF) and music background (MB). ON PLAY, PLAY ON/OFF/STOP, and PLAY(*n*) are used only when Music Background is active.

Program 16-1.

```
1 REM ** Play Beethoven While Circling **
2 ' GW-BASIC: The Reference, Chapter 16.  File: GWRF1601.BAS
3 ' Demonstrates Music Foreground

100 REM ** Initialize **
110 SCREEN 1: CLS: KEY OFF: DEFINT A-Z
120 ON PLAY(2) GOSUB 1010
130 PLAY ON

200 REM ** Start the music **
210 PLAY "T160 MB ML L8 O4 E E- E E- E <B >D C <A"
220 PLAY "O2 E A >C E A B"
230 PLAY "O2 E G# >E G# B >C"
240 PLAY "O2 E A >E"
250 stanza = 1

300 REM ** Draw random circles **
310 WHILE INKEY$ = ""
320    col = INT(RND * 280) + 20: row = INT(RND * 160) + 20
330    kolor = INT(RND * 3) + 1: radius = INT(RND * 15) + 3
340    CIRCLE (col, row), radius, kolor
350    start! = TIMER: WHILE TIMER < start! + .125: WEND
360 WEND

400 REM ** Disable music buffer on keypress **
401 ' Wait until music stops before ending
410 PLAY OFF
420 WHILE PLAY(0) > 0: WEND
430 CLS: SCREEN 0: CLS: WIDTH 80: KEY ON
440 END

1000 REM ** SUBROUTINE: Switch stanzas **
1010 IF stanza = 2 THEN GOTO 1060
1020 PLAY "MB ML L8 O4 E E- E E- E <B >D C <A"
1030 PLAY "O2 E A >C E A B"
1040 PLAY "O2 E G# >E >C <B A2. L8 N0"
1050 stanza = 2: GOTO 1110
1060 PLAY "MB ML L8 O4 E E- E E-E <B >D C <A"
1070 PLAY "O2 EA >C E A B"
1080 PLAY "O2 E G# >E G# B >C"
1090 PLAY "O2 E A >E"
1100 stanza = 1
1110 RETURN
```

Play Beethoven While Circling (GWRF1601.BAS)

CHAPTER

Memory
Access and
Control

When GW-BASIC is accessed, an area of memory is set aside as a workspace for it. This 64K area of memory is known as GW-BASIC's *data segment* and is used to store the program, variables, and other data needed to execute the program. The DEF SEG statement (with no argument) specifies GW-BASIC's current data segment. A specific memory location within this segment is accessed by an offset from the beginning of the segment. Several of the statements, commands, and functions discussed in this chapter require that you specify both DEF SEG and the offset to access a specific memory location. See Figure 17-1.

The following statements, commands, and functions are discussed in this chapter.

BLOAD	BSAVE	CLEAR	DEF SEG	FRE
PEEK	POKE	VARPTR	VARPTR$	

DEF SEG Statement, VARPTR and VARPTR$ Functions

The DEF SEG statement (with no value assigned for an address) and the VARPTR and VARPTR$ functions are used to locate variables, both simple and array types, in GW-BASIC's memory.

Figure 17-1.

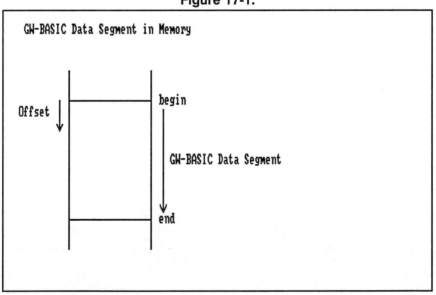

GW-BASIC data segment

DEF SEG Statement

The DEF SEG statement is needed to assign the current segment address to be referenced by subsequent uses of BLOAD, BSAVE, CALL, PEEK, POKE, or USR. If no argument is used with DEF SEG, GW-BASIC's data segment is used as the default segment. When you follow DEF SEG with an equal sign and a value, you can address other areas in memory, such as the display screen.

DEF SEG   **Statement**

Syntax: DEF SEG [= *address*]

Purpose: Assigns the current segment address to be referenced by a subsequent BLOAD, BSAVE, CALL, PEEK, POKE, or USR command, function, or statement.

Notes: Entry of any value outside the address range (0 to FFFF hexadecimal, 0 to 65535 decimal) results in an "Illegal function call" error. If the address option is specified, it should be based on a 16-byte boundary.

Parameters: *address* is a numeric expression in the range 0 to 65535 in decimal notation, or 0 to FFFF in hexadecimal notation (which is usually used because of the boundary requirements).

Although the address of the DEF SEG statement may be specified in decimal, hexadecimal, or octal form, hexadecimal form is often used because segments begin on 16-byte boundaries. Here are some examples of the DEF SEG statement, one with no address and others with an address.

```
DEF SEG                (Sets GW-BASIC's data segment)
DEF SEG = &HB800       (Color video memory; hexadecimal)
DEF SEG = 47104        (Color video memory; decimal)
DEF SEG = &HB000       (Monochrome video memory; hexadecimal)
DEF SEG = 45056        (Monochrome video memory; decimal)
```

VARPTR Function

The VARPTR function is frequently used to locate the address of a simple variable or an array variable. It can also be used to locate the starting address of the GW-BASIC File Control Block (FCB) assigned to a file number.

VARPTR   **Function**

Syntax:

VARPTR(*variable name*)
or
VARPTR(*#file number*)

Purpose: Returns the address in memory of the variable or the File Control Block (FCB). The FCB contains information about data files currently in use.

Notes: A value must be assigned to a variable name before VARPTR(*variable name*) is used. The variable name may be any type: numeric, string, or array. All simple variables should be assigned before VARPTR is executed for an array, because the addresses of arrays change whenever a new simple variable is assigned. The address returned will be an integer in the range 32767 to -32768. If a negative address is returned, add 65536 to it to obtain the actual address.

Parameters: *variable name* may be any variable type (numeric, string, or array); *file number* is any valid numeric expression that evaluates to the number under which the file was opened.

To locate a simple variable, use GW-BASIC's DEF SEG statement, and then use the variable as an argument following VARPTR, as shown here:

```
110 DEF SEG
120 AddrRow = VARPTR(row)
```

The address of the first byte of the data identified by the variable (row) would be returned and assigned to the variable AddrRow.

The address of the lowest-addressed element of an array is found by using an argument of the smallest element. In Chapter 15 under the BSAVE command, the VARPTR function was used to locate the beginning location of an array so that it could be saved to a disk file.

```
320 DEF SEG
330 SAVE "B:BURST.DAT", VARPTR(star%(0))
```

Table 17-1 shows the offsets to information in the FCB from the address returned by VARPTR.

VARPTR$ Function

The VARPTR$ function can be used to assign a variable to a command in a DRAW or PLAY string. VARPTR$ locates the address of the variable and returns its value in string form.

Table 17-1.

Offset*	Length**	Name	Description
0	1	Mode	Mode in which the file was opened. 1 Input only, 2 Output only, 4 Random I/O, 16 Append only, 32 Internal use, 64 Future use, 128 Internal use.
1	38	FCB	Disk file control block.
39	2	CURLOC	Number of sectors read or written for sequential access. The last record number + 1 for random access files.
41	1	ORNOFS	Number of bytes in sector when read or written.
42	1	NMLOFS	Number of bytes left in INPUT buffer.
43	3	—	Reserved for future use.
46	1	DEVICE	Device number. 0 to 9 Disks A through J, 248 LPT3:, 249 LPT2:, 250 COM2:, 251 COM1:, 252 CAS1:, 253 LPT1:, 254 SCRN:, 255 KYBD:.
47	1	WIDTH	Device width.
48	1	POS	Position in buffer for PRINT.
49	1	FLAGS	Internal use during BLOAD/BSAVE. Not used for data files.
50	1	OUTPOS	Output position used during tab expansion.
51	128	BUFFER	Physical data buffer. Used to transfer data between DOS and BASIC. Use to examine data in sequential I/O mode.
179	2	VRECL	Variable-length record size. Default is 128. Set by length option in OPEN statement.

*The Offset is measured in bytes from the beginning of the File Control Block.

**Length of data is also measured in bytes.

Offsets to File Control Block Information (continued on next page)

Table 17-1.

Offset*	Length**	Name	Description
181	2	PHYREC	Current physical record number.
183	2	LOGREC	Current logical record number.
185	1	—	Reserved for future use.
186	2	OUTPOS	Disk files only. Output position for PRINT, INPUT, and WRITE.
188	*n*	FIELD	FIELD data buffer. Size is determined by S: switch. VRECL bytes are transferred between BUFFER and FIELD on I/O operations. Use to examine file data in random access I/O mode.

*The Offset is measured in bytes from the beginning of the File Control Block.

**Length of data is also measured in bytes.

Offsets to File Control Block Information

VARPTR$ **Function**

Syntax: VARPTR$(*variable*)

Purpose: Returns the address of a variable in string form and the value at that address.

Notes: Assign all simple variables before executing a VARPTR$ function for an array element, because the array addresses change when a new simple variable is assigned.

Parameters: *variable* is the name of a variable that exists in the program.

The DRAW statement contains commands in string format. You can use the VARPTR$ function in a DRAW statement to get the value of a variable in string form, by using the variable as the argument in the VARPTR$ function.

The DRAW statement has a scale subcommand (S) that can be used to change the scale of the commands that follow it in a DRAW string. In the following short program, the scale is changed with each pass through a FOR/NEXT loop. The variable scale% is accessed from memory with the VARPTR$ command in string form so that it can be used in the DRAW statement. It is important that no space follow the equal (=) sign in line 30. An "Illegal function call" error will occur if an extra space is used.

```
10 SCREEN 1: CLS: KEY OFF
20 FOR scale% = 2 TO 10 STEP 2
30    DRAW "S =" + VARPTR$(scale%)
40    DRAW "BM160, 100 BE10 D20 L20 U20 R20"
50 NEXT scale%
```

Figure 17-2 shows the five rectangles drawn by the program.

BSAVE and BLOAD Commands

The BSAVE and BLOAD commands were discussed in Chapter 15, but they are so closely associated with memory access that they are included again here for your convenience.

BSAVE Command

To save an image of memory to a disk file, write the image by using the BSAVE command. You do not have to OPEN a file for this purpose. BSAVE automatically opens and closes the file.

Figure 17-2.

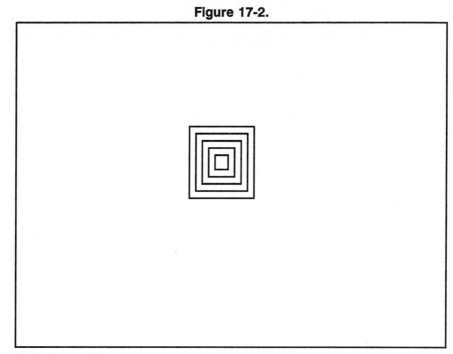

Scaled rectangles

BSAVE   **Command**

Syntax: BSAVE *file name, offset, length*

Purpose: Saves a portion of memory to a disk file.

Notes: Execute a DEF SEG statement before the BSAVE. The last known DEF SEG is always used for the save.

> **Parameters:** *file name* includes a valid disk drive and file name; *offset* is a numeric expression in the range 0 to 65535 (decimal) or 0 to FFFF (hexadecimal), an offset into the segment declared by the last DEF SEG statement where saving is to begin; *length* is a valid numeric expression in the range 0 to 65535 (0 to FFFF hexadecimal), specifying the length of the memory image to be saved.

One use for BSAVE is to save a graphics image of a portion of the screen to a disk file, as was done in Chapter 15. A complete screen may also be saved. The length of the memory area of a video screen depends on the screen mode being used. SCREEN 0 requires approximately 2000 bytes of memory for its screen when WIDTH 40 is in effect, and approximately 4000 bytes of memory when WIDTH 80 is in effect. SCREEN 1 requires approximately 16,000 bytes of memory.

With SCREEN 1 the entire screen is saved, as shown in the following example:

```
10 DEF SEG = &HB800        (Segment in hexadecimal)
20 BSAVE "DISPLAY.DAT", 0, 16384   (Length in decimal)
30 DEF SEG                 (Reset segment)
```

BLOAD Command

The BLOAD command is used to load a disk file that has previously been saved in memory.

BLOAD   **Command**

Syntax: BLOAD *file name* [*,offset*]

Purpose: Loads an image file from disk to memory.

Notes: BLOAD does not perform an address range check. You should be warned *not* to use an address with BLOAD that loads in the memory area of GW-BASIC stack space, your GW-BASIC program, or the GW-BASIC variable area or you may destroy or lose parts of the programs.

Parameters: *file name* includes a valid disk drive and filename; *offset* is a numeric expression in the range 0 to 65535, an offset into the segment declared by the last DEF SEG statement where loading is to begin.

To load the full display screen saved by the previous BSAVE example, execute the following statements:

```
40 DEF SEG = &HB800
50 BLOAD "DISPLAY.DAT", 0
60 DEF SEG
```

PEEK Function and POKE Statement

PEEK and POKE are useful for efficient data storage and retrieval. They are often used for loading assembly language subroutines, and for passing arguments and results to and from assembly language subroutines.

PEEK Function

PEEK performs an action complementary to the POKE statement. The argument for PEEK is an address from which a byte is to be read.

PEEK   **Function**

Syntax: PEEK(*address*)

Purpose: Reads from a specified memory location.

Notes: The DEF SEG statement last executed determines the absolute address that will be peeked into. The byte returned is a decimal integer in the range 0 to 255.

Parameters: *address* is a numeric expression, an offset value, in the range 0 to FFFF hexadecimal or 0 to 65535 decimal.

The following short program assigns values 1 through 10 to the variable used in the FOR/NEXT loop. On each pass through the loop, the PEEK function peeks at the memory location where the value of the variable number% is stored and then the value is printed.

```
10 CLS: KEY OFF
20 FOR number% = 1 TO 10
30   PRINT PEEK(VARPTR(number%));
40 NEXT number%
```

Enter and run this program. You will see

```
RUN
 1  2  3  4  5  6  7  8  9  10
```

POKE Statement

POKE performs an action that is complementary to that of the PEEK function. The arguments for POKE are a memory address (with the appropriate DEF SEG) and the data to be written into that address.

POKE   **Statement**

Syntax: POKE *address, data*

Purpose: Writes a byte of data into a specified memory location.

Notes: The DEF SEG statement last executed determines the absolute address that will be poked into. The byte entered (or poked) must be a decimal integer in the range 0 to 255.

Parameters: *address* is a numeric integer expression, an offset, in the range 0 to 65535; *data* is a numeric integer expression in the range 0 to 255.

Use the POKE statement with great caution. Take care not to poke some value into a location that will destroy information vital to your program, or to the environment in which the program is running.

Add the following lines to the foregoing short program example for the PEEK statement:

```
50 PRINT
60 POKE VARPTR(number%), 50
70 PRINT PEEK(VARPTR(number%))
```

Run the program again with these additions. Notice that line 60 pokes a new value (50) into the location that stores the value of the number variable. Line 70 prints the new value. This time, the result will be

```
RUN
 1  2  3  4  5  6  7  8  9  10
 50
Ok
_
```

CLEAR Command and FRE Function

The CLEAR command initializes variables, closes files, and can be used to set the end of memory used by GW-BASIC and reserve the amount of string and stack space available. The FRE function returns the amount of memory space available for GW-BASIC and can be used to initiate a "garbage collection."

CLEAR Command

The CLEAR command clears out all values previously assigned to variables and closes all open files. It also includes options to change the default values of memory allocation.

CLEAR   **Command**

Syntax:

CLEAR [,[*numeric expression1*][, *numeric expression2*]]

Purpose: Sets all numeric variables to zero, all string variables to null, and closes all open files. Command options set the end of memory used by GW-BASIC and reserve string and stack space.

Notes: GW-BASIC allocates string space dynamically. An "Out of String Space" error occurs only if there is no free memory left for GW-BASIC to use. If this happens, you can increase the space available for use with the CLEAR command. The *numeric expression1* argument is used to ensure that the GW-BASIC memory use does not extend into an area where an assembly language subroutine may be placed.

Parameters: *numeric expression1*, if specified, sets the maximum number of bytes available for use by GW-BASIC; the value cannot exceed the memory available in your computer. The *numeric expression2* parameter sets aside stack space for GW-BASIC. When GW-BASIC is first accessed, the stack space is set to 512 bytes, or one-eighth the available memory, whichever is smaller. GW-BASIC uses the stack space for keeping track of internal data that it uses.

The CLEAR command performs the following tasks:

- Closes all files
- Clears all COMMON and user variables

- Resets the stack

- Releases all disk buffers

- Turns off any sound

- Resets sound to Music Foreground

- Resets PEN to off

- Resets STRIG to off

- Disables ON ERROR trapping

Here are several forms of the CLEAR command, along with the related action performed.

CLEAR	Zeros variables and nulls strings
CLEAR 32768	Zeros variables, nulls strings, and protects memory above 32768
CLEAR ,, 2000	Zeros variables, nulls strings, allocates 2000 bytes for stack space, and uses all available memory in the segment
CLEAR, 32768, 2000	Zeros variables, nulls strings, protects memory above 32768, and allocates 2000 bytes for stack space

FRE Function

The FRE function allows you to check the amount of memory space available for GW-BASIC. It also can initiate a process called "garbage collection," which reorganizes the use of memory space into a more efficient form.

FRE   **Function**

Syntax:

FRE(*string expression*)
or
FRE(*numeric constant*)

Purpose: Returns the number of available bytes in allocated string memory (*numeric constant* as parameter), and/or initiates a "garbage collection" activity (*string expression* as parameter).

Notes: Before FRE(*string expression*) returns the amount of space available in allocated string memory, GW-BASIC initiates an activity called "garbage collection." Data in string memory space is collected and reorganized—unused portions of fragmented strings are discarded to make room for new input. If FRE is not used, GW-BASIC will not initiate garbage collection until all available space has been used. Garbage collection may take 1 to 1.5 minutes. Using FRE("") or any string forces garbage collection periodically, resulting in shorter delays for each garbage collection.

Parameters: *string expression* and *numeric constant* are dummy arguments. Any valid string may be used for *string expression*, and any valid number for *numeric constant*.

Program 17-1, Monitor Memory, uses FRE in both syntaxes. FRE(0) is used to check the use of memory as the program progresses. Just before the program ends, FRE("") is used to

Program 17-1.

```
1 REM ** Monitor Memory **
2 ' GW-BASIC: The Reference, Chapter 17.  File: GWRF1701.BAS
3 ' Demonstrate FRE function

100 REM ** Initialize and check memory **
110 CLS: KEY OFF: DEFINT A-Z
120 PRINT FRE(0)

200 REM ** Dimension strings and check memory **
210 DIM astring$(100)
220 PRINT FRE(0)

300 REM ** Assign array elements and check memory **
310 FOR number = 1 TO 100
320   astring$(number) = STRING$(10, "a")
330 NEXT number
340 PRINT FRE(0)

400 REM ** Assign new elements to array and check memory **
410 FOR count = 1 TO 50
420   astring$(count) = STRING$(5, "b")
430 NEXT count
440 PRINT FRE(0)

500 REM ** Initiate garbage collection and check memory **
510 PRINT FRE(" ")
520 END
```

Monitor Memory (GWRF1701.BAS)

initiate a garbage collection and print the available memory after the collection.

```
RUN
  59360              (Initial memory)
  59043              (Memory after dimensioning array)
  58033              (Memory after entering array elements)
  57774              (Memory after entering new elements)
  58274              (Memory after garbage collection)
```

Then the program ends. The values printed are machine specific; therefore, your results will probably be different than the preceding values printed (on the authors' machines) at various stages of the program.

18

System Routines

The commands, functions, and statements discussed in this chapter are related to the computer system. Some of them duplicate DOS commands, but are more convenient to use when operating within GW-BASIC. Some of them (such as DATE$, TIME$, and TIMER) have been discussed earlier, but their formal syntax is included in this chapter.

The following statements, commands, and functions are discussed in this chapter.

CHDIR   DATE\$ ENVIRON ENVIRON\$ MKDIR
ON TIMER RMDIR SYSTEM   TIME\$ TIMER
TIMER ON/OFF/STOP

MKDIR, CHDIR, and RMDIR Commands

These three commands are duplicates of the same commands from DOS. MKDIR is used to make a new directory or subdirectory. CHDIR is used to change from one working directory to another. RMDIR is used to remove a directory or subdirectory.

MKDIR Command

The MKDIR command creates a new directory. The MKDIR command in GW-BASIC is equivalent to the MKDIR command of DOS. Although the DOS command can be executed with a shortcut (MD), the GW-BASIC MKDIR command has no shortcut.

MKDIR   **Command**

Syntax: MKDIR *path name*

Purpose: Creates a directory or subdirectory.

Notes: There is no shortcut for the MKDIR command, as there is in DOS.

Parameters: *path name* is a string expression, not exceeding 63 alphanumeric characters, naming the directory or subdirectory to be created.

Here are two examples of the MKDIR command. The first makes a new directory (ORDERS on the disk in drive C). The second makes a new subdirectory within that directory (SMITH, within the directory ORDERS on the disk in drive C).

```
MKDIR "C:ORDERS"
MKDIR "C:ORDERS\SMITH"
```

Once a directory is made, you can save files to it. For example, the following SAVE command saves the file named BOLTS.DAT to subdirectory SMITH in the ORDERS directory:

```
SAVE "C:ORDERS\SMITH\BOLTS.DAT"
```

CHDIR Command

The CHDIR command is used to change the current default directory. The CHDIR is another command that duplicates the DOS command of the same name. The DOS command can be executed with a shortcut (CD), but the GW-BASIC CHDIR command has no shortcut.

CHDIR   **Command**

Syntax: CHDIR *path name*

Purpose: Changes from one working directory or subdirectory to another.

Notes: There is no shortcut for the CHDIR command, as there is in DOS.

Parameters: *path name* is a string expression, not exceeding 63 alphanumeric characters, naming the directory or subdirectory to which you are changing.

Assuming you are working in drive C, the following command changes to the SMITH subdirectory of the ORDERS directory of the disk in that drive:

```
CHDIR "ORDERS\SMITH"
```

If you are already in the ORDERS directory of the disk in drive C, you can omit ORDERS.

```
CHDIR "SMITH"
```

To move to a directory (SALES) in drive B from a different drive, use

```
CHDIR "B:SALES"
```

RMDIR Command

The RMDIR command is used to remove a directory or subdirectory from a disk. To do so, you must first delete all files in the directory or subdirectory, using the KILL command from GW-BASIC or the ERASE command from DOS.

RMDIR   **Command**

Syntax: RMDIR *path name*

Purpose: Removes a directory or subdirectory from a disk.

Notes: There is no shortcut for the GW-BASIC RMDIR command, as there is for the equivalent DOS command.

Parameters: *path name* is a string expression, not exceeding 63 alphanumeric characters, naming the directory or subdirectory to be removed.

To delete all the files from the SMITH subdirectory of the ORDERS directory (both are in a disk on drive C), use the following command from within GW-BASIC:

```
KILL "ORDERS\SMITH\*.*"
```

 CAUTION GW-BASIC (unlike DOS) does not display an "Are you sure (Y/N)" prompt when you delete groups of files by using the *.* wildcard designation. Use the *.* wildcard with care so that you do not unintentionally delete files you want to keep.

When all the files in the SMITH subdirectory have been deleted, you can use the RMDIR command to remove the subdirectory.

```
RMDIR "C:ORDERS\SMITH"
```

If all files and all subdirectories have been deleted from the ORDERS directory of the disk on drive C (and the current default drive is C), you can use the following RMDIR command to remove the ORDERS directory:

```
RMDIR "ORDERS"
```

SYSTEM Command

GW-BASIC can perform many operations, but there are some tasks it cannot do (at least not easily). These include formatting or copying a disk, finding the available remaining space on a disk, and running commercial software. To perform such functions it is necessary to return to DOS. This is accomplished with the SYSTEM command.

SYSTEM **Command**

Syntax: SYSTEM

Purpose: Returns to DOS from GW-BASIC.

> **Notes:** The SYSTEM command closes all data files that are open.
>
> **Parameters:** None.

When a SYSTEM command is executed, the GW-BASIC program currently in memory is lost. Therefore, if you need the program in memory, remember to save it before executing the SYSTEM command. As an alternative, you can invoke DOS with the SHELL command (available in GW-BASIC 3.0 and later versions). The SHELL command is discussed in Chapter 9, "Program Control." With SHELL, you can return to GW-BASIC with your program intact.

ENVIRON$ Function and ENVIRON Statement

DOS has an *environment table* that stores equations that define various parameters used in perfoming DOS functions. These parameters include such things as the path used to find files and the form used to display DOS prompts. When you start GW-BASIC, the environment table is set up for GW-BASIC. This table initially is a copy of the DOS environment table. You can retrieve items from the table with the ENVIRON$ function. The ENVIRON statement lets you add or change items in the table.

ENVIRON$ Function

The ENVIRON$ function is used to read items from the environment table. The ENVIRON$ function is not valid for versions of GW-BASIC preceding version 3.0.

ENVIRON$ **Function**

Syntax:

ENVIRON$ (*string expression*)
or
ENVIRON$ (*numeric expression*)

Purpose: Returns the specified environment string from the environment table.

Notes: Not valid for GW-BASIC versions earlier than 3.0. The string argument must be entered exactly as it appears in the table, because the ENVIRON$ function distinguishes between uppercase and lowercase characters.

Parameters: The environment value to be returned is contained in *string expression*, a valid string expression; or *numeric expression*, a valid integer expression in the range 1 to 255.

Here is a short program that uses both forms of the EN-VIRON$ function.

```
10 CLS: KEY OFF: DEFINT A-Z
20 PRINT ENVIRON$("PATH")
30 PRINT ENVIRON$(2)
40 END
```

When this program was run on a Tandy 1000 TX computer with GW-BASIC version 3.20, and MS-DOS version 3.20, the following values were displayed. The results shown are from a specific computer. Your results may not be the same.

```
PATH=
COMSPEC=C:\COMMAND.COM
```

From this result, you can see that no environment value for PATH has been defined. The second item (COMSPEC=) in the environment table for this computer tells GW-BASIC where the COMMAND.COM file is located—in the root directory of hard disk C.

If you want to look at the complete environment table, you can run a FOR/NEXT loop to display the items.

```
10 CLS: KEY OFF: DEFINT A-Z
20 FOR number = 1 to 5
30    PRINT ENVIRON$(number)
40 NEXT number
```

The table items from the Tandy computer were printed as follows. Your display may show something different.

```
PATH=
COMSPEC=C:\COMMAND.COM
PROMPT=$P$G
```

Since there were only three items in this environment table, two blank lines appear following the PROMPT= item. If the table contained more items, they would be printed in the order in which they appear in the table. The third item in the table (PROMPT=PG) indicates that the normal DOS prompt has been changed to display the current drive and directory ($P), followed by the right-pointing arrowhead ($G). Therefore, the prompt for the root directory of the C drive on this computer will be

```
C:\>_
```

ENVIRON Statement

You can add or change items in the environment table with the ENVIRON statement, provided you have GW-BASIC version 3.0 or higher. This statement is not valid for earlier versions.

ENVIRON   **Statement**

Syntax: ENVIRON *string expression*

Purpose: Modifies parameters in GW-BASIC's environment table.

Notes: The ENVIRON statement is not valid for GW-BASIC versions earlier than 3.0.

Parameters: *string expression* must have one of these two forms:

"*name = text*" or "*name text*"

where *name* is the name of the parameter (such as PATH), and *text* is the new parameter text (*text* must not contain any embedded blanks).

If the *text* parameter is a null string, or consists only of a single semicolon, then the item is removed from the table, and the table is compressed. If the *name* parameter does not currently exist in the table, then the item is added at the end of the table. If the *name* parameter does exist, it is deleted, the table is compressed, and the new item is added at the end of the table.

To create a new path to the root directory of drive A, you can use the following ENVIRON statement:

```
ENVIRON "PATH=A:\"
```

Now, using the same environment table from the earlier example, the following program can be run to change the PATH item and then print the first three items in the modified table:

```
10 CLS: KEY OFF: DEFINT A-Z
20 ENVIRON "PATH=A:\"
```

```
30 FOR number = 1 to 3
40   PRINT ENVIRON$(number)
50 NEXT number
```

When the program is run, the new environment table is printed as follows:

```
COMSPEC=C:\COMMAND.COM
PROMPT=$P$G
PATH=A:\
```

DATE$ and TIME$ Statements

Uses of DATE$ and TIME$ were demonstrated in Chapter 2, "Direct Mode Operations," and Chapter 3, "The Program Mode." Here the description of these statements includes their formal syntax.

DATE$ Statement

The computer stores a date in memory. You can read the computer's date, and you can set a new date with the DATE$ statement.

DATE$ **Statement**

Syntax:

   DATE$ = *string expression*
   or
   *today$* = DATE$

Purpose: Sets or retrieves the current date.

Notes: The *string expression* parameter must be in the form shown under Parameters in this box.

Parameters: *string expression* is a string in one of these forms:

mm-dd-yy
mm/dd/yy
mm-dd-yyyy
mm/dd/yyyy

where *mm* is the month (1 through 12), *dd* is the day (1 through 31), *yy* is the last two digits of the year (00 through 99), and *yyyy* is the year (1980 through 2099). The *today$* parameter is a valid string variable to which the computer's date is assigned, in the form *mm-dd-yyyy*.

You can read the date and assign it to a variable in a program:

```
10 now$ = DATE$
```

You can also read the date by using a direct PRINT statement:

```
PRINT DATE$
```

You can set the date by using a direct DATE$ statement:

```
DATE$ = "12/20/90"
```

You can also set the date from within a program:

```
10 today$ = "12/24/90"
20 DATE$ = today$
```

As seen in the following direct statements, the earliest possible date is 1-1-1980:

```
DATE$ = "1-1-1980"
Ok
DATE$ = "12-31-1979"
Illegal function call
Ok
```

The latest possible date is 12 31 2099, as shown in the following direct statements:

```
DATE$ = "12-31-2099"
Ok
DATE$ = "1-1-2100"
Illegal function call
Ok
```

TIME$ Statement

As well as keeping track of the date, the computer also stores the time in memory. The TIME$ statement is used to set or retrieve the computer's time.

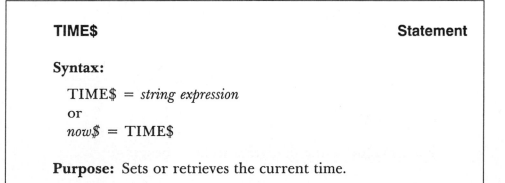

TIME$ **Statement**

Syntax:

   TIME$ = *string expression*
   or
   *now$* = TIME$

Purpose: Sets or retrieves the current time.

Notes: The *string expression* parameter must be one of the forms shown under Parameters in this box.

Parameters: *string expression* is a string in one of these forms:

hh	*hh* is the hour (00 through 23); minutes and seconds default to 00.
hh:mm	*hh* is the hour (00 through 23); *mm* is the minutes (00 through 59); seconds default to 00.
hh:mm:ss	*ss* is the seconds (00 to 59); *hh* and *mm* have the values expressed above.

The *now$* parameter is a variable to which the computer's date is assigned, in the form *hh:mm:ss*.

You can read the time and assign it to a variable in a program:

```
10 instant$ = TIME$
```

You can also read the time by using a direct PRINT statement:

```
PRINT TIME$
```

You can set the time by using a direct TIME$ statement:

```
TIME$ = "8:43:00"
```

You can also set the time from within a program:

```
10 instant$ = "13:22:15"
20 TIME$ = instant$
```

TIMER Function, ON TIMER and TIMER ON/OFF/STOP Statements

The computer not only keeps track of the time, but also has a TIMER function that keeps track of the number of seconds that have passed since midnight or a system reset. The ON TIMER and TIMER ON/OFF/STOP statements use this function to allow you to trap events that happen during a program.

TIMER Function

The TIMER function is used to time events. Quite often it is used when a time delay is required in a program. When the TIMER is used in this way, a delay is independent of the speed of the computer system being used.

TIMER   **Function**

Syntax: TIMER

Purpose: Returns a single precision number representing the elapsed number of seconds since midnight or a system reset.

Notes: Fractions of a second are printed to the nearest hundredth.

Parameters: None.

Enter the following program lines and execute them to see the TIMER count:

```
10 CLS
20 WHILE akey$ <> CHR$(27)
30    LOCATE 1, 60: PRINT TIMER;
40 WEND
```

The TIMER function is used in the following program to find out the time used to perform a FOR/NEXT loop that calculates a running sum of the integers from 1 to 2000:

```
10 start! = TIMER
20 FOR number% = 1 TO 2000
30    total% = total% + number%
40 NEXT number%
50 PRINT USING "##.##"; TIMER - start!
```

Enter and run the program. See how long it takes your computer to perform the loop 2000 times.

The next program performs a time delay of 0.75 seconds as it plays some random sounds. TIMER is used in the time delay, and also to "seed" the random number generator.

```
10 RANDOMIZE TIMER
20 FOR number% = 1 TO 20
30    note% = INT(RND * 500) + 250
40    SOUND note%, 7
50    start! = TIMER: WHILE TIMER < start! + .75: WEND
60 NEXT number%
```

TIMER ON/OFF/STOP
Statement

The TIMER ON statement enables clock event trapping, TIMER OFF disables clock event trapping, and TIMER STOP suppresses event trapping. A form of this statement is used in tandem with the ON TIMER statement, which defines the clock event trap.

TIMER ON/OFF/STOP   **Statement**

Syntax: TIMER {ON|OFF|STOP}

Purpose: Enables (ON), disables (OFF), or suppresses (STOP) clock events that depend on the TIMER.

Notes: This statement is used in conjuction with ON TIMER.

Parameters: ON enables an event trap; OFF disables an event trap; STOP suppresses an event trap.

ON TIMER Statement

The ON TIMER statement defines how often the event should be trapped and the location of the event trap.

ON TIMER   **Statement**

Syntax: ON TIMER *(seconds)* GOSUB *address*

Purpose: Defines how often an event should be trapped (in seconds) and specifies the location of the trap.

Notes: Used in conjunction with TIMER ON/OFF/STOP.

Parameters: *seconds* is the number of seconds between traps; *address* is the line number of the first executable line of the event trap subroutine.

Program 18-1, Number Guess, picks a random integer from 1 to 50. You are asked to guess whether the number is over 25, under 25, or equal to 25. A menu is displayed with these prompts:

Press + for over   25
Press − for under   25
Press = for equal to 25

The program uses TIMER ON and ON TIMER to define a clock event trap that prints the number of elapsed seconds on the screen.

```
120 TIMER ON                 (Enables timer)
130 ON TIMER(1) GOSUB 1010   (Trap each second)
```

The event—printing the time in seconds—takes place in the following subroutine:

```
1000 REM ** SUBROUTINE: Print elapsed time **
1010 LOCATE 2, 36: PRINT now
1020 RETURN
```

While a loop that allows you to press a key is executing, the event trap prints the elapsed time at each second. When your keypress matches the number comparison (num > 25, num < 25, or num = 25), the event trapping is turned off so that you can see

Program 18-1.

```
1 REM ** Number Guess **
2 ' GW-BASIC: The Reference, Chapter 18.  File: GWRF1801.BAS
3 ' Demonstrates TIMER, TIMER ON, TIMER OFF, and ON TIMER

100 REM ** Initialize **
110 SCREEN 1: CLS: DEFINT A-Z: RANDOMIZE TIMER
120 TIMER ON
130 ON TIMER(1) GOSUB 1010

200 REM ** Draw the menu **
210 LOCATE 8, 5: PRINT "Guess the number (1 to 50)"
220 LOCATE 10, 8: PRINT "Press + for over  25"
230 LOCATE 11, 8: PRINT "Press - for under 25"
240 LOCATE 12, 8: PRINT "Press = for equal 25"
250 LINE (52, 68)-(218, 100), , B

300 REM ** Get number and play **
310 num = INT(RND * 50) + 1: start! = TIMER
320 WHILE akey$ <> CHR$(27)
330    WHILE akey$ = ""
340      akey$ = INKEY$
350      now = TIMER - start!
360    WEND
370    IF akey$ = "+" AND num > 25 THEN PLAY OFF: GOTO 510
380    IF akey$ = "-" AND num < 25 THEN PLAY OFF: GOTO 510
390    IF akey$ = "=" AND num = 25 THEN PLAY OFF: GOTO 510
400    IF akey$ <> CHR$(27) THEN akey$ = ""
410 WEND

500 REM ** Play again or end? **
510 LOCATE 22, 2: PRINT "Press ESC to quit";
520 LOCATE 23, 2: PRINT "Press another key to play more";
530 LOCATE 24, 2: PRINT "The number was"; num;: akey$ = INPUT$(1)
540 IF akey$ <> CHR$(27) THEN akey$ = "": CLS: GOTO 120
550 END

1000 REM ** SUBROUTINE: Print elapsed time **
1010 LOCATE 2, 36: PRINT now
1020 RETURN
```

Number Guess (GWRF1801.BAS)

the number of seconds it took to identify the magnitude of the number. A GOTO statement passes control to line 510, where you can decide whether to quit or play again.

```
370   IF akey$ = "+" AND num > 25 THEN PLAY OFF: GOTO 510
380   IF akey$ = "-" AND num < 25 THEN PLAY OFF: GOTO 510
390   IF akey$ = "=" AND num = 25 THEN PLAY OFF: GOTO 510
```

You can press the ESC key to get out of the loop at any time.

Figure 18-1 shows the screen after a correct guess has been made. The elapsed time in seconds is displayed near the upper-right corner of the screen. The menu is at the approximate center of the screen, and the ending prompts are at the bottom of the screen.

Figure 18-1.

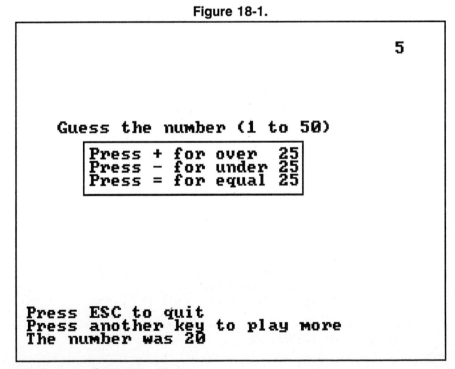

Final screen of Program 18-1

Error Handling

The commands and statements discussed in this chapter are related to error handling. Many kinds of errors occur when programs are being written and used. Appendix D contains a list of GW-BASIC error codes and the messages they print. Some errors can be anticipated, but others cannot. Where you think an error may occur, you can write error-handling routines into the program.

The following statements and commands are discussed in this chapter:

ERRDEV	ERRDEV$	ERL	ERR
ERROR	EXTERR	ON ERROR	RESUME

ON ERROR and RESUME Statements

The ON ERROR statement is the primary statement for error handling. The RESUME statement, contained in the error-handling routine, specifies where program execution should continue after the error-handling chores are completed.

ON ERROR Statement

The ON ERROR statement enables error trapping, and contains a GOTO keyword that specifies the error-handling section of the program. When you want to trap an error, you normally place an ON ERROR statement near the beginning of the program. The statement must be executed before an anticipated error might occur.

ON ERROR   **Statement**

Syntax: ON ERROR GOTO *line number*

Purpose: Enables error trapping and specifies the first line of the error-handling routine.

Notes: GW-BASIC branches to the line specified by the ON ERROR statement, and continues until a RESUME statement is found. If the specified line number is not found, an "Undefined line" error occurs. To disable error trapping, execute an ON ERROR GOTO 0 statement. Then subsequent errors will print an error message and execution will halt.

Parameters: *line number* is the number of the first line of the error-handling routine.

A typical ON ERROR statement is

```
ON ERROR GOTO 1010
```

Here the error-handling routine begins at line 1010. The last executable statement in the error-handling routine will be a RESUME statement specifing where the program should continue.

RESUME Statement

The RESUME statement continues program execution after an error-handling procedure has been performed. The statement has four formats.

RESUME   **Statement**

Syntax:

> RESUME
> RESUME 0
> RESUME NEXT
> RESUME *line number*

Purpose: Continues program execution after error handling.

Notes: RESUME statements are used only in error-trapping routines. A RESUME statement that is not in an error-trapping routine, or a RESUME statement executed prior to the execution of an ON ERROR GOTO statement, causes a "RESUME without error" message to be printed.

> **Parameters:** *line number* is a valid line number identifying the
> point where execution will resume following the error-handling
> routine.

The format used for the RESUME statement determines where
program execution will continue.

RESUME or RESUME 0	Continues execution at statement that caused the error.
RESUME NEXT	Continues execution at statement following the statement that caused the error.
RESUME *line number*	Continues execution at first statement in the specified line.

Program 19-1, Scan a File, is similar to Program 14-2, Scan the
NotePad.TXT File, but contains an error-handling routine for the
anticipated error of entering a filename not on disk in the
currently active drive. ON ERROR executes early in the program.

At the top of the opening screen is a prompt to insert a disk
into drive A.

```
Insert a disk with NotePad.TXT file in drive A.
Then press ENTER to continue.
```

If the file is not found on the disk in drive A, the error occurs, and
the error-handling routine is called. A BEEP statement sounds a
warning from the speaker, and an error message is added to the
previously printed prompt.

```
Insert a disk with NotePad.TXT file in drive A.
Then press ENTER to continue.
File not found.
```

The RESUME statement at line 1020 sends control back to line
210, where the original prompt is repeated. The screen now
displays

Insert a disk with NotePad.TXT file in drive A.
Then press ENTER to continue.
File not found.
Insert a disk with NotePad.TXT file in drive A.
Then press ENTER to continue.

Program 19-1.

```
1 REM ** Scan a File **
2 ' GW-BASIC: The Reference, Chapter 19.  File:GWRF1901.BAS
3 ' Scans a previously created unstructured sequential file
4 ' Includes error handling routine

100 REM ** Initialize **
110 CLS: KEY OFF: DEFINT A-Z
120 ON ERROR GOTO 1010

200 REM ** Open file and enter data **
210 PRINT "Insert a disk with NotePad.TXT file in drive A."
220 PRINT "Then press ENTER to continue.": akey$ = INPUT$(1)
230 OPEN "A:NotePad.TXT" FOR INPUT AS #1
240 ON ERROR GOTO 0
250 CLS
260 LOCATE 24, 1: PRINT "Press a key to see the next record";
270 VIEW PRINT 1 TO 22
280 WHILE EOF(1) = 0                'Loop until end of file
290   LINE INPUT #1, record$: PRINT record$
300   akey$ = INPUT$(1)            'Wait for a key press
310 WEND

400 REM ** Print file size, close file, and end **
410 PRINT : PRINT "NotePad.TXT has"; LOF(1); "bytes"
420 PRINT "Press a key to close the file and end"
430 VIEW PRINT
440 LOCATE 24, 1: PRINT SPACE$(34);
450 akey$ = INPUT$(1)
460 CLOSE #1: CLS: KEY ON: END

1000 REM ** Disk Error Handler **
1010 BEEP: PRINT "File not found."
1020 PRINT: RESUME 210
```

Scan a File (GWRF1901.BAS)

This gives you a second chance to place the correct disk in drive A. The error will keep repeating until you put the correct disk in the drive.

When the correct disk is in drive A, the error does not occur, and the error-handling routine is therefore not executed. The file is opened at line 230, and the error-handling routine is disabled at line 240. The first record of the file appears at the top of the screen:

```
This is a NotePad.TXT file.
```

and this prompt appears at the bottom of the screen:

```
Press a key to see the next record.
```

Each time you press a key, a new record is printed below the previous record. Figure 19-1 shows the screen after the complete file has been printed. Notice that the prompt at the bottom of the screen has been erased.

ERL and ERR Variables, and ERROR Statement

The ERL variable returns the line number associated with an error, and the ERR variable returns the error code. These variables are usually used in IF/THEN, ON ERROR . . . GOTO, or GOSUB statements to direct program flow in error trapping. The ERROR statement is used to simulate the occurrence of an error, or to let you define error codes.

Figure 19-1.

```
This is a NotePad.TXT file.
It is an unstructured sequential file.
Each record is one string, up to 128 characters.
Use the file for notes of any kind.
Doctor appt. 10:30 AM
Meet Kit for lunch 12:30 PM

NotePad.TXT has 208 bytes
Press a key to close the file and end
```

Output of Program 19-1

ERL Variable

You can use the ERL variable to help determine the location of an error. The ERL variable returns the number of the line where the error was detected, but does not tell you what caused the error.

ERL   **Variable**

Syntax: ERL

Purpose: Returns the line number associated with an error.

Notes: ERL is used as a variable and is assigned the number of the line in which an error is detected. ERL is often used in an IF/THEN statement. If an error occurs in a Direct mode statement, ERL returns a value of 65535.

Parameters: None.

ERR Variable

You can use the ERR variable to help determine the exact cause of an error. The ERR variable is assigned the error code of the last error that occurred. Error codes and messages are listed in Appendix D.

ERR   **Variable**

Syntax: ERR

Purpose: Returns the error code associated with an error.

Notes: ERR is used as a variable and is assigned the error code of a detected error. ERR is often used in an IF/THEN statement.

Parameters: None.

To see how ERR and ERL work, change line 1010 of the error-handling routine in Program 19-1 to the following:

```
1010 PRINT "File not found.  Error"; ERR; "in line"; ERL
```

When Program 19-1 is run with this change to line 1010, and the correct disk is not in drive A, the error-handling routine will print

```
File not found.  Error 53 in line 230
```

The error message now tells you the error code (53) and the line in which the error occurred (230). Appendix D lists the message for error code 53 as "File not found," meaning "A LOAD, KILL, NAME, FILES, or OPEN statement refers to a nonexistent file on the current disk."

ERROR Statement

If you want to force a program to terminate, you can create an error with the ERROR statement. Forcing an error can be useful during program development, to test error-handling routines.

ERROR   **Statement**

Syntax: ERROR *integer expression*

Purpose: Allows you to define an error code or to simulate the occurrence of an error.

Notes: If the value of *integer expression* equals an error code already in use by GW-BASIC, the ERROR statement simulates the occurrence of that error, and the corresponding error message is printed. You can also use this statement to define an error of your own. A user-defined error code must use a value greater than any value used by the GW-BASIC error codes. Currently, 76 is the highest value given in Appendix D; you should use a number high enough to remain valid in case more error codes are added to GW-BASIC.

Parameters: *integer expression* is a valid integer expression greater than 0 and less than 255.

The following short program simulates an error with error code number 1:

```
10 ON ERROR GOTO 40
20 ERROR 1
30 END
40 PRINT ERL, ERR
50 RESUME 30
```

Run the program. You will see this:

```
RUN
 20             1
Ok
_
```

Line 10 enables the error trap. Line 20 simulates error 1. Line 30 contains the END statement of the program. Lines 40 and 50 contain the error-trapping routine and its RESUME statement. Because of the simulated error in line 20, the trap is executed before the program ends.

Use a simulated error when you are developing a program, such as Program 19-1, and want to be sure the error-handling routine works. Assume you have written the following lines:

```
100 REM ** Initialize **
110 CLS: KEY OFF: DEFINT A-Z
120 ON ERROR GOTO 1010
```

and this error-handling routine:

```
1000 REM ** Disk Error Handler **
1010 PRINT "File not found."
1020 RESUME 210
```

You look up the error code for "File not found" and find that it is code 53. You can simulate the error by adding a temporary line 130, and an END statement to which the program cxecution will return after the error handler, as shown here:

```
100 REM ** Initialize **
110 CLS: KEY OFF: DEFINT A-Z
120 ON ERROR GOTO 1010
130 ERROR 53
210 END
```

Now test the error-handling routine by running the partial program. This is the displayed result:

```
RUN
File not found.
Ok
_
```

Line 130 forced the error—even though the program does not yet have lines to open a file. The disk-handling section worked as planned. Lines 130 and 210 can now be deleted, and program development can continue.

You can define your own error codes for use with ON ERROR and an error-handling routine. In the example below, line 150 defines an error that detects a color number that is too large. The number 185 is used for the error code. (When defining your own error codes, use a number larger than the highest already assigned—currently 76—so there will be no conflicting numbers.)

```
130 ON ERROR GOTO 1010
140 INPUT "What color number"; kolor
150 IF kolor > 8 THEN ERROR 185
```

If the entry is greater than 8, the ERROR 185 clause forces an error. Your error-handling routine beginning at line 1010 could contain the following lines to handle this specific error:

```
1010 IF ERR = 185 THEN PRINT "Color number too large."
1020 IF ERL = 150 THEN RESUME 140
```

If the error occurs at line 150, the IF/THEN statement at line 1020 will resume program execution at line 140 so that you can enter a number in the correct range. You can write other lines into the error-handling routine to handle other errors.

If an ERROR statement specifies a code for which no error message has been defined, the message "Unprintable Error" is returned.

ERDEV and ERDEV$ Variables

These variables return the actual value of a device error (ERDEV), and the name of the device causing the error (ERDEV$). There are two types of devices, named to indicate how they handle data. The display screen (SCRN), keyboard (CON), printer (LPT1), and modem (AUX) are examples of *character devices*. Character devices process characters serially. Disk drives (A:, B:, C:, and so forth) are examples of *block devices*, which process random input and output to and from sectors of a disk.

ERDEV Variable

The ERDEV variable returns numeric values that reveal information about the type of error and the device causing it.

ERDEV   **Variable**

Syntax: ERDEV

Purpose: Returns an integer indicating the device that caused the error

Notes: ERDEV contains the error code in the lower eight bits. Bits 8 to 15 contain information about the device causing the crror.

Parameters: None.

If the device causing the error is a character device, the value returned by ERDEV will be a negative integer. If the device causing the error is a block device, the value returned by ERDEV will be a positive integer.

ERDEV$ Variable

The ERDEV$ variable returns a string (up to eight characters) that is the name of the device causing a device error.

ERDEV$ **Variable**

Syntax: ERDEV$

Purpose: Returns the name of the device causing a device error.

Notes: ERDEV$ contains the character device name (up to eight bytes), such as LPT1, if the error was a character device. If the device was not a character device, ERDEV$ contains the two-byte block device name (A:, B:, C:, and so on).

Parameters: None.

The following short program demonstrates how ERDEV and ERDEV$ can be used in an error-handling routine:

```
10 CLS: KEY OFF: DEFINT A-Z
20 ON ERROR GOTO 1010
30 LPRINT "If this is printed, no error occurred."
40 END
1010 PRINT "ERDEV ="; ERDEV, "ERDEV$ = "; ERDEV$
1020 RESUME 40
```

If you have not turned your printer on when you run this program, the following message is printed, and the program ends.

```
ERDEV =-32758          ERDEV$ = LPT1
Ok
_
```

Since the printer that caused the error is a character device, the value of ERDEV is negative (−32758). ERDEV$ contains the name of the device, the printer LPT1.

The messages printed in the error-handling routine are not very specific. If you want more detailed information, use lines 10,

20, and 30 as they are, but change the error-handling program as shown here:

```
1010 PRINT "ERDEV ="; ERDEV, "ERDEV$ = "; ERDEV$
1020 DEF SEG: device = ERDEV
1030 memory = VARPTR(device)
1040 PRINT PEEK(memory); PEEK(memory + 1)
1050 END
```

Now run the revised program. The memory location storing the device name is found using the VARPTR function at line 1030. Then the PEEK function is used to find the two-byte integer stored as ERDEV. Here are the results:

```
ERDEV =-32758              ERDEV$ = LPT1
 10   128
```

The first line contains the information illustrated earlier. In the second printed line, the first number (10) is the first byte of the two-byte integer value of ERDEV. This number identifies the type of error, as shown in Table 19-1. Since the printer was not turned on when line 30 tried to write to the printer, error 10 (write fault) is indicated.

The second byte of the value of ERDEV is a little more complex. You must interpret this number (128) in its binary format.

128 decimal = 10000000 binary

The three leftmost bits (binary digits) of the second byte provide the following information:

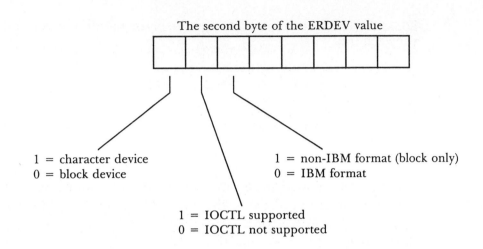

The second byte of the ERDEV value

1 = character device
0 = block device

1 = non-IBM format (block only)
0 = IBM format

1 = IOCTL supported
0 = IOCTL not supported

Since the printer caused the error and is a character device, the leftmost bit is a 1. The second bit is zero, indicating that IOCTL (Input/Output Control) is not supported. The third bit has meaning only if a block device caused the error.

Table 19-1.

Integer	Error Description
0	Attempt to write on a write-protected disk
1	Unknown unit
2	Drive not ready
3	Unknown command
4	Data error (CRC)
5	Bad request-structure length
6	Seek error
7	Unknown media type
8	Sector not found
9	Printer out of paper
10	Write fault
11	Read fault
12	General failure

First Byte Returned by ERDEV

EXTERR Function

Some GW-BASIC statements—such as LOAD, SAVE, and LPRINT—call on DOS to perform a specific task. If DOS is unable to perform the task, the EXTERR function returns extended error information.

EXTERR   **Function**

Syntax: EXTERR(*integer expression*)

Purpose: Returns extended error information. The type of information depends on the value of the *integer expression* parameter.

Notes: EXTERR always returns zero for GW-BASIC versions earlier than 3.0.

Parameters: *integer expression* is an integer in the range 0 through 3.

The *integer argument* of the EXTERR function determines which of the following types of information is returned:

Integer	Return Value
0	Extended error code (see Table 19-2)
1	Extended error class (see Table 19-3)

    2   Extended error suggested action (see Table 19-4)

    3   Extended error locus (see Table 19-5)

Here is a short program that attempts to load a program from disk drive B. It contains an ON ERROR statement at line 20.

```
10 CLS: KEY OFF: DEFINT A-Z
20 ON ERROR GOTO 1010
30 LOAD "B:GWRF1902"
40 END
```

An error-handling routine is added, beginning at line 1010, to print out each type of EXTERR argument for the error that will occur if the file is not found.

```
1010 FOR number = 0 TO 3
1020    PRINT EXTERR(number)
1030 NEXT number
1040 RESUME NEXT
```

If the program specified in line 30 is not on the disk in drive B, the following is printed by the For/Next loop of the error-handling routine:

```
2
8
3
2
```

Table 19-2 shows that the first value printed (2) indicates "File not found." In Table 19-3, you can see that the second value printed (8) indicates "Not found." Table 19-4 lists the third value printed (3) as "Ask user to re-enter input." In Table 19-5, the fourth value (2) indicates "Related to disk."

Table 19-2.

Code	Meaning
1	Invalid function number
2	File not found
3	Path not found
4	Too many open files
5	Access denied
6	Invalid handle
7	Memory control-block address
8	Insufficient memory
9	Invalid memory-block address
10	Invalid environment
11	Invalid format
12	Invalid access code
13	Invalid data
14	Reserved
15	Invalid drive
16	Attempt to remove the current directory
17	Not same device
18	No more files
19	Attempt to write to write-protected disk
20	Unknown unit
21	Drive not ready
22	Unknown command
23	Data error (CRC)
24	Bad request-structure length
25	Seek error
26	Unknown media type
27	Sector not found
28	Printer out of paper

Error Codes from the EXTERR Function (continued on next page)

Table 19-2.

Code	Meaning
29	Write fault
30	Read fault
31	General failure
32	Sharing violation
33	Lock violation
34	Invalid disk change
35	FCB unavailable
36	Sharing buffer overflow
37-49	Reserved
50	Network request not supported
51	Remote computer not listening
52	Duplicate name on network
53	Network name not found
54	Network busy
55	Network device no longer exists
56	Net BIOS command limit exceeded
57	Network adapter hardware error
58	Incorrect response from network
59	Unexpected network error
60	Incompatible remote adapter
61	Print queue full
62	Not enough space for print file
63	Print file was deleted
64	Network name was deleted
65	Access denied
66	Incorrect network device type
67	Network name not found
68	Network name limit exceeded

Error Codes from the EXTERR Function (continued)

Table 19-2.

Code	Meaning
69	Net BIOS session limit exceeded
70	Temporary paused
71	Network request not accepted
72	Print or disk redirection is paused
73-79	Reserved
80	File exists
81	Reserved
82	Cannot make directory entry
83	Fail on INT 24
84	Too many directives
85	Duplicate redirection
86	Invalid password
87	Invalid parameter
88	Network data fault

Error Codes from the EXTERR Function

Initially, the values of EXTERR(0), EXTERR(1), EXTERR(2), and EXTERR(3) are zero. If an error occurs, the value of an EXTERR function returns to zero after the error-handling routine is completed. The EXTERR function only reports errors that occur within GW-BASIC. Any errors that occur within DOS after a SHELL command have no effect on the values of EXTERR.

Table 19-3.

Number	Classification
1	Out of resource
2	Temporary situation
3	Authorization
4	Internal
5	Hardware failure
6	System failure
7	Application program error
8	Not found
9	Bad format
10	Locked
11	Media
12	Already exists
13	Unknown

Error Classes of the EXTERR Function

Table 19-4.

Number	Suggested Action
1	Retry
2	Delay retry
3	Ask user to reenter input
4	Abort
5	Immediate exit
6	Ignore
7	Retry after user intervention

Suggested Actions for EXTERR Function Errors

Table 19-5.

Number	Location
1	Unknown
2	Related to disk
3	Related to network
4	Related to serial devices
5	Related to random access memory

Locations for EXTERR Function Errors

CHAPTER

20

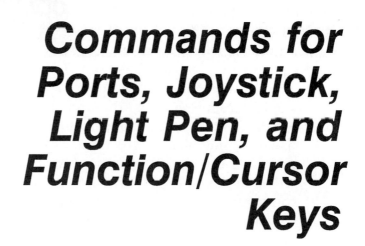

Commands for Ports, Joystick, Light Pen, and Function/Cursor Keys

You have previously studied four major input/output (I/O) devices: the screen, keyboard, printer, and disk drive. The statements and functions discussed in this chapter are related to the activities of less common I/O devices. You will learn how to control the light pen, the joystick, KEY(*n*), COM ports, and I/O ports.

The statements and functions discussed in this chapter are

COM	INP	KEY(*n*)	ON COM	ON KEY(*n*)
ON PEN	ON STRIG	OPEN COM	OUT	PEN
STICK	STRIG	WAIT		

OPEN COM, COM, and ON COM Statements

The COM (communication) ports on your computer are used to communicate with the world outside the computer. These ports use the RS-232 standard for asynchronous communication. If you have an application that requires the use of the COM1 or COM2 port, you can use GW-BASIC to write that application. These statements assume you have a communications adapter in your computer. Modems (communication devices external to your computer) used for communications vary, so consult your modem manual for specific instructions.

OPEN COM Statement

The OPEN statement for COM ports is slightly different from the OPEN statements used previously with disk files. You can specify various communications options with OPEN COM.

OPEN COM(*n*)   **Statement**

Syntax:

> OPEN "COM*n*:[*speed*][, *parity*][, *data*][, *stop*][, *line signals*]"
> AS [#]*file number* [LEN = *number*]

where *parity* may be E, O, N, S, or M and *line signals*
represents [, RS][, CS[*n*]][, DS[*n*]][, CD[*n*]][, LF][, PE]

Purpose: Allocates a buffer to support RS-232 asynchronous
communications with other computers and devices.

Notes: COM*n* is a valid communications device: COM1 or
COM2.

Parameters:

speed is an integer specifying the transmit/receive baud rate
(75, 110, 150, 300, 600, 1200, 1800, 2400, 4800, or 9600);
default is 300.

parity is a single-character literal specifying the parity for
transmitting and receiving.

data is an integer indicating the number of transmit/receive
data bits (4, 5, 6, 7, and 8); default is 8.

stop the number of bits required to tell the receiving computer that transmission of the character is completed, is an
integer expression that evaluates to 1 or 2, depending on the
baud rate. Typically 1 is needed, but 2 is needed at baud rates
of 110 and below.

file number is a number between 1 and the maximum number of files allowed. (A communication device may be opened to
only one file number at a time.)

number is the maximum number of bytes that can be read
from the communications buffer when using the GET or PUT
default of 128 bytes.

The *line signal* options are as follows:

RS	Suppresses RTS (Request To Send)
CS[*n*]	Controls CTS (Clear To Send)
DS[*n*]	Controls DSR (Data Set Ready)
CD[*n*]	Controls CD (Carrier Detect)
LF	Sends a line feed at each carriage return
PE	Enables parity checking
n	The number of milliseconds to wait (0 to 65535) for the specified signal before a device timeout error occurs. Defaults are CS 1000, DS 1000, and CD 0. If RS is specified, CS 0 is the default. If *n* is omitted, then timeout is set to 0.

Baud rate is the transmit/receive speed of data between the computer and the peripheral device. A wide range of baud rates is provided; the default rate is 300. *Baud* refers to the number of signal elements per second. Because a signal element can represent more than one bit, baud is not synonymous with bits-per-second (bps); however, bps is often used loosely in communications literature to indicate baud.

The *parity* options are N (None), S (Space), and M (Mark) for no parity checking; or E (Even) and O (Odd) for enabled parity checking (see table below). Each character transmitted is composed of eight bits (one byte). When parity checking is enabled, the highest bit of the byte is used as the parity bit. If you need to use all eight data bits, you must select no parity. Both the transmitting device and the receiving device must use the same type of parity.

Parity	Action
E	The parity bit is used to make the sum of all eight bits (including the parity bit) even.
O	The parity bit is used to make the sum of all eight bits (including the parity bit) odd.
N	The parity bit is not used. All eight data bits are used to transmit the character.
S	The parity bit is not used for parity checking; it is always transmitted as 0 (zero).
M	The parity bit is not used for parity checking; it is always transmitted as 1 (one).

Table 20-1 shows some forms of the OPEN COM statement.

COM Statement

The COM statement has three forms. A COM ON statement is usually executed to enable event trapping, before the ON COM statement that creates the trap.

COM Statement

Syntax:

COM(*n*) ON
COM(*n*) OFF
COM(*n*) STOP

Purpose: Enables or disables trapping of communications to the specified communications adapter.

Notes: COM(*n*) is a valid communications device.

Parameters: *n* is the number of the communications adapter: 1 or 2.

If a nonzero number is specified for *n* in a COM ON statement, GW-BASIC checks every statement executed from there on to see if any characters have come from the communications adapter.

Table 20-1.

Statement:	OPEN "COM1:" AS 1
Description:	Opens communications port 1 as file 1 with default settings.
Statement:	OPEN "COM2: 2400" AS #1
Description:	Opens communications port 2 as file 1 at 2400 baud rate; other settings at default values.
Statement:	OPEN "COM1: 1200, E, 7, PE" AS 3
Description:	Opens communications port 1 as file 3 at 1200 baud rate, even parity, 7 data bits, parity checking enabled; other settings at default values.
Statement:	OPEN "COM1: 2400, N, 8, CD3000" AS #2
Description:	Opens communications port 2 as file 2 at 2400 baud rate, no parity, 8 data bits; carrier detect line is checked and will cause an error interrupt 3 seconds (3000 milliseconds) after the line is off (carrier is lost); other settings at default values.

Examples of OPEN COM Statements

A COM OFF statement disables trapping, and any subsequent communications activity will be lost.

After a COM STOP statement, no trapping takes place, but any communications event that takes place is remembered so that immediate trapping will occur after COM ON is executed. Once an event is trapped, a COM(n) STOP statement is automatically executed, even though it is not contained in the code. Trapping is then temporarily suspended until the RETURN statement in the error-handling routine is executed (see Chapter 19).

ON COM Statement

The ON COM statement is used to specify an event trap line number for a communications event. If 0 (zero) is used for the line number, the communications event trap is disabled.

ON COM   **Statement**

Syntax: ON COM(n) GOSUB *line number*

Purpose: Specifies an event trap line number for a specified communications event.

Notes: Typically, the COM trap routine will read an entire message from the COM port before returning to the program. Avoid using the COM trap for single-character messages, because at high baud rates the time to trap and read each individual character may allow the interrupt buffer for COM to overflow.

> **Parameters:** *n* is the number of the COM channel (1 or 2); *line number* is the first line number of the error-trapping subroutine. A line number of 0 (zero) disables trapping for this event.

A COM port must be opened before any communications activity can take place. Event trapping is created by an ON COM statement and enabled by a COM ON statement. The ON COM and COM ON statements may appear in any order, but the event trapping will not be activated until both statements are executed. When the COM event occurs, trapping is suspended until the RETURN statement in the error-handling routine is executed.

Here is an example that uses COM port 1, a baud rate of 2400, even parity, seven data bits, one stop bit, and default values for the *line signal* parameters.

```
10 OPEN "COM1: 2400, E, 7, 1" AS #1
20 ON COM(1) GOSUB 1010
30 COM(1) ON
```

STRIG, ON STRIG, and STICK
Statements and Functions

A typical joystick has a lever (stick), attached by a swivel, that can be pushed in any direction. It also has two buttons (triggers). The STRIG statement enables or disables trigger status checking, and the STRIG function returns status information about the triggers. STICK returns status information about the stick. GW-BASIC joystick statements and functions provide for the use of two joysticks (A and B).

Statements and functions relating to the joystick require that hardware be built into a computer, or added by a special board called the Game Controller Adapter, to which the joysticks are connected.

STRIG Statement and Function

The STRIG statement enables or disables checking of the status of the two joystick triggers. When STRIG ON is executed, GW-BASIC checks the status of the triggers before every statement is executed, until a STRIG OFF statement is executed.

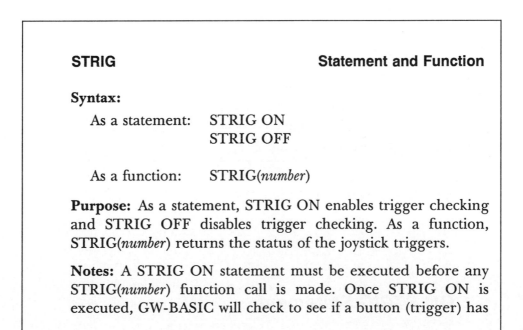

STRIG   **Statement and Function**

Syntax:

As a statement: STRIG ON
                  STRIG OFF

As a function: STRIG(*number*)

Purpose: As a statement, STRIG ON enables trigger checking and STRIG OFF disables trigger checking. As a function, STRIG(*number*) returns the status of the joystick triggers.

Notes: A STRIG ON statement must be executed before any STRIG(*number*) function call is made. Once STRIG ON is executed, GW-BASIC will check to see if a button (trigger) has been pressed before any other statement is executed. The STRIG OFF statement disables the checking (resets the triggers to OFF). The CLEAR command also resets the triggers to OFF.

Parameters: *number* is a numeric expression within the range 0 to 7 that returns the following values, each pertaining to a condition of one of the two joystick triggers (A1 and A2 for joystick A; B1 and B2 for joystick B):

Number	Value Returned
0	−1 if trigger A1 was pressed since the last STRIG(0) statement; 0 if not.
1	−1 if trigger A1 is currently pressed; 0 if not.
2	−1 if trigger B1 was pressed since the last STRIG(2) statement; 0 if not.
3	−1 if trigger B1 is currently pressed; 0 if not.
4	−1 if trigger A2 was pressed since the last STRIG(4) statement; 0 if not.
5	−1 if trigger A2 is currently pressed; 0 if not.
6	−1 if trigger B2 was pressed since the last STRIG(6) statement; 0 if not.
7	−1 if trigger B2 is currently pressed; 0 if not.

ON STRIG Statement

The ON STRIG statement sets up an event trap for a joystick trigger, specifying the line number for the trap.

ON STRIG **Statement**

Syntax: ON STRIG(*number*) GOSUB *line number*

Purpose: Creates an event trap line number for a specified joystick trigger event.

Notes: STRIG(*number*) is a valid joystick trigger: A1, A2, B1, or B2. ON STRIG will not be enabled until a STRIG ON statement has been executed.

Parameters: *number* is the number of the trigger: 0, 2, 4, or 6 (where 0 = trigger A1, 2 = trigger B1, 4 = trigger A2, and 6 = trigger B2). The *line number* parameter is the first line number of the error-trapping subroutine; a *line number* of 0 (zero) disables trapping for this event.

STICK Function

The position of the joystick lever (stick) is described by a pair of numbers called the *x-coordinate* and the *y-coordinate* of the stick. The range of values returned by the STICK function varies for different joysticks.

STICK **Function**

Syntax: STICK(*number*)

Purpose: Returns the x-coordinates and the y-coordinates of two joysticks.

Notes: Valid joysticks are A and B. Values returned by STICK(*number*) vary for different joysticks.

Parameters: *number* is a valid numeric expression within the range 0 to 3. The numbers return the following quantities:

Number	Quantity
0	x-coordinate of joystick A. Stores the x and y values for both joysticks, in order to use the remaining three function calls (1, 2, and 3).
1	y-coordinate of joystick A
2	x-coordinate of joystick B
3	y-coordinate of joystick B

You can use the following short program to experiment with the values returned by your joystick as you move joystick A:

```
10 CLS: KEY OFF: DEFINT A-Z
20 WHILE akey$ <> CHR$(27)
30   LOCATE 2, 2: PRINT "X ="; STICK(0)
40   LOCATE 3, 2: PRINT "Y ="; STICK(1)
50   akey$ = INKEY$
60 WEND
```

Notice that STICK(0) must be executed first because it stores the values for all four STICK functions. If you want to check the movements of joystick B, change lines 30 and 40 to

```
30   X = STICK(0): LOCATE 2, 2: PRINT "X ="; STICK(2)
40   LOCATE 3, 2: PRINT "Y ="; STICK(3)
```

Joysticks are used primarily for games. In graphics modes, you can use PUT and GET statements to move an object about the screen.

PEN Statement, PEN Function, and ON PEN Statement

PEN statements and functions are used for enabling, disabling, and reading a *light pen*. A light pen is about the size and shape of a small flashlight. Its cord is attached to the computer. To use PEN statements and functions, you must have a Color Graphics Adapter (CGA). Light pens have limited popularity and software support.

PEN Statement

The PEN statement enables and disables the PEN function, and disables PEN event trapping, depending on which keyword (ON, OFF, or STOP) is used. You must enable the light pen input with a PEN ON statement before you can read light pen values with the PEN function.

PEN   **Statement**

Syntax:

PEN ON
PEN OFF
PEN STOP

Purpose: Enables and disables the PEN(*n*) read function, or disables event trapping.

Notes: PEN ON enables the PEN read function, causing GW-BASIC to check the light pen after each program statement to see if the pen is active. PEN OFF disables the PEN read function. PEN STOP disables event trapping, but remembers the events so that immediate trapping occurs when PEN ON is executed. The PEN function is initially off. If a PEN read function call is made before PEN ON is executed, an "Illegal function call" error occurs.

Parameters: None.

PEN Function

The PEN function reads the current status of the light pen if a PEN ON statement has been previously executed. An argument (0 to 9) is used to provide specific information.

PEN   **Function**

Syntax: PEN(*number*)

Purpose: Reads the light pen.

Notes: A PEN ON statement must be executed before a PEN(*number*) function call can be made, or an "Illegal function call" error occurs. To improve execution speed, use PEN OFF when the light pen is not in use. If the pen is in the border area of the screen, values returned will not be accurate.

Parameters: *number* is an integer expression within the range 0 to 9. The values returned by PEN(*number*) are as follows.

Number	Value Returned
0	−1 if PEN was down since the last poll; 0 if not.
1	Column pixel coordinate when PEN was last activated; range is 0 to 319 for medium-resolution graphics and 0 to 639 for high-resolution graphics.
2	Row pixel coordinate when PEN was last activated; range is 0 to 199.
3	−1 if current PEN switch value is down; 0 if up.
4	Last known valid column pixel coordinate.
5	Last known valid row pixel coordinate.
6	Text character row position when PEN was last activated; range 1 to 24.
7	Text character column position when PEN was last activated; range 1 to 40, or 1 to 80, depending on the current screen width.
8	Last known valid text character row; range 1 to 24.
9	Last known valid text character column; range 1 to 40, or 1 to 80, depending on screen width.

The following program lines might be used in a game of tic-tac-toe. Player$(1) is assigned the letter *X*, and Player$(2) is assigned the letter *O*. The light pen is enabled with PEN ON. Then a loop is executed until a pen press PEN(0) occurs. When the light pen is pressed, a LOCATE statement uses the location of the pen (PEN(6) and PEN(7)) to print an *X* or an *O* in that location.

```
10 Player$(1) = "X": Player$(2) = "O"
20 PEN ON
30 WHILE NOT press%: press% = PEN(0): WEND
40 LOCATE PEN(6), PEN(7)
50 PRINT Player$(n);
```

ON PEN Statement

The ON PEN statement provides the line number where the light pen event trap occurs.

ON PEN   **Statement**

Syntax: ON PEN GOSUB *line number*

Purpose: Creates a trap line number for a light pen event.

Notes: Because there is only one light pen, no number argument follows ON PEN.

Parameters: *line number* is the first line number of the error trapping subroutine. A line number of 0 (zero) disables trapping for this event.

The following two lines enable the light pen and provide the line number where the pen event trapping routine begins.

```
10 PEN ON
20 ON PEN GOSUB 1010
```

The event trapping routine might detect the x- and y-coordinates of the light pen, and then call another subroutine that used the coordinates to select an item from a menu.

```
1000 REM ** SUBROUTINE: PEN event handler **
1010 press = -1
1020 x% = PEN(1): y% = PEN(2)
1030 GOSUB 2010          (Select menu item subroutine)
1040 RETURN
```

KEY(n) and ON KEY(n) Statements

In Chapter 2, you learned to list and change the function key assignments. The formal syntax for the KEY statement that accomplishes those tasks was given in Chapter 8. The KEY(*n*) and ON KEY(*n*) statements are also used in conjunction with function keys, but are not otherwise related to the KEY statement discussed earlier.

The KEY(*n*) statement is used to enable, suspend, and disable event trapping for the function keys or the cursor control keys. ON KEY(*n*) specifies the key to capture, and the opening line of the event trapping routine.

KEY(n) Statement

The KEY(*n*) statement enables, suspends, or disables the capture presses of the function keys or the cursor control keys. The KEY(*n*) ON statement enables key capture; KEY(*n*) STOP suspends key capture; and KEY(*n*) OFF disables key capture. Use a KEY(*n*) ON statement to enable the detection of a specific keypress before it is used in a key event trap.

KEY(*n*)   **Statement**

Syntax:

> KEY(*n*) ON
> KEY(*n*) OFF
> KEY(*n*) STOP

Purpose: Enables, disables, or suppresses the keystroke capture of the function keys or cursor control keys.

Notes: Once the KEY(*n*) ON statement is executed, GW-BASIC checks to see if a keystroke has been made after each statement executed in the program. If KEY(*n*) STOP is executed, no keystroke capture occurs. However, if the specified key is pressed, the keystroke is retained so that immediate capture occurs when a KEY(*n*) ON statement is executed. After KEY(*n*) OFF is executed, the specified keystrokes are neither captured nor retained.

Parameters: *n* is an integer from 1 through 20 that indicates which key is to be captured. The key numbers are as follows.

Value of *n*	Keys
1-10	Function keys F1 through F10
11	Cursor up
12	Cursor left
13	Cursor right
14	Cursor down
15-20	Keys defined by this KEY statement: KEY *n*, CHR$(*hexcode*) + CHR$(*scancode*)

Key numbers 15-20 allow you to define other keys that can be captured. The hex codes and scan codes necessary to define key numbers 15-20 are given in Appendix C.

ON KEY(n) Statement

The ON KEY(*n*) statement provides the number of the line where the KEY event trap occurs.

ON KEY(*n*)   **Statement**

Syntax: ON KEY(*n*) GOSUB *line number*

Purpose: Specifies a trap line number for a function key or cursor key event.

Notes: A KEY(*n*) ON statement must be executed to enable the event trap.

Parameters: *n* is the number of the key to be captured (defined in the Parameters section of the KEY(*n*) syntax box); *line number* is the first line number of the error-trapping subroutine. A line number of 0 (zero) disables trapping for this event.

When you are running a program, it is possible to accidentally press a key that might affect the program. Suppose you define the F10 function key as the one that terminates a program. Accidentally pressing this key at the wrong time would interrupt your program. To detect an accidental keypress and recover from the accident, you can write an event trapping routine into your program.

The following lines set up the trap and print a blinking block character:

```
10 CLS: ON KEY(10) GOSUB 1010
20 KEY(10) ON
30 WHILE -1: COLOR 23: LOCATE 1,1: PRINT CHR$(219);: WEND
```

In this example, the event trapping routine asks whether you really want to quit. If not, it resumes execution of the program.

```
1000 REM ** SUBROUTINE: F10 key event handler **
1010 LOCATE 1, 1: COLOR 7: PRINT "You pressed F10.   ";
1020 INPUT "Are you sure you want to quit"; akey$
1030 IF akey$ = "Y" OR akey$ = "y" THEN CLS: END
1040 LOCATE 1, 1: PRINT SPACE$(78)
1050 RETURN
```

If you press the F10 key while the block character is blinking, the following message is displayed by the event handler:

```
You pressed F10.   Are you sure you want to quit? _
```

If you then enter a Y (uppercase or lowercase) at line 1030, the program will end. Press any other key, and the message is erased. Control returns to the main program, with the keypress trap once again active.

OUT Statement, INP Function, and WAIT Statement

Peripheral devices like the keyboard, disk drives, speaker, and screen each have an assigned I/O port. An I/O port is a channel through which the computer interacts with an external device. OUT, INP, and WAIT allow you to manipulate your computer's I/O ports directly. If your computer monitors a security system, alarm clock, coffeepot, or other external event, you probably have an interface card in your computer to access through an I/O port.

Use extreme care when using an I/O port. Improper use can damage the peripheral device. *Before* using OUT or INP, study the manuals that came with the interface cards and peripheral devices through which you communicate.

OUT Statement

The OUT statement outputs data to a port one byte at a time. Therefore, integers larger than 255 must be broken into two parts. You can then use two output statements to output the complete integer.

OUT   **Statement**

Syntax: OUT *port number, databyte*

Purpose: Sends one byte of data to an output port.

Notes: OUT is the complementary statement to the INP function.

Parameters: *port number* is an integer expression that evaluates to an integer in the range 0 to 65535; *databyte* is a single byte of data to be sent to the output port.

Here is an OUT statement that sends a one-byte integer (223) to an open output port (45).

```
OUT 45, 223
```

To send an integer larger than 255, such as 400, you must use two OUT statements, as follows:

```
OUT 45, mynumber% MOD 256    (Remainder of integer division)
OUT 45, mynumber% \ 256      (Quotient of integer division)
```

For example, If *mynumber%* = 400, then *mynumber%* MOD 256 = 144, and *mynumber%* \ 256 = 1.

Using the OUT statement is not as simple as it first appears. When using multiple OUT statements (as shown above or within a loop), you must be sure the receiving device can handle the data as fast as you send it. This is usually not the case. In most cases, two-way communication between your program and the device therefore employs a technique called *handshaking*. An example of handshaking is shown after the description of the INP function.

INP Function

The INP function returns a byte of data from the specified input port. This provides a way for a peripheral device to communicate with a GW-BASIC program.

INP   **Function**

Syntax: INP(*integer*)

Purpose: Returns a byte read from the port whose number is the value of the *integer* argument.

Notes: The INP function is the complement to the OUT statement.

Parameters: *integer* is a valid machine port number in the range 0 to 65535.

Here is a series of statements that demonstrates use of INP and OUT to perform a handshaking routine between the computer and a peripheral device. Port 17 is used to send the data, port 18 is used to tell the device that data is waiting on port 17, and port 19 is used for the device to tell the program that it has received the data.

Send a byte of data:

```
1010 OUT 17, onebyte%
```

Tell the device that data is ready:

```
1020 OUT 18, 1
```

Wait until the device acknowledges data is received, then reset the data ready signal:

```
1030 WHILE INP(19) = 0: WEND
1040 OUT 18, 0
```

Wait for the device to acknowledge that the data ready signal has been reset:

```
1050 WHILE INP(19) <> 0: WEND
```

WAIT Statement

The WAIT statement suspends program execution until a specified input port develops a specified bit pattern.

WAIT   **Statement**

Syntax: WAIT *port number, integer1*[, *integer2*]

Purpose: Suspends program execution while monitoring the status of an input port.

Notes: WAIT suspends program execution until a specified input port develops a specified bit pattern. An XOR operation is performed on the data read at the port, and the second integer expression (*integer2*). An AND operation is then performed on the result of the XOR operation and the first integer expression (*integer1*). If the result is zero, GW-BASIC reads the data port again. If the result is nonzero, execution continues at the next statement. It is possible to enter an infinite loop with WAIT. You can exit the loop by pressing CTRL+BREAK, or by resetting the system.

Parameters: *port number* is a valid port number in the range 0 to 65535; *integer1* and *integer2* are integer expressions in the range 0 to 255.

The WAIT statement eliminates the need for the WHILE/WEND loops in the series of statements in the previous handshaking example. Here is the same series of statements, using WAIT instead of WHILE/WEND.

```
1010 OUT 17, onebyte%
1020 OUT 18, 1
1030 WAIT 19, 1
1040 OUT 18, 0
1050 WAIT 19, 1, 1
```

The WAIT statement at line 1030 checks port 19 and ANDs the data with 1. It waits until this result is not zero. The WAIT statement at line 1050 checks port 19, XORs it with 1, and ANDs it with 1. In other words, it waits until the data is zero again.

PART

III

BASIC

Applications

Part III contains three chapters with detailed discussions of application programs that make use of a wide variety of GW-BASIC commands, functions, and statements. In particular, the programs show expanded uses of the PAINT statement for tiling, the SCREEN function and PUT and GET for making menu windows, and the DRAW statement for making original drawings.

Programs in this section include a step-by-step tile generator that allows you to create a tile pattern. When the pattern is completed, the program displays the codes needed to create the pattern and the PAINT statement that will fill a closed figure with the pattern. Also included are two menu-making programs: one demonstrates the use of the SCREEN function to save the image of a screen area, and the other demonstrates the use of PUT and GET to display and erase menu windows. Part III concludes with a drawing utility that allows you to use DRAW commands from the keyboard to create your own drawings and paintings dynamically.

21

Tiling Generator

In Chapter 15, "Graphics," you learned that you could use a tile pattern with the PAINT statement. You can tile enclosed geometric figures with multicolored patterns in graphics modes that provide color (such as SCREEN 1), or in two-colored patterns for other graphics modes (such as SCREEN 2). The difficulty with using tiles is in determining the values used as arguments to the CHR$ function that creates the tile pattern.

Values of CHR$ function arguments are usually expressed in hexadecimal notation, since this notation is closely associated with binary numbers used to form the tile patterns. Each hexadecimal value contains two characters (eight binary digits, or one byte). A tile string may contain up to 64 bytes.

Since SCREEN 2 has only one drawing color, a byte represents a block that is eight pixels wide by one pixel high. A binary 1 represents a pixel turned on, and a binary 0 represents a pixel turned off. Thus the following tile string creates a four-row pattern:

```
Tile$ = CHR$(&H88) + CHR$(&H44) + CHR$(&H22) + CHR$(&H11)
```

The hexadecimal values in the Tile$ string form the following binary values:

&H88 = 10001000 binary
&H44 = 01000100 binary
&H22 = 00100010 binary
&H11 = 00010001 binary

Thus, the four-row pattern of diagonal lines produced by the string is

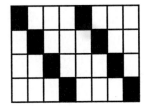

A geometric figure filled with this pattern would have a pattern composed of diagonal lines.

In SCREEN 1, each byte represents a block that is four pixels wide and one pixel high. Each byte represents four sets of two bits. Each two bits contains the color information for its own set (one pixel). In palette 1, the binary values for each color are

00 = color 0, background
01 = color 1, cyan
10 = color 2, magenta
11 = color 3, white

A hexadecimal code of A5, converted to binary, represents a pixel row made up of two magenta pixels followed by two cyan pixels.

A5 hexadecimal = 1 0 1 0 0 1 0 1

Color number = 2 2 1 1

Pixel color = magenta magenta cyan cyan

You can see that tiling a figure in SCREEN 1 is much more complex than tiling a figure in SCREEN 2. Program 21-1, Tile Generator, makes this task easier.

Discussion of Program 21-1

The program uses the text mode (SCREEN 0) to let you choose the background color and palette that you want to use in developing the values used to create a pattern. Then it switches to SCREEN 1 so that you can see the pattern as it is created.

After you have chosen the colors, you select the number of rows (1 through 16) for a grid that has four columns. You then create a pattern by moving a circular cursor within the grid, using the four arrow keys. When the cursor is on a section of the grid

Program 21-1.

```
1 REM ** TILE GENERATOR **
2 ' GW-BASIC: The Reference, Chapter 21.  File: GWRF2101.BAS
3 ' Generates statements for tile production

100 REM ** Initialize **
110 DEFINT A-Z
120 DIM Size(12), Cschm(80), Forgrnd$(1, 3), Backgrnd$(8)
130 SCREEN 0: CLS: KEY OFF: WIDTH 80: RESTORE

200 REM ** Read color arrays **
210 FOR palet = 0 TO 1
220    FOR kolor = 1 TO 3
230       READ Forgrnd$(palet, kolor)
240    NEXT kolor
250 NEXT palet
260 DATA green, red, brown, cyan, magenta, white
270 FOR bgcolor = 0 TO 7
280    READ Backgrnd$(bgcolor)
290 NEXT bgcolor
300 DATA black, blue, green, cyan
310 DATA red, magenta, brown, white

400 REM ** Get palette data **
410 LOCATE 5, 1: PRINT "Which palette, please (0 or 1)?"
420 LOCATE 7, 3: PRINT "0  green, red, and brown"
430 LOCATE 8, 3: PRINT "1  cyan, magenta, and white"
440 akey$ = "2"
450 WHILE INSTR("01", akey$) = 0
460    akey$ = INPUT$(1)
470 WEND
480 Pal = VAL(akey$)

500 REM ** Get background color **
510 CLS: PRINT "Palette is "; Forgrnd$(Pal, 1); ", ";
520 PRINT Forgrnd$(Pal, 2); ", and "; Forgrnd$(Pal, 3)
530 LOCATE 3, 1: PRINT "Which background color?"
540 PRINT TAB(3); "(0-7,  but not in the palette)": PRINT
550 FOR bgcolor = 0 TO 7
560    PRINT TAB(2); bgcolor; " "; Backgrnd$(bgcolor)
570 NEXT bgcolor
580 a$ = "8"
```

Tile Generator (GWRF2101.BAS) (continued on next page)

Program 21-1.

```
590 IF Pal = 0 THEN Ok$ = "01357" ELSE Ok$ = "01246"
600 WHILE INSTR(Ok$, a$) = 0
610    a$ = INPUT$(1)
620 WEND
630 Back = VAL(a$): Forgrnd$(Pal, 0) = Backgrnd$(Back)

700 REM ** Get boundary color **
710 CLS: PRINT "Which color boundary do you want?": PRINT
720 FOR num = 1 TO 3
730    PRINT TAB(2); num; " "; Forgrnd$(Pal, num)
740 NEXT num
750 akey$ = "0"
760 WHILE INSTR("123", akey$) = 0
770    akey$ = INPUT$(1)
780 WEND
790 PRINT akey$: bordcol = VAL(akey$)

800 REM ** Pick and Choose **
810 GOSUB 2010: GOSUB 3010

900 REM ** Display Result and PAINT Statement **
910 SCREEN 1: COLOR Back, Pal: CLS
920 LINE (1, 1)-(80, 40), bordcol, B
930 PAINT (40, 20), Tile$, bordcol
940 LOCATE 3, 14: PRINT "This is the pattern"
950 LOCATE 4, 14: PRINT "you generated."
960 LOCATE 10, 1: PRINT "The values for this pattern are:"
970 PRINT: PRINT "Tile$ = ";
980 FOR number = 1 TO pics + 1
990    PRINT MID$(TileH$, (number - 1) * 13 + 1, 13);
1000 NEXT number
1010 PRINT: PRINT
1020 PRINT "PAINT (X, Y), Tile$, " + MID$(STR$(bordcol), 2)

1100 REM ** Go Again? **
1110 LOCATE 20, 1: PRINT "Try another pattern (Y or N)?"
1120 WHILE INSTR("YyNn", akey$) = 0
1130    akey$ = INPUT$(1)
1140 WEND
1150 IF akey$ = "Y" OR akey$ = "y" THEN GOTO 130
1160 CLS: SCREEN 0: COLOR 7, 0, 0: WIDTH 80: END
```

Tile Generator (GWRF2101.BAS) (continued)

Program 21-1.

```
2000 REM ** SUBROUTINE: Customize Choice Screen **
2010 CLS: pics = 0
2020 WHILE pics > 16 OR pics < 1
2030   INPUT "Number of pixel rows (1-16)"; pics
2040   IF pics < 1 THEN PRINT "Too small, try again"
2050   IF pics > 16 THEN PRINT "Too big, try again"
2060 WEND
2070 pics = pics - 1: SCREEN 1: COLOR Back, Pal: CLS
2080 CIRCLE (5, 4), 2, 3: GET (1, 1)-(9, 7), Size: CLS
2090 PRINT TAB(2); "Possible colors:": PRINT
2100 FOR kolor = 0 TO 3
2110   PRINT TAB(2); kolor; "  "; Forgrnd$(Pal, kolor)
2120 NEXT kolor
2130 LOCATE 20, 2: PRINT "Use arrow keys to move cursor."
2140 LOCATE 21, 2: PRINT "Use color number to color square."
2150 LOCATE 23, 2: PRINT "Press ENTER if pattern is final."
2160 FOR trow = 0 TO pics
2170   FOR tcol = 0 TO 3
2180     col = tcol * 10 + 200: row = trow * 8
2190     LINE (col, row)-(col + 10, row + 8), 3, B
2200     PAINT (col + 5, row + 4), 1, 3
2210     Cschm(tcol + trow * 4) = 1
2220   NEXT tcol
2230 NEXT trow
2240 GOSUB 4010
2250 RETURN

3000 REM ** SUBROUTINE: Choose Action **
3010 tcol = 0: trow = 0
3020 row = trow * 8: col = tcol * 10 + 200
3030 PUT (col + 1, row + 1), Size, XOR
3040 WHILE a$ <> CHR$(13)
3050   a$ = INKEY$
3060   IF a$ = "" THEN 3050
3070   IF a$ = CHR$(0) + "M" AND tcol < 3 THEN GOSUB 5010
3080   IF a$ = CHR$(0) + "K" AND tcol > 0 THEN GOSUB 6010
3090   IF a$ = CHR$(0) + "P" AND trow < pics THEN GOSUB 7010
3100   IF a$ = CHR$(0) + "H" AND trow > 0 THEN GOSUB 8010
3110   IF a$ >= "0" AND a$ <= "3" THEN GOSUB 9010
3120 WEND
```

Tile Generator (GWRF2101.BAS) (continued)

Program 21-1.

```
3130 Tile$ = "": TileH$ = ""
3140 FOR trow = 0 TO pics
3150    des1 = Cschm(3 + 4 * trow) + 4 * Cschm(2 + 4 * trow)
3160    des2 = 16 * Cschm(1 + 4 * trow) + 64 * Cschm(4 * trow)
3170    Descrip = des1 + des2
3180    Tile$ = Tile$ + CHR$(Descrip)
3190    TileH$ = TileH$ + "CHR$(&H" + HEX$(Descrip) + ") + "
3200 NEXT trow
3210 TileH$ = LEFT$(TileH$, LEN(TileH$) - 3)
3220 RETURN

4000 REM ** SUBROUTINE: Set Tile **
4010 Tile$ = ""
4020 FOR trw = 0 TO pics
4030    csc1 = Cschm(3 + 4 * trw) + 4 * Cschm(2 + 4 * trw)
4040    csc2 = 16 * Cschm(1 + 4 * trw) + 64 * Cschm(4 * trw)
4050    Tile$ = Tile$ + CHR$(csc1 + csc2)
4060 NEXT trw
4070 LINE (260, 0)-(300, 40), 0, BF
4080 LINE (260, 0)-(300, 40), 3, B
4090 PAINT (280, 20), Tile$, 3
4100 RETURN

5000 REM ** SUBROUTINE: Move Right **
5010 PUT (col + 1, row + 1), Size, XOR
5020 tcol = tcol + 1: col = tcol * 10 + 200
5030 PUT (col + 1, row + 1), Size, XOR
5040 RETURN

6000 REM ** SUBROUTINE: Move Left **
6010 PUT (col + 1, row + 1), Size, XOR
6020 tcol = tcol - 1: col = tcol * 10 + 200
6030 PUT (col + 1, row + 1), Size, XOR
6040 RETURN

7000 REM ** SUBROUTINE: Move Down **
7010 PUT (col + 1, row + 1), Size, XOR
7020 trow = trow + 1: row = trow * 8
7030 PUT (col + 1, row + 1), Size, XOR
7040 RETURN
```

Tile Generator (GWRF2101.BAS) (continued)

Program 21-1.

```
8000 REM ** SUBROUTINE: Move Up **
8010 PUT (col + 1, row + 1), Size, XOR
8020 trow = trow - 1: row = trow * 8
8030 PUT (col + 1, row + 1), Size, XOR
8040 RETURN

9000 REM ** SUBROUTINE: Change Colors **
9010 PUT (col + 1, row + 1), Size, XOR
9020 ppt = VAL(a$)
9030 LINE (col, row)-(col + 10, row + 8), 0, BF
9040 LINE (col, row)-(col + 10, row + 8), 3, B
9050 PAINT (col + 5, row + 4), ppt, 3
9060 Cschm(tcol + trow * 4) = ppt
9070 PUT (col + 1, row + 1), Size, XOR
9080 GOSUB 4010
9090 RETURN
```

Tile Generator (GWRF2101.BAS)

that you want to color, you press a number corresponding to the desired color number. That section is colored with your selection, and you move the cursor to the next section that you want to color. If you change your mind, you can move the cursor back and recolor any section. As you are creating the pattern, a rectangular area next to the selection area is tiled in the temporary pattern. Thus you can see how each color change affects the overall pattern.

When you have the desired pattern, press the ENTER key. A new screen appears showing the final pattern, and the values for the CHR$ function used as the Tile$ variable in a PAINT statement.

The Prompt Screens

The text mode is used for selecting values to set up the tile selection screens. The opening prompt requests one of two color palettes and names the colors in each palette.

```
Which palette, please (0 or 1)?

0  green, red, and brown
1  cyan, magenta, and white
```

If you press 0, you will have the use of green, red, and brown, plus the background color (selected in the next screen). If you press 1, you will have the use of cyan, magenta, white, and the background color. Because of the better contrast in colors, palette 1 is used in this demonstration. When 1 is pressed, the second screen appears, as shown in Figure 21-1.

Since cyan, magenta, and white are in palette 1, you cannot use color numbers 3, 5, and 7 for the background. If you did, you would only have two foreground colors to work with. The

Figure 21-1.

```
    Palette is cyan, magenta, and white

    Which background color?
      (0-7, but not in the palette)

      0  black
      1  blue
      2  green
      3  cyan
      4  red
      5  magenta
      6  brown
      7  white
```

Screen 2 of Program 21-1

program will only let you use the color numbers 0, 1, 2, 4, and 6. For this demonstration, color 1 (blue) was selected for the background color.

The next screen prompts you for the color boundary desired. This color is used to draw the grid lines on the tile selection grid.

```
Which color boundary do you want?

   1  cyan
   2  magenta
   3  white
```

Notice that the background color is not among these selections, in order to give you a clear distinction between the boundaries and the grid lines of the tile selection grid.

The next screen prompts you for the number of rows that you want to use (1 to 16) in the tile selection grid.

```
Number of pixel rows (1-16)? _
```

The number of rows is the last entry before the tile selection process begins. If you make an entry less than 1, the message "Too small, try again" appears. If your entry is greater than 16, the message "Too big, try again" appears. Eight rows were selected for this demonstration.

Tile Selection Screens

When all the preliminary entries have been made, the computer switches from SCREEN 0 to SCREEN 1 so that you have the use of four colors for creating your tile pattern. These colors are listed in the upper-left section of the first selection screen, shown in Figure 21-2.

Figure 21-2.

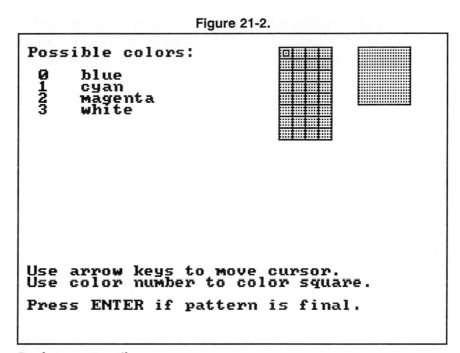

Ready to create a tile

Two rectangular areas are displayed in the upper-right section of the screen. The one on the left is the grid, made up of four columns and the number of rows you selected in the prompt screen procedure (eight rows in this demonstration). The cursor appears in the first column of the first row of the grid.

Three messages appear at the bottom of the screen.

```
Use arrow keys to move the cursor.
Use color number to color square.

Press ENTER if pattern is final.
```

You can move the cursor within this grid with the cursor keys, as the first message says. When the cursor is in a square of the grid that you want to color, press the number of the desired color, as the second message says. The color of that square immediately changes.

 CAUTION *Do not* press ENTER until you have colored all the squares you want. Pressing ENTER finalizes the pattern and displays a new screen.

As you make each change in the grid colors, the rectangular area to the right of the grid also changes to give you a preview of what the pattern now looks like. If you decide to change the color of a given square, move the cursor to the square and press another color number. The square will change to the color of the new selection. Figure 21-3 shows a partially completed tile pattern. Columns 1 and 2 of the first row have been colored, as have columns 3 and 4 of the eighth row. The cursor has been moved to the third column of the second row.

Figure 21-4 shows a completed pattern. Note that the cursor is still on the screen, and additional changes can be made until you press the ENTER key.

When you press ENTER, a new display screen appears, as shown in Figure 21-5. This final screen showns the completed pattern at the top left of the screen. The values used in the string assigned to the Tile$ variable are listed below the pattern. Below the Tile$ string is the PAINT statement that can be used in a program with the Tile$ variable to create the pattern.

PAINT(X, Y),   Tile$,   3

Column and row   Tile   Border color
to start PAINT   string

Figure 21-3.

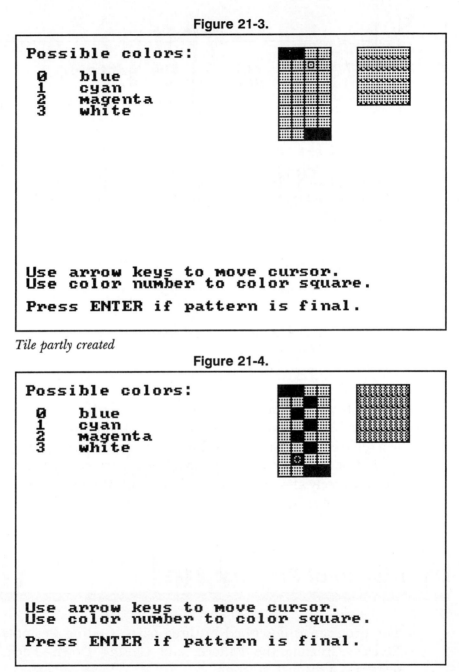

Tile partly created

Figure 21-4.

Pattern complete

Figure 21-5.

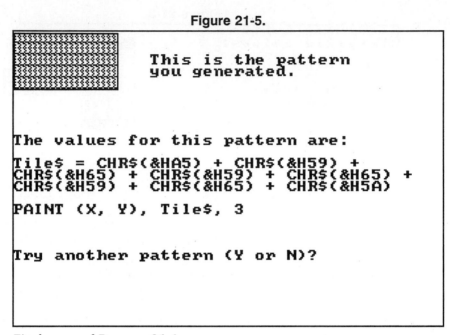

Final screen of Program 21-1

The boundary color (3) of the figure to be painted is printed by Program 21-1. If the geometric figure you want to paint is drawn in a different color, use that color number in the PAINT statement instead of 3. Remember, the geometric figure to be painted must be completely closed so that it will contain the paint. Otherwise, paint will overflow the figure and color the entire screen.

Description of Program 21-1

The program is described in three parts: Getting Prompts and Entries, Creating the Pattern, and Closing Down. Each part performs a distinct function.

Getting Prompts and Entries

The opening program description block is followed by the initialization block, which sets the default variable type to integer, dimensions four arrays, initializes the text screen, and restores the DATA pointer to the beginning of the first DATA statement in the program.

```
100 REM ** Initialize **
110 DEFINT A-Z
120 DIM Size(12), Cschm(80), Forgrnd$(1, 3), Backgrnd$(8)
130 SCREEN 0: CLS: KEY OFF: WIDTH 80: RESTORE
```

Four arrays are dimensioned at line 120. The Size array is an integer array that holds the image of the cursor (a small circle). The cursor is later moved about with PUT statements. The Cschm( ) array is an integer array that holds the color scheme of the created pattern. The Forgrnd$( ) array is a two-dimensional string array that holds the names of the colors in each palette (palette 0: green, red, and brown; palette 1: cyan, magenta, and white). The Backgrnd$( ) array is a one-dimensional string array that holds the names of the background colors: 0 (black), 1 (blue), 2 (green), 3 (cyan), 4 (red), 5 (magenta), 6 (brown), and 7 (white).

The RESTORE statement in line 130 is necessary to move the DATA pointer back to the beginning data item when the program is repeated for multiple patterns in the same run. After the first pattern has been finalized, an option to try a new pattern is offered. If the RESTORE statement were not there, a second attempt would create an "Out of DATA" error message.

The next block of code first reads the color names into the Forgrnd$( ) array.

```
200 REM ** Read color arrays **
210 FOR palet = 0 TO 1
220    FOR kolor = 1 TO 3
230       READ Forgrnd$(palet, kolor)
```

```
240   NEXT kolor
250 NEXT palet
```

Notice that the FOR/NEXT loops are nested. Since "palette" is a reserved keyword, it cannot be used for a variable name; therefore, "palet" is used as the variable.

The palet variable is first set to 0 (in the outer loop), and the inner loop reads the first three names from the data in line 260.

260 DATA green, red, brown, cyan, magenta, white

The names are assigned to elements in column 0 of the Forgrnd$( ) array by line 230, as follows:

Forgrnd$(0, 1) = "green"
Forgrnd$(0, 2) = "red"
Forgrnd$(0, 3) = "brown"

The palet variable (in the outer loop) is then set to 1. The inner loop reads the last three values from the data in line 260 and assigns them to elements in column 1 of the Forgrnd$( ) array by line 230, as follows:

Forgrnd$(1, 1) = "cyan"
Forgrnd$(1, 2) = "magenta"
Forgrnd$(1, 3) = "white"

The block continues with another FOR/NEXT loop that reads background color names into the Backgrnd$( ) array.

```
270 FOR bgcolor = 0 TO 7
280   READ Backgrnd$(bgcolor)
290 NEXT bgcolor
300 DATA black, blue, green, cyan
310 DATA red, magenta, brown, white
```

The FOR/NEXT loop at lines 270 through 290 reads in the values for the elements of the Backgrnd$( ) array from the DATA statements in lines 300 and 310. The elements of the array are assigned names as follows:

Backgrnd$(0) = "black"
Backgrnd$(1) = "blue"
Backgrnd$(2) = "green"
Backgrnd$(3) = "cyan"
Backgrnd$(4) = "red"
Backgrnd$(5) = "magenta"
Backgrnd$(6) = "brown"
Backgrnd$(7) = "white"

The color names are now in elements whose subscripts correspond to the color number of the color, so that they can be easily accessed when needed by the program.

You enter the palette desired for creating the tile pattern in the next block of code. First, the screen prompts you for the palette number and shows the colors available in each palette.

```
400 REM ** Get palette data **
410 LOCATE 5, 1: PRINT "Which palette, please (0 or 1)?"
420 LOCATE 7, 3: PRINT "0  green, red, and brown"
430 LOCATE 8, 3: PRINT "1  cyan, magenta, and white"
```

After the prompt and messages are printed, your entry of 0 or 1 is accepted in a WHILE/WEND loop.

```
440 akey$ = "2"
450 WHILE INSTR("01", akey$) = 0
460    akey$ = INPUT$(1)
470 WEND
480 Pal = VAL(akey$)
```

The akey$ variable is assigned a string of "2" at line 440. Then the WHILE/WEND loop begins. Line 460 accepts a single keystroke.

The INSTR function in line 450 will not allow an exit from the loop unless your keypress is either a 0 or a 1. (The INSTR function is discussed in Chapter 13, "String Manipulation.") If you press a 0, akey$ will equal 0; the value of INSTR("01", akey$) will change from 0 to 1 (the position of 0 in the string "01"). If you press a 1, akey$ will equal 1; the value of INSTR("01", akey$) will change from 0 to 2 (the position of 1 in the string "01"). When you make an acceptable entry, the string "0" or "1" is changed to numeric form by the VAL function and assigned to the Pal variable at line 480.

The next block of code displays prompts and information. Then it accepts an entry of the background color number. The prompts are printed by the following lines:

```
500 REM ** Get background color **
510 CLS: PRINT "Palette is "; Forgrnd$(Pal, 1); ", ";
520 PRINT Forgrnd$(Pal, 2); ", and "; Forgrnd$(Pal, 3)
530 LOCATE 3, 1: PRINT "Which background color?"
540 PRINT TAB(3); "(0-7, but not in the palette)": PRINT
```

The colors in the palette are printed by lines 510 and 520 from the Forgrnd$( ) array that holds the color names read earlier from DATA statements. The Pal variable has a value that was assigned earlier at line 480. Line 530 prompts you for the background color desired, and line 540 displays the range of numbers that you can enter.

A FOR/NEXT loop is used next to read in the list of acceptable background colors and their numbers.

```
550 FOR bgcolor = 0 TO 7
560   PRINT TAB(2); bgcolor; " "; Backgrnd$(bgcolor)
570 NEXT bgcolor
```

The color number (the bgcolor variable) ranges from 0 through 7 and is printed along with the name of the color (obtained from the Backgrnd$( ) array) by the PRINT statement in line 560. The display screen now looks like the one shown previously in Figure 21-1.

After the color numbers and names are printed, the constraints of a WHILE/WEND loop are set up.

```
580 a$ = "8"
590 IF Pal = 0 THEN Ok$ = "01357" ELSE Ok$ = "01246"
```

The variable a$, used in the WHILE/WEND loop to accept your entry, is now set to a number outside the color number range so that the condition in the WHILE statement will be false (to allow entry into the loop). The variable Ok$ is assigned a string of acceptable foreground color numbers based on the palette that was selected earlier.

When the WHILE/WEND loop is entered, a color number is selected for the foreground. The value of the selected number is assigned to the variable named Back. This variable is then used to assign the appropriate background color to the appropriate palette.

```
600 WHILE INSTR(Ok$, a$) = 0
610    a$ = INPUT$(1)
620 WEND
630 Back = VAL(a$): Forgrnd$(Pal, 0) = Backgrnd$(Back)
```

When a correct entry is made (your entry is in the string Ok$), an exit is made from the WHILE/WEND loop. The number selected is converted to numeric form by the VAL function and assigned to the variable Back in line 630. The value of the background color chosen is obtained from the appropriate element of the Backgrnd$( ) array — Backgrnd$(Back) — and assigned as color number 0 of the appropriate palette — Forgrnd$(Pal, 0).

The next block of code allows you to select a boundary color that will not be used until the final pattern has been selected. It is the boundary of the rectangle that will contain your pattern at the end of the program. First, a prompt and the appropriate color number and names are printed.

```
700 REM ** Get boundary color **
710 CLS: PRINT "Which color boundary do you want?": PRINT
720 FOR num = 1 TO 3
730   PRINT TAB(2); num; " "; Forgrnd$(Pal, num)
740 NEXT num
```

The possible boundary colors are chosen from the Forgrnd$( ) array, using the palette that was previously selected.

In the same block of code, the input variable (akey$) is set to "0". This ensures that the value of akey$ is not one of the numbers in the string "123" used as a condition in the WHILE/WEND loop where you choose the boundary color. If akey$ was equal to 1, 2, or 3, the loop would not be entered at all.

```
750 akey$ = "0"
760 WHILE INSTR("123", akey$) = 0
770   akey$ = INPUT$(1)
780 WEND
790 PRINT akey$: bordcol = VAL(akey$)
```

Once again the INSTR function is used to void an exit from the WHILE/WEND loop until an appropriate selection from the string "123" is made. When you have entered 1, 2, or 3, the entry is printed, and the numeric value of your entry is assigned to the variable bordcol by line 790.

All entries have now been made, and you are ready to create the desired pattern.

Creating the Pattern

The next block calls two subroutines that are the heart of the pattern creation.

```
800 REM ** Pick and Choose **
810 GOSUB 2010: GOSUB 3010
```

You will choose the size of the pattern-creation grid in the subroutine of block 2000. The cursor is drawn and saved as an array with the GET statement. The possible colors are listed, and the grid is drawn. Another subroutine is then called to draw the pattern preview area.

The screen is first cleared, and the variable named pics is set to zero.

```
2000 REM ** SUBROUTINE: Custom Choice Screen **
2010 CLS : pics = 0
```

Then you pick the number of rows that you want in the pattern-creation grid (1 to 16). If you pick a number less than 1 or greater than 16, a message is printed that selection is either too small or too big.

```
2020 WHILE pics > 16 OR pics < 1
2030    INPUT "Number of pixel rows (1-16)"; pics
2040    IF pics < 1 THEN PRINT "Too small, try again"
2050    IF pics > 16 THEN PRINT "Too big, try again"
2060 WEND
```

Your selection for the number of rows is reduced by one for use in a later calculation. The graphics screen is now invoked with the background and palette colors you selected earlier. The screen is cleared, the cursor is drawn, and its image saved in the Size array. The screen is cleared again.

```
2070 pics = pics - 1: SCREEN 1: COLOR Back, Pal: CLS
2080 CIRCLE (5, 4), 2, 3: GET (1, 1)-(9, 7), Size: CLS
```

Next, the colors that you can use to color squares in the grid are printed by these lines:

```
2090 PRINT TAB(2); "Possible colors:": PRINT
2100 FOR kolor = 0 TO 3
2110    PRINT TAB(2); kolor; "  "; Forgrnd$(Pal, kolor)
2120 NEXT kolor
```

Two nested FOR/NEXT loops follow. They draw and color individual squares in the pattern-creation grid. The outside loop uses a variable named trow (text row) to control the row in which the square is drawn.

```
2160 FOR trow = 0 TO pics
   .
   .
   .
2230 NEXT trow
```

The inside loop uses a variable named tcol to select a text column for the four-column grid. Each square in the grid is the size of a text character. The variable trow designates the text row. The variables named col and row are used for graphics columns and rows.

```
2170    FOR tcol = 0 TO 3
2180       col = tcol * 10 + 200: row = trow * 8
2190       LINE (col, row)-(col + 10, row + 8), 3, B
2200       PAINT (col + 5, row + 4), 1, 3
2210       Cschm(tcol + trow * 4) = 1
2220    NEXT tcol
```

The values of the graphics column and row variables (col and row) are calculated from the text row and column variables (tcol and trow) at line 2180. A value of 200 is added to the col variable to place the grid on the right part of the screen. Individual squares of the grid are drawn at line 2190, and painted at line 2200.

When all squares in the grid have been drawn, another subroutine is called at line 2240 before the program returns to the main program at line 2250.

```
2240 GOSUB 4010
2250 RETURN
```

The subroutine of the 4000 block builds a string (Tile$) that describes the current pattern. Originally, Tile$ reflected only the background color. As squares are colored, this subroutine is called from another point in the program to update the Tile$ string as needed to fill in the pattern preview area.

The Tile$ string is first set to the null string.

```
4000 REM ** SUBROUTINE: Set Tile **
4010 Tile$ = ""
```

Then the Tile$ string is created by catenating the CHR$ function with the calculated values needed for the two-character code, in these lines:

```
4020 FOR trw = 0 TO pics
4030    cscl = Cschm(3 + 4 * trw) + 4 * Cschm(2 + 4 * trw)
4040    csc2 = 16 * Cschm(1 + 4 * trw) + 64 * Cschm(4 * trw)
4050    Tile$ = Tile$ + CHR$(cscl + csc2)
4060 NEXT trw
```

When the Tile$ string is complete, the current pattern preview area is erased, redrawn, and painted. Then the program returns to the statement following the statement that called the Set Tile subroutine.

```
4070 LINE (260, 0)-(300, 40), 0, BF
4080 LINE (260, 0)-(300, 40), 3, B
4090 PAINT (280, 20), Tile$, 3
4100 RETURN
```

When this subroutine is called from line 2240, no squares have been colored. The RETURN in line 4100 goes to line 2250 of the Customize Choice Screen block. From there, a RETURN is executed to take you to line 810.

A second subroutine, Choose Action, is called at line 810. In this subroutine, you either move the cursor or select a color for the square in which the cursor lies. The variables named tcol (text column) and trow (text row) are set to zero at line 3010. Then the graphics row (row) and graphics column (col) are calculated at line 3020, to place the cursor at the first column and first row of the grid.

```
3000 REM ** SUBROUTINE: Choose Action **
3010 tcol = 0: trow = 0
3020 row = trow * 8: col = tcol * 10 + 200
3030 PUT (col + 1, row + 1), Size, XOR
```

The screen now looks like the display shown previously in Figure 21-2. Most of the action takes place within a WHILE/WEND loop that follows. The only escape from the loop is when you have completed your pattern and pressed the ENTER key (whose ASCII code is 13 as used in line 3040).

```
3040 WHILE a$ <> CHR$(13)
3050    a$ = INKEY$
3060    IF a$ = "" THEN 3050
```

The INKEY$ function is used at lines 3050 and 3060 to intercept a keystroke. INKEY$ is used instead of INPUT$(1) because the arrow keys must be detected. The arrow keys have extended ASCII codes that cannot be detected by the INPUT$ function. The following combinations of characters are returned by the arrow keys:

Right arrow = CHR$(0) + "M"
Left arrow   = CHR$(0) + "K"
Down arrow   = CHR$(0) + "P"
Up arrow   = CHR$(0) + "H"

Included in the WHILE/WEND loop are five IF statements that call different subroutines to perform the necessary cursor movement or square coloring.

```
3070    IF a$ = CHR$(0) + "M" AND tcol < 3 THEN GOSUB 5010
3080    IF a$ = CHR$(0) + "K" AND tcol > 0 THEN GOSUB 6010
3090    IF a$ = CHR$(0) + "P" AND trow < pics THEN GOSUB 7010
3100    IF a$ = CHR$(0) + "H" AND trow > 0 THEN GOSUB 8010
3110    IF a$ >= "0" AND a$ <= "3" THEN GOSUB 9010
3120 WEND
```

The subroutine called in lines 3070, 3080, 3090, and 3100 performs the cursor movements right, left, down, and up, respectively. If a number key (1, 2, or 3) is pressed, a subroutine is called at line 3110 to change the color of the square in which the cursor lies. The WEND statement at line 3120 marks the end of the WHILE/WEND loop. On return from the selected subroutine, program execution continues at the top of the loop (unless the ENTER key has been pressed).

The subroutines that perform the cursor movement are similar to one another. Each contains a PUT statement to erase the cursor, a statement that calculates the new cursor position, and a second PUT statement to place the cursor at the new position. For example:

```
5000 REM ** SUBROUTINE: Move Right **
5010 PUT (col + 1, row + 1), Size, XOR
5020 tcol = tcol + 1: col = tcol * 10 + 200
5030 PUT (col + 1, row + 1), Size, XOR
5040 RETURN
```

Only the column position needs to be calculated in the Move Right subroutine. The cursor stays in the same row, but its column position is increased.

In the Move Left subroutine, only the column position needs to be calculated. The cursor stays in the same row, but its column position is decreased.

```
6000 REM ** SUBROUTINE: Move Left **
6010 PUT (col + 1, row + 1), Size, XOR
6020 tcol = tcol - 1: col = tcol * 10 + 200
6030 PUT (col + 1, row + 1), Size, XOR
6040 RETURN
```

Only the row position needs to be calculated in the Move Down subroutine. The cursor stays in the same column, but its row position is increased.

```
7000 REM ** SUBROUTINE: Move Down **
7010 PUT (col + 1, row + 1), Size, XOR
7020 trow = trow + 1: row = trow * 8
7030 PUT (col + 1, row + 1), Size, XOR
7040 RETURN
```

In the Move Up subroutine, only the row position needs to be calculated. The cursor stays in the same column, but its row position is decreased.

```
8000 REM ** SUBROUTINE: Move Up **
8010 PUT (col + 1, row + 1), Size, XOR
8020 trow = trow - 1: row = trow * 8
8030 PUT (col + 1, row + 1), Size, XOR
8040 RETURN
```

The Change Colors subroutine uses a PUT statement to erase the cursor. Then the square is erased, redrawn, and painted with the color selected at line 3050.

```
9000 REM ** SUBROUTINE: Change Colors **
9010 PUT (col + 1, row + 1), Size, XOR
9020 ppt = VAL(a$)
9030 LINE (col, row)-(col + 10, row + 8), 0, BF
9040 LINE (col, row)-(col + 10, row + 8), 3, B
9050 PAINT (col + 5, row + 4), ppt, 3
```

Next, the color scheme of the square is reset to the new color, and the cursor is placed back in the square by a second PUT statement. The pattern preview area is updated by the subroutine in block 4000. Then the program returns to the WEND statement at line 3120.

```
9060 Cschm(tcol + trow * 4) = ppt
9070 PUT (col + 1, row + 1), Size, XOR
9080 GOSUB 4010
9090 RETURN
```

When the pattern is complete and you press the ENTER key, an exit is made from the WHILE/WEND loop (lines 3040 to 3120).

The tile string is now calculated, using intermediate variables to describe the string (des1, des2, and Descrip). A FOR/NEXT loop is used to compile the string, row by row.

```
3130 Tile$ = "": TileH$ = ""
3140 FOR trow = 0 TO pics
3150   des1 = Cschm(3 + 4 * trow) + 4 * Cschm(2 + 4 * trow)
3160   des2 = 16 * Cschm(1 + 4 * trow) + 64 * Cschm(4 * trow)
3170   Descrip = des1 + des2
3180   Tile$ = Tile$ + CHR$(Descrip)
3190   TileH$ = TileH$ + "CHR$(&H" + HEX$(Descrip) + ") + "
3200 NEXT trow
```

Table 21-1 shows the values of the variables des1, des2, and Descrip for each pass through the FOR/NEXT loop. It also shows how the hexadecimal string for the tile pattern grows. The Tile$ string is converted to hexadecimal format.

The hexadecimal string (TileH$) in Table 21-1 ends with a space, a plus sign (+) and another space. These three characters are clipped from the end of the TileH$ string, and a return is made to the main program.

```
3210 TileH$ = LEFT$(TileH$, LEN(TileH$) - 3)
3220 RETURN
```

Closing Down

After the TileH$ string is completed, the main program displays the results (shown previously in Figure 21-5). SCREEN 1 is used with the background and foreground colors you selected earlier. A rectangular area in the upper-left corner displays your pattern.

```
900 REM ** Display Result and PAINT Statement **
910 SCREEN 1: COLOR Back, Pal: CLS
920 LINE (1, 1)-(80, 40), bordcol, B
```

```
930 PAINT (40, 20), Tile$, bordcol
940 LOCATE 3, 14: PRINT "This is the pattern"
950 LOCATE 4, 14: PRINT "you generated."
```

A rectangle, 80 pixels by 40 pixels, is drawn at line 920 with the selected border color. The rectangle is filled with your pattern by the PAINT statement at line 930. Lines 940 and 950 print text to the right of the pattern.

Next, a message is printed (line 960), along with the string that should be assigned to the Tile$ variable to create the selected pattern (lines 970 to 1000).

```
960 LOCATE 10, 1: PRINT "The values for this pattern are:"
970 PRINT: PRINT "Tile$ = ";
980 FOR number = 1 TO pics + 1
990    PRINT MID$(TileH$, (number - 1) * 13 + 1, 13);
1000 NEXT number
```

Table 21-1.

des1	*des2*	*Descrip*	*TileH$*
5	160	165	CHR$(&HA5) +
9	80	89	CHR$(&HA5) + CHR$(&H59) +
5	96	101	CHR$(&HA5) + CHR$(&H59) + CHR$(&H65) +
9	80	89	CHR$(&HA5) + CHR$(&H59) + CHR$(&H65) + CHR$(&H59) +
5	96	101	CHR$(&HA5) + CHR$(&H59) + CHR$(&H65) + CHR$(&H59) + CHR$(&H65) +
9	80	89	CHR$(&HA5) + CHR$(&H59) + CHR$(&H65) + CHR$(&H59) + CHR$(&H65) + CHR$(&H59) +
5	6	101	CHR$(&HA5) + CHR$(&H59) + CHR$(&H65) + CHR$(&H59) + CHR$(&H65) + CHR$(&H59) + CHR$(&H65) +
10	80	90	CHR$(&HA5) + CHR$(&H59) + CHR$(&H65) + CHR$(&H59) + CHR$(&H65) + CHR$(&H59) + CHR$(&H65) + CHR$(&H5A) +

Building a Tile String

The PAINT statement that will use the pattern to fill a figure is also displayed, by line 1020.

```
1020 PRINT "PAINT (X,Y), Tile$, " + MID$(STR$(bordcol), 2)
```

In the next block of code, a prompt is printed to see if you want to create another pattern.

```
1100 REM ** Go Again? **
1110 LOCATE 20, 1: PRINT "Try another pattern (Y or N)"
```

Then a WHILE/WEND loop gets the first letter (Y, y, N, or n) of your response. If the response is Y or y, line 1150 passes control back to line 130, near the beginning of the program. If your response is N or n, the screen is cleared and you are returned to the text screen, where the program ends.

```
1120 WHILE INSTR("YyNn", akey$) = 0
1130    akey$ = INPUT$(1)
1140 WEND
1150 IF akey$ = "Y" OR akey$ = "y" THEN GOTO 130
1160 CLS: SCREEN 0: COLOR 7, 0, 0: WIDTH 80: END
```

Program 21-1 can be modified to use SCREEN 2. Since the pixels in SCREEN 2 would either be on or off (no color variety), you would want your pattern-creation grid to be eight columns wide (to represent one byte). You would have to remove all color selections from the program. The program would be much shorter and simpler to use. The program can also be modified for other graphics modes.

22

Menu Maker

This chapter contains two programs that you may find useful in creating menus and using windows to display them. The first program is used in the text mode, SCREEN 0. The second program is used in the graphics mode, SCREEN 2, but can be rewritten for any graphics mode.

You learned in Chapter 8, "Terminal I/O," how to use the SCREEN function to read the ASCII code of a character at a specified position on the screen. In the first program of this chapter, you will use the SCREEN function to create a text array from the characters in a specified area of the screen. The text array will then be used to save information on the original screen that a menu will overlay. When you are finished using the menu, the information in the array can then replace the menu, restoring the original screen conditions.

Making a Menu in the Text Mode

Program 22-1, Menu Window in the Text Mode, allows you to create a menu window. You make entries specifying the number of menu items, the location of the window on the screen, a title for the menu, and the text for each menu item.

The SCREEN function is used to copy that part of the original screen that the menu will overlay. The menu used in this demonstration contains a list of items, from which you choose one item by number. The program then prints the number of your choice. Next it prompts you to press the spacebar to erase the menu. When you do, the original area of the screen that was saved to the array replaces the menu, thus restoring the original screen. You can modify this section of the program to perform whatever task the selected menu item specifies.

When the original screen is restored, a prompt tells you to press the ESC key to end the program.

Program 22-1.

```
1 REM ** Menu Window in the Text Mode **
2 ' GW-BASIC: The Reference, Chapter 22. File: GWRF2201.BAS
3 ' Demonstrates a window used for a menu

100 REM ** Initialize **
110 SCREEN 0: CLS: KEY OFF: WIDTH 80: DEFINT A-Z
120 ON ERROR GOTO 5010

200 REM ** Print entry information **
210 LOCATE 2, 1
220 PRINT "This program allows you to create menu windows."
230 PRINT "Enter the information requested": PRINT: PRINT

300 REM ** Get window information **
310 FOR number = 1 TO 3
```

Menu Window in the Text Mode (GWRF2201.BAS) (continued on next page)

Program 22-1.

```
320    ON number GOSUB 2010, 3010, 4010
330 NEXT number
340 DIM Menu$(MenuNumber): PRINT

400 REM ** Get data for window **
410 LINE INPUT "Enter Menu title: "; Title$
420 IF MenuCol + LEN(Title$) > 75 THEN ERROR 80
430 longest = LEN(Title$)
440 FOR num = 1 TO MenuNumber
450    PRINT "Menu item"; num; " " ;: LINE INPUT item$
460    IF MenuCol + LEN(item$) > 75 THEN ERROR 81
470    Menu$(num) = STR$(num) + " " + item$
480    chars = LEN(Menu$(num))
490    IF chars > longest THEN longest = chars
500 NEXT num
510 rows = MenuNumber + 6: cols = longest + 4
520 EndRow = MenuRow | MenuNumber | 5
530 EndCol = MenuCol + longest + 3
540 DIM Block(rows, cols)

600 REM ** Copy window area and wait for keypress **
610 FOR row = MenuRow TO EndRow
620    FOR col = MenuCol TO EndCol
630       lyne = row - MenuRow: colmn = col - MenuCol
640       Block(lyne, colmn) = SCREEN(row, col)
650    NEXT col
660 NEXT row
670 LOCATE 21, 1, 0: PRINT "Press spacebar to see menu.";
680 WHILE akey$ <> CHR$(32): akey$ = INPUT$(1): WEND
690 LOCATE 21, 1: PRINT SPACE$(28);: GOSUB 1010 'Call menu

700 REM ** Show menu choice and erase menu prompt **
710 COLOR 7, 0
720 LOCATE 21, 1: PRINT "You chose "; Choice$; "."; SPACE$(17)
730 PRINT "Press spacebar to erase menu."; SPACE$(2)
740 WHILE akey$ <> CHR$(32): akey$ = INPUT$(1): WEND

800 REM ** Return to original screen **
810 COLOR 7, 0
820 FOR row = MenuRow TO EndRow
830    FOR col = MenuCol TO EndCol
840       lyne = row - MenuRow: colmn = col - MenuCol
```

Menu Window in the Text Mode (GWRF2201.BAS) (continued)

Program 22-1.

```
850     LOCATE row, col: PRINT CHR$(Block(lyne, colmn));
860   NEXT col
870 NEXT row

900 REM ** Prompt for end, wait for keystroke, end **
910 LOCATE 21, 1: PRINT SPACE$(12)
920 LOCATE 22, 1: PRINT "Press ESC key to end program. "
930 WHILE akey$ <> CHR$(27): akey$ = INPUT$(1): WEND
940 CLS: KEY ON: END

1000 REM ** SUBROUTINE: Menu **
1009 ' Menu background
1010 COLOR 1, 0
1020 FOR row = MenuRow + 1 TO EndRow - 1
1030    LOCATE row, MenuCol: PRINT STRING$(longest + 4, 219)
1040 NEXT row
1049 ' Menu border, top and bottom
1050 COLOR 11, 0: LOCATE MenuRow, MenuCol
1060 PRINT STRING$(longest + 4, 220)
1070 LOCATE EndRow, MenuCol: PRINT STRING$(longest + 4, 223)
1079 ' Menu border, sides
1080 COLOR 11, 1
1090 FOR row = MenuRow + 1 TO EndRow - 1
1100    LOCATE row, MenuCol: PRINT CHR$(221)
1110    LOCATE row, EndCol: PRINT CHR$(222)
1120 NEXT row
1129 ' Menu Title and items
1130 LOCATE MenuRow + 2, MenuCol + 2: PRINT Title$;
1140 FOR row = 1 TO MenuNumber
1150    LOCATE MenuRow + row + 3, MenuCol + 2
1160    PRINT Menu$(row);
1170 NEXT row
1179 ' Menu Choice
1180 Choice$ = ""
1190 WHILE VAL(Choice$) < 1 OR VAL(Choice$) > MenuNumber
1200    Choice$ = INPUT$(1): akey$ = Choice$
1210 WEND
1220 RETURN

2000 REM ** Get number of menu items **
2010 MenuNumber = 0
2020 WHILE MenuNumber < 2 OR MenuNumber > 10
```

Menu Window in the Text Mode (GWRF2201.BAS) (continued)

Program 22-1.

```
2030    INPUT "How many items (2-10) "; MenuNumber
2040 WEND
2050 RETURN

3000 REM ** Get top row of menu **
3010 MenuRow = 0
3020 WHILE MenuRow < 1 OR MenuRow > 16
3030    INPUT "Top row of menu (1-16) "; MenuRow
3040    IF MenuRow + MenuNumber > 18 THEN ERROR 82
3050 WEND
3060 RETURN

4000 REM ** Get first column of menu **
4010 MenuCol = 0
4020 WHILE MenuCol < 1 OR MenuCol > 70
4030    INPUT "First column of menu (1-70) "; MenuCol
4040 WEND
4050 RETURN

5000 REM ** Error-handling routine **
5010 IF ERR = 80 THEN PRINT "Title too long. Try again."
5020 IF ERR = 81 THEN PRINT "Item too long. Try again."
5030 IF ERR = 82 THEN PRINT "Row value too large. Try again."
5040 IF ERL = 420 THEN RESUME 410
5050 IF ERL = 460 THEN RESUME 450
5060 IF ERL = 3040 THEN RESUME 3030
```

Menu Window in the Text Mode (GWRF2201.BAS)

Display Screens

The opening screen of Program 22-1 includes a two-line prompt and a request for the number of items to be included in the menu.

```
This program allows you to create menu windows.
Enter the information requested.


How many menu items (2-10) ? _
```

For this demonstration, three menu items are requested. The next three prompts request the number of the row for the top of the menu, and the leftmost column of the menu. Here are the prompts and the items selected for our example.

```
How many items (2-10) ? 3
Top row of menu (1-16) ? 5
First column of menu (1-70) ? 12
```

After these three items are entered, you are prompted for the menu title. The title for this demonstration is

```
Enter Menu title: Pick Program by Number
```

Next, requests are made for each menu item by number. The first request is

```
Menu item 1  _
```

Notice that the prompt provides the item number. All you have to do is enter the text for the item.

```
Menu item 1  GWRF1101.BAS_
```

The menu items in our example are filenames of three programs from Chapter 11. When all three items have been entered, the text in the area that the window will overlay is copied to an array. A prompt then appears, near the bottom of the screen, to press the spacebar to see the menu. Figure 22-1 shows the screen with this prompt.

When you press the spacebar, the menu overlays the prompts and entries that have been made, as shown in Figure 22-2. Notice that the upper-left corner of the menu window is placed, as requested, at row 5 and column 12. The title is displayed two rows

Figure 22-1.

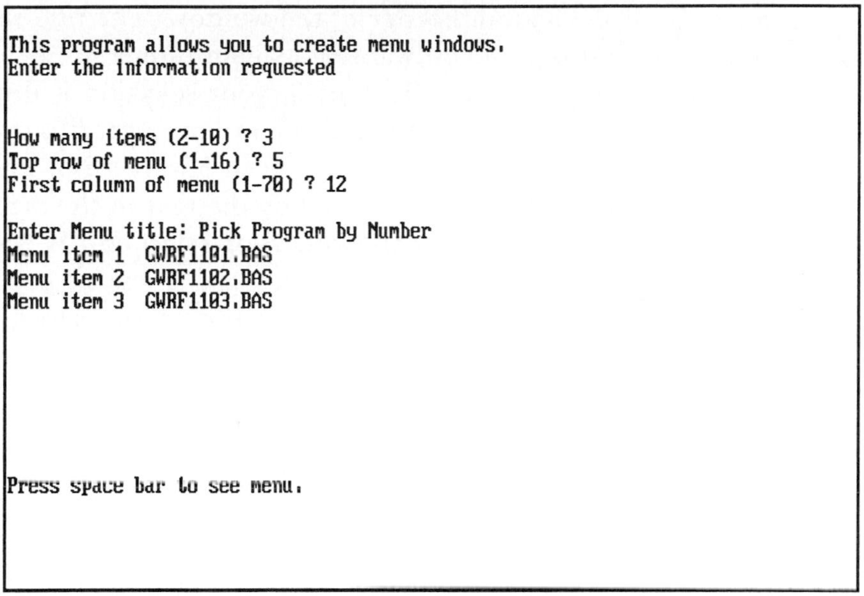

```
This program allows you to create menu windows.
Enter the information requested


How many items (2-10) ? 3
Top row of menu (1-16) ? 5
First column of menu (1-70) ? 12

Enter Menu title: Pick Program by Number
Menu item 1  GWRF1101.BAS
Menu item 2  GWRF1102.BAS
Menu item 3  GWRF1103.BAS




Press space bar to see menu.
```

Menu items entered

Figure 22-2.

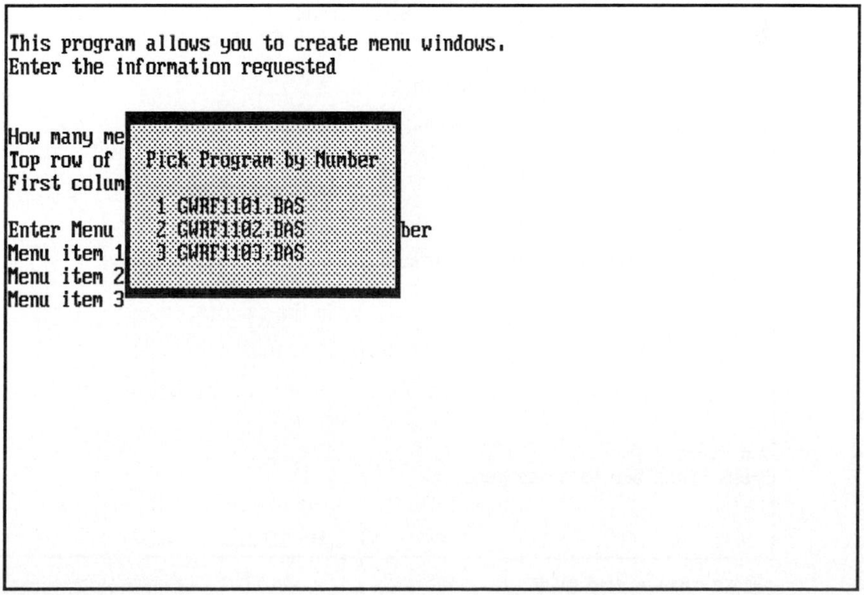

```
This program allows you to create menu windows.
Enter the information requested


How many me
Top row of    Pick Program by Number
First colum
              1 GWRF1101.BAS
Enter Menu    2 GWRF1102.BAS         ber
Menu item 1   3 GWRF1103.BAS
Menu item 2
Menu item 3
```

Menu displayed

below the top border of the window. The last item is displayed two rows above the bottom border of the window. The title suggests you pick the program you want by its item number.

When you press either 1, 2, or 3, your selection is displayed near the bottom of the screen, and you are prompted to press the spacebar to erase the menu, as shown in Figure 22-3. Press the spacebar, and the menu is replaced by the text in the array that was saved earlier. The screen, with your selections, is restored. Near the bottom of the screen, the message "Press ESC key to end program." is added. Figure 22-4 shows the screen before the ESC key is pressed.

Program Description

After the program identification lines (1, 2, and 3), the screen is initialized and integers are specified as the default variable type.

Figure 22-3.

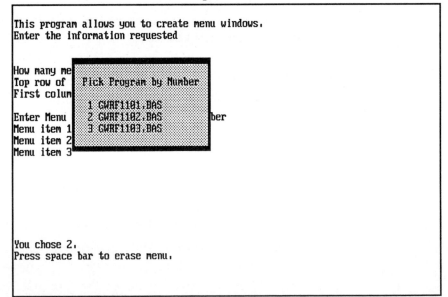

Menu choice displayed

Figure 22-4.

```
This program allows you to create menu windows.
Enter the information requested


How many items (2-10) ? 3
Top row of menu (1-16) ? 5
First column of menu (1-70) ? 12

Enter Menu title: Pick Program by Number
Menu item 1  GWRF1101.BAS
Menu item 2  GWRF1102.BAS
Menu item 3  GWRF1103.BAS




Press ESC key to end program.
```

Menu erased

An error-handling routine is enabled, with the first line of the routine specified as 5010.

```
100 REM ** Initialize **
110 SCREEN 0: CLS: KEY OFF: WIDTH 80: DEFINT A-Z
120 ON ERROR GOTO 5010
```

Two instruction lines are then printed near the top of the screen (at rows 2 and 3).

```
200 REM ** Print entry information **
210 LOCATE 2, 1
220 PRINT "This program allows you to create menu windows."
230 PRINT "Enter the information requested": PRINT: PRINT
```

The next block of code (block 300) calls subroutines that request and accept information about the desired placement of the menu window. Then the dimension of the Menu$( ) array (which will hold the item number and name) is specified at line 340 from the data entered as MenuNumber.

```
300 REM ** Get window information **
310 FOR number = 1 TO 3
320   ON number GOSUB 2010, 3010, 4010
330 NEXT number
340 DIM Menu$(MenuNumber): PRINT
```

The first subroutine called (block 2000) gets the number of menu items. A WHILE/WEND loop is used with a condition that the entry is in the range 2 to 10.

```
2010 MenuNumber = 0
2020 WHILE MenuNumber < 2 OR MenuNumber > 10
2030   INPUT "How many items (2-10) "; MenuNumber
2040 WEND
2050 RETURN
```

Another subroutine is then called to get the top row of the menu. Its WHILE/WEND loop includes an error check (ERROR 82) at line 3040 to make sure the value for the top row is not so large that the menu will not fit on the screen.

```
3010 MenuRow = 0
3020 WHILE MenuRow < 1 OR MenuRow > 16
3030   INPUT "Top row of menu (1-16) "; MenuRow
3040   IF MenuRow + MenuNumber > 18 THEN ERROR 82
3050 WEND
3060 RETURN
```

Even when your top row value is in the correct range (1-16), the number of menu items to be entered might be too large for the menu to fit on the screen. The error check prevents this.

A third subroutine (block 4000) is then called to get the leftmost column of the menu.

```
4010 MenuCol = 0
4020 WHILE MenuCol < 1 OR MenuCol > 70
4030   INPUT "First column of menu (1-70) "; MenuCol
4040 WEND
4050 RETURN
```

After all three subroutines have been successfully completed, the next block of code requests and accepts the menu title and item entries. It assigns a number to each entry, and stores the number and item in the Menu$( ) array. The ending row and column of the window are calculated, and the Block( ) array is dimensioned. The Block( ) array will hold the text of the original screen area replaced by the window.

First, the title is entered at line 410. Then an error check at line 420 ensures that the length of the title is not so long that the menu will not fit on the screen. If the title fits, its length is assigned to the variable named longest. This variable is used to hold the length of the longest text line from the title and menu items, so that the length of the longest line can be used for automatically providing the correct number of columns for the window.

```
400 REM ** Get data for window **
410 LINE INPUT "Enter Menu title: "; Title$
420 IF MenuCol + LEN(litle$) > 75 THEN ERROR 80
430 longest = LEN(Title$)
```

If the title is too long, line 420 invokes the error-handling routine (block 5000), which prints this message:

```
Title too long.   Try again.
```

The error-handling routine's RESUME statement returns control to line 410, where you can enter a different title.

Next, a FOR/NEXT loop is used to enter each item, check the item's length, assign a number to it, and verify that each item is longer than the current number assigned to the variable, longest. When an item is longer than the current value, the length of this item becomes the new value of longest.

```
440 FOR num = 1 TO MenuNumber
450   PRINT "Menu item"; num; " ";: LINE INPUT item$
460   IF MenuCol + LEN(item$) > 75 THEN ERROR 81
470   Menu$(num) = STR$(num) + " " + item$
```

```
480    chars = LEN(Menu$(num))
490    IF chars > longest THEN longest = chars
500 NEXT num
```

The prompt for a menu item is printed next, and a LINE INPUT statement accepts the entry at line 450. The error check at line 460 makes sure the item name will fit on the screen. If not, the error-handling routine (block 5000) prints this message:

```
Item too long.  Try again.
```

A RESUME statement in the error-handling routine passes control back to line 450 for a different item entry. Once an item entry is accepted, it is catenated to the string form of the number (STR$(num)) at line 470. The length of the menu item entry is assigned to the chars variable at line 480. The values of the variables, chars and longest, are compared at line 490. If the new value is greater than the current value, the new value is assigned to longest.

When all menu items have been successfully entered, the location for the last row and the rightmost column of the menu's border is calculated. These values are used to dimension the Block( ) array that is used to store the original screen where the menu window will be placed.

```
510 rows = MenuNumber + 6: cols = longest + 4
520 EndRow = MenuRow + MenuNumber + 5
530 EndCol = MenuCol + longest + 3
540 DIM Block(rows, cols)
```

In the sample run of this demonstration program (see Figures 22-1 and 22-2), the first row of the menu window (MenuRow) is 5, the number of items (MenuNumber) is 3, the leftmost column (MenuCol) is 12, and the longest text string is the title (longest = 22). Therefore:

EndRow = 5 + 3 + 5 = 13
EndCol = 12 + 22 + 3 = 37

This means that the menu (including its border) will occupy rows 5 through 13 (9 rows) and columns 12 through 37 (26 columns).

rows = (MenuNumber + 6) = 3 + 6 = 9
cols = (longest + 4) = 22 + 4 = 26

The Block( ) array is then dimensioned with

DIM Block(9, 26)

Now that the placement of the menu window is known, the text in that area is copied and saved in the Block( ) array. The outer FOR/NEXT loop specifies the row to be copied and saved, using the values of the top row (MenuRow) and the bottom row (EndRow) as the beginning and ending values of the row variable.

```
610 FOR row = MenuRow TO EndRow
  .
  .
  .
660 NEXT row
```

The inner FOR/NEXT loop specifies the column and copies the ASCII codes of each character, returned by the SCREEN function, into the Block( ) array.

```
620    FOR col = MenuCol TO EndCol
630      lyne = row - MenuRow: colmn = col - MenuCol
640      Block(lyne, colmn) = SCREEN(row, col)
650    NEXT col
```

When the text has been copied and saved, a prompt is printed to press the spacebar and see the menu. A WHILE/WEND loop waits for the spacebar keypress. When it occurs, the prompt is erased and the Menu subroutine is called.

```
670 LOCATE 21, 1, 0: PRINT "Press space bar to see menu.";
680 WHILE akey$ <> CHR$(32): akey$ = INPUT$(1): WEND
690 LOCATE 21, 1: PRINT SPACE$(28);: GOSUB 1010 'Call menu
```

The menu-drawing subroutine first selects blue as the foreground color to use with the STRING$ function (and ASCII code 219) to lay down a background for the menu.

```
1009 ' Menu background
1010 COLOR 1,  0
1020 FOR row = MenuRow + 1 TO EndRow - 1
1030    LOCATE row, MenuCol: PRINT STRING$(longest + 4, 219)
1040 NEXT row
```

If the computer were interrupted at this point, the screen would look like Figure 22-5. However, with no pause, it immediately

Figure 22-5.

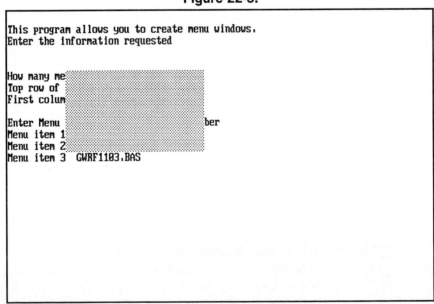

Background for menu

prints a light cyan border around the menu background. The top and bottom of the border are printed first, in these lines:

```
1049 ' Menu border, top and bottom
1050 COLOR 11, 0: LOCATE MenuRow, MenuCol
1060 PRINT STRING$(longest + 4, 220)
1070 LOCATE EndRow, MenuCol: PRINT STRING$(longest + 4, 223)
```

Then the sides of the border are printed, as follows.

```
1079 ' Menu border, sides
1080 COLOR 11, 1
1090 FOR row = MenuRow + 1 TO EndRow - 1
1100    LOCATE row, MenuCol: PRINT CHR$(221)
1110    LOCATE row, EndCol: PRINT CHR$(222)
1120 NEXT row
```

At this point, the menu background and border overlay the original screen as shown in Figure 22-6. The title and menu items are then printed in light cyan on the blue background.

```
1129 ' Menu Title and items
1130 LOCATE MenuRow + 2, MenuCol + 2: PRINT Title$;
1140 FOR row = 1 TO MenuNumber
1150    LOCATE MenuRow + row + 3, MenuCol + 2
1160    PRINT Menu$(row);
1170 NEXT row
```

The LOCATE statements in lines 1130 and 1150 place the text within the menu border so they can be easily read. The screen now looks like the one shown previously in Figure 22-2.

The computer now waits for you to enter the number of your selection: 1, 2, or 3. When you press one of those keys, a return is made to the main program.

```
1179 ' Menu Choice
1180 Choice$ = ""
1190 WHILE VAL(Choice$) < 1 OR VAL(Choice$) > MenuNumber
1200    Choice$ = INPUT$(1): akey$ = Choice$
1210 WEND
1220 RETURN
```

The WHILE statement at line 1190 will not allow an exit from the loop until the keypress is greater than zero, and less than or equal to the greatest number in the item list. When a valid entry is made, control returns to the main program at the 700 block of code. The menu is still on the screen. The number of your choice is printed near the bottom of the screen along with a prompt to press the spacebar to erase the menu. The screen at this point looks like the one in Figure 22-3.

```
700 REM ** Show menu choice and erase menu prompt **
710 COLOR 7, 0
720 LOCATE 21, 1: PRINT "You chose "; Choice$; "."; SPACE$(17)
730 PRINT "Press spacebar to erase menu."; SPACE$(2)
740 WHILE akey$ <> CHR$(32): akey$ = INPUT$(1): WEND
```

The PRINT statement at line 720 prints your menu choice at the same location of a previous prompt. The SPACE$ functions at the

Figure 22-6.

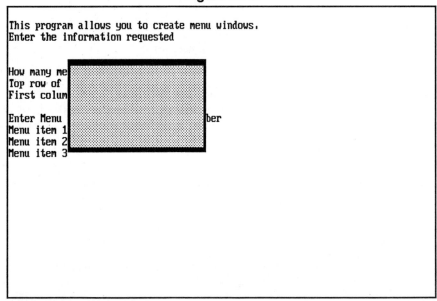

Border for menu added

end of both lines 720 and 730 erase the ends of the lines previously located at screen rows 21 and 22 that were not overwritten by the new display. The WHILE/WEND loop at line 740 is executed until you press the spacebar, whose ASCII code is 32.

In the 800 block of code, the color of the screen is returned to the default colors (white on black). The text that was previously saved in the Block( ) array is replaced, one character at a time.

```
810 COLOR 7, 0
820 FOR row = MenuRow TO EndRow
830    FOR col = MenuCol TO EndCol
840       lyne = row - MenuRow: colmn = col - MenuCol
850       LOCATE row, col: PRINT CHR$(Block(lyne, colmn));
860    NEXT col
870 NEXT row
```

The last block of code erases the previous prompts and displays a new prompt to press the ESC key and end the program. When you do, the screen is cleared and the program ends.

```
900 REM ** Prompt for end, wait for keystroke, end **
910 LOCATE 21, 1: PRINT SPACE$(12)
920 LOCATE 22, 1: PRINT "Press ESC key to end program. "
930 WHILE akey$ <> CHR$(27): akey$ = INPUT$(1): WEND
940 CLS: KEY ON: END
```

The error-handling routine contains PRINT statements that print the messages caused by entry errors in the main program. It uses ERR variables to determine the error number so that the correct message is printed, and ERL variables to determine where the program should resume using the RESUME command.

```
5010 IF ERR = 80 THEN PRINT "Title too long.  Try again."
5020 IF ERR = 81 THEN PRINT "Item too long.  Try again."
5030 IF ERR = 82 THEN PRINT "Row value too large.  Try again."
5040 IF ERL = 420 THEN RESUME 410
5050 IF ERL = 460 THEN RESUME 450
5060 IF ERL = 3040 THEN RESUME 3030
```

Closing Down Program 22-1

Program 22-1 contains a minimum amount of error checking to demonstrate how it can be done. In a professionally designed program, the error checking would be more extensive. This makes a program longer and more complex. Therefore, in the interest of simplicity, error checking in our example program is kept to a minimum.

Although the menu display method used in Program 22-1 does not write the menu or replace the screen with blazing speed, it works fast enough for most situations. If you want faster speed and can do without the colors of the previous menu, you can write your program in a two-color graphics mode. The next program uses SCREEN 2, and has PUT and GET statements to save the text as a graphics array.

Making Menu Windows in a Graphics Mode

Program 22-2, Menu Windows in a Graphics Mode, creates two menus with borders. It uses a GET statement to save each menu. It then displays the first window, with a message to press the plus (+) key to see the next window. When you press the plus key, the second window overlays most of the first window. The second window contains a message to press the minus (−) key to see the previous window. Another message appears at the bottom of the screen prompting you to press the ESC key to quit. You can thus switch back and forth between the windows by alternately pressing the plus and minus keys, or ESC to quit.

Program 22-2.

```
1 REM ** Menu Windows in a Graphics Mode **
2 ' GW-BASIC: The Reference, Chapter 22. File: GWRF2202.BAS
3 ' Demonstrates windows with PUT and GET

100 REM ** Initialize **
110 SCREEN 2: CLS: KEY OFF: DEFINT A-Z
120 DIM one(765), two(765), temp(765)

200 REM ** Print first window, then GET it **
210 LOCATE 5, 2: PRINT "This is the original window."
220 LOCATE 6, 2: PRINT "A border surrounds the text."
230 LOCATE 7, 2: PRINT "Press the plus (+) key to "
240 LOCATE 8, 2: PRINT "see the next window."
250 LOCATE 4, 1
260 PRINT CHR$(218); STRING$(28, 196); CHR$(191);
270 LOCATE 9, 1
280 PRINT CHR$(192); STRING$(28, 196); CHR$(217);
290 FOR row = 5 TO 8
300   LOCATE row, 1: PRINT CHR$(179);
310   LOCATE row, 30: PRINT CHR$(179);
320 NEXT row
330 GET (0, 24)-(240, 72), one: CLS

400 REM ** Print second window, then GET it **
410 LOCATE 5, 2: PRINT "This is the second window."
420 LOCATE 6, 2: PRINT "A border surrounds the text."
430 LOCATE 7, 2: PRINT "Press the minus (-) key to "
440 LOCATE 8, 2: PRINT "See the previous window."
450 LOCATE 4, 1
460 PRINT CHR$(218); STRING$(28, 196); CHR$(191);
470 LOCATE 9, 1
480 PRINT CHR$(192); STRING$(28, 196); CHR$(217);
490 FOR row = 5 TO 8
500   LOCATE row, 1: PRINT CHR$(179);
510   LOCATE row, 30: PRINT CHR$(179);
520 NEXT row
530 GET (0, 24)-(240, 72), two: CLS

600 REM ** Switch windows with + or - key, or quit **
```

Menu Windows in a Graphics Mode (GWRF2202.BAS) (continued on next page)

Program 22-2.

```
610 PUT (4, 4), one
620 akey$ = INPUT$(1)
630 IF akey$ = CHR$(27) THEN 810
640 IF akey$ <> "+" THEN 620
650 LOCATE 22, 1: PRINT "Press ESC to quit."
660 GET (44, 20)-(284, 68), temp
670 PUT (44, 20), two, PSET
680 akey$ = INPUT$(1)
690 IF akey$ = CHR$(27) THEN 810
700 IF akey$ <> "-" THEN 680
710 PUT (44, 20), two, XOR: PUT (44, 20), temp: GOTO 620

800 REM ** Restore screens and end **
810 CLS: SCREEN 0: CLS: KEY ON: END
```

Menu Windows in a Graphics Mode (GWRF2202.BAS)

Display Screens

In this program the menus are created quickly, and the screen is cleared after each menu is printed. You will probably see the windows flicker on and off before the first window is displayed a second time by a PUT statement. The first window is shown in Figure 22-7, placed near the upper-left corner of the screen.

When you press the plus (+) key, the second window overlays most of the first window. The upper-left corner of the second window is placed slightly to the right and below the upper-left corner of the original window. The second window includes instructions to press the minus (−) key to see the previous window, and another message near the bottom of the screen to press the ESC key to quit. See Figure 22-8.

Press the minus key to see the second window erased and the original window replaced. When you press the minus key, the prompt message remains at the bottom of the screen, the second window is replaced, and the first window is restored—as shown in Figure 22-9. Once again, you have the choice of pressing the plus key to overlay the original window with the second window, or ESC to quit.

Figure 22-7.

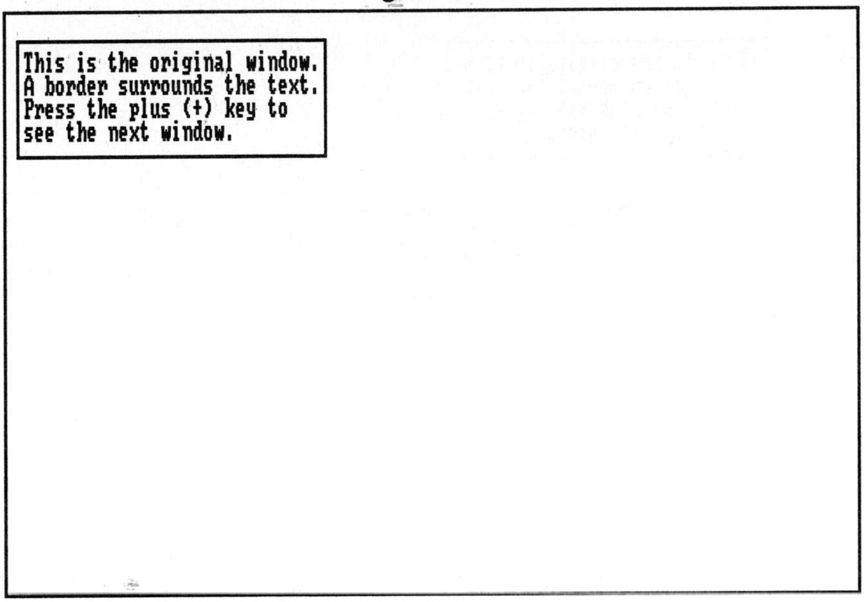

```
┌─────────────────────────────┐
│This is the original window. │
│A border surrounds the text. │
│Press the plus (+) key to    │
│see the next window.         │
└─────────────────────────────┘
```

First window

Figure 22-8.

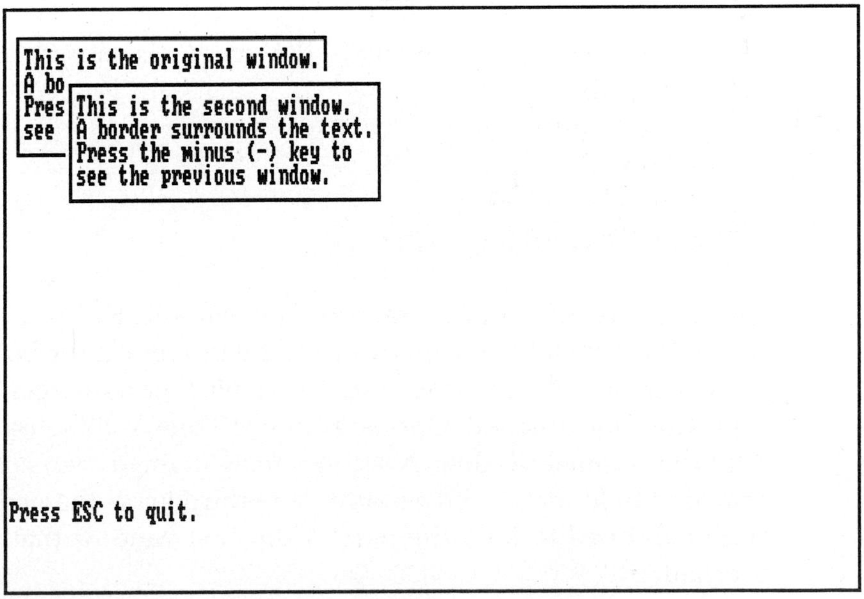

```
┌─────────────────────────────┐
│This is the original window. │
│A bo                         │
│Pres│This is the second window. │
│see │A border surrounds the text.│
│    │Press the minus (-) key to  │
│    │see the previous window.    │
│    └───────────────────────────┘




Press ESC to quit.
```

Second window overlays first window

Figure 22-9.

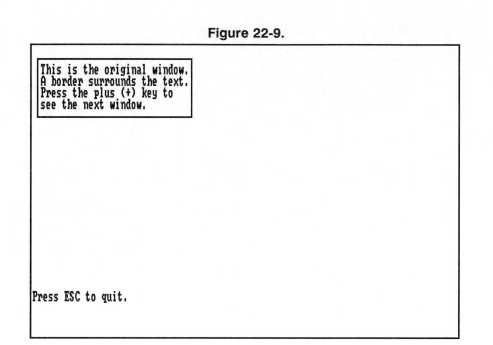

```
This is the original window.
A border surrounds the text.
Press the plus (+) key to
see the next window.
```

```
Press ESC to quit.
```

Second window erased

If you do press the ESC key, the screen is erased and the
program ends.

Program Description

The Initialize block of Program 22-2 specifies SCREEN 2 (graphics mode), clears the screen, turns off the key line at the bottom of
the screen, and declares the default variable type as integer. Three
arrays are dimensioned. One array (named one) is dimensioned to
hold the original window. A second array (named two) is dimensioned to hold the second window. The third array (named temp)
is dimensioned to hold the part of the first window that will be
overlaid.

```
100 REM ** Initialize **
110 SCREEN 2: CLS: KEY OFF: DEFINT A-Z
120 DIM one(765), two(765), temp(765)
```

The approximate dimensions needed for the arrays are calculated in these ways using the following variables for SCREEN 2:

colrange = colmax − colmin + 1
rowrange = rowmax − rowmin + 1
dimension = INT(colrange / 8 + 1) * rowrange * 1 / 2 + 4

where the expression 1 / 2 represents the ratio of color bits to array bits. The value of array bits is 2 for integer arrays, 4 for single precision, and 8 for double precision arrays. The value of color bits depends on the graphics mode, as shown in the following table:

Mode	Color Bits
2	1
1, 10	2
7, 8	4
9	2 if screen memory = 64K
9	4 if screen memory > 64K

The approximate dimension for the array named one can thus be calculated from the values of the variables colmax (240), colmin(0), rowmax (72), and rowmin (24) of line 330.

```
330 GET (0, 24)-(240, 72), one: CLS
```

Here are the calculations for the dimension.

colrange   = 240 − 0 = 240
rowrange   = 72 − 24 = 48
dimension   = INT(240 / 8 + 1) * 48 * .5 + 4
             = 31 * 24 + 4
             = 748

NOTE   These calculations produce only the approximate dimension needed. To be safe, a value of 765 is used for one, two, and temp. This is adequate for holding the arrays. In this program, all three arrays are the same size. In other programs, you might have to calculate the dimensions of more than one array.

The text of the first window is printed next.

```
200 REM ** Print first window, then GET it **
210 LOCATE 5, 2: PRINT "This is the original window."
220 LOCATE 6, 2: PRINT "A border surrounds the text."
230 LOCATE 7, 2: PRINT "Press the plus (+) key to "
240 LOCATE 8, 2: PRINT "see the next window."
```

Then a border is drawn around the text. The top and bottom lines are drawn first.

```
250 LOCATE 4, 1
260 PRINT CHR$(218); STRING$(28, 196); CHR$(191);
270 LOCATE 9, 1
280 PRINT CHR$(192); STRING$(28, 196); CHR$(217);
```

Then the sides are drawn.

```
290 FOR row = 5 TO 8
300    LOCATE row, 1: PRINT CHR$(179);
310    LOCATE row, 30: PRINT CHR$(179);
320 NEXT row
```

When the window is complete, a GET statement is used to store the information of the window in the array named one. The screen is immediately cleared.

```
330 GET (0, 24)-(240, 72), one: CLS
```

Figure 22-10.

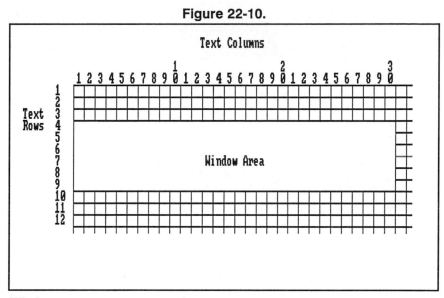

Window area

The graphics coordinates needed in the GET statement must include the window area shown in Figure 22-10. The coordinates are calculated based on the relationship between a graphics pixel's position and a given text character's position. This is calculated as follows:

graphcol = 8 * (textcol − 1)
graphrow = 8 * (textrow − 1)

In text coordinates, the leftmost column and top row of the window are column 1 and row 4 (obtained from the LOCATE statement in line 250). Therefore, the graphics coordinates of the leftmost column and top row are calculated as follows:

graphcol = 8 * (1 − 1) = 0
graphrow = 8 * (4 − 1) = 24

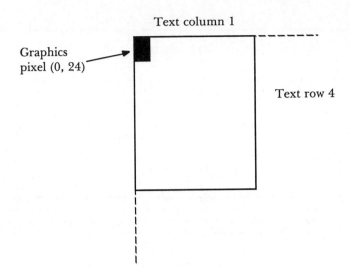

The lower-right corner of the border of the window is positioned at text column 30 and text row 9, as obtained from the LOCATE statement in line 470 and the number of characters printed in line 480. However, one more column and one more row must be included because of the position of the pixel in the text area.

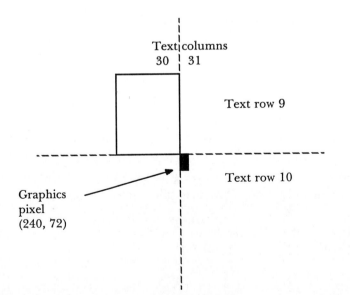

Therefore, the graphics coordinates of the rightmost column and bottom row are calculated as follows:

$$graphcol = 8 * (31 - 1) = 240$$
$$graphrow = 8 * (10 - 1) = 72$$

In specifying graphics coordinates, the order is column first, then row. Therefore, the calculated coordinates for the upper-left and lower-right corners are (0, 24) and (240, 72). These coordinates will hold the desired rectangular window.

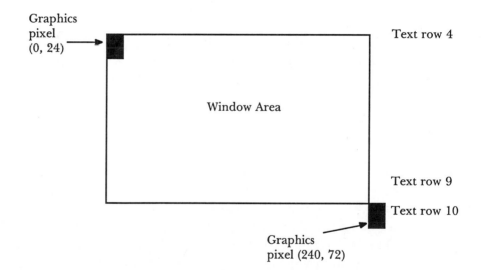

Graphics pixel (0, 24)

Text row 4

Window Area

Text row 9

Text row 10

Graphics pixel (240, 72)

The second window is created in the same way. First the text is printed.

```
400 REM ** Print second window, then GET it **
410 LOCATE 5, 2: PRINT "This is the second window."
420 LOCATE 6, 2: PRINT "A border surrounds the text."
430 LOCATE 7, 2: PRINT "Press the minus (-) key to "
440 LOCATE 8, 2: PRINT "see the previous window."
```

Then a border is drawn around the text. The top and bottom lines are drawn first.

```
450 LOCATE 4, 1
460 PRINT CHR$(218); STRING$(28, 196); CHR$(191);
470 LOCATE 9, 1
480 PRINT CHR$(192); STRING$(28, 196); CHR$(217);
```

Then the sides are drawn.

```
490 FOR row = 5 TO 8
500   LOCATE row, 1: PRINT CHR$(179);
510   LOCATE row, 30: PRINT CHR$(179);
520 NEXT row
```

When the window is complete, a GET statement is used to store the information of the window in the array named two. The screen is immediately cleared.

```
530 GET (0, 24)-(240, 72), two: CLS
```

In the next block, the first window is placed on the screen by a PUT statement. The screen now looks like the one shown in Figure 22-7. The instructions in the window tell you to press the plus (+) key to see the next window. The INPUT$(1) function at line 620 causes the computer to wait for you to press a key.

The IF/THEN statement at line 630 allows an exit to the end of the program if you press the ESC key. If you press any key other than ESC or +, line 640 passes control back to line 620 for another keystroke. The only way to escape this loop is to press ESC or +. When you press the + key, line 650 prints the prompt for the ESC key. This line was placed at this point in the program so it would not be displayed the first time a window appears.

```
600 REM ** Switch windows with + or - keys, or quit **
610 PUT (4, 4), one
620 akey$ = INPUT$(1)
630 IF akey$ = CHR$(27) THEN 810
```

```
640 IF akey$ <> "+" THEN 620
650 LOCATE 22, 1: PRINT "Press ESC to quit."
```

After the ESC key prompt is printed, the area for the second window is saved in an array named temp. This array can be used later to restore the first window. The second window is then placed so it will overlay most of the first window, as shown previously in Figure 22-8.

```
660 GET (44, 20)-(284, 68), temp
670 PUT (44, 20), two, PSET
```

The instructions in the second window tell you to press the minus (−) key to see the previous window, or the ESC key to quit. The computer waits for your choice at line 680. If you press the ESC key, line 690 passes control to line 810, where the program ends. Line 700 ensures that the keypress was not something other than ESC or minus (−). When the minus key is pressed, line 710 erases the second window, and then replaces that part of the first window that was saved in the array named temp.

```
680 akey$ = INPUT$(1)
690 IF akey$ = CHR$(27) THEN 810
700 IF akey$ <> "-" THEN 680
710 PUT (44, 20), two, XOR: PUT (44, 20), temp: GOTO 620
```

The screen now appears as shown previously in Figure 22-9. If you press the ESC key, the program will move on to the last block of the program, where the graphics screen is restored. Then the text screen is accessed and cleared, and the program ends.

```
800 REM ** Restore screens and end **
810 CLS: SCREEN 0: CLS: KEY ON: END
```

You can practice moving back and forth between windows by alternately pressing the + key when the first window is displayed, and the − key when the second window overlays the first one; press ESC to quit.

Closing Down Program 22-2

Placing and replacing windows with PUT and GET (as in Program 22-2) is a lot faster than using the SCREEN function (as in Program 22-1). To use PUT and GET, you must be in a graphics mode. However, graphics mode SCREEN 2 provides the same text width as text mode SCREEN 0 with WIDTH 80. The only thing lost is the number of colors. If you want color in your windows, you can use SCREEN 1 for a CGA graphics adapter, or SCREEN 7, 8, or 9 for EGA or VGA graphics adapters.

You can modify either program to provide more windows and to place the windows wherever you want on the screen.

23

The DRAW Utility

The DRAW statement and its formal syntax were first used in Chapter 15, "Graphics." This chapter contains a more detailed description of the commands that can be used in the DRAW statement. It also contains a program that you can use to quickly create original drawings. The program is written so that you may use simple keystrokes to perform cursor movements much like those of turtle graphics in the LOGO programming language.

The DRAW statement includes a string that contains one or more commands. This allows you to write compact statements that can perform several graphics functions.

Commands in a DRAW String

There are eight letter commands that, used with DRAW, move the
cursor and draw lines.

Command: U   D   L   R   E   F   G   H

Direction: ↑   ↓   ←   →   ↗   ↘   ↙   ↖

Before any graphics statements have been executed, the
graphics cursor originally is located at the center of the display
screen (160, 100 for SCREEN 1). The graphics cursor is invisible
and in graphics terminology is referred to as the *last referenced
point*. The program in this chapter draws a visible graphics cursor,
so that you can see where the last referenced point is located.

Normally, a distance is specified with a basic cursor movement
(the default value is 1). The value specified for the distance is in
graphics pixels of the graphics mode being used. The eight basic
cursor movements cause the cursor to move, in the direction
indicated, a *relative distance*. This movement is relative to the last
referenced point.

For example, the following short program draws a rectangle
with its lower-right corner at the center of the screen:

```
10 SCREEN 1: CLS
20 DRAW "U20 L40 D20 R40"
```

The DRAW statement at line 20 moves the cursor up 20 pixels
from the center of the screen, drawing a line as it goes; it draws left
40 pixels, then down 20 pixels, and finally right 40 pixels,
bringing the cursor back to its original position.

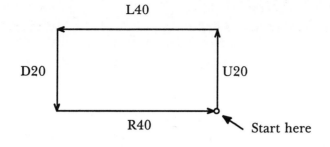

The E, F, G, and H direction commands move the cursor diagonally. The following command moves the cursor to the right and up 10 pixels, as shown in Figure 23-1:

```
DRAW "E10"
```

Figure 23-1.

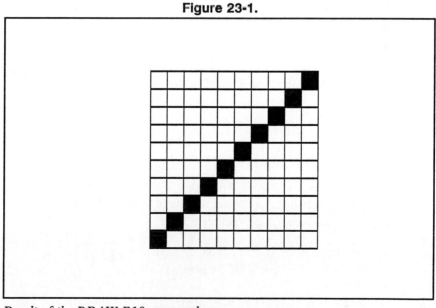

Result of the DRAW E10 command

The B Command

If you want to move the cursor without drawing a line, place a B (Blank) command immediately in front of the direction command. For example:

BD20 moves the cursor down 20 pixels, without drawing a line.
BL40 moves the cursor left 40 pixels, without drawing a line.
BE40 moves the cursor diagonally, right and up 40 pixels, without drawing a line.

The N Command

If you want to draw a line and have the cursor return to the position from which it started, use the N command in front of the direction command. This lets the last referenced point remain the same as it was before the line was drawn. The N command is useful for making a figure like the starburst used in Chapter 15, "Graphics." Here is how a starburst can be drawn using the N command in a DRAW string.

```
10 SCREEN 1: CLS
20 DRAW "NU14 NE10 NR14 NF10 ND14 NG10 NL14 NH10"
```

The M Command

The M command moves the cursor to a new location on the screen in one step. M can be used to make a move relative to the last referenced point, or to an absolute screen location.

To make a *relative* movement:

```
DRAW "M+10, 20"    (Move to a point that is right 10 pixels,
                    and down 20 pixels)
```

To make an *absolute* movement:

DRAW "M10, 20"   *(Move to a point with the coordinates (10, 20))*

Although the numbers used in both the relative and the absolute M commands were the same, the plus (+) sign used with the column coordinates in the relative command tells the computer the move is relative to the last referenced point. Figure 23-2 shows the difference in the results of the two commands when each one is executed with the cursor at the center of the screen (160, 100).

The C Command

If you are using a multicolor graphics mode such as SCREEN 1, you can change your drawing color by using the C command in

Figure 23-2.

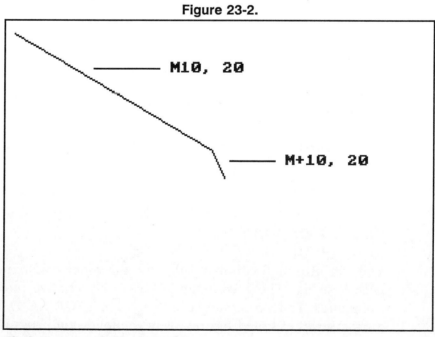

Absolute versus relative movements

the DRAW string. The following program uses DRAW commands that draw a cyan rectangle near the center of the screen, then move to the right and draw a magenta rectangle.

```
10 SCREEN 1: CLS: COLOR 0, 1
20 DRAW "C1 U10 R20 D10 L20 BM+40,0 C2 U10 R20 D10 L20"
```

When you change colors, the new color stays in effect until a new color command is given.

The P Command

The P command in a DRAW statement has results similar to those of the graphics PAINT command. To use the P command, first use BM (Blank Move) to move the cursor inside the closed figure to be painted. The P command then specifies the painting color number and the color number of the boundary of the figure. For example, assume you have just drawn two rectangles with the DRAW statement in line 20 of the previous example. Use a BM command to move the cursor inside the rectangle drawn with color number 1 (C1). Since the rectangle was drawn using color 1, use color 2 for painting.

```
DRAW "BM165, 95 P2,1"     (Move without drawing to inside rectangle;
                            paint)
```

The S Command

You can use the S command to scale the other commands in a DRAW string. The S command affects only relative movement commands. The S command can be used in a FOR/NEXT loop to draw a series of scaled figures, as in the following program:

```
10 SCREEN 1: CLS
20 FOR scale = 2 TO 8 STEP 2
30   DRAW "S" + STR$(scale) + "R8 U8 L8 D8 BM+16,0"
40 NEXT scale
```

This program draws a series of squares, each one placed to the right of the preceding square. Each square is larger than the preceding one. The S command multiplies the relative movements by a fractional factor formed in this way:

scale / 4

where *scale* is the integer specified in the DRAW string

Thus, the program uses successive scale factors of 2/4, 4/4, 6/4, and 8/4, giving successive values for the sides of the squares of 4, 8, 12, and 16. This is illustrated in Figure 23-3.

Figure 23-3.

Scaled squares

The A and TA Commands

The basic directional commands U, E, R, F, D, G, L, and H draw lines that have an increment of 45 degrees from the previous command, as shown here .

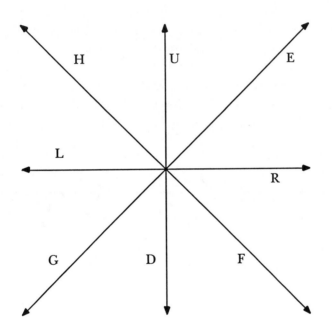

The A command of the DRAW statement allows you to use the same eight directional commands, rotating them *counterclockwise* in 90-degree increments. The amount of rotation in increments is determined by the numbers 0, 1, 2, or 3 appended to the A command. This rotation affects all subsequent commands until a new A command is given.

A0 = rotate 0 degrees
A1 = rotate counterclockwise 90 degrees
A2 = rotate counterclockwise 180 degrees
A3 = rotate counterclockwise 270 degrees

Table 23-1 shows the A (angle) commands equivalent to all eight direction commands used with a value of 20 pixels.

The following short program uses the command NR20 with A0, A1, A2, and A3 to draw a line at four different angles. Notice that a semicolon must follow the value assigned to the variable in line 30.

```
10 SCREEN 1: CLS: DEFINT A-Z
20 FOR angle = 0 TO 3
30   DRAW "A-angle; NR20"
40   akey$ = INPUT$(1)
50 NEXT angle
```

Enter and run the program. After each line is drawn, the computer waits for you to press a key to continue so you can see

Table 23-1.

Direction Command	Equivalent Angle Commands			
R20	A0 R20	A1 D20	A2 L20	A3 U20
U20	A0 U20	A1 R20	A2 D20	A3 L20
L20	A0 L20	A1 U20	A2 R20	A3 D20
D20	A0 D20	A1 L20	A2 U20	A3 R20
E20	A0 E20	A1 F20	A2 G20	A3 H20
F20	A0 F20	A1 G20	A2 H20	A3 E20
G20	A0 G20	A1 H20	A2 E20	A3 F20
H20	A0 H20	A1 E20	A2 F20	A3 G20

Equivalent DRAW Commands

the result of changing the angle each time. Here is the final result.

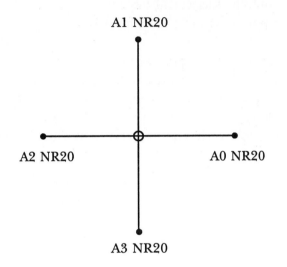

Notice that the result is the same as if the following single DRAW statement were executed:

```
DRAW "NR20 NU20 NL20 ND20"
```

If you place a T in front of the A command, you have a far more versatile drawing tool. The TA command allows you to rotate a direction command either clockwise (with a minus sign in front of the rotation angle value), or counterclockwise (with no sign or a plus sign in front of the rotation angle value). These two statements:

```
DRAW "TA20 NU20"       (Rotate 20 degrees counterclockwise)
DRAW "TA-20 NU20"      (Rotate 20 degrees clockwise)
```

will produce lines drawn at this angle:

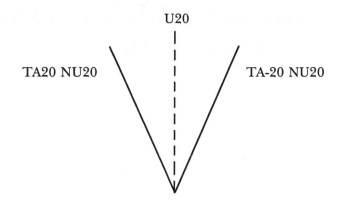

The following short program draws a starburst by using the TA command with NU40. Once again, notice the semicolon following the value assigned to a variable, as in line 30.

```
10 SCREEN 1: CLS: DEFINT A-Z
20 FOR angle = 0 TO 340 STEP 20
30    DRAW "TA=angle; NU40"
40 NEXT angle
```

When you run this program, notice the lengths of the lines are all the same (having the same radius) in contrast with lines drawn by the longer direction lines E, F, G, and H when compared to the shorter R, D, L, and U (as in the basic directional-line illustration shown earlier).

The X Command

A DRAW statement can contain a "call" to a substring that has been predefined. The string variable assigned to the substring is appended to the X command that calls the substring.

```
10 wee$ = "R4 D4 L4 U4"
20 DRAW "R12 Xwee$;"
```

A substring must always be followed by a semicolon, as shown in line 20. This two-line example defines the substring, wee$. It then calls wee$ after drawing a line to the right 12 pixels long. The result is a small square at the end of the line.

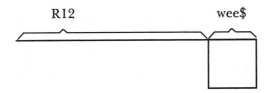

Here is a short program that draws a rectangle, calling the wee$ substring at each corner of the rectangle.

```
10 SCREEN 1: CLS: KEY OFF: DEFINT A-Z
20 wee$ = "R4 D4 L4 U4"
30 DRAW "BM20, 20"                       (Start position)
40 DRAW "R32 Xwee$; BF4 D12 BL4 Xwee$;"  (Right and down)
50 DRAW "BD4 L32 BU4 Xwee$; U16 Xwee$;"  (Left and up)
```

The foregoing program draws a small square in each corner of the large rectangle.

Substrings like wee$ can be used to shorten very long DRAW strings. When used like subroutines, they are helpful when you want to draw a shape many times in a program.

Overview of Program 23-1

Program 23-1, DRAW Utility, uses all of the DRAW commands except the substring command (X). When you run the program, you are prompted to execute the direction commands desired. Available commands are displayed at the bottom of the screen at all times.

For multiple-letter commands (those using B, N, M, or T with the direction command), respond to the first prompt with the first letter. The computer then prompts you for the second letter. There is one exception: The A command is automatically appended to the T command.

A cursor is displayed so that you can see the result of each command. You can erase lines by changing to the background color (0) and executing a command that retraces the unwanted line. To exit the program at any time, press the ESC key when the "What Command ?" prompt is given in the main program.

Prompt Lines in Program 23-1

The commands available are shown at the bottom of the screen.

```
Commands:
D U L R E F G H B N C M P S A T
```

For each new command, a prompt is printed at the top left of the screen.

```
What Command ?
```

Program 23-1.

```
1 REM ** DRAW Utility **
2 ' GW-BASIC: The Reference, Chapter 23.  File: GWRF2301.BAS
3 ' Uses DRAW commands

100 REM ** Setup **
110 SCREEN 1: CLS: KEY OFF: DEFINT A-Z
120 DIM cursor(4)

200 REM ** Print Commands **
210 LINE (2, 2)-(3, 3), 1, B
220 GET (2, 2)-(4, 4), cursor: CLS
230 LOCATE 23, 1
240 PRINT "Commands:"
250 PRINT "D U L R E F G H B N C M P S A T";
260 DRAW "C3"

300 REM ** Main Program **
310 WHILE 1
320   col = POINT(0): row = POINT(1): Letter$ = "Z"
330   PUT (col, row), cursor, XOR
340   Ok$ = "DULREFGHBNCMPSAT"
350   WHILE INSTR(Ok$, Letter$) = 0
360     LOCATE 1, 1: PRINT SPACE$(80): LOCATE 1, 1
370     PRINT "What command ? ";
380     Letter$ = INPUT$(1): PRINT Letter$;
390     IF Letter$ = CHR$(27) THEN CLS: END
400     GOSUB 5010
410   WEND
420   choose = INSTR("BNMPT", Letter$)
430   ON choose + 1 GOSUB 6010, 1010, 2010, 3010, 4010, 7010
440   Move$ = Letter$ + Number$
450   PUT (col, row), cursor, XOR: DRAW Move$
460 WEND

1000 REM ** SUBROUTINE: Blank Move **
1010 Letter$ = INPUT$(1): PRINT Letter$;: GOSUB 5010
1020 Letter$ = "B" + Letter$
1030 IF Letter$ = "BM" THEN GOSUB 3010
1040 IF MID$(Letter$, 2, 1) <> "M" THEN GOSUB 6010
1050 RETURN
```

DRAW Utility (GWRF2301.BAS) (continued on next page)

Program 23-1.

```
2000 REM ** SUBROUTINE: Move Back to Start **
2010 Letter$ = INPUT$(1): PRINT Letter$;
2020 Letter$ = "N" + Letter$
2030 GOSUB 6010
2040 RETURN

3000 REM ** SUBROUTINE: M Command **
3010 LOCATE 2, 1: INPUT "column number "; ColNumber$
3020 Letter$ = Letter$ + ColNumber$ + ","
3030 LOCATE 2, 1: PRINT SPACE$(40);
3040 LOCATE 2, 1: PRINT "row number "; ColNumber$; ",";
3050 INPUT "", Number$
3060 RETURN

4000 REM ** SUBROUTINE: Paint **
4010 LOCATE 2, 1: INPUT "Paint number "; num1$
4020 LOCATE 1, 1: PRINT SPACE$(80): LOCATE 1, 1
4030 PRINT "What command ? "; Letter$; num1$
4040 Letter$ = Letter$ + num1$ + ","
4050 LOCATE 2, 1: INPUT "Paint to number "; Number$
4060 RETURN

5000 REM ** SUBROUTINE: Change to Uppercase **
5010 code = ASC(Letter$)
5020 IF code > 96 AND code < 123 THEN code = code - 32
5030 Letter$ = CHR$(code)
5040 RETURN

6000 REM ** SUBROUTINE: Get Number **
6010 LOCATE 2, 1: INPUT "Number "; Number$
6020 RETURN

7000 REM ** SUBROUTINE: Turn Angle **
7010 Letter$ = Letter$ + "A": PRINT "A";
7020 LOCATE 2, 1: INPUT "Turn Angle number "; Number$
7030 RETURN
```

DRAW Utility (GWRF2301.BAS)

At this point, you can enter any of the commands listed at the bottom of the screen. When you make an entry it is printed on the screen following the prompt.

All of the commands except B, N, M, P, and T are single-letter commands. For single-letter commands, a second prompt appears on the line below the "What Command ?" prompt. This second prompt is for the pixel distance value.

```
What Command ? D          (D entered)
Number ? ▮                (Prompt for a number)
```

After you type in the number and press ENTER, the command is carried out. The cursor moves as commanded and draws a line down the number of pixels specified.

Multiple-Letter Command Prompt Lines

If you enter any of the commands B, N, M, P, or T, a second command letter is required. You are guided by the prompts for the necessary entries.

The BM command is the most complicated. For example, a blank move to an absolute screen location requires the following information:

```
What Command ? B          (A second command letter needed)
```

A second letter command is needed with the B command; no prompt is displayed. If you enter an M, a new prompt appears on the second line.

```
What Command ? BM
column number ? ▮         (Column number requested)
```

When you enter the column number (40 in this example), the second prompt line changes to reflect the entry. You are then prompted for the row number.

```
What command ? BM
row number 40,■              (Row number requested)
```

When you enter the row number, the cursor moves accordingly without drawing a line. Other multiple-letter commands contain similar step-by-step prompts for the required entries.

Program Description

Program 23-1 contains a description block; a Setup block; a block to get the square cursor, print the commands available, and set the drawing color number to 3; and a main program block. In addition, there are seven subroutines that combine the letter commands and appended numbers.

Opening Program Blocks

In the Setup block after the program description, the screen (SCREEN 1) is initialized, the default variable type is set to integer, and the cursor is dimensioned. The cursor is small, with a maximum subscript of 4.

```
110 SCREEN 1: CLS : KEY OFF: DEFINT A-Z
120 DIM cursor(4)
```

The Print Commands block contains statements that draw the cursor (line 210), save the cursor image in an array named cursor (line 220), print the commands at the bottom of the screen (lines 230, 240, and 250), and set the drawing color to 3 (line 260).

```
210 LINE (2, 2)-(3, 3), 1, B
220 GET (2, 2)-(4, 4), cursor: CLS
230 LOCATE 23, 1
240 PRINT "Commands:"
250 PRINT "D U L R E F G H B N C M P S A T";
260 DRAW "C3"
```

The Main Program

The Main Program consists of one long WHILE/WEND loop whose only exit is when an ESC keystroke is detected at the command prompt. The ESC keystroke causes the screen to clear and the program to end. As the WHILE/WEND loop is entered, the column and row of the cursor's position are detected by POINT statements. The Letter$ variable is set to an invalid command letter, the cursor is placed at its position by a PUT statement, and the valid commands are defined by a variable named Ok$.

```
310 WHILE 1
320   col = POINT(0): row = POINT(1): Letter$ = "Z"
330   PUT (col, row), cursor, XOR
340   Ok$ = "DULREFGHBNCMPSAT"
```

A nested WHILE/WEND loop is used to obtain your entry for a DRAW command. No exit can be made from the loop until a valid entry is made, because of the WHILE statement that compares your entry, Letter$, to the valid commands in the Ok$ string.

```
350   WHILE INSTR(Ok$, Letter$) = 0
  .
  .
  .
410   WEND
```

Inside the loop, your command entry is requested and printed.

```
360     LOCATE 1, 1: PRINT SPACE$(80): LOCATE 1, 1
370     PRINT "What command ? ";
380     Letter$ = INPUT$(1): PRINT Letter$;
```

A check is made to see if you have pressed the ESC key. If so, the screen is cleared and the program ends. If a key other than ESC was pressed, a subroutine (5010) is called that changes your entry to uppercase if you have entered a lowercase letter. On return from the subroutine, the WEND statement is encountered. If your entry is invalid, the loop is repeated (requesting a new entry). If your entry is valid, an exit is made from the loop.

```
390     IF Letter$ = CHR$(27) THEN CLS: END
400     GOSUB 5010
410 WEND
```

When you enter a valid letter command, the program checks your entry (Letter$) to see if it is in the string "BNMPT." If not, the value of the variable named choose will be 0 (zero). If the entry is one of the characters in the string, the value of choose will be 1, 2, 3, 4, or 5—depending on the position of the character in the string. The value of choose + 1 determines the subroutine that will be called in line 430.

```
420    choose = INSTR("BNMPT", Letter$)
430    ON choose + 1 GOSUB 6010, 1010, 2010, 3010, 4010, 7010
```

As shown in Table 23-2, the value of choose + 1 selects the subroutine in the ON . . . GOSUB statement of line 430.

On return from the selected subroutine, the necessary command letters and/or values will have been selected. They are then catenated in line 440 and assigned to the variable Move$. The cursor is erased by the PUT statement in line 450, and the DRAW statement with the Move$ string is executed. The WEND statement marks the end of the outside loop of the nested loop pair. Control is passed back to the beginning of the outer loop.

```
440    Move$ = Letter$ + Number$
450    PUT (col, row), cursor, XOR: DRAW Move$
460 WEND
```

The Subroutines

If the first letter of the command entry was a B, the Blank Move subroutine at line 1010 is called. This subroutine accepts the second command letter entry at line 1010, prints the entry, and calls the subroutine at line 5010 to assure the entry is in upper-case.

```
1010 Letter$ = INPUT$(1): PRINT Letter$; : GOSUB 5010
```

The Letter$ variable is changed to a two-letter string at line 1020. If the second letter is an M, line 1030 calls the subroutine at line 3010 to get the column and row coordinates that must be supplied with a BM command. If the second letter is not an M (as

Table 23-2.

Variable choose	Expression choose + 1	Subroutine Called
0	1	6010, first in the list
1	2	1010, second in the list
2	3	2010, third in the list
3	4	3010, fourth in the list
4	5	4010, fifth in the list
5	6	7010, sixth in the list

Subroutines in Program 23-1

in BD, BR, or BE), line 1040 calls the subroutine at line 6010 to get a pixel number that must be appended. A return is then made to the Main Program.

```
1020 Letter$ = "B" + Letter$
1030 IF Letter$ = "BM" THEN GOSUB 3010
1040 IF MID$(Letter$, 2, 1) <> "M" THEN GOSUB 6010
1050 RETURN
```

If the N command is entered, the subroutine at line 2010 is called. This subroutine needs a second command letter, obtained at line 2010. It also needs a pixel number, obtained by calling the subroutine at line 6010. It then returns to the Main Program.

```
2010 Letter$ = INPUT$(1): PRINT Letter$;
2020 Letter$ = "N" + Letter$
2030 GOSUB 6010
2040 RETURN
```

If the M command is entered in the Main Program or after a B command, the subroutine at line 3010 is called. This subroutine first gets the column number coordinate, and appends it and a comma to the variable Letter$.

```
3010 LOCATE 2, 1: INPUT "column number "; ColNumber$
3020 Letter$ = Letter$ + ColNumber$ + ","
```

The subroutine then erases the line where the column number was entered, prompts you for the row number, and prints the value entered for the column number, followed by a comma to indicate the partial entry. It then accepts your entry for the row number coordinate and returns to the Main Program or to the calling subroutine.

```
3030 LOCATE 2, 1: PRINT SPACE$(40);
3040 LOCATE 2, 1: PRINT "row number "; ColNumber$; ",";
3050 INPUT "", Number$
3060 RETURN
```

If a P command was entered in the Main Program, the subroutine at line 4010 is called. It first requests the painting color number at line 4010. Then the command line is erased, and the command prompt with the P and its appended color number is printed.

```
4010 LOCATE 2, 1: INPUT "Paint number "; num1$
4020 LOCATE 1, 1: PRINT SPACE$(80): LOCATE 1, 1
4030 PRINT "What command ? "; Letter$; num1$
```

In line 4040, the variable Letter$ is changed to include the P, the number, and a comma. Then an INPUT statement prints a prompt, "Paint to number ", and accepts the boundary color in line 4050. Then a return is made to the Main Program.

```
4040 Letter$ = Letter$ + num1$ + ","
4050 LOCATE 2, 1: INPUT "Paint to number "; Number$
4060 RETURN
```

The subroutine at line 5010 is called whenever there is a need for uppercase letter entries. This allows both uppercase and lowercase entries to be made; the program will automatically change the entries as needed. In this way, the program doesn't have to test for both upper- and lowercase letters when making its decisions. Uppercase letters have ASCII codes that are 32 less than their lowercase counterparts.

```
5010 code = ASC(Letter$)
5020 IF code > 96 AND code < 123 THEN code = code - 32
5030 Letter$ = CHR$(code)
5040 RETURN
```

The subroutine at line 6010 is called when a single number entry is required for the command. It merely accepts the entry and returns to the line following the line that called it.

```
6000 REM ** SUBROUTINE: Get number **
6010 LOCATE 2, 1: INPUT "Number "; Number$
6020 RETURN
```

The final subroutine, Turn Angle, is used when the T command is entered in the Main Program. It appends the letter A to the T entry, and requests and accepts a number for the turn angle value. It then returns to the Main Program.

```
7010 Letter$ = Letter$ + "A": PRINT "A";
7020 LOCATE 2, 1: INPUT "Turn Angle number "; Number$
7030 RETURN
```

Closing Down Program 23-1

Program 23-1 is written so that the prompts guide you through the necessary entries. Do not enter more information than the prompt requests. Letter entries are executed immediately; you don't have to press the ENTER key. Number entries, on the other hand, may require more than one keypress, so you must press the ENTER key after entering the complete number.

When you use a color number for painting, or when you change the drawing color number with the C command, that color remains in effect until a new color number is invoked.

A typical command (U40) would be entered in the following steps:

1. The command prompt appears with the cursor.

   ```
   What command ? ▮
   ```

2. When the command U is typed (no ENTER necessary), the letter is printed and a new prompt appears. You can enter either U or u. It will be printed as you enter it, but the program will

change lowercase letters to uppercase for its own use.

```
What command ? U
Number ? ■
```

3. The digits 4 and 0 are typed.

```
What command ? U
Number ? 40■
```

4. When the ENTER key is pressed, the command is executed, and a new command line appears.

```
What command ? ■
```

Figure 23-4 shows a sample result from a run of Program 23-1. All commands were entered in uppercase. The top triangle was drawn and painted using the sequence of entries shown in Table 23-3. The last three commands (C, S, and TA) prepare the color, scale, and turn angle for drawing the small dark triangle on the left. The command sequence of Table 23-3 is repeated for each triangle, with the following modifications to P, S, and TA values:

First Pass	Second Pass	Third Pass	Last Pass
P1, 3	P2, 3	P1, 3	P2, 3
S2	S4	S2	S4
TA90	TA180	TA270	TA0

The modifications to S and TA in the last pass return the scale and turn angle to the default values (S4 and TA0).

 REMEMBER You can erase unwanted, previously drawn portions of a figure by using the background color and retracing the DRAW movements.

You are encouraged to experiment with the DRAW Utility and modify it in any way you want. For example, you may want to add

Figure 23-4.

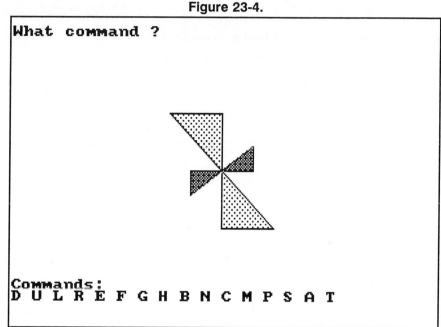

Sample figure from Program 23-1

a BSAVE command to save an image of your creation for use in another program. You could alter line 390 so that the computer branches to a new section of code, instead of clearing the screen and ending the program, as follows:

```
390 IF Letter$ = CHR$(27) THEN 510
```

The code you write at line 510, and subsequent lines, would dimension the array to hold your image. The size for the dimension would be indicated as described in Chapter 15. The method is repeated here for your convenience.

$$size = \text{INT}(colrange / 8 + 1) * rowrange * colorbits / arraybits + 4$$

where

$colrange = columnmax - columnmin + 1$
$rowrange = rowmax - rowmin + 1$
$arraybits = 2$ for integer
$colorbits = 2$ for SCREEN 1

Table 23-3.

Prompt	*Response*
What command ?	U
Number ?	40 ENTER
What command ?	L
Number ?	40 ENTER
What command ?	F
Number ?	40 ENTER
What command ?	BU
Number ?	8 ENTER
What command ?	BL
Number ?	4 ENTER
What command ?	P
Paint number ?	1 ENTER
Paint to number ?	3 ENTER
What command ?	BR
Number ?	4 ENTER
What command ?	BD
Number ?	8 ENTER
What command ?	C
Number ?	3 ENTER
What command ?	S
Number ?	2 ENTER
What command ?	T
Turn angle number ?	90 ENTER

NOTE: The A command is automatically appended to the T command.

Sample DRAW Prompts and Entries

You would use GET and BSAVE as done previously in Program 15-7, BSAVE and BLOAD an Image. Once an image is saved, it can be used in any program that uses the same screen mode. Just load it into the new program with a BLOAD statement, and then place it anywhere on the screen with a PUT statement (also shown in Program 15-7). After the image has been loaded, you can move the image around by the technique shown in Program 15-6, GET and PUT Starburst.

IV

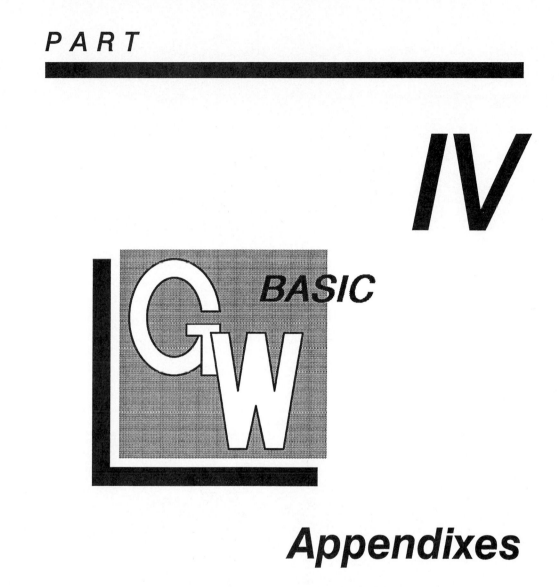

BASIC

GW

Appendixes

A P P E N D I X

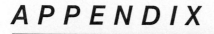

GW-BASIC Keywords

Keyword	Chapter	Keyword	Chapter
CVI	13, 14	IF	6
CVS	13, 14	IMP	5
DATA	6	INKEY$	8
DATE$	2, 18	INP	20
DEF FN	12	INPUT	8
DEF SEG	17	INPUT#	14
DEF USR	12	INPUT$	8
DEFDBL	7	INSTR	13
DEFINT	7	INT	12
DEFSNG	7	IOCTL	14
DEFSTR	7	IOCTL$	14
DELETE	10	KEY	2, 8, 20
DIM	5, 11	KEY ON/OFF/STOP	20
DRAW	15, 23	KEY$	reserved but not used as function or state-ment
EDIT	4, 10		
ELSE	6		
END	9		
ENVIRON	18		
ENVIRON$	18		
EOF	14	KILL	14
EQV	5	LEFT$	13
ERASE	11	LEN	13
ERDEV	19	LET	6
ERDEV$	19	LINE	15
ERL	19	LINE INPUT	8
ERR	19	LINE INPUT#	14
ERROR	19	LIST	3, 9
EXP	12	LLIST	3, 9
EXTERR	19	LOAD	3, 9
FIELD	14	LOC	14
FILES	9	LOCATE	8
FIX	12	LOCK	14
FOR	6	LOF	14
FRE	17	LOG	12
GET (files)	14	LPOS	8
GET (graphics)	15	LPRINT	8
GOSUB	6	LPRINT USING	8
GOTO	6	LSET	13, 14
HEX$	5, 7	MERGE	4, 9

Keyword	Chapter	Keyword	Chapter
MID$	13	PMAP	15
MKD$	13, 14	POINT	15
MKDIR	18	POKE	17
MKI$	13, 14	POS	8
MKS$	13, 14	PRESET	15
MOD	5	PRINT	2, 8
MOTOR	9	PRINT USING	8
NAME	14	PRINT#	14
NEW	9	PRINT# USING	14
NEXT	6	PSET	15
NOT	5	PUT (files)	14
OCT$	5, 7	PUT (graphics)	15
OFF	16, 18, 20	RANDOMIZE	12
ON	6, 16, 18, 20	READ	6
		REM	1, 4, 7
ON COM	20	RENUM	4, 10
ON ERROR	19	RESET	14
ON. . .GOSUB	6	RESTORE	6
ON. . .GOTO	6	RESUME	19
ON KEY	20	RETURN	6
ON PEN	20	RIGHT$	13
ON PLAY	16	RMDIR	18
ON STRIG	20	RND	12
ON TIMER	18	RSET	13, 14
OPEN	14	RUN	3, 9
OPEN COM	20	SAVE	1, 3, 9
OPTION BASE	11	SCREEN (function)	8, 22
OR	5	SCREEN (statement)	2, 8, 15, App. H
OUT	20		
PAINT	15	SGN	12
PAINT (tiling)	21	SHARED	14
PALETTE	15	SHELL	9
PALETTE USING	15	SIN	12
PCOPY	15	SOUND	16
PEEK	17	SPACE$	8
PEN	20	SPC	8
PLAY	16	SQR	12
PLAY ON/OFF/ STOP	16	STEP	6
		STICK	20
PLAY(n)	16	STOP	10

Keyword	Chapter	Keyword	Chapter
STR$	13	USING	8, 14, 15
STRIG	20	USR	12, App. F
STRIG ON/OFF	20	VAL	13
STRING$	13	VARPTR	17
SWAP	11	VARPTR$	17
SYSTEM	1, 18	VIEW	15
TAB	8	VIEW PRINT	8
TAN	12	WAIT	20
THEN	6	WEND	6
TIME$	2, 18	WHILE	6
TIMER	18	WIDTH	2, 8, 14
TO (*see* FOR/NEXT box)	6	WINDOW	15
		WRITE	8
TROFF	10	WRITE#	14
TRON	10	XOR	5
UNLOCK	14		

ASCII Codes

ASCII Value	Character	ASCII Value	Character
0	Null	12	Form-feed
1	☺	13	Carriage return
2	☻	14	♫
3	♥	15	☼
4	♦	16	►
5	♣	17	◄
6	♠	18	↕
7	Beep	19	‼
8	◘	20	¶
9	Tab	21	§
10	Linefeed	22	▬
11	Cursor home	23	↨

ASCII Value	Character	ASCII Value	Character
24	↑	58	:
25	↓	59	;
26	→	60	<
27	←	61	=
28	Cursor right	62	>
29	Cursor left	63	?
30	Cursor up	64	@
31	Cursor down	65	A
32	Space	66	B
33	!	67	C
34	"	68	D
35	#	69	E
36	$	70	F
37	%	71	G
38	&	72	H
39	'	73	I
40	(	74	J
41	)	75	K
42	*	76	L
43	+	77	M
44	,	78	N
45	-	79	O
46	.	80	P
47	/	81	Q
48	0	82	R
49	1	83	S
50	2	84	T
51	3	85	U
52	4	86	V
53	5	87	W
54	6	88	X
55	7	89	Y
56	8	90	Z
57	9	91	[

ASCII Value	Character	ASCII Value	Character
92	\	126	~
93	]	127	⌂
94	^	128	Ç
95	—	129	ü
96	'	130	é
97	a	131	â
98	b	132	ä
99	c	133	à
100	d	134	å
101	e	135	ç
102	f	136	ê
103	g	137	ë
104	h	138	è
105	i	139	ï
106	j	140	î
107	k	141	ì
108	l	142	Ä
109	m	143	Å
110	n	144	É
111	o	145	æ
112	p	146	Æ
113	q	147	ô
114	r	148	ö
115	s	149	ò
116	t	150	û
117	u	151	ù
118	v	152	ÿ
119	w	153	Ö
120	x	154	Ü
121	y	155	¢
122	z	156	£
123	{	157	¥
124	¦	158	Pt
125	}	159	ƒ

ASCII Value	Character	ASCII Value	Character
160	á	194	┬
161	í	195	├
162	ó	196	─
163	ú	197	┼
164	ñ	198	╞
165	Ñ	199	╟
166	ª	200	╚
167	º	201	╔
168	¿	202	╩
169	⌐	203	╦
170	¬	204	╠
171	½	205	═
172	¼	206	╬
173	¡	207	╧
174	«	208	╨
175	»	209	╤
176	░	210	╥
177	▒	211	╙
178	▓	212	╘
179	│	213	╒
180	┤	214	╓
181	╡	215	╫
182	╢	216	╪
183	╖	217	┘
184	╕	218	┌
185	╣	219	█
186	║	220	▄
187	╗	221	▌
188	╝	222	▐
189	╜	223	▀
190	╛	224	α
191	┐	225	β
192	└	226	Γ
193	┴	227	π

ASCII Value	Character	ASCII Value	Character
228	Σ	242	$\geq$
229	σ	243	$\leq$
230	μ	244	$\lceil$
231	τ	245	$\rfloor$
232	ϕ	246	$\div$
233	θ	247	$\approx$
234	Ω	248	$\circ$
235	δ	249	$\bullet$
236	∞	250	$\cdot$
237	$\varnothing$	251	$\sqrt{}$
238	ϵ	252	^{n}
239	$\cap$	253	^{2}
240	$\equiv$	254	■
241	$\pm$	255	(blank 'FF')

Key HEX Codes and Scan Codes

Key HEX Codes

Key	HEX Code
EXTENDED	&H80
CAPS LOCK	&H40
NUM LOCK	&H20
ALT	&H08
CTRL	&H04
SHIFT	&H01, &H02, &H03

Scan Codes

Main Keyboard

Key	Scan Code Decimal	HEX	Key	Scan Code Decimal	HEX
a or A	30	1E	ESC	01	01
b or B	48	30	1 or !	02	02
c or C	46	2E	2 or @	03	03
d or D	32	20	3 or #	04	04
e or E	18	12	4 or $	05	05
f or F	33	21	5 or %	06	06
g or G	34	22	6 or ^	07	07
h or H	35	23	7 or &	08	08
i or I	23	17	8 or *	09	09
j or J	36	24	9 or (	10	0A
k or K	37	25	0 or)	11	0B
l or L	38	26	– or _	12	0C
m or M	50	32	= or +	13	0D
n or N	49	31	[or {	26	1A
o or O	24	18	] or }	27	1B
p or P	25	19	; or :	39	27
q or Q	16	10	' or "	40	28
r or R	19	13	` or ~	41	29
s or S	31	1F	\ or ¦	43	2B
t or T	20	14	, or <	51	33
u or U	22	16	. or >	52	34
v or V	47	2F	/ or ?	53	35
w or W	17	11	* or PRTSC	55	37
x or X	45	2D			
y or Y	21	15			
z or Z	44	2C			

Extended ASCII Codes for Function Keys & Keypad Keys

Key	Normal Code		Code with SHIFT		Code with CTRL		Code with ALT	
	Dec	HEX	Dec	HEX	Dec	HEX	Dec	HEX
F1	59	3B	84	54	94	5E	104	68
F2	60	3C	85	55	95	5F	105	69
F3	61	3D	86	56	96	60	106	6A
F4	62	3E	87	57	97	61	107	6B
F5	63	3F	88	58	98	62	108	6C
F6	64	40	89	59	99	63	109	6D
F7	65	41	90	5A	100	64	110	6E
F8	66	42	91	5B	101	65	111	6F
F9	67	43	92	5C	102	66	112	70
F10	68	44	93	5D	103	67	113	71
HOME	71	47	55	37	119	77		
UP ARROW	72	48	56	38				
PGUP	73	49	57	39	132	84		
LEFT ARROW	75	4B	52	34	115	73		
5*	76	4C	53	35				
RIGHT ARROW	77	4D	54	36	116	74		
END	79	4F	49	31	117	75		
DOWN ARROW	80	50	50	32				
PGDN	81	51	51	33	118	76		
INS	82	52	48	30				
DEL	83	53	46	2E				
Gray+	78	4E	43	2B				
Gray −	74	4A	45	2D				

* On the numeric keypad

Error Codes and Messages

Error Code	Message and Meaning
1	*NEXT without FOR.* A NEXT statement occurs without a matching FOR statement. Check variables for match.
2	*Syntax error.* A line contains a syntax error, such as unmatched parenthesis, misspelled command or statement, incorrect punctuation. The incorrect line is displayed in Edit mode.

Error Code	Message and Meaning
3	*RETURN without GOSUB.* A RETURN occurs without a matching GOSUB.
4	*Out of DATA.* No items available in DATA statements for an executed READ statement.
5	*Illegal function call.* Out-of-range value is passed to a function. Also: Subscript is negative or too large; LOG with negative or zero argument; SQR with negative argument; negative mantissa with noninteger power; call to a USR function without a starting address; MID$, LEFT$, RIGHT$, INP, OUT, WAIT, PEEK, POKE, TAB, SPC, STRING$, SPACE$, INSTR, or ON. . .GOTO with improper argument.
6	*Overflow.* Calculation result too large to represent in GW-BASIC's number format. Underflow results in zero.
7	*Out of memory.* Program too large; too many FOR loops, GOSUBs, or variables; or expressions too complicated. Use CLEAR to set aside more stack space or memory.
8	*Undefined line number.* GOTO, GOSUB, IF/THEN/ELSE, or DELETE references a nonexistent line.
9	*Subscript out of range.* An array element is referenced with the wrong number of subscripts, or with a subscript outside the array's dimensions.
10	*Duplicate definition.* DIM statement for an array occurs after the default dimension (10) has been established, or two DIM statements are used for the same array.
11	*Division by zero.* A division by zero, or zero raised to a negative power.

Error Code	Message and Meaning
12	*Illegal direct.* Illegal statement used in Direct mode.
13	*Type mismatch.* A string variable assigned to a numeric value; a numeric variable assigned to a string value; a function that needs a numeric argument is given a string argument, or vice versa.
14	*Out of string space.* Storage of string variables exceeds the amount of free memory.
15	*String too long.* Attempt to use a string longer than 255 characters.
16	*String formula too complex.* A string expression is too long or too complex. Break it into smaller parts.
17	*Can't continue.* You attempted to continue a program that has halted because of an error, has been modified during a break, does not exist.
18	*Undefined user function.* A USR function is called before a defining DEF statement.
19	*No RESUME.* A RESUME statement does not occur in an executed error-trapping routine.
20	*RESUME without error.* A RESUME occurs before an error-trapping routine is entered.
21	*Unprintable error.* No error message available for the existing error; usually caused by an error with an undefined error code.
22	*Missing operand.* An expression contains an operator with no following operand.
23	*Line buffer overflow.* You attempted to input a line containing too many characters.
24	*Device timeout.* Information not received from an I/O device within a predetermined amount of time.

Error Code	Message and Meaning
25	*Device fault.* Hardware error in printer or interface card.
26	*FOR without NEXT.* A FOR statement occurs without a matching NEXT. Check variables in FOR and NEXT for a match.
27	*Out of paper.* Printer out of paper, or some other printer fault.
28	*Unprintable error.* No error message available for the existing error; usually caused by an error with an undefined error code.
29	*WHILE without WEND.* WHILE does not have a matching WEND.
30	*WEND without WHILE.* WEND does not have a matching WHILE.
31-49	*Unprintable error.* No error message available for the existing error; usually caused by an error with an undefined error code.
50	*FIELD overflow.* A FIELD statement is attempting to allocate more bytes than specified for record length of a random access file.
51	*Internal error.* Internal malfunction occurred in GW-BASIC; report to your dealer the conditions under which the message appeared.
52	*Bad file number.* A file number is referenced for a file that is not open, or is out of range of file numbers specified at initialization.
53	*File not found.* A LOAD, KILL, NAME, FILES, or OPEN statement references a file not on the current disk.
54	*Bad file mode.* You have attempted to use PUT, GET, or LOF with a sequential file, or to load a random file, or to execute an OPEN with a file mode other than I, O, A, or R.

Error Code	Message and Meaning
55	*File already open.* You have attempted to open (for sequential output mode) a file already open, or to use KILL for a file that is open.
56	*Unprintable error.* No error message available for the existing error; usually caused by an error with an undefined error code.
57	*Device I/O error.* Usually a disk I/O error, but may be any I/O device error; the operating system cannot recover from the error.
58	*File already exists.* Filename specified in NAME statement is identical to a filename already in use on the disk.
59-60	*Unprintable error.* No error message available for the existing error; usually caused by an error with an undefined error code.
61	*Disk full.* No space left on the disk in use.
62	*Input past end.* INPUT statement executed after all data in the file has been input, or for a null (empty) file. To avoid, use the EOF function.
63	*Bad record number.* Record number in PUT or GET statement is either greater than the maximum allowed or equal to zero.
64	*Bad filename.* Illegal form used for filename with LOAD, SAVE, KILL, or OPEN.
65	*Unprintable error.* No error message available for the existing error; usually caused by an error with an undefined error code.
66	*Direct statement in file.* Direct statement found while loading an ASCII format file; the LOAD aborts.

Error Code	Message and Meaning
67	*Too many files.* You have attempted to create a new file with SAVE or OPEN when all directory entries are full, or the file specifications are invalid.
68	*Device unavailable.* You have attempted to open a file to a nonexistent or unsupported device.
69	*Communication buffer overflow.* Occurs when a communications input statement is executed, but the input queue is already full.
70	*Permission denied.* Hard disk error returned from the disk controller; you have attempted to write to a disk that is protected; or another process has attempted to access a file already in use; or the UNLOCK range specified does not match the preceding LOCK statement.
71	*Disk not ready.* Disk drive door is open, or there is no disk in the drive.
72	*Disk media error.* Disk controller detects a hardware media fault; usually indicates damaged media.
73	*Advanced feature.* You have attempted to use a reserved word that is not available in this version of GW-BASIC.
74	*Rename across disks.* You have attempted to rename a file to a new name on a disk other than the disk specified for the old name.
75	*Path/File access error.* DOS is unable to make a correct path-to-filename connection during an OPEN, MKDIR, CHDIR, or RMDIR operation.

Error Code	**Message and Meaning**
76	*Path not found.* DOS is unable to find the specified path during an OPEN, MKDIR, CHDIR, or RMDIR operation.

Decimal/Octal/ Hexadecimal Equivalents

Decimal	Octal	Hexadecimal	Decimal	Octal	Hexadecimal
0	0	0	11	13	B
1	1	1	12	14	C
2	2	2	13	15	D
3	3	3	14	16	E
4	4	4	15	17	F
5	5	5	16	20	10
6	6	6	17	21	11
7	7	7	18	22	12
8	10	8	19	23	13
9	11	9	20	24	14
10	12	A	21	25	15

Decimal	Octal	Hexadecimal	Decimal	Octal	Hexadecimal
22	26	16	62	76	3E
23	27	17	63	77	3F
24	30	18	64	100	40
25	31	19	65	101	41
26	32	1A	66	102	42
27	33	1B	67	103	43
28	34	1C	68	104	44
29	35	1D	69	105	45
30	36	1E	70	106	46
31	37	1F	71	107	47
32	40	20	72	110	48
33	41	21	73	111	49
34	42	22	74	112	4A
35	43	23	75	113	4B
36	44	24	76	114	4C
37	45	25	77	115	4D
38	46	26	78	116	4E
39	47	27	79	117	4F
40	50	28	80	120	50
41	51	29	81	121	51
42	52	2A	82	122	52
43	53	2B	83	123	53
44	54	2C	84	124	54
45	55	2D	85	125	55
46	56	2E	86	126	56
47	57	2F	87	127	57
48	60	30	88	130	58
49	61	31	89	131	59
50	62	32	90	132	5A
51	63	33	91	133	5B
52	64	34	92	134	5C
53	65	35	93	135	5D
54	66	36	94	136	5E
55	67	37	95	137	5F
56	70	38	96	140	60
57	71	39	97	141	61
58	72	3A	98	142	62
59	73	3B	99	143	63
60	74	3C	100	144	64
61	75	3D	101	145	65

Decimal	Octal	Hexadecimal	Decimal	Octal	Hexadecimal
102	146	66	142	216	8E
103	147	67	143	217	8F
104	150	68	144	220	90
105	151	69	145	221	91
106	152	6A	146	222	92
107	153	6B	147	223	93
108	154	6C	148	224	94
109	155	6D	149	225	95
110	156	6E	150	226	96
111	157	6F	151	227	97
112	160	70	152	230	98
113	161	71	153	231	99
114	162	72	154	232	9A
115	163	73	155	233	9B
116	164	74	156	234	9C
117	165	75	157	235	9D
118	166	76	158	236	9E
119	167	77	159	237	9F
120	170	78	160	240	A0
121	171	79	161	241	A1
122	172	7A	162	242	A2
123	173	7B	163	243	A3
124	174	7C	164	244	A4
125	175	7D	165	245	A5
126	176	7E	166	246	A6
127	177	7F	167	247	A7
128	200	80	168	250	A8
129	201	81	169	251	A9
130	202	82	170	252	AA
131	203	83	171	253	AB
132	204	84	172	254	AC
133	205	85	173	255	AD
134	206	86	174	256	AE
135	207	87	175	257	AF
136	210	88	176	260	B0
137	211	89	177	261	B1
138	212	8A	178	262	B2
139	213	8B	179	263	B3
140	214	8C	180	264	B4
141	215	8D	181	265	B5

Decimal	Octal	Hexadecimal	Decimal	Octal	Hexadecimal
182	266	B6	221	335	DD
183	267	B7	222	336	DE
184	270	B8	223	337	DF
185	271	B9	224	340	E0
186	272	BA	225	341	E1
187	273	BB	226	342	E2
188	274	BC	227	343	E3
189	275	BD	228	344	E4
190	276	BE	229	345	E5
191	277	BF	230	346	E6
192	300	C0	231	347	E7
193	301	C1	232	350	E8
194	302	C2	233	351	E9
195	303	C3	234	352	EA
196	304	C4	235	353	EB
197	305	C5	236	354	EC
198	306	C6	237	355	ED
199	307	C7	238	356	EE
200	310	C8	239	357	EF
201	311	C9	240	360	F0
202	312	CA	241	361	F1
203	313	CB	242	362	F2
204	314	CC	243	363	F3
205	315	CD	244	364	F4
206	316	CE	245	365	F5
207	317	CF	246	366	F6
208	320	D0	247	367	F7
209	321	D1	248	370	F8
210	322	D2	249	371	F9
211	323	D3	250	372	FA
212	324	D4	251	373	FB
213	325	D5	252	374	FC
214	326	D6	253	375	FD
215	327	D7	254	376	FE
216	330	D8	255	377	FF
217	331	D9			
218	332	DA			
219	333	DB			
220	334	DC			

F

Assembly Language Use

This appendix discusses the interface between assembly language subroutines and GW-BASIC programs. A comprehensive discussion of assembly language program techniques cannot be supplied here. For this you can consult an assembly language text (such as *80386/80286 Assembly Language Programming*, Murray and Pappas, Osborne/McGraw-Hill). This appendix addresses only the GW-BASIC techniques for interfacing the two languages.

The term *assembly language* is used in this discussion to represent the machine code produced by an assembler—the binary code that the computer understands. Although GW-BASIC only accepts data in decimal, hexadecimal, and octal number systems,

the data is stored in binary format. You can interface assembly
language (machine code) subroutines in a GW-BASIC program by
using either the USR function or the CALL statement.

The USR Function

The USR function allows you to call assembly language subroutines in the same way you call GW-BASIC intrinsic functions (such
as SIN, LEFT$, INSTR, and so on). Before a USR function is
called, a corresponding DEF USR statement must be executed to
define the USR function call offset.

The DEF USR statement takes the following general form:

DEF USR[*n*] = *Offset*

where *n* is the subroutine's number identification (0 through 9),
and *Offset* is the offset (to the current DEF SEG) of the first byte of
the assembly language subroutine. If *n* is omitted, the number 0
(zero) is assumed.

The same subroutine number identifier is used in the associated USR function call, as shown here:

variable = USR*n*(*argument*)

where *variable* is any valid variable name to which the value
returned by the assembly language subroutine is assigned; *argument* is any valid numeric expression (integer, single precision, or
double precision) or any valid string expression. The value of the
argument expression is passed to the subroutine. If no value is to be
passed to the subroutine, a dummy argument must be used in the
USR function call; zero is a good choice.

Only one argument can be passed by a USR function, and that argument cannot be an array. Usually the value returned by an assembly language subroutine (called by a USR function) is the same type as the argument passed to the subroutine. The value to be returned must be placed in the *floating point accumulator* (FAC) by the subroutine before a return is made to GW-BASIC from the subroutine.

Since the USR function is restricted to passing a single argument, its use is limited to simple applications. The CALL statement is more versatile. The USR function is provided for compatibility with programs written in earlier versions of BASIC.

The CALL Statement

The CALL statement is the recommended tool for interfacing assembly language programs with GW-BASIC. CALL is compatible with more computer languages than the USR function. In addition, with CALL you can pass multiple arguments to the assembly language subroutines.

The CALL statement takes this general form:

CALL *name(argument list)*

where *name* is the variable that has been assigned the offset (in the current segment) of the assembly language subroutine being called; *argument list* contains the variables or constants (separated by commas) that are to be passed to the subroutine.

For each parameter in the *argument list,* the 2-byte offset of the parameter's location within the data segment (DS) is pushed onto the stack. The GW-BASIC return address code segment (CS) and offset (IP) are also pushed onto the stack.

A call to the segment address given in the last DEF SEG statement, and the offset given in the *name* variable of the CALL statement, transfers control to the user's assembly language routine. The user routine must preserve internal information as it existed at the time of the call, including: the stack segment (SS), data segment (DS), extra segment (ES), and the stack pointer (SP).

The user routine may reference parameters by moving the stack pointer (SP) to the base pointer (BP) and adding a positive offset to the base pointer.

The following lines set up DEF SEG, the offset within the segment, and call the assembly language subroutine. Three parameters are passed.

```
110 DEF SEG = &H6000
120 Offset = &HFF0
130 CALL Offset (age%, name$, year%)
```

The CALL statement was used in Chapter 9, "Program Control," to call a machine language program that rotated the bits in the lower byte of an integer one place to the right.

```
0 1 0 0 0 0 0 1    = 65 Number entered

1 0 1 0 0 0 0 0    = 160 Rotated right
```

Program F-1, Rotate Bits Left, is a similar program that rotates all bits in the lower byte of an integer one place to the left, instead of the right. In addition, the value entered is displayed in binary form. The result is expressed in both binary and decimal form so that you can see the rotation of the individual bits.

The subroutine in the 1000 block converts the number you entered to binary form and prints it as a string of binary bits. The

Program F-1.

```
1 REM ** Rotate Bits Left **
2 ' GW-BASIC Reference, Appendix F. File: GWRF0F01.BAS
3 ' Enters and runs a machine language program

100 REM ** Initialize **
110 CLS: KEY OFF: DEFINT A-Z
120 anumber = 0; bite = 0; count = 0
130 DEF SEG : DIM ByteHold(7)
140 RotateL = VARPTR(ByteHold(0))

200 REM ** Read and store subroutine **
210 FOR count = 0 TO 15
220    READ bite: POKE RotateL + count, bite
230 NEXT count
240 DATA &H55, &H8B, &HEC, &H8B
250 DATA &H76, &H06, &H8B, &H04
260 DATA &HD0, &HC0, &H89, &H04
270 DATA &H5D, &HCA, &H02, &H00

300 REM ** Enter, rotate, and print **
310 INPUT "Enter an integer (between 1 and 255): "; anumber
320 GOSUB 1010
330 PRINT "Your number in binary is: "; binary$
340 RotateL = VARPTR(ByteHold(0))
350 CALL RotateL(anumber)
360 PRINT: PRINT "The result in decimal is: "; anumber
370 GOSUB 1010
380 PRINT "The result in binary is: "; binary$: PRINT

400 REM ** Quit or go on ? **
410 PRINT "Press ESC to quit; another key to go on"
420 akey$ = INPUT$(1): PRINT
430 IF akey$ = CHR$(27) THEN END ELSE 310

1000 REM ** Convert decimal to binary **
1010 a = 128: binary$ = "": num = anumber
1020 FOR bit = 8 TO 1 STEP -1
1030    bit$ = STR$(num \ a)
1040    IF bit$ = " 1" THEN num = num - 2 ^ (bit - 1)
1050    binary$ = binary$ + bit$
1060    a = a \ 2
1070 NEXT bit
1080 RETURN
```

Rotate Bits Left (GWRF0F01.BAS)

machine language routine is located by line 340 and called at line 350. The rotated result is printed in decimal form. Then the conversion subroutine is called again, and the result is printed as a string of binary bits.

Here are some typical entries and results for Program F-1. First, the number 3 is entered.

```
Enter an integer (between 1 and 255): ? 3
Your number in binary is:  0 0 0 0 0 0 1 1

The result in decimal is:  6
The result in binary is:  0 0 0 0 0 1 1 0
```

You can see from a comparison of the binary form of the number entered and the binary form of the result that the bits have been rotated to the left one place. A prompt is displyed to see if you want to go on or quit.

```
Press ESC to quit; another key to go on
```

When the number 33 is entered, the following is displayed:

```
Enter an integer (between 1 and 255): ? 33
Your number in binary is:  0 0 1 0 0 0 0 1

The result in decimal is:  66
The result in binary is:  0 1 0 0 0 0 1 0
```

To see what happens when the leading bit is a 1, try entering 160 for the number to be rotated. Here are the results.

```
Enter an integer (between 1 and 255): ? 160
Your number in binary is:  1 0 1 0 0 0 0 0

The result in decimal is:  65
The result in binary is:  0 1 0 0 0 0 0 1
```

This is what happened to each bit of the number that was entered:

```
1 0 1 0 0 0 0 0    = 160 Number entered



  0 1 0 0 0 0 0 1    = 65 Rotated left
```

To find out more about assembly language programming, scan the shelves of the computer section in your local bookstores. Look for an assembly language book that is appropriate for the CPU of your computer.

APPENDIX

Glossary of Terms

Absolute Coordinates The row and column coordinates used to locate a point on the screen. See also Relative Coordinates.

Absolute Value The magnitude of a number without regard to whether it is positive or negative.

Argument A variable or expression. It can represent the location of a number in an operation, or a number with which a function works to produce its results, or a reference factor required to find a desired item in a table.

Arithmetic Operations   The GW-BASIC operations that perform arithmetic: addition (+), subtraction (−), multiplication (*), division (/), exponentiation (^), integer division (\), and remainder on an integer division (MOD).

Array   A group of values that share a common name. A single member of an array is called an element of the array.

Array Subscript   Denotes the number assigned to an element of an array.

ASCII   An acronym for American Standard Code for Information Interchange; a standard 8-bit code used to represent characters used in interfacing the computer to peripheral devices.

ASCII Format   A format GW-BASIC uses to store data to a file using ASCII codes.

BASIC   An acronym for Beginner's All-purpose Symbolic Instruction Code; a computer language.

Batch Files   Files that are executed in a series, one at a time.

Baud Rate   A measurement of data processing speed in signal elements per second. A signal element can represent more than one bit.

Binary   A number system having a base of 2, using the digits 0 and 1.

Boolean Expression   An expression that evaluates to true or false, based on a system formulated by British mathematician George Boole.

Booting a System   A machine procedure that allows the computer system to begin operations.

Bubble Sort   A method of sorting data by "bubbling" each item from its current position in a list to its sorted position.

Buffer   An area of computer memory used to store data used for a specific purpose.

Bug   Something in a program that produces erroneous results.

Byte   A group of eight binary digits.

Catenate   Join together (append one to another); sometimes referred to as concatenate.

Chaining   A process that passes control from one program to another via the CHAIN command.

Child Process   A process initiated by using a string with the SHELL command to execute one program (the child) from within another (the parent).

Command Level   The computer level where GW-BASIC commands are entered (as compared to the Program Level).

Compiler   A computer program that translates a high-level language into instructions the computer can understand, before the program is run.

Compressed Binary Format   A format using binary codes to save GW-BASIC programs. It is the default format when using the SAVE command.

Control Structures   Program structures, such as WHILE/ WEND, used to control the execution order of GW-BASIC statements.

Coordinates   A pair of numbers (row and column) that defines a position on the display screen.

Data Pointer   A method the computer uses internally to keep track of the next item in the list of a DATA statement to be accessed by a READ statement.

Data Type   May be either string or numeric. Numeric types are integer, single precision, and double precision.

Debug   To inspect a block of program code and correct errors found.

Decimal   A number system having a base of 10, using the digits 0, 1, 2, 3, 4, 5, 6, 7, 8, and 9.

Default Disk Drive   The disk drive that is currently in use.

Default Value   A value used when an optional value is not provided.

Delimiter   A character that marks the beginning or end of a block of data.

Device Driver   Software code that provides information so the computer can communicate with external devices.

Dimension of an Array   The maximum subscript that may be used in an array.

Direct Entry Mode   A computer operating mode where commands are executed immediately; no program is necessary.

Disk   A flat platter, coated with magnetic material, used to store computer programs and data.

Disk File   A unit of information stored on a disk which the computer accesses by its filename; may contain a program (program file) or data (data file).

Disk Directory   A table of information about the files on a disk; usually gives the name, size, and date of creation (or last revision) of the files on a disk.

Disk Drive   The device that holds and manipulates a disk so that the computer can read or write data to a file.

Disk Operating System   A collection of procedures that enable the computer to operate its disk drives for data entry and storage.

DOS Command Line   The line of the screen on which you enter DOS commands.

Double Precison Value   A GW-BASIC decimal value that is precise up to 16 digits.

Dummy Argument   An argument that is required in a command, statement, or function, but has no functional meaning.

Element of an Array   A specific item in a group of items, in an array designated by a unique subscript.

Ellipsis   Three consecutive periods (. . .) indicating that an action or series of events continues.

Encoded Binary Format A format used to save GW-BASIC programs; protects a file so that you may not use the LIST command or edit it.

Error-Handling Routine A block of code that performs a specific function when an error is encountered.

Error Trap A process that detects an error.

Event Trap A process that detects a specific event (such as a specified keypress).

.EXE File A program file with the three-letter filename extension, EXE, that can run from DOS rather than from within GW-BASIC.

Exponent The power to which a number is raised.

Extension Up to three characters, preceded by a period, appended to a filename to distinguish the file type (GW-BASIC's default extension is BAS).

External Devices A device that is connected to the computer so that it works with, but is not a part of, the computer.

Field A unit within either a file record or a printed line, containing a specified number of characters.

File A unit of information stored on a disk and accessed by the computer via filename; may contain a program (program file) or data (data file).

Filename Extension Up to three characters, preceded by a period, appended to a filename to distinguish the file type (GW-BASIC's default extension is BAS).

Floating Point A term applied in computer computation when the computer automatically tracks the location of the decimal point.

Floating Point Notation The notation used to express floating point numbers; it specifies a mantissa and an exponent.

Formatting a Disk A procedure that determines how data will be arranged when it is stored on the disk.

Function Keys Special keys on the computer keyboard that, when pressed, perform predetermined functions.

Functional Block A block of program code that performs a specific function.

Garbage Collection A process that reorganizes the use of memory space into a more efficient form.

Graphics Adapter The hardware component that determines the type of graphics displayed by a display monitor.

Handshaking The communication process between the computer and an external device to make sure both are ready to transfer information.

Hard Disk A special type of disk drive capable of holding more data than a diskette or floppy disk.

Hertz A unit of measurement of frequency equal to one cycle per second; abbreviated Hz.

Hexadecimal A number system with a base of 16, using the digits 0, 1, 2, 3, 4, 5, 6, 7, 8, 9, A, B, C, D, E, and F.

Indirect Entry Mode   The computer entry mode used to write programs, as compared to the Direct Entry Mode where commands are immediately executed.

Insert Edit Mode   The edit mode used to insert data at the current cursor position. All characters to the right of the cursor are shifted right as new characters are entered.

Integer Division   An arithmetic operation in which the result is expressed as an integer, and the remainder is ignored.

Interpreter   A computer program, such as GW-BASIC, that translates (interprets) each instruction *as it is encountered* when a program is run.

Key Line   The line at the bottom of the display screen where GW-BASIC displays a short description of the functions performed by the function keys.

Keyword   A word that is *reserved* by GW-BASIC for use in functions, statements, and commands; it cannot be used as a variable.

Line Number   The number used before GW-BASIC program lines that determines the order in which the lines are executed.

Logarithm of a Number   The exponent to which it is necessary to raise the logarithm's base to produce the number.

Logical Operators   Operators that return a bit-wise result (-1 or 0) that can be interpreted as true or false. Logical operators in GW-BASIC include AND, EQV, IMP, NOT, OR, and XOR.

Machine Language   A low-level language understood by the computer (as compared to a high-level language such as GW-BASIC).

Mantissa   The decimal portion of a floating point number (as compared to its exponent). It is greater than or equal to one, but less than 10.

Member of an Array   A specific item in a group of items, in an array designated by a unique subscript.

Merging Programs   A process that combines lines of two programs. Lines in the program being incorporated replace lines with the same line numbers in the program in memory.

MOD Operation   The arithmetic operation (modulus arithmetic) that returns the remainder when an integer division operation is performed.

Multiple Statements   The name applied to the statements of a program line when it has more than one statement.

Network   A system of connected computers that work together.

Null String   A GW-BASIC string with nothing in it, denoted by adjacent double quotation marks ("") with no space between them; also called the empty string.

Octal   A number system having a base of 8, using the digits 0, 1, 2, 3, 4, 5, 6, and 7.

Offset Address   The part of the memory address added to the segment address to obtain a location in memory.

Operand   A quantity used in an operation.

Operational Symbol   Symbols used to indicate an arithmetic operation (the process to be performed); for example, +, −, *, /, ^, \, and MOD.

Overflow   The condition when the result of an entry or calculation is larger than the computer can handle.

Overtype Edit Mode   The edit mode used to replace data at the current cursor position.

Parameter   A constant or variable used in an expression.

Parity Bit   An extra bit in a byte of information; used to detect data errors.

Path Name   A series of characters used to tell the computer where to find a file.

Peripheral Device   An external device connected to a computer.

Pi   The ratio of a circle's circumference to its diameter (approximately 3.141593).

Pixel   The smallest element of a graphics screen that can be turned on and off.

Pointer   An internal method of tracking some series of sequential information.

Port   The channel to and from the computer, used to connect a communication line or other peripheral device.

Prompt   A symbol or phrase that means the computer expects some action from the user.

Radian A unit of angular measure (2 * Pi radians = 360 degrees).

Random Access File A type of file whose records may be accessed in any order.

Record A unit of information within a file, measured in bytes.

Relational Operators Operators that perform tests on the relation of two quantities. GW-BASIC relational operators include: equal (=), unequal (< >), less than (<), greater than (>), less than or equal to (< =), and greater than or equal to (> =).

Relative Coordinates Row and column numbers of a point relative to the last graphics point referenced. Also see Absolute Coordinates.

Remark A GW-BASIC term that contains information but no computer action; remarks are not executed when a program is run. Represented by REM or an apostrophe.

Reserved Word A GW-BASIC word that cannot be used as a variable; commonly used by GW-BASIC as (or as part of) commands, statements, and functions.

Root Directory The main directory of a disk; it may contain other directories, called subdirectories.

Screen Coordinates A system of numbering the row and column values that locate a point on the screen. Rows are numbered from top to bottom, and columns from left to right.

Screen Mode The type of display supported by GW-BASIC; may be text only (SCREEN 0), or graphics (SCREEN 1, 2, 7, 8, 9, and 10).

Search Key   The key on which a search (for a particular data item in a group of items) is based.

Seed Value   A number used to start the random number generator at a unique place in the sequence of the numbers it contains.

Segment Address   The part of the memory address that locates a specific segment of memory (begins on 16-byte boundaries).

Sequential File   A type of file in which records of the file are accessed in sequential order.

Single Precision Value   A GW-BASIC decimal value that is precise up to seven digits.

Sort Key   The key on which a sort of data items is based.

String   A combination of letters, numbers, and other characters; usually enclosed in double quotation marks.

String Variable   A variable to which a string is assigned.

Subdirectory   A directory of files on a disk drive that is contained within, and accessed from, the root directory.

Subroutine   A computer routine that is "called" from the main program, and contains a RETURN statement that passes control back to the main program when the subroutine execution is completed.

Switch   Information included in a command, designating that special (nondefault) actions should be carried out when the command is executed.

Syntax Rules of structure used in GW-BASIC and other programming languages.

System-Formatted Disk A disk that is formatted so that it includes information to start (boot) the computer system.

Terminal The device used to communicate with the computer; the keyboard and display monitor combination is commonly referred to as the terminal.

Time-sharing Computer A term applied to a computer that allows more than one person to access it at the same time, from different terminals. The computer shares its use, but appears to work with more than one person at the same time.

Trace The technique of displaying line numbers as they are executed, so you can see the order of program execution (used to debug a program).

Type Declaration Character A symbol appended to a variable or a number, to indicate whether it is an integer (%), a single precision value (!), or a double precision value (#).

Variable A name for a quantity that can assume changing values as data is processed.

Variable Type Either string or numeric. Numeric types are integer, single precision, and double precision.

Viewport A specific area of the display screen.

Window A specific area of the display screen.

World Coordinates   A system of numbering the row and column values that locate a point on the screen. Rows are numbered from bottom to top, and columns from left to right.

Screen
Descriptions
and Colors

Screen Descriptions

Screen	Text Format	Graphics Pixel	Color Numbers
0	40 by 25 OR 80 by 25	Text only	0 through 15
1	40 by 25	320 by 200 2 bits/pixel	0 through 3

Screen	Text Format	Graphics Pixel	Color Numbers
2	80 by 25	640 by 200 1 bit/pixel	0 and 1
7	40 by 25	320 by 200 4 bits/pixel	0 through 15
8	80 by 25	640 by 200 4 bits/pixel	0 through 15
9	80 by 25	640 by 350 2 bits/pixel*	0 through 15 for 64K EGA memory;
		4 bits/pixel**	0 through 63 for EGA memory >64K
10	80 by 25	640 by 350 2 bits/pixel	0, 1, 2, 3

* bits/pixel (64K EGA memory)
** 4 bits/pixel (> 64K EGA memory)

 NOTE   Screens 0, 1, and 2 used by CGA, EGA, and VGA; screens 7, 8, 9, and 10 require EGA or VGA. Screen 10 is for monochrome displays.

Screen Colors for Color Displays

Screen Modes	Palette	Color Number	Color
0, 7, 8, 9†	NA	0	Black
		1	Blue
		2	Green
		3	Cyan

†Colors 0 through 63 if > 64K EGA memory

Screen Modes	Palette	Color Number	Color
		4	Red
		5	Magenta
		6	Brown
		7	White
		8	Gray
		9	Light blue
		10	Light green
		11	Light cyan
		12	Light red
		13	Light magenta
		14	Yellow
		15	Bright white
1	0	0	Background
		1	Green
		2	Red
		3	Brown
	1	0	Background
		1	Cyan
		2	Magenta
		3	White
2	NA	0	Background
		1	Foreground
10	NA	0	Off
		1	Blink, off to on
		2	Blink, off to high-intensity
		3	Blink, on to off
		4	On

Screen Modes	Palette	Color Number	Color
		5	Blink, on to high-intensity
		6	Blink, high-intensity to off
		7	Blink, high-intensity to on
		8	High-intensity

BASIC

Index

A

W

X

The manuscript for this book was prepared and submitted to Osborne/McGraw-Hill in electronic form. The acquisitions editor for this project was Elizabeth Fisher, the associate editor was Gwen Goss, the technical reviewer was Paul Sevigny, and the project editor was Janis Paris.

Text design by Stefany Otis and Lance Ravella, using Baskerville for text body and Swiss boldface for display.

Cover art by Bay Graphics Design, Inc. Color separation and cover supplier, Phoenix Color Corporation. Screens produced with InSet, from InSet Systems, Inc. Book printed and bound by R.R. Donnelley & Sons Company, Crawfordsville, Indiana.